China: The Next Decades

Edited by Denis Dwyer

Addison Wesley Longman Limited
Edinburgh Gate, Harlow
Essex, CM20 2JE, England
and Associated Companies throughout the world.

Copublished in the United States with
John Wiley & Sons, Inc., 605 Third Avenue, New York, NY 10158

© Longman Group UK Limited 1994

First published 1994
Reprinted 1996

ISBN 0-582-10164-6

British Library Cataloguing in Publication Data
A CIP record for this book is available from the British Library

Library of Congress Cataloging-in-Publication Data
A CIP record for this book is available from the Library of Congress

Set by 13 in 10/11 pt Palatino
Produced through Longman Malaysia, TCP

CONTENTS

Preface

The Keele Geographical Symposia are held annually to bring together geographers and other social scientists to consider a subject of current major significance. The Fourth Symposium, organized by the editor of the present volume, was held in December 1991 in order to review China's development experience both generally during the period of its Communist government since 1949 and particularly since the Dengist economic reforms were instituted in the late 1970s. Within that broad remit, one theme was identified as being of particular importance: the prospects for China's socio-economic and political future in the one or two decades immediately ahead. The present volume consists of a re-working of the papers presented at the Symposium, with an additional contribution from Professor Jack Williams on the rapidly changing relationship between China and Taiwan. Abbreviations used in individual chapters are found in the reference section at the end of each chapter.

It is a pleasure to acknowledge the enthusiasm for the Symposium of colleagues in the Department of Geography at Keele and their willing cooperation in making the meeting a success. In particular, Ms Jill Eyre played a major role in day-to-day administration and preparation. In addition to that of the Department of Geography, financial sponsorship for the Symposium was received from Cambridge University Press and Messrs Routledge as well as from the publishers of the present volume. Both the University and the Department are grateful for the support given by these leading international publishers.

It hardly needs to be said that the present book does not present a consensus view on China's future prospects but rather reflects the lively diversity of views expressed both in the papers and in the subsequent discussions at the Symposium. As editor, it has been not only a considerable pleasure but also a profitable education to be able to exchange views and opinions on China with such a stimulating and cooperative group of authors.

Denis Dwyer

Contributors

John Cole, Professor, Department of Geography, University of Nottingham

Ian Douglas, Professor, School of Geography, University of Manchester

Denis Dwyer, Research Professor, Department of Geography, Keele University

Richard Louis Edmonds, Senior Lecturer, Department of Geography, School of Oriental and African Studies, University of London

Gu Hengyue, Professor, Xilin General Development Institute, Chongqing University, People's Republic of China

Sarah Harper, Lecturer, Department of Geography, Royal Holloway and Bedford New College, University of London

He Min, graduate student, Department of Geography, University of Manchester

Sheila Hillier, Professor, Joint Department of Human Science and Medical Ethics, St Bartholomews and the London Hospital Medical Colleges

Rupert Hodder, Lecturer, Department of Geography, London School of Economics, University of London

Brian Hook, Senior Lecturer, Department of East Asian Studies, University of Leeds

Athar Hussain, Reader, Department of Economics, Keele University

Richard Kirkby, Lecturer, Department of Civic Design, University of Liverpool

Frank Leeming, formerly Senior Lecturer, School of Geography, University of Leeds

Jack F. Williams, Director of the Center of Asian Studies, Michigan State University, U.S.A

Xiang Zheng, Lecturer, Department of Health Planning and Management, Shanghai Medical University

CHAPTER 1

Introduction: China, steps forward and steps back

Denis Dwyer

In 1986 Deng Xiaoping, China's paramount leader and the architect of revolutionary reforms, was selected as Man of the Year by *Time* magazine. Less than three years later, in June 1989, Deng was ordering the massacre of his fellow citizens in Tiananmen square. China's period of reform since 1979 had come to an abrupt halt with the emphatic statement by the Communist Party through the guns of the People's Liberation Army that there could only be economic not political change.

This extreme brutality occurred in the midst of a period of severe austerity and restriction on investment introduced in the autumn of 1988 to combat the development of runaway inflation. By then, laxity in spending, both official and personal, was leading to price rises in excess of 30 per cent a year. State projects were suspended or even discontinued; funding for the new township and rural industries outside of the state sector, the rapid growth of which had been such a positive feature of the reform period, was severely curtailed, resulting in mass closures; and urban workers' incomes were cut, with part of their salaries being invested in government bonds. Following the massacre, Western countries imposed their own sanctions; and the World Bank suspended several loans. The response from the ruling group of the Chinese Communist Party was a return to more centralized planning and control – a rolling back of the frontiers of the Dengist economic reforms – the overthrow of Deng's protégé and heir apparent, Zhao Xiyang, who was held responsible for allowing the situation to develop that led to the massacre, and the growth in influence of the more Stalinist element within the leadership typified by the Prime Minister, Li Peng, and the veteran economist Chen Yun.

Today, however, the situation is considerably different. By the beginning of 1992, the internal balance of power had so changed that the octogenarian Deng Xiaoping was able to make a massively publicized visit to southern China, with a particularly symbolic stop in the Shenzen

Special Economic Zone, in order to preach again the virtues of his version of market reform with Chinese characteristics – the latter including the continued dictatorship of the Party. At the Fourteenth Party Congress in November of the same year, Deng and his policies received a level of adulation reminiscent of that accorded to Mao at the height of his own personality cult. And the economic news had become universally good. GNP growth in 1992, it was reported, was likely to reach 12 per cent, or double the official target set in March the same year. Foreign investment, it was expected, would exceed all previous levels. The number of tourists was the highest ever. This renewed confidence was coming at a time when the grain harvest was set to exceed that of 1990, which itself was a record.

The extreme nature of the swings both of policy and of economic fortune that have characterized China since 1989 is by no means unusual; indeed such swings are typical of China's history under the Communist Party since 1949. Following an initial period of national rehabilitation after the war years, the First Five Year Plan (1953–57) has since generally been held to have been reasonably successful in its own terms, which largely concerned industrial development, and the concentration of investment upon heavy industry. The First Five Year Plan was followed, however, by the Great Leap Forward in which all economic logic was abandoned in an excess of Maoism which ordained completely unrealistic economic goals, and relied for their accomplishment to a significant degree upon the primitive force of China's huge population often, as with the well-publicized 'backyard steel furnaces', working in the smallest of units.

The effects of the policies of the Great Leap Forward upon agriculture, including the initial reaction of the peasantry to the introduction of the people's communes, was directly responsible for the mass famine of the early 1960s in which as many as 30 million people may have died. A period of rehabilitation followed but then, in 1966, for political reasons Mao launched the Cultural Revolution, a renewed period of national turmoil that lasted, in varying degrees, for almost ten years. The death of Mao in 1976 saw a struggle for succession marked first by the overthrow of the Maoist 'Gang of Four' led by Mao's widow, Jiang Qing, and then by the rise to ascendancy of Deng Xiaoping. Finally, at the Third Plenum of the Eleventh Central Committee in December 1978 the decisions were made to embark upon unprecedented economic reforms. It was widely, but wrongly, assumed outside China that this might well involve the liberalization of the country as a whole, and Deng Xiaoping was soon being glorified in the Western media as the saviour of his country. The introduction of the family responsibility system in agriculture and the abolition of the communes, the mushrooming of industry outside the state sector in townships and villages, together with the attraction of significant foreign investment, produced unprecedented rates of national economic growth and a general perception of improvement in China's prospects that was fundamentally to be called into question by the events in Tiananmen Square.

The chapters that follow assess the impact of this turbulent history on China's overall socio-economic development through the detailed examination of key topics. They pass judgement on significant aspects of

2

the record of policy formulation and execution, and on the basis of such assessments make predictions for the country in the immediate future. There is no consensus view but, in sum, from within the diverse presentations that comprise the book a sufficient number of serious reservations emerges to throw considerable doubt upon China's ability – as at present governed, and organized in the socio-economic sense – to achieve its stated objective of an early ascent into the ranks of the middle income countries. In some respects, there are even indications of possible catastrophe in the making.

In the first contribution (Chapter 2), Hussain presents an overall review and assessment of the economic reforms of the 1980s and identifies the items he considers need to be at the top of a reform agenda for the 1990s. He places the Chinese reforms in a comparative perspective, drawing comparisons between China and the ex-Soviet Union and its former East European satellites, the other East Asian economies, and with some large developing countries such as India. Hussain gives full weight to the positive aspects of the reforms and claims they have been a success in three respects: first, the achievement of high rates of economic growth; second, during the course of the reforms, protecting the mass of the population from deprivation; and third, the promotion of a significant rise in foreign trade and investment. However, as he states, success in the last direction is also bringing with it increased external pressures, both to liberalize trade further, by ending hidden subsidies for exports and protectionist measures against imports, and to improve China's currently appalling record in respect of human rights. The stage may currently be in process of being set for a higher level of international confrontation in these matters, particularly confrontation with the administration of newly elected President Clinton in the United States. For China, in Hussain's view, there can be only one future path: further forward in terms of the implementation of the Dengist reforms. Further progress in China's development could not be achieved by reverting back to a command economy. The way forward must involve the solution of major problems that have so far proved intractable, such as the reform of the pricing system; the contradictions inherent in the family responsibility system in agriculture; the gross inefficiency of state-run industries; and the need both to reform and to widen the social security system.

These major problems are among those identified and discussed by several other contributors to this volume, but in Chapter 3 John Cole shifts the focus towards an examination of one of the fundamentals, namely China's endowment of natural resources for development, in particular in comparison with that of the former USSR. While such assessments are always fraught with difficulties, and estimates must if necessity be gross, nevertheless instructive comparisons in terms of orders of magnitude can be made. Cole examines China's resources in two revealing ways. The first is by adopting a time-lag approach, so that a comparison is made between the current use of resources in China and that in the former USSR 25 years previously, this being the time difference between 1928, the first year of the First Soviet Five Year Plan, and 1953, the first year of the Chinese one. Secondly, Cole examines comparative resource endowment not only on an absolute but also on a per capita basis. To summarize his findings, he constructs an index which assesses the overall resource endowment of China against that of the former USSR. The conclusion he reaches is that if the former USSR is represented by 1000 on the index, China would rank only at 150.

However the exact statistics may be argued, it is apparent that both absolutely, and certainly in per capita terms, China is a country poor in the natural resources necessary for development. If China is to modernize further, Cole argues, and eventually industrialize as intensively as Japan, or even the former USSR, it will have to consume much more fuel and other raw materials than it does now. Its resource inventory for this task is far from adequate, so it will have to draw increasingly upon other parts of the world for primary products. This is a further reason both why there can be no return to an isolationist command economy and why its international relations will become ever more vital to China in the future.

Population is the other fundamental resource of any nation. In China, attitudes towards the size and growth of the population have changed drastically between the earlier years of the Communist period, when during the Great Leap Forward particularly a large and rapidly increasing population was perceived in the Maoist scheme of things as being a considerable asset for rapid development, and the present day when the situation is one of considerable alarm over the 16 million people each year that continue to be added to the population. This is despite unprecedented efforts to curb the rate of population growth more recently, including the introduction in 1979 of the highly publicized One Child Family policy, and the imposition of such draconian measures as widespread forced abortions. Official policy towards population limitation has suffered many shifts during the period since 1949. These are analysed by Sarah Harper in Chapter 4 who also assesses the One Child Family policy in some detail, illustrating how a range of exceptions came to be accepted within the system which in the rural areas greatly diluted its effect. She discusses the contention that the One Child Family policy as a whole was an aberration out of context with the general spirit of the post-1978 reform period. As Harper demonstrates, since the mid-1980s the One Child Family policy has become at best a modified one-child policy the degree of success of which will be mediated by an intricate mesh of social and cultural as well as economic and political factors within the country. In particular, Harper draws attention to China's fundamentally partiarchical society with its inherent structural emphasis on male children and patrilocal residence, the cultural emphasis on pronatalism and familialism, and reliance an inter-generational support for care in illness and old age as exceedingly strong forces encouraging the procreation of children. Harper also analyses a significant problem arising from the degree of success of the more recent policies: that of the ageing of the population in general. Her observations reinforce Hussain's earlier contention that the whole question of social security provision must come to occupy a higher place in China's list of priorities if the present reforms are to proceed significantly further.

China's population remains, of course, predominantly a peasant population and food security has always been high on the political agenda, not only during the Communist period but historically, since the rulers of China have traditionally derived legitimacy from their ability to guarantee food supply. Frank Leeming in Chapter 5 illustrates how, for a few years after the 1978 reforms, the countryside was a great success story. The introduction of the family responsibility system into agricultural production not only released latent rural energies, it also placed decision making much more directly into the hands of those who would most fully feel the impact of the decisions upon their own living standards and welfare. Official procurement prices were increased and income for farmers rose. For some years, it seemed like the start of a new golden age in the countryside.

The problems that have arisen since have been substantial however. Grain is cheap, but the industrial inputs necessary to produce it, such as fertilizers and pesticides, are no longer cheap, or at least were not so until 1990 when renewed official efforts were made through price manipulation to obtain an improvement in grain output, which had stagnated in the second half of the 1980s. Despite such recent efforts, official investment in the agricultural sector remains exceptionally low in proportional terms, and collective investment weakened sharply in the 1980s, in large part because of the attractive financial returns to be obtained from the rapidly developing township industries. Meanwhile, both halves of what Leeming terms 'the forbidding equation' – namely that China maintains about 22 per cent of the world's population from only 7 per cent of the world's arable land – are tending to deteriorate. Not only is population growing more rapidly than was planned at the beginning of the 1980s but also the amount of arable land is falling steadily due to its conversion to other uses such as housebuilding and non-agricultural enterprises, and also due to its unwise use in some areas leading to soil erosion and desertification. In the 1950s, Leeming states, there were 1800 square metres of arable land per person. This figure is now around 900 square metres, and even on very favourable assumptions by the year 2000 it is bound to be lower than 800 square metres, with some writers arguing for a figure nearer to 650 square metres. By the end of the century, China will need to produce 500 million tonnes of foodgrains even to maintain current levels of supply to its, by then, increased population. Leeming argues that only a radical restructuring of financial allocations to the advantage of the countryside, together with several other major reforms, would allow such a target to be approached.

The present difficulties in the countryside do not only concern food production. In a detailed examination of rural health care, Sheila Hillier in Chapter 6 shows the ways in which the introduction of market prices has altered systems of provision which, though by no means perfect, had involved substantial progress towards a goal of accessible and affordable health care for all the people; an emphasis on disease prevention; control of the medical dominance of the health care system; the incorporation of traditional medicine into the mainstream of care; and a strong emphasis on citizen participation, epitomized by the 'barefoot doctors'. In particular, Hillier claims, the demise of the collectivist system and the abolition of the communes removed the organizational basis for collective health care in the villages. The official response has been to introduce a 'multitype' health system into the rural areas, a variety of forms of care, including private doctors and private clinics and hospitals, within a freer more market-oriented system. Even by the early 1980s, free health care had become a thing of the past and nine-tenths of the rural population were paying for treatment on a fee-for-service basis. By the late 1980s, almost half of all rural clinics were privately owned, and surveys showed that low-income rural families were spending about 10 per cent of their annual income on medical care. Hillier observes that in addition to the new policies hitting hardest those least able to pay, the years of reform have also produced a serious reversal in preventive health work. For example, schistosomiasis, which had been the subject of huge labour-intensive campaigns to wipe out the snail vector during the first three decades of communism, is now on the increase again, as are several other serious diseases such a plague, cases of which increased by over 60 per cent between 1986 and 1990. The overall responsibility for the provision of health services now rests more than it ever did before in the hands of the people themselves, who must finally decide what they wish to spend. Whether this is the best basis for future policy must be doubtful.

A principal reason for the difficulties of the countryside during the Communist period has been the emphasis placed by the regime on industrial development, especially that of heavy industry, and the subsidization of the politically vital urban population through cheap food policies and the operation of a jobs-for-life policy within state industries. In Chapters 7 and 8, Rupert Hodder and Richard Kirkby, respectively, examine the industrial structure and the urban structure. As Hodder observes, China could probably have achieved a steady but slow rate of progress in industrial output without the need for significant structural adjustments but by the end of the century this would still have left China a predominantly peasant economy in a region, East Asia, containing several examples of rapid industrialization and comparative economic prosperity. The Dengist reforms, therefore, included significant demands for faster industrial growth and greater industrial efficiency. One of their main practical aims was to replace vertical channels of command in industry, which had coordinated administrative units, with horizontal linkages, which would facilitate more efficient flows of funds, raw materials, equipment, labour and goods, and also reduce the wasteful duplication of industrial activities by separate administrative units. Other important objectives included the wider introduction of taxation, so that rather than handing nearly all profits over to the state, enterprises could pay taxes at rates stipulated before production began; the granting of the right of determining wages, and even introducing bonuses, to individual factories; and the giving to them of the authority to set ex-factory prices for certain goods.

These and other vital reforms within the state-run industrial sector have been a good deal less than successful, and while this sector has tended to stagnate, it is in the township and rural industries, and in joint ventures with foreign capital particularly in the areas immediately adjacent to Hong

Kong, that rapid development has been experienced. As do other contributors to this volume, Hodder stresses that emphasis is no longer on the social dimensions of economic policy, nor on the need to ensure regional equality. This latter is most apparent in industry of all the major economic activities since the espousal of policies of regional comparative advantage has led to a marked concentration of new industrial development at or near the coasts, in direct contrast to the interior-oriented policies of the Maoist period. Hodder speculates whether China will become Asia's next economic giant, and advances the view that significant political change would not be necessary for this. Much more important to him is the seeming intractability of certain major industrial problems, for a sufficient development of state industry would certainly be an indispensable condition for China's advance to such a status.

All modern advanced societies and economies are predominantly urban–industrial. China's urban future is thus a critical consideration in terms of its prospects. Could China control and manage a future urbanization of its huge peasant population; their movement out of a very much more efficient and productive agriculture? Upon what national financial basis could such a fundamental transition be achieved; and what are the prospects for so expanding the economic bases of the urban areas that mass unemployment and destitution could be avoided? What form should physical planning for possible urbanization on such an unprecedented scale take? Alternatively, is it possible to envisage realistically the economic transformation of the peasantry on a basis of rural and small settlement development?

Kirkby examines the components of urban population increase since 1979, in the process unravelling and analysing urban population data of recent years that have become increasingly confusing due to changes in the official definition of urban population. He estimates that at least one-third of the overall urban population increase is due to migration, thus confirming widespread reports during the period of reform of the loosening of the bonds holding the peasantry in the countryside. As Kirkby states, the official line on urbanization policy laid down in the early 1980s has by now become a familiar refrain: strictly control the growth of the large cities, rationally develop the medium sized cities and actively promote the small cities. Yet, as he demonstrates, several countervailing policies have had the effect, economically at least, of promoting the growth of the large cities. During the period 1980–90, in fact, million-population cities doubled in number to 30. Significant inward migration is a new element in the urban situation, and the former close relationship between grain harvests and the permissible urbanization rate is now no longer so controllable. This gives rise to the very real fear that China may well face a future scenario of further urbanization of staggering proportions, especially as at least one-third of the huge agricultural workforce is already surplus to the needs of cultivation. As yet, there is no indication that the economic bases of the towns and cities could be so expanded as to make such an urbanization tolerable either in human or in political terms. In a possibly realistic, if catastrophic, future scenario, by 2040 AD of a population of 1.5 billion, two-thirds could be concentrated in several hundred cities, perhaps even straddling eastern, southern and north-eastern China in virtually contiguous linear belts.

Richard Edmonds in Chapter 9 reinforces the general tenor of this latter observation, but with respect to the environment in general. He demonstrates that China experiences virtually every type of environmental degradation to a gross degree and the situation is worsening. Environmental policy was born out of the ashes of the Cultural Revolution around 1972 but is weak in terms of enforcement and has frequently been ignored in the development of heavy industrial projects. In the countryside, the household responsibility system, and the accompanying official encouragement of a get-rich-quick mentality, has in places encouraged cultivation practices not of a sustainable nature. Further, a proportion of the new township and village industry has been established without reference to consequences in terms of pollution, while the remarkable increase in foreign investment of recent years has been characterized to some degree by the export of pollution-producing industries to China from Hong Kong and Taiwan. The factual record of environmental deterioration presented by Edmonds is an indictment of stewardship of the Chinese Communist Party that is even more damning than what has now become known of that of the Party in eastern Europe.

As Edmonds states, it would take a total optimist to predict that within the next two decades China will be able to halt the deterioration now occurring: the overall trend, he asserts, will be for conditions to continue to worsen not only because of the inability of the Party to reform the situation but also because as population increases so also does the ability to consume and pollute. Yet a halt in further environmental degradation is absolutely necessary if China is to feed and otherwise sustain its people to a reasonable standard in the next century. These general conclusions are supported by Douglas, Gu and He in Chapter 10 on water resources and environmental problems of China's great rivers. *Inter alia* they examine the controversial plans for the Three Gorge dam project on the Chang Jiang (Yangtze River), an attempt to tame nature by massive engineering means which will involve the resettlement of between 700 000 and 1.2 million people and, to sustain them, the conversion of 20 000 hectares of wild mountain land to cash crop cultivation and the use of a further 10 000 hectares of hillside for the cultivation of grain crops. The environmental risks of this aspect of the project alone are obviously severe.

In Chapters 11 and 12 Brian Hook and Jack Williams, respectively, examine two significant aspects of China's external relations: with Hong Kong and Taiwan. The two are linked since even though China has successfully accomplished the return of Hong Kong, which is to take place at the end of June 1997, the more important item on its reunification agenda, that of Taiwan, still remains to be resolved. Hook uses the statistics of emigration from Hong Kong as an index for registering the changing sentiment within the territory towards China. He demonstrates how China is increasingly seeking influence and a degree of control in Hong Kong before the agreed secession, in part because of the reaction of Beijing to the massive spontaneous protests that occurred in Hong Kong after the Tiananmen Square massacre.

The present situation in Hong Kong can only discourage reunification as far as the Taiwan government is concerned, yet the facts of current economics are dictating ever closer contacts with the mainland. Williams traces the evolution of the political relationship between China and Taiwan over the period since 1949. Taiwan would be the second smallest province in land area in China if reunited. Its population is only 21 million, yet its export trade is somewhat larger than that of China and its per capita income 20 times that of the mainland. During the past five years, both mutual trade and investment from Taiwan in China have grown significantly. Williams analyses this situation and draws attention to the fact that if present trends continue China could possibly become dependent upon Taiwan for perhaps a proportion of its export manufacturing, particularly in Fujian province. About half of Taiwanese investment capital entering China has gone into the Xiamen Special Economic Zone, and Taiwan capital accounts for half of all contracted foreign capital in this SEZ. A new factor in the relationship since 1986 has been the more public expression within Taiwan of attitudes of independence towards the mainland. These now appear to be growing, and in response China has publicly stated that any major moves in such a direction would be opposed by force. In this situation, as Williams states, despite the rapidly developing economic links, reunification would appear to be a very distant prospect.

In the final chapter the Editor, Denis Dwyer, assesses the general prospects for China. He emphasizes the need to examine carefully both the statistical base and the other development information supplied by Chinese sources at all levels because, not only in the international press but also within the academic community in the West, over the period since 1949 rather uncritical attitudes towards China's constant claims of substantial progress can be identified. In common with several other contributors to the present volume, he identifies population – its present size and future projected growth – as the issue central to China's future fortunes. Population issues, either directly or indirectly, can be shown to be key factors in many of the most critical problems now facing China. There can be no going back on the economic reforms but, as yet, they have provided only very partial solutions, to such a degree that, taking into account the continued political ossification of the country, it remains an open question whether Dengism is in process of creating a viable political legitimacy to replace Maoism. Opinions on China's future remain polarized. Many clearly remain impressed. 'You have here the most dramatic shift in the world balance of economic power in I don't know how many centuries', Mr Claude Smadja, director of the Geneva-based World Economic Forum, is reported as saying (*South China Morning Post*, Hong Kong, 8/11/92). On the other hand, Chevrier (1992, p. 118) has recently claimed that 'A bureaucracy without a state, official corruption, disorganised competition, inefficient authoritarian rule: the descending phase of Deng's decade is not unlike the end of the Ming and Qing dynastic cycles.' After reading this volume, let the reader decide.

Reference

Chevrier Yves (1992) 'From modernisation to involution: failed pragmatism and lost opportunities in Deng Xiaoping's China', in Marta Dassu and Tony Saich (eds), *The Reform Decade in China: From Hope to Dismay*, Kegan Paul, London, pp. 115–31.

CHAPTER 2

The Chinese economic reforms: an assessment*

Athar Hussain

This chapter provides a retrospective review of the Chinese reforms and discusses some items at the top of the reform agenda for the 1990s. As well as outlining the changes which have taken place, the retrospective review also compares China with the economies of Eastern Europe and the ex-Soviet Union and occasionally with East Asian and developing economies. The chapter goes on to explore reasons for the relative success of the Chinese economic reforms, and then analyses the motor forces of the reforms. This is followed by an analysis of particular areas for reform. The chapter ends with a brief speculation on the future prospects of economic and political reform.

The Chinese reforms from a comparative perspective

The Chinese economy invites comparisons with three groups of countries with which it shares partial resemblances: East European economies and the ex-Soviet Union; East Asian; and developing economies, especially large ones such as India. China once shared with Eastern Europe and the ex-Soviet Union various hallmarks of a socialist state and economy, such as the monopoly of power and control by one party, output planning, price controls and the state ownership of industrial enterprises. The last it still shares, but little else other than the fact that it too is in transit to a market economy. The post-1978 China shares with East Asian economies rapid growth rates of GNP, a high household savings ratio, a dynamic small-scale industrial sector, and, also lately, rapidly expanding exports. Finally, China displays some characteristic features of a developing

* This chapter is a revised and abridged version of a lecture delivered at the East Asia Institute of Copenhagen University in December 1991.

economy such as a large percentage of the population in rural areas and dependent on agriculture and a low income per capita. Among the erstwhile and still surviving communist countries, China, Cuba and Vietnam are, according to the World Bank classification, the only low-income economies.

China came to economic reforms relatively late. By 1978, when they officially started, East European economies and the then Soviet Union had already been on what has been referred to as the 'treadmill' of economic reforms for a decade or more. As it had done with the building of a socialist economy, China took its own particular road to economic reforms and drew little, if anything, from the experience of reforms in socialist economies. The initial instalment of the Chinese reforms was highly selective, but they proceeded quickly in the areas on which they were focused, such as agriculture, international trade and foreign investment. From the mid-1980s on, the Chinese economic reforms appeared both radical and more successful than the then still cautious reforms in Eastern Europe and the Soviet Union. The events of June 1989 in China and, soon after, the collapse of the one-party states and democratization in Eastern Europe and the ex-Soviet Union cast China in a very different light. It began to appear less as an exemplar of successful reforms in a socialist economy and more as one of the few remaining bastions of a discredited political system in the unedifying company of Cuba, North Korea and Vietnam.

Most of the East European economies and the ex-Soviet Republics seem to have opted for a 'great leap' into a market economy. In contrast, the Chinese are persisting with their 'long march' to a market economy, with its approach of step-by-step, though sometimes radical, reforms, while still retaining features of the old command economy, such as output planning, albeit selective, and the state ownership of medium- and large-size enterprises. In discussions of Eastern Europe it is now a commonplace that the two-track approach of grafting elements of a market economy to the command economy, which characterized earlier attempts at economic reform in Eastern Europe and the Soviet Union, failed and left behind a legacy of pervasive economic inefficiency, and, in some cases, also a large foreign debt and money stock and a high inflation rate (Kornai 1986; Brus and Laski 1989). In such discussions it is almost axiomatic that failure must logically follow from any attempt at 'mixing systems' or from any route other than the rapid one (Lipton and Sachs 1990(a), 1990 (b)). Yet the Chinese economic reforms, in contrast, have been an outstanding success in three respects: first, economic growth; second, protecting the population from deprivation; and, third, foreign trade and investment. I take these in turn and then draw some positive and negative lessons from the Chinese economic reforms.

Economic growth

In the period from 1978 to 1991, gross national product (GNP) grew by 8.6 per cent per year (ZTN 1991, p. 31; ZTZ 1992, p. 3). Given the population growth rate of around 1.4 per cent per annum (ZTN 1991, p. 79), the annual growth rate of per capita income comes to 7.3 per cent, which means that in the 13 years to 1991 average per capita income increased by around two-and-half times. The growth rates of total and per capita GNP over the reform period are significantly higher than those for any 13-year period since 1952; high not only by China's own historical standards but also internationally. The GNP growth rates of 6 to 7 per cent per annum over a decade are exceptional, especially for populous and diverse economies. Except in the 1950s, the ex-Soviet and East European economies have not been able to achieve growth rates as seen in China since 1978. In fact, China's growth rates would not look out of place among the growth records of the legendary 'high performance' Asian economies. They stand out all the more if one takes into account the fact that the so-called 'four dragons' – Hong Kong, South Korea, Singapore and Taiwan – are all homogeneous, and comparatively small, in terms of the population. It would be more appropriate to compare the 'four dragons' with Chinese provinces. For example, Guangdong's economic growth during the reform period is as impressive as theirs (for a discussion of reforms in Guangdong see Vogel 1989). Between 1980 and 1991 its gross product (equivalent to GNP) grew by 12.4 per cent per annum (*BR* 1992, No. 21, p. 4). Deng Xiaoping has recently elevated Guangdong to the rank of the dragons.

Looking into the future, what are the implications of the Chinese per capita income growing at an annual rate of 6 per cent, or doubling every 12 years? With such a growth rate over the next two decades, the Chinese population will graduate from a low-income status, with a per capita income of US$370 in 1990 (*WDR* 1992), to a middle-income status with a per capita income of around US$1200 by 2010. Thus the Chinese economy will have repeated, a bit more slowly, the performance of other Far Eastern economies in the 1960s and 1970s. The consequences of this for the world economy, however, would be far greater, given the huge size of China's population relative to those of its Far Eastern neighbours (for a discussion see Perkins 1986). For example, Guangdong alone with 63.5 million inhabitants has a slightly larger population than South Korea and Taiwan combined. The atlas of world poverty will look very different, given that around 37 per cent of the current low-income population in the world is in mainland China (see *WDR* 1992).

Turning to the sources of growth since 1978, during the first reform phase (1978–83) almost half the acceleration in the growth rate was due to agriculture (see Hussain and Stern 1991). The rural economy was de-collectivized almost as quickly as it was collectivized in 1958 during the Great Leap Forward, but this time with no upheaval. The de-collectivized agriculture immediately registered an impressive growth, well beyond expectations, and spurred the leadership to embark on reforms in the urban and industrial economy (see, for example, Deng Xiaoping 1987, pp. 120–5). It is hard to find many parallel cases of such a fundamental organizational change leading to a quick improvement in economic performance. It is, however, an open question as to how much of the accelerated growth in agriculture was due to the household responsibility system and how much was due to an increased supply of inputs and higher prices for agricultural produce – an issue to which I return later.

As the growth rate of agriculture began to slacken in 1985, the growth rate of industry accelerated. As a result, the overall growth rate for the economy stayed high. In fact, it was higher in the second reform phase (1984–88) than in the first, though accompanied with an inflationary spiral which began to career out of control in the summer–autumn of 1988 (see Hussain and Stern 1991). Faced with popular discontent and panic purchases by the population, the leadership embarked on a stabilization policy which, although decided in the autumn of 1988, was implemented in its full rigour only in June 1989, following the change in the leadership. In one sense, the 1989 stabilization policy was similar to the earlier ones in 1980–81 and 1986: geared to bringing down the inflation rate by reining in investment. But what made it different was the change in the ideological climate. It seemed then that Chinese economic reforms would end up the same way as those in Eastern Europe and the then Soviet Union in the 1970s to 1980s: an initial spurt followed by a lacklustre performance.

The growth rate dropped sharply, from 11.3 per cent in 1988 to 3.7 per cent in 1989 and stayed comparatively low at 4.8 per cent in 1990. The 1990 growth rate would have been much lower but for an exceptionally high growth rate of 7.5 per cent in agriculture (ZTN 1991, p. 34). The inflation rate too fell sharply but a year later than the national income growth rate (see ZTN 1991, p. 229). Also the international balance of payments which had been in deficit over most of the 1980s turned into a surplus (ZTN 1991, p. 615). A notable change in the stabilization period (1989–91) has been an acceleration in the growth rates of agriculture and of exports. By international standards, the stabilization policy, although heavy-handed, succeeded in its aim remarkably well and quickly. More important, the stabilization period saw no significant reversal in reforms. The 'household responsibility system' in agriculture remained intact and the door to the international economy stayed wide open. The economy began to climb out of recession from the end of 1990 and grew by 7.3 per cent in 1991, but the inflation rate remained low at 3.0 per cent (ZTZ 1992, p. 39). The growth rate for 1992 is expected to be even higher and so too is the inflation rate. The reform process resumed in 1991, but on a cautious note. It has been given a further impetus by Deng Xiaoping's call to accelerate reforms issued early in 1992 in the Shenzhen SEZ. In retrospect, it seems very much that 1989 was not a watershed as originally feared.

The Chinese government is projecting annual GNP growth rate of around 6 to 7 per cent for the 1990s as compared to growth rates of around 10 per cent from 1980 to 1988. For example, Li Peng in a speech to the National People's Congress suggested a growth rate of 7 per cent for 1992 (see BR 1992, No. 12). Given the recent performance of the economy, there would seem to be little doubt that the Chinese economy will be able to achieve the growth rate target. On the contrary, the problem is more likely to be the economy overshooting the target and an acceleration in inflation. The growth rate of agriculture is bound to be lower than that of industry. From the experience of 1991 and 1992, it would seem that a notable feature of industrial growth in the 1990s is likely to be rural industry growing significantly faster than urban industry dominated by state-owned enterprises.

Social protection and living standards

Economic growth is not the only relevant factor; improvement in the living standards and the protection of the population from deprivation are as important for assessing the Chinese reforms. In contrast to what is happening in Eastern Europe and the ex-Soviet Union now, and earlier in the developing economies which underwent economic restructuring and liberalization in the 1980s, the Chinese economic reforms have not brought economic hardship to a significant segment of the population. On the contrary, they have brought in their wake a record rise in personal incomes and living standards for both the rural and the urban population. As measured by household consumption, the increase in the general standard of living in the first nine years (1979–87) of the reform was the same as the improvement in the 26 years between 1952 and 1978 (see ZTN 1991, p. 271). The losers from the economic reforms in the absolute sense would appear to be few, if any. The increase in personal incomes, however, has been unevenly distributed and a rise in income inequality in urban areas and among provinces is likely to remain a major source of social discontent in the 1990s as it was in the period immediately prior to May–June 1989. It is, however, difficult to provide an unambiguous answer to the general question of whether the reforms have widened income inequalities all round. The answer, I suspect, would be mixed and would depend crucially on the scope of analysis (see, for example, Hussain et al. 1991; Griffin and Zhao Renwei 1992).

For the rural population the reforms began with the household responsibility system and the removal of restraints on private economic activities, and for the urban population with the abolition of rationing on a wide range of consumer goods. Breaking with the pre-reform ethos of frugal living in the pre-reform period, the reformist leadership attached a special importance to widening the range of consumer goods available to households. From the early 1980s there has been a remarkable increase in the ownership of consumer durables, which is still continuing apace. In 1978, the four treasured consumer goods were the thermos flask, the bicycle, the wrist watch and the sewing machine, but by the middle 1980s these were replaced by the TV set, the washing machine, the refrigerator and the radio cassette player. For example, the colour television set has changed from being a rare to a commonplace household item: colour sets per 1000 households rose from 172 in 1985 to 684 in 1991 (ZTN 1992, p. 286). (For a statistical summary of consumer durable ownership in Chinese cities see BR 1991, No. 42, p. 29.)

Although the reforms have been introduced from the top and have not relied on 'mass mobilization', as revolutionary campaigns in the pre-reform period did, they have commanded general support, though this support is far from coherent and inter-mixed with discontent with particular aspects of the reforms. The general support for reforms is due not merely to a record rise in personal income and the availability of a wide range of consumer goods, but also to a concerted attempt on the part of the leadership to keep the numbers of losers small. It would seem the leadership largely succeeded in this until the summer of 1988, when the inflation rate within a year climbed from 7 per cent to around 19 per cent, and a sizeable section of the urban population experienced a significant decline in its real income. This together with the perception of widespread corruption provided the social background for the demonstrations of May 1989.

The policy of keeping down the numbers of losers has been and still remains an important consideration in decisions about the speed and form of reforms, especially in the cases of price and enterprise reforms. For example, the procurement prices of agricultural commodities have since 1978 been raised continually in order to provide economic incentives to farmers but the government has passed on only a part of the increase to urban consumers and absorbed the remainder from the budget. Similarly, the government has reduced its 'tax-take' from profitable enterprises but has kept loss-making enterprises afloat in order to maintain employment. The bankruptcy law promulgated in 1988 remains yet to be enforced. In the year to April 1992, grain prices charged to urban inhabitants were raised 240 per cent (see *BR* 1992, No. 12, p. 7), but wages and salaries have also been raised to compensate for the rise. As price reforms go this was as significant as any attempted in Eastern Europe or the ex-Soviet Union except they went through smoothly and as a result did not receive much notice outside China.

The government has, as it were, provided an open-ended 'social insurance' to shield the population from the adverse consequences of the economic reforms, while at the same time reducing its revenue share in national income. For 'social insurance', the Chinese leadership, rather than introducing a new social security framework, has relied on the protective features of the pre-reform economy, such as guaranteed employment and low-price rations of staples for the urban population. As discussed later, this combination is becoming increasingly costly to sustain and an overhaul of the social security system is urgently needed. Further, guaranteed lifetime employment, which no longer formally holds but still applies in practice, poses the hardest problem for reform. The guarantee has to be rescinded if the industrial reforms involving possible bankruptcy of enterprises is to go ahead, but as yet the government has only chipped away at the guarantee shying away from abolishing it altogether.

Open-door policy and international trade

In China, the combination of the command and a market economy has hindered neither the expansion of foreign trade nor the inflow of foreign investment. On the contrary, the Chinese performance in these fields compares very favourably with those of other developing economies and ex-communist economies (see Hussain and Stern 1991; Lardy 1992). As with economic growth, the rise in Chinese exports seems to be a replication of the East Asian pattern. There has been a massive expansion in foreign trade relative to GNP. The ratio of imports and exports to GNP has risen from around 5 per cent in 1978 to over 15 per cent in 1990, which is higher than those for the Indian or Brazilian economies. Further, this has gone together with a radical change in the composition of exports away from primary goods towards manufactured goods.

Since 1978, the leadership, discarding the previous watchword of 'self-reliance', has welcomed loans from international agencies and governments and foreign direct investment, which between 1979 and 1990 totalled around US$68 billion (*ZTN* 1991; p. 629). As compared to developing economies such as India and East European economies, China has been extremely successful in attracting foreign investment. With the expansion of the Chinese market and the improvement of relations with South Korea and Taiwan, the flow seems to be rising. China's foreign borrowing is mainly from international organizations and governments rather than from banks. It would appear to have contributed to the combination of a significantly higher growth than in the pre-reform period while maintaining an unprecedented increase in household consumption. China's foreign debt at the end of 1991 was US$52 billion (*BR* 1992, No. 14; pp. 18–19), significantly less than its exports of around US$72 billion in 1991 (*BR* 1992, No. 12; p. 40). By international standards, the Chinese economy does not face a significant debt servicing problem.

The open-door policy consisting of export promotion, attracting foreign capital and resort to foreign borrowing has played a central role in the process of reforms and has already left a deep imprint on the economy. Large segments of the Chinese economy are dependent on international trade, and tourism and foreign-owned enterprises are a significant source of employment in urban areas, not only in southern China but also increasingly in other coastal provinces. Loans from international organizations have been an important channel for outside influence on the design and the course of Chinese reforms. Some of the important reforms in recent years have been prompted directly by the open-door policy. These include the sale of land-use rights, the institution of a white market in foreign currency, the acceptance of ownership forms other than the traditional state and collective ownership and the grant of direct trading rights to enterprises.

China, East Asia and transitional economies

In terms of economic growth and the expansion of foreign trade, the Chinese economy since 1978 seems to be repeating the East Asian pattern. However, the Chinese economy differs markedly from East Asian economies in the fields of social security and social protection. The urban labour force in China enjoys a far more extensive level of social benefits than its counterparts in those economies. The concern for social protection together with a large state-owned sector is what marks out the Chinese economy from its East Asian neighbours.

In comparison with the East European economies and the ex-Soviet Republics, the Chinese economic performance since 1978 looks extremely impressive. The purpose of this contrast is not, however, to argue that their salvation lies in the adoption of the Chinese approach. The initial

17

economic and social conditions for a transition to a market economy are very different. Comparatively speaking, the Chinese economy was stable, albeit highly inefficient and traumatized by the ten years of the Cultural Revolution, when it embarked on the reform process in 1978. Moreover, political conditions are very different also: in China the economic reforms have preceded democratization, which has yet to happen. The reforms have been introduced from the top and the Communist Party retains its monopoly of political power, though it has to be emphasized that the Chinese leadership is far from indifferent to the reaction of the population to reforms, especially since the events of June 1989. In contrast, in the Soviet Union and Eastern Europe the break-up of the traditional political order has preceded, or been contemporaneous with, the transition process. In some of these economies, the main problem is no longer pervasive government interference in economic activities and the lives of citizens, but a breakdown of law and order and the inability of the government to take and implement decisions. It is this rather than the survival of the elements of the command economy which may turn out to be the main obstacle in the transition to a well-functioning market economy.

The Chinese experience provides both positive and negative lessons for other transitional economies. One negative lesson from the Chinese experience is that combining elements of the command and the market economy, although it reduces uncertainty and helps to maintain economic and social stability in the initial stages of transition, also creates problems which become more acute with the passage of time. Two notable examples are the two-track pricing system introduced in 1984 and the grant of financial and operational autonomy to state-owned enterprises without also exposing them to a risk of bankruptcy. The two-track system of letting output in excess of the plan quota to be sold at negotiated prices has not only undermined the state supply system but, more important, also stunted the development of markets. On the one hand, it gives enterprises a strong incentive to default on plan deliveries, with a knock-on effect of the government also defaulting on the delivery of inputs at plan prices to enterprises. On the other hand, it spawns segmented markets of various shades from white to black, which have provided a fertile ground for a 'hundred crooked flowers to bloom'. Similarly, protecting enterprises from the downside risk of bankruptcy, while allowing them considerable discretion over wages and investment, has encouraged them to be generous in granting wage increases to their employees at the state's expense, on the one hand, and to 'over-invest' on the other. Over-investment has been further facilitated by a loosening of administrative controls on bank lending to enterprises since the mid-1980s. Throughout the 1980s the propensity to over-invest on the part of enterprises has been, and still remains, a major source of macroeconomic problems in the Chinese economy (for a discussion see Hussain and Stern 1991).

The Chinese example also provides some positive lessons for other transitional economies. Prominent among these are two: first, piecemeal reforms can be cumulative and do not necessarily run out of impetus. Second, delegating economic decision-making to individuals and households, without an immediate and complete overhaul of the traditional economic order and wholesale privatization, can bring speedy and impressive effects. A large state industrial sector does not necessarily crowd out an incipient non-state sector. In some cases they may even be complementary. The relative importance of the state sector in the Chinese economy has decreased steadily since 1978 due not to privatization, however, but to the fast growth rate of the non-state sector, especially of rural industrial enterprises. The Chinese experience also indicates that in a large economy there may be benefits in going for a geographical or sectoral decentralized approach to reforms: letting particular regions and sectors race ahead.

Comparative success of the Chinese reforms

The above discussion has projected the Chinese economic reforms in a favourable light and raises the question of why they have succeeded whereas the comparable economic reforms in Eastern Europe and the ex-Soviet Union during the communist era failed. I attempt to answer the question by first drawing up a balance sheet of the Chinese reforms and then outlining the factors which would appear to have contributed to the success of the Chinese reforms in particular areas.

It is important to emphasize that Chinese reforms have been far from an unqualified success. There are many areas where they seem to have failed. For example, the attempts at reforming the state-owned enterprises have not made much progress towards transforming them into market-oriented firms, responsible for their profits and losses. Many of them are loss-making, and government intervention in their running remains ubiquitous (for a discussion see Perkins 1988). As many as one third of state-owned enterprises are currently running at a loss (BR 1991, No. 34, p.5). The Chinese record in this area appears no better than those of discredited reforms in Eastern Europe and the ex-Soviet Union during the Communist era. Another area where the economic reforms have yet to make much headway is in the reform of the financial system. The lending operations of banks are governed more by administrative directives than by commercial criteria and a significant percentage of bank loans are write-offs (World Bank 1991).

On the positive side of the balance sheet, the Chinese reforms have been remarkably successful on four counts: first, accelerating the growth rate and sustaining it at a high level over a comparatively long period; second, transforming collective agriculture; third, spurring the growth of rural industry and household-based activities; and, fourth, the expansion of exports. What this list suggests is that the success of the reforms is due in large measure, but not exclusively, to the rural economy – a feature which seems to be central in explaining the comparative success of the Chinese reforms.

Turning to the main differences in the style of reforms between China and the erstwhile Communist economies, some of the major Chinese economic reforms have not been pre-planned. Rather they began as local experiments and have been open-ended. In many cases, they went further than originally intended. For example, the household responsibility system was initially intended for poor areas and for those localities where collective agriculture was not performing well. But given their initial success, they spread to the whole of the countryside within a few years. Similarly, the rapid growth of rural industry, which has been a notable feature since the mid-1980s and is likely to be of even greater importance in the 1990s, was neither planned nor foreseen. The government did little more than remove restraints. The open-ended approach to reforms can both help and hinder their progress. In the Chinese case, they have helped where reforms have borne fruit quickly such as the household responsibility system – an issue which I discuss further in the next section.

The Chinese economy was fairly decentralized in the pre-reform period, and the reforms have involved a further devolution of economic administration from higher to lower government tiers: from the central to provincial governments and to the government tiers below. This has deepened the segmentation of the economy and brought with it a number of problems, but it has also helped to speed up the reforms (for a discussion of the problems see White 1991). Given the vast size of China and resistance to the economic reforms from various quarters, a reform package for the whole economy in concert runs the risk of being determined by the 'lowest common denominator'. For example, allowing provinces such as Anhui to replace collective farming with household farming in 1979, and letting Guangdong and special economic zones forge ahead in the 1980s, have facilitated the introduction of radical reforms which were not politically feasible for the whole country. In retrospect, the strategy of decentralized reforms has succeeded in two respects: first, it has served to outflank resistance to the reforms and has also made it difficult to reverse them. Second, the provinces and areas which have taken the lead in reforms such as Guangdong, rather than remaining isolated examples, have become a model for emulation elsewhere. Thus many reforms which were radical when they were introduced, such as special incentives to attract foreign investment and the leasing of land to foreigners, within a few years spread to other parts of the country. It has also to be said that decentralized reforms have some severe limitations. There are areas where some centralization and uniformity throughout the economy are necessary for the success of reforms. This applies particularly to a reform of the taxation system, the public finances, the financial system and the social security system. These happen to be the areas where the Chinese reforms thus far have been particularly deficient.

Another reason for the difference between the performance of the Chinese reforms and other 'socialist reforms' would also seem to lie in the features which distinguished the Chinese economy from the economies of Eastern Europe and the ex-Soviet Union in the Communist era. These may be attributed to three interrelated factors: first, the revolutionary route taken by China since the late 1950s; second, the structure of the Chinese command economy; and, third, China being a developing economy. It may be argued that the Great Leap Forward and the Cultural Revolution, although fundamentally hostile to any form of market economy, embodied features which have played a positive role in the success of the Chinese economic reforms. The paradox is that the movements which set out to push collectivism to its limits and cut off the 'capitalist tail' furnished some of the ingredients responsible for the relative success of market-oriented reforms in China.

The Great Leap Forward relied heavily on the initiation of institutional change from the grassroots rather than from the top. Neither spontaneous nor unconstrained, such initiatives were encouraged, if not instigated, and assured of protection by sections of the top leadership. They were also permeated with coercion. Notwithstanding all these, they marked a radical departure from the hierarchical principle of organization which has been the hallmark of Leninist or Stalinist organizations. The initiation of major institutional changes from below has been an important strand in the Chinese economy not only during the Cultural Revolution but also in the reform period. This holds especially for two success stories of the reform: the household responsibility system in agriculture and the explosive growth of rural industry from the mid-1980s. The initiation and the spread of de-collectivization of agriculture from 1979 mirrors the pattern of the collectivization of agriculture from 1956. Rural industrialization dates back to the pre-reform period. Although it was not particularly successful then, it did bring some tangible economic benefits. The experience of setting up and operating industrial plants developed in rural areas the capacity to engage and organize industrial production which, it may be argued, facilitated the development of rural industry in the 1980s.

The pre-reform command economy in China differed from the command economies of the erstwhile Soviet Union and Eastern Europe in some important respects. Central planning had a comparatively limited remit and the economy was highly decentralized with a great deal of discretion to provinces and the lower government tiers. The process of decentralization which began with the Great Leap Forward marked an important break from the Soviet-style planning. It was initially prompted by an economic strategy of development, albeit ill-conceived, but later (especially in the 1960s) it was underpinned by the military considerations of fighting a prolonged war on Chinese soil. The economy which the Chinese economic reforms set out to transform was planned coarsely, though permeated with government intervention. In China, improving the performance of the economy through a reform of planning rather than market-oriented reforms did not have the support it had in the ex-Soviet Union (for a discussion see Sutela 1991). Neither was the planning apparatus in China a serious obstacle to market-oriented reforms as it was in the ex-Soviet Union.

This pre-reform 'administrative decentralization with Chinese characteristics' segmented the economy into semi-independent cells and went in tandem with massive inefficiencies, which have been much commented on (for a discussion see Tidrick 1987). But this cellular segmentation also gave the economy resilience to shocks and considerable flexibility, which is crucial to an understanding of the Chinese economy pre- and post-1978. The Great Leap, after an initial flutter, led immediately to a steep fall in national income and claimed tens of millions of victims. In contrast, the Cultural Revolution, even at its height when the government machinery was paralysed and planning moribund, led to a comparatively minor decline in national income. It is instructive to contrast the economic effects of the Cultural Revolution, which at its peak would rank high on the Richter scale of economic shocks, with the effects of economic and political dislocation in the present-day ex-Soviet Union and some East European economies. While falls in national income of 10 to 15 percentage points have been common in Russia and some East European economies in recent years, national income in China declined by 7 per cent in 1967 and 6 per cent in 1968 but more than rebounded to the 1966 level in 1969 (see ZTN 1991, pp. 33–4). We see a recurrence of a similar mixture of resilience to economic shocks and powers of a quick recovery in the interregnum, 1976–78, and the period since June 1989. The cellular segmentation of the economy also gave the post-Mao leadership the flexibility to introduce radical reforms in particular areas without disruption to the rest of the economy.

Turning to China being a developing economy, on the eve of the economic reforms an overwhelming percentage of the labour force (around 76 per cent in 1978) was in rural areas and most of it employed in agriculture (see ZTN 1991, pp. 99–100). In the pre-reform period, the agricultural labour force was largely organized at the household level, even though the overall deployment of labour was determined by collective institutions. Tasks were assigned to households rather than to individuals; so too were work points and payments (for an account see Parish and Whyte 1978). Agriculture accounted for a comparatively high proportion of national income, around one-third in 1978 (ZTN 1991, p. 35). Chinese agriculture was efficient by the standards of developing economies and, organized around households as it was, it could be de-collectivized very easily (for a discussion of the relative efficiency of Chinese agriculture see Hussain 1989). In comparison with large-scale industry and economic organizations, market-oriented reforms in respect to household-based economic activities are much easier. They do not require the building of new institutions, but merely the lifting of restraints on economic activities.

The fact that an overwhelming percentage of the labour force was, and still is, employed in the non-state sector (mostly in rural areas) gave the Chinese labour market considerable flexibility, which it still retains. Rural labour has been available for a much lower wage rate than in the state sector or the urban collective sector. The actual gap in the labour cost is larger than the difference in cash wages because the rural labour force is not entitled to the extensive social insurance provided for the urban labour force. Moreover, rural workers, unlike their urban counterparts, do not enjoy lifetime employment. An important contributory factor to the explosive growth of rural industry from the mid-1980s is the highly flexible labour market it faces. The rural labour force has also given flexibility at the margin in the urban labour markets. Although permanent migration from rural to urban areas in China has remained strictly controlled, 'temporary' labour migration from rural to urban areas has risen sharply during the reform period (see, for example, NPCO 1991, pp. 6–11). A large percentage of the workforce in building construction in China's large cities is made up of, for example, temporary migrants from the countryside.

The large share of agriculture in national income and the overwhelming percentage of the rural labour force in the total, features which are normally associated with developing economies, are crucial to an understanding of the relative success of the Chinese economic reforms. They began with agriculture, while the reforms in Eastern Europe and the ex-Soviet Union during the Communist era were focused on state-owned industry, which, as indicated earlier, has proved to be particularly difficult to reform. These two features are central to two of the four success stories of the reforms: the household responsibility system in agriculture and its impact on the economy and the growth of rural industry. Moreover, the third success story, the high growth of national income in the reform period, is due in part to an improvement in the performance of agriculture and the growth of rural industry.

Turning to the fourth success story of the reforms, the expansion of exports and a large inflow of foreign investment, Hong Kong has played a crucial role. It is the most important conduit for Chinese exports, and its highly developed international trading and financial links have provided China with a highly valuable staging post for its exports. In 1990, Hong Kong accounted for almost one-third of Chinese exports (ZTN 1991, p. 620). It has also been the largest source of foreign investment in the Chinese economy, accounting for over half in 1990 (ZTN 1991, p. 630), for example. The opening of the economy and its rapid growth, its geographical proximity to the fastest growing economic region in the world and its ethnic and cultural links with countries in East and South East Asia, have become important factors in China's foreign trade and investment, especially in the coastal regions.

Pattern and dynamics of the reform

The reforms since 1978 have followed a Chinese version of a stop–go cycle, alternating between a loosening of administrative controls and bold economic reforms in the 'go' phase and reimposition of administrative controls and a cautious attitude towards further reforms in the 'stop' phase. The principal 'stop phases' have been three: the curb on investment in 1981–82, the short-lived restraint on investment and bank credit in 1986; and the stabilization period 1989–91. One can identify a similar oscillation between the tightening and the loosening of ideological controls on discussions and speech which have not always coincided with the cycle of economic reforms.

The change in the leadership in June 1989 marked the onset of a stop phase in economic reforms and also the tightening of ideological and political controls. Although it seemed then to be a decisive turning point, there were no significant reversals of economic reforms. The process of economic reforms restarted in 1991 with a major rise in prices of grain and cooking oil for urban inhabitants. It received a further fillip from Deng

Xiaoping's speech in Shenzhen in January 1992 (for an account in English of the speech see *BR* 1992, No. 15, pp. 4–6). Deng's speech was made outside the official channels and not published in China until several months later. It is interesting to note that its reverberations bear some striking resemblance to Mao's famous speech on the eve of the Cultural Revolution in 1966 (Mao 1974, pp. 253–5). However, ideological and political controls introduced in the wake of the change in the leadership in June 1989 still remain in force.

Among the motor forces of the reforms, three may be singled out: first, the commitment to modernization; second, the opendoor policy; and, third, a conjunction of factors which may be termed the internal dynamics of the economic reforms. That is, reforms have been propelled in part by the success of initial reforms and in part by the problems they themselves have created.

The commitment to modernize China, which predates the reforms, has been shared by all Chinese leaders. It has been, as it were, the river bed which has shaped the course of reforms. As with the flow of water, the reforms may vary over time in their speed or extent, yet follow the direction set by the underlying commitment to reforms. As with a river bed, the theme of modernization has undergone changes over time and occasionally abruptly, as it has done in the 1980s. Unlike in the pre-reform period, all Chinese leaders since 1978 have accepted that modernization involves emulation of developed market economies, at least in some major respects, and that it is not possible without the 'open-door' policy, involving extensive reliance on international trade and foreign technology and investment. Unlike in the pre-reform period, modernization through self-reliance has few, if any, adherents among the top leadership. It is also commonly accepted that the 'open-door' policy for the most part means economic relations with Japan and other East Asian market economies, North America and Western Europe, and, more important, largely on terms which China has to take as given. It is interesting to note that the change in the leadership in June 1989 left the open-door policy intact; there was no attempt to revise the elements of the policy.

As argued earlier, the effects of the open-door policy on the reforms have gone well beyond the acquisition of technology and capital, the expansion of exports and attracting foreign capital. The desire to keep the door open to the outside world has prompted the leadership to break some cherished taboos. Notable among these are allowing foreign-owned and managed companies, granting them a privileged status, and the leasing of land to foreigners. Initially introduced in the special economic zones, these innovations are no longer restricted to them. As with other East Asian economies such as South Korea and Taiwan, the Chinese government is also discovering that success in increasing exports brings with it pressure from foreign governments, in particular the United States, to liberalize the economy. For example, the desire of the Chinese government to join the General Agreement on Trade and Tariffs (GATT) to benefit automatically from the 'most-favoured nation treatment' in international trade has led the government to restrict further the monopoly of foreign trade corporations, to reduce subsidies to them and to recognize international intellectual property rights (see interview with the Minister of Foreign Trade in BR 1992, No.10, pp. 8–10). Such pressure is likely to increase with a growth in Chinese exports and the inflow of foreign investment.

Turning to the internal dynamics of the reform, the reforms until the mid-1980s were propelled by the immediate success of the first set of reforms, especially in rural areas. It may be argued that the economic take-off of the household responsibility system in the early 1980s was due partly to the rich legacy of collective agriculture. This included all the main ingredients needed for a 'Green Revolution': irrigation, high yield variety seeds and fertilizers. Due to massive hydraulic construction in the two decades of 1958–78, the proportion of irrigated area was exceptionally high – twice as high as in India, for example. High yield varieties of grain were as widely spread in China as in any developing economy. Chinese scientists had pioneered high yield varieties of rice in the early 1960s, and in the 1970s the government imported high yield varieties of wheat for planting or cross-breeding. Finally, the leadership put special emphasis on the use of fertilizers, both natural and chemical. Between 1973 and 1975 the government imported 20 large chemical fertilizer plants, which came on stream just as the household responsibility system was being introduced (for a discussion see Hussain 1989). How much of the growth in agricultural output was due to the incentives provided by the household responsibility system and how much was due to increase in the procurement prices of agricultural produce is an interesting issue for further research (see Lin 1991 for further discussion).

However, the reform process could be sustained only for a limited period by the immediate success of earlier reforms. The first set of reforms exhausted the easy possibilities for an immediate improvement. The urban and industrial reforms from 1984, especially of the state industrial sector, have turned out to be far more intractable and less successful than rural reforms. The reforms such as the two-track pricing system and the grant of financial and operational autonomy to industrial enterprises have brought some improvements but have also created problems. Many of the major problems facing the Chinese economy since the mid-1980s do not date from the pre-reform period, but have arisen from the piecemeal reforms themselves. These include the anomalies of the two-track pricing system, increased corruption, losses of state-owned enterprises and the erosion of the public finances. Together with the exigencies of the open-door policy, it is these problems which have been the main driving force behind the reforms from the late 1980s.

The problems facing the Chinese economy cannot be solved by reverting to the command economy, though the government has periodically resorted to administrative controls to keep them in check. The reforms have weakened the structures of the command economy and the planning machinery to a degree where a reversal is no longer possible. For example, it is simply not feasible to replace the two-track pricing system with a planned pricing system. Moreover, in many cases doing nothing is not a feasible option either. For example, the losses of state-owned enterprises are currently such that they cannot be sustained without creating other serious problems. The only option left for the government is to introduce further reforms.

Outstanding problems

The Chinese economy still has a long way to go towards a full transition to a market economy and faces serious problems which require major reforms. Prominent on the agenda for immediate reforms are the two-track pricing system; state-owned enterprises; the public finances; and the social security system. Missing from the list are agriculture or the rural economy and foreign trade and investment. The household responsibility system is a makeshift set-up and sooner or later the leadership will have to address the problem of a long-term organization of agriculture. However, it still seems capable of generating a respectable growth rate for farm output, given appropriate incentives such as higher prices for agricultural goods and the availability of inputs, as evidenced by the improvement in the growth rate of agriculture in 1990–91. Foreign trade and investment do not appear on the list, not because the present arrangements are satisfactory but given the commitment to the open-door policy the leadership has little option but to introduce the reforms necessary for expanding exports and attracting foreign investment.

The two-track pricing system for both agricultural and manufactured commodities has over time become increasingly untenable. Starting in 1990, the Chinese government has followed a cautious strategy of price reforms, and a large number of government-controlled prices have been raised (for an account see BR 1992, No. 18, pp. 14–17). For agricultural commodities, the gap between government-controlled and market prices has been heavily reduced and a few more good harvests may encourage the government to abolish government-controlled prices altogether. However, it appears that the abolition of the two-track pricing for industrial inputs such as coal, petroleum and steel would take some time. The two-track pricing, as other systems of price controls, has created a strong vested interest in its continuation. However, it would seem that the two-track pricing system is already extensively frayed and would in time disappear with a further development of markets.

Central to the transition from a command to a market economy is transformation of the state-owned enterprises into institutions akin to firms in market economies and an overhaul of their relations with the state. In China, as in East European economies and the ex-Soviet Union, this has proved to be the most intractable part of economic reforms. Looking to the future, two questions arise: first, where is the main impetus for a radical reform of state-owned enterprises coming from, and, second, what is the likely form of such a reform in China? Following the imposition of the stabilization policy in 1989, the losses of state-owned enterprises have mounted and they have remained high despite the upturn in the economy. As pointed out earlier, as many as one-third of state-owned enterprises are running at a loss (see BR 1991, No. 34, p. 5). Added to this there is also a major problem of default on inter-enterprise debts. The cost to government of keeping loss-making SOEs afloat is very high now. There is a sense of urgency about the reform of state-owned enterprises, as evidenced by a high-level meeting on the reform of state-owned enterprises held in September 1991 and the announcement of a package of reforms (BR 1991, No. 40, pp. 4–5). A reform of state-owned enterprises in China would, however, not take the form of wholesale privatization, at least not in the foreseeable future.

An oft-recurring theme in recent economic discussions in China is the stringency of the public finances. The reform period has seen a dramatic decline in the ratio of government revenue to GNP, from 34.4 per cent in 1978 to around 20 per cent in 1989 and 1990. The ratio of government expenditure to GNP too has fallen but with a lag. As a result, there has usually been a budget deficit every year since 1979, the period of stabilization since June 1989 included. Almost all of the decrease in the ratio of government revenue to GNP is accounted for by the decrease in profit taxes relative to GNP. A decrease in the profit tax-take is as intended by reforms, but the extent of the fall has come as a surprise to the government. The main problem on the expenditure side is the change in the composition of government expenditure in the 1980s. An increasing share of government expenditure has been devoted to price subsidies, mostly on grain and cooking oil, and subsidies to loss-making enterprises. Heavily reliant as it remains on enterprises (especially state owned) for revenue, the Chinese tax system is increasingly like a building resting on eroding foundations. There is an urgent need to diversify the sources of government revenue. However, as yet there is little concerted discussion of the reform of the taxation system in China (see Hussain and Stern 1992).

A reform of the social security system is currently high on the reform agenda, but the attention is almost exclusively on labour insurance for the wage-employed labour force in urban areas. Since the start of the Cultural Revolution in 1966, enterprises have been responsible for the financing of labour insurance for their labour force. Until the onset of industrial reforms, this responsibility was of purely nominal significance as enterprise budgets were integrated with the government budget: enterprises handed over their revenue to the government, which in turn covered their costs. With the grant of financial autonomy to enterprises as part of the reforms, many enterprises are not able to cover their labour insurance liabilities. The problem is most acute in the case of old-age pensions, where the ratio of retired workers to the labour force varies widely across enterprises and across provinces. Of the large number of problems which a social security reform in China has to address, two are of special importance: first, old-age support and, second, a potentially large problem of unemployment (for a discussion see Hussain and Liu 1989; Ahmad and Hussain 1991). The first is by far the largest issue in terms of number of persons and financial burden. For a low-income economy, China has an unusually large percentage of elderly people, and the percentage is expected to continue rising and likely to accelerate. The Chinese social security system still remains tied to pre-reform distinctions even though changes brought about by the reforms are rendering them obsolete. The general tenor of the reforms is to reduce security of employment or income where it comes into conflict with efficiency, as illustrated by the replacement of permanent employment with terminable employment and the concern with reducing disguised unemployment. Further, the reforms have given rise to phenomena which increase the risk of deprivation, such as migration from rural areas on a large scale. The general implication is that the Chinese social security system is in need of a major overhaul if the population is to continue enjoying the level of security it enjoyed in the past.

Future prospects

The process of reforms looks set to continue but it will be piecemeal and proceed in stop–go cycles, as it has since 1978. Deng Xiaoping's speeches in Guangdong would seem to have paved the way for an acceleration of reforms (see BR 1992, No. 12, pp. 5–7). Both the form of Deng's intervention and the content of his speech are of some significance. The fact that his intervention was in the form of public speeches outside the official channels, rather than the usual private talk to leaders, suggests that it was intended to outflank the cautious reformers in the ranks of the top leadership who, it appears in retrospect, were winning the battle over the course and pace of the future reforms. The notable feature of Deng's speeches is not so much the call for an acceleration of reform as the reaffirmation of his earlier pragmatic approach to reforms. For him, the main danger now is from left ideologues rather than from the right seeking a further liberalization of the economy. He also rehabilitated the accelerated reform policy between 1986 and 1988, which was completely discredited after June 1989, and thus by implication all those associated with it, and regretted not having made Shanghai a special economic zone. The reference to Shanghai is important because, having lagged behind Guangdong in reforms in the 1980s, it is now the most important test-case for reforms.

Turning to the pattern of development in the Chinese economy, as pointed out earlier, the economic reforms have been decentralized and certain provinces and regions have raced ahead of others. An acceleration of reforms following Deng's speech would accentuate a regionalization of the Chinese economy around the south Chinese economy centred around Hong Kong and Guangdong; the east Chinese economy centred around Shanghai and the surrounding provinces of Jiangsu and Zhejiang; and the northern Chinese economy. As until now, regionalization would go together with uneven growth rates and thereby exacerbate problems which have surfaced in the 1980s. Principal among them is the migration of the population from poorer to richer regions. Adminstrative controls on migration, which still remain in force, are increasingly in conflict with the growing migration of the population.

References

Ahmad, E, and Hussain A (1991) 'Social security in China: a historical perspective', in Ahmad E, Dreze J, Hills J and Sen A (eds). *Social Security in Developing Countries*, Clarendon Press, Oxford, pp. 247–304.

BR *(Beijing Review)* various references specified in text.

Brus W and Laski K (1989) *From Marx to the Market Socialism*, Clarendon Press, Oxford.

Deng Xiaoping (1987) *Fundamental Issues in Present-Day China*, Foreign Languages Press, Beijing.

Griffin K and Zhao Renwei (eds) (1992) *The Distribution of Income in China*, Oxford University Press, Oxford.

Hussain A (1989) 'Science and technology in the Chinese countryside', in Goldman, M. and Simon, F. (eds). *Science and Technology in Post-Mao China*, Harvard University Press, Cambridge, Mass.

Hussain A and Liu Hong (1989) 'Compendium of literature on the Chinese social security system', *China Programme Papers*, No. 3, STICERD, London School of Economics.

Hussain A and Stern N (1991) 'Effective demand, enterprise reforms and public finance in China', *Economic Policy*, April, pp. 142–86.

Hussain A and Stern N (1992) 'Economic reforms and public finance in China', in *Public Finance in a Changing World*, International Public Finance Association.

Hussain A, Lanjouw P. and Stern N (1991) 'Income inequalities in China: evidence from household survey data', *China Programme Papers*, No. 17, STICERD, London School of Economics.

Kornai J (1986) 'The Hungarian reform process: visions, hopes and reality', *Journal of Economic Literature*, **24** 1687–737.

Lardy N R (1992) *Foreign Trade and Economic Reform in China*, Cambridge University Press, Cambridge.

Lin Y (1991) 'Rural reform and agricultural growth in China', *American Economic Review*.

Lipton D and Sachs J (1990a) 'Creating a market economy in Eastern Europe', *Brookings Papers on Economic Activity*, 1, 75–147.

Lipton D and Sachs J. (1990b) 'Privatization in Eastern Europe: the case of Poland', *Brookings Papers on Economic Activity*, 2, 293–341.

Mao Zedong (1974) In Schram S (ed.) *Mao Unrehearsed*, Penguin, Books Harmondsworth, London, pp. 253-5.

NPCO (The National Population Census Office) (1991) *The Major Figures of the Fourth National Population Census of China*, The Statistical Publishing House, Beijing.

Parish W P and Whyte M (1978) *Village and Family in Contemporary China*, Chicago University Press, Chicago.

Perkins D H (1986) *China – Asia's Next Economic Giant?*, University of Washington Press, Seattle.

Perkins D H (1988) 'Reforming China's economic system', *Journal of Economic Literature* **XXVI**, 601–45.

Sutela P (1991) *Economic Thought and Economic Reform in the Soviet Union*,

Cambridge University Press, Cambridge.

Tidrick G (1987) 'Planning and supply' in Tidrick G and Chen Jiyuan (eds). *China's Industrial Reform*, Oxford University Press, Oxford, pp. 175–209.

Vogel E (1989) *One Step Ahead – Guangdong Under Reform*, Harvard University Press, Cambridge, Mass.

White G (ed) (1991) *The Chinese State in the Era of Economic Reforms – The Road to Crisis*, Macmillan, London.

World Bank (1991) *China – Financial Sector Review: Financial Policies and Institutional Development*, World Bank, Washington, DC.

WDR (*World Development Report*) (1992) World Bank, Washington, DC.

ZTN *Zhongguo Tongji Nianjian 1991 (Statistical Yearbook of China 1991)*, (1991), State Statistical Bureau, Beijing.

ZTN *Zhongguo Tongji Nianjian 1992 (Statistical Yearbook of China 1992)*, State Statistical Bureau, Beijing.

ZTZ *Zhongguo Tongji Zhaiyao 1992 (Statistical Survey of China 1992)* (1992), State Statistical Bureau, Beijing.

CHAPTER 3

China and the former USSR: a comparison in time and space

John Cole

Before the disintegration of the former USSR in 1991, following several years of change and restructuring in the late 1980s, it could be argued that the Soviet experience of development contained lessons for China's leaders. The problems arising from the break-up of the USSR and the prospect that China could follow a similar path in the future, one of several 'alternative futures' for it, now make a comparison even more thought-provoking. There have, however, been few serious attempts to compare the two great socialist powers, whereas comparisons of the USSR with the USA have been numerous, and some have been made between the USSR and Japan (e.g. Maddison 1969). Likewise, China and India have frequently been compared.

In 1957 the present author wrote a paper 'China surmounting a late start: limitations of Russian model' (Cole 1957). The justification for the comparison was the assumption, reasonable at the time, that with an appropriate time-lag, development in China could follow the Soviet experience. More recently, the comparison was followed up by the author in a study of post-war production and consumption trends in the USSR and China (Cole 1987), and of the cities of the two countries (Cole 1990). Until the late 1980s, such a comparison seemed valid in a positive sense. China and the USSR were broadly similar in certain respects, above all in the presence of a command economy, with a single political party in control, a large population and area, and a high degree of economic self-sufficiency as measured by their very low import coefficients of a few per cent in each case. Differences in performance, therefore, might to a large extent be attributable to their different natural resource endowments (in relation to population) and to different cultural features.

Currently, Chinese leaders cannot avoid observing two aspects of rapid change in the former Soviet system: the attempt to change from a centrally planned to a market economy and the survival, after seven decades of Soviet power, of strong ethnic feelings in the populations of the fifteen former Soviet Socialist Republics and, indeed, even in non-Russian ethnic groups not separated into such republics. Before the visit of Gorbachev to China in 1989, and the accompanying manifestations in Beijing in favour of a more open and democratic system for China, it appeared that China was, in a pragmatic way, making greater progress than the USSR towards *perestroyka* and a market economy, whereas in the USSR *glasnost*, with greater freedom of expression, was coming more quickly than in China. Since 1991 it is no longer possible to generalize about the USSR because each of the 15 former Soviet Socialist Republics has followed its own path politically and economically. It is of interest, however, to speculate about a possible future in which China becomes less centralized, or even breaks up as the USSR has done.

To allow a valid comparison through time between China and the former USSR it is necessary to decide how far China lagged behind the USSR in the 1950s, when it adopted the Soviet model and received advice and technical assistance from its new partner. A time-lag of 25 years is assumed, this being the difference between 1928, the first year of the First Soviet Five Year Plan, and 1953, the first year of the first Chinese one. Such a time-lag is preferred to the more obvious one of 1917 against 1949, the years in which the Communist Parties of the two countries came to power. To illustrate the comparison, Fig. 3.1 shows the production of steel per inhabitant in the two countries, both contemporaneously and with the 25 year time-lag. It can be seen that not only was steel output per inhabitant in the late 1980s much higher in the USSR than in China, as to be expected, but also that even in 1964 it was almost 10 times higher in the USSR than it was in China in 1989. Cole (1987) compared various products in this way. Examples of the gaps are discussed later in this chapter. The clear message is that China has far less production per inhabitant for development and

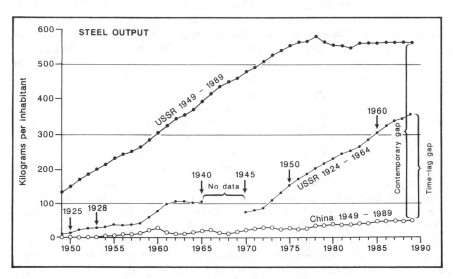

Fig. 3.1 A comparison of steel output per inhabitant in China and the USSR 1949–89.

consumption than the USSR had at roughly an equivalent stage in its development.

It is appropriate to compare the natural resource endowment of the two countries since the former USSR is more than twice as large in area as China but China has more than four times as many inhabitants. As will be shown below, per inhabitant the former USSR has somewhere between five and ten times as many natural resources as China. Such a disparity seems bound to restrict the room for manoeuvre in China, especially as its population is expected to increase by another 200–300 million before it stabilizes, and its leaders have ambitious plans for further economic growth.

To achieve a spatial comparison is more difficult, partly at least because while the two countries pass along a common time scale, the various bioclimatic and mineral resources, people and places of production are uniquely distributed over different two-dimensional spaces. Cartographical comparisons can be made of such spatial features as for example distance from the national capital or from the coast, and the distribution of total population or of large cities (Figs 3.3 and 3.4).

In the sections that follow, China and the former USSR will be compared with regard to population, natural resources and production. Spatial features of the two countries are then compared. Finally, the prospect that China may disintegrate in the way the USSR has done will be examined, and a compromise reorganization of the management of space in China will be proposed. Since much of the material in this chapter refers to the USSR before its break-up in 1991, the term 'former USSR' is only used when the 1991–92 situation is being referred to.

Population

According to Population Reference Bureau (1992), the mid-1992 population of China was estimated to be 1166 million, compared with 292 million in the former USSR. In the mid-1950s China only had three times as many inhabitants as the USSR, compared with four times as many now. In the early 1990s the population of China was growing by about 1.3 per cent per year, or by 15 million, whereas with an annual natural increase rate of 0.7 per cent, that of the former USSR was only growing by about 2 million per year.

Since the USSR is more than twice the area of China, the difference in density of population is very large: 13 compared with 122 per square kilometre. To be sure, even the 122 per square kilometre in China is far below the density of population in some countries that in per capita terms are much more wealthy (e.g. Japan about 330, the Netherlands 430). Therefore, it is not immediately obvious that the density of population alone greatly influences differences in development between China and the USSR. Countries such as Japan and the Netherlands depend heavily on foreign trade for their economic development, whereas both the USSR and China, partly through the policy of their political leaders and partly through sheer size and quantity and variety of natural resources, have tended to follow a policy of self-sufficiency. Foreign trade was used largely when it was necessary to import goods needed at home rather than as a means of using their comparative advantage to sell products abroad at favourable prices to boost economic production and growth. For this reason, therefore, it is relevant to compare the population/natural resource balance of the two countries. It is not implied that because each person in the former USSR has available almost 10 times as much land area as each person in China, the availability of natural resources is necessarily exactly 10 times as great. This issue will be taken up again below.

Soviet policy on population since the 1920s has broadly been to encourage growth, especially with a view to settling more people in the eastern half of the country, which looked distinctly 'empty' when compared with neighbouring China and Japan. The population 'explosion' in the Central Asian Republics since the 1950s appears, however, to have alarmed the slow-growing Russian population recently. In contrast, in the 1970s and 1980s Chinese policy has been directed with varying intensity and thoroughness to bringing down the rate of increase, with considerably different results in different parts of the country. Table 3.1 shows a selection of the 30 major administrative divisions of China (3 municipalities, 5 autonomous regions and 22 provinces) and of the 30 major administrative divisions of the former USSR (3 large predominantly urban oblasts, 13 'other' Soviet Socialist Republics, and 11 and 3 regions, respectively, of the Russian Republic (RSFSR) and Ukraine). In each country the regions selected (every fourth in rank) are ranked from low to high according to the rate of natural growth of population, the average value in 1989 being 14.3 per 1000 for China, and 7.6 per 1000 for the USSR.

In terms of demographic 'performance' there is much greater diversity in the former USSR than in China, with extremes in growth (change) of −0.8 per 1000 in the Northwest region of Russia and +32.2 per 1000 in Tadjikistan, but +5.9 per 1000 for Shanghai compared with +20.8 for Xinjiang. While it is conceivable that the removal of the demographic 'threat' to Russia of Central Asian Republics was regarded as a positive result of the break-up of the USSR, non-Han regions of China with above average rates of natural increase are both a smaller proportion of the total population of the country and, in spite of the absence of severe restrictions on family size imposed on the Han population, much less distinguished by exceptionally fast growth, than is the case with Central Asia and certain other parts of the USSR.

In Table 3.1 the percentage of total population defined as urban is also shown, but some caution must be used in the comparison of this variable on account of a drastic redefinition of urban China in the late 1980s. The figure of 66 per cent urban for the USSR is considered by the author to compare more realistically with 32 per cent urban for China at the end of 1984 rather than with 52 per cent for 1989, the result of the redefinition *en masse* of many largely rural counties, making the population of large areas surrounding many cities artificially 'urban'. Again, if the three municipalities of China (Beijing, Tianjin and Shanghai) and the highly urbanized oblasts of Moscow, Leningrad and Kiyev are excluded from consideration, not only is there a much lower level of urbanization in China than in the USSR, but the range between extremes is greater in China: Shanxi 56 per cent urban, Tibet 10 per cent, compared with Donets-

Table 3.1 Natural growth of population and level of urbanization in selected regions of China and the USSR

Rank	China	Natural growth per thousand	Per cent urban	Rank	USSR		Natural growth per thousand	Per cent urban
1	Shanghai	5.9	61	1	Northwest[1]	(R)	−0.8	66
5	Liaoning	9.4	55	5	Donets-Pridnepr	(U)	0.3	79
9	Heilongjiang	13.4	51	9	South	(U)	2.8	66
13	Guizhou	14.1	29	13	Volga	(R)	4.4	73
17	Hebei	14.8	28	17	North	(R)	5.9	77
21	Shaanxi	15.9	37	21	East Siberia	(R)	8.6	72
25	Fujian	17.7	37	25	Armenia		15.6	68
30	Xinjiang	20.8	40	30	Tadjikistan		32.2	32

(*Sources*: For China, CSY 1990, p. 83; SYC 1985, p. 188. For USSR, Goskomstat 1990, pp. 7–13, 149–54.)
Note: 1. Includes Leningrad
R, Russia; U, Ukraine.

Pridnepr 79 per cent and Tadjikistan 32 per cent. The USSR was more highly urbanized in the 1960s than China was in the late 1980s, another indicator of the more sophisticated nature of Soviet development.

In the world as a whole, a broad negative correlation is observed between level of urbanization and rate of natural increase of population. In Fig. 3.2 the relationship of the two variables in China, the USSR and other selected countries is represented graphically. While most of the divisions of the USSR fall fairly close together, the 'less developed' Republics of Transcaucasia and Central Asia are a great distance away in 'demographic space'. In China, the mass of 'less developed' divisions crowd to the left, the few more sophisticated ones to the right. The correlation (negative) between urbanization and natural increase is not great. It may be inferred from the comparison that most of the population of the USSR resides in regions in which the achievement of a stable population is not far off, with Central Asia, Kazakhstan and Transcaucasia (54–60) the exceptions, whereas in China a massive number of people live in divisions in which the annual rate of natural increase is between about ten and twenty per 1000, and a reduction to five per 1000 or less a distant

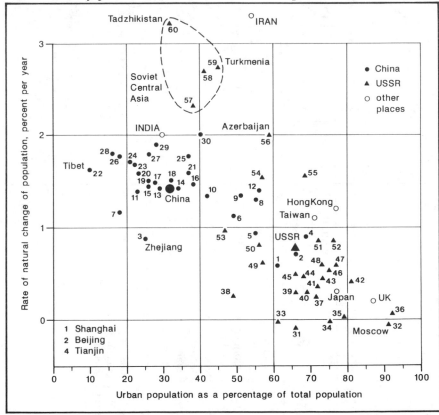

Fig. 3.2 The relationship of level of urbanization and natural increase of population in regions of China, USSR and other selected countries in the late 1980s.

prospect. A population of 1591 million is projected for China in 2025 compared with 363 million for the former USSR (Population Reference Bureau 1992).

One of the influences proposed as responsible for the break-up of the USSR has been the persistence of strong national feeling among the many nationalities of the country. In a comparison of the USSR and China it is essential to underline the differences with respect to national minorities. In 1989 the Han Chinese, the dominant nationality in China, accounted for over 90 per cent of the total population, whereas Russians made up barely half of the population of the USSR (see Table 3.2). Even if the fellow Slavs of the Ukraine and Belarus are added to the Russians, the three nationalities still only account for 70 per cent of the population of the country. In China, only the Zhuang among the non-Han have more than 1 per cent of the total population of the whole country, whereas there are nine non-Russian groups in the USSR with over 1 per cent. While some of the former Soviet Socialist Republics are large enough to bear comparison in size and location with smaller countries of Central and Western Europe, most Chinese minority nationalities are too small in population size and accompanying production to exist independently. The three territorially extensive autonomous regions of Inner Mongolia, Xinjiang and Tibet are small in population, heavily infiltrated by Han Chinese and geographically isolated from the rest of the world.

Table 3.2   The twelve largest national groups in China and the USSR in 1989

China	Population (millions)	%	USSR	Population (millions)	%
1 Han	1007.9	90.6	Russians	145.2	50.8
2 Zhuang	14.4	1.3	Ukrainians	44.2	15.5
3 Hui	7.9	0.7	Uzbeks	16.7	5.8
4 Uygur	6.5	0.6	Belorussians	10.0	3.5
5 Yi	5.9	0.5	Kazakhs	8.1	2.8
6 Miao	5.4	0.5	Azeris	6.8	2.4
7 Manchu	4.6	0.4	Tatars	6.6	2.3
8 Tibetan	4.1	0.4	Armenians	4.6	1.6
9 Mongolian	3.7	0.3	Tadzhiks	4.2	1.5
10 Tujia	3.0	0.3	Georgians	4.0	1.4
11 Buyi	2.3	0.2	Moldavians	3.4	1.2
12 Korean	1.8	0.2	Lithuanians	3.1	1.1
Total	1111.9	100.0	Total	288.6	100.0

Sources: For China, *CSY* 1990. For USSR, Goskomstat 1991, p. 5.

One final aspect of population may be noted here: the matter of economically active population. The drive to industrialize has dominated policy and planning in both countries ever since the start of their Five Year Plans. In the USSR 36.4 million people were employed in the production side of industry in the late 1980s, while the figure was almost 100 million in

China. It is, however, in the agricultural sector that an enormous contrast occurs. Figures from FAO (1990) credit China with 458 million economically active persons engaged in agriculture compared with 18.7 million in the USSR, giving roughly 450 persons on average working every 100 hectares of arable compared with fewer than 10 in the USSR (but only one in Australia). While employment in agriculture has fallen in the USSR in both relative and absolute terms ever since the 1920s, in China the absolute number has actually risen, with an increase of almost 90 million in 1975–90 alone, in spite of a reduction in the sector's share of total employment from 76 to 68 per cent during that period. With 68 per cent of China's economically active population in the agricultural sector, the proportion is higher than the 60 per cent in the Russian Empire in the 1890s (Mitchell 1981). While much of the sown area in China is capable of intensive cultivation, so is that of Japan and The Netherlands, yet even in these countries the relationship of agricultural workers to sown area is about one per hectare and one per four hectares respectively. To follow the Soviet path, even with a delay of several decades, Chinese planners would have to work out how to move at least half of the present labour force in the agricultural sector into other jobs, an undertaking of massive proportions.

Natural resources

The importance of natural resources in the development of economies is a matter of some controversy and speculation. The economic success of Canada and Australia could be attributed to some extent at least to their huge natural resource endowment in relation to population size. The no less conspicuous economic success of Japan and Switzerland, on the other hand, cannot be attributed to an abundance of indigenous natural resources; both these countries import most of the fuel and raw materials they consume, as well as much of the food. The vast natural resources of the USSR, and of Russia in particular, have been noted by many, while some have also attributed to China a generous natural resource endowment, conveniently forgetting to divide it among more than one-fifth of the population of the world. In this section both absolute and per capita quantities of natural resources are examined, but any meaningful comparison between China and the USSR must take into account not only the difference in population size but also the difference in the actual rate at which the non-renewable natural resources are being used.

Estimates of the quantity of natural resources in the world and in various parts of it must be sought in a variety of sources. The area of land under different types of use, and the volume of water flowing through river basins, can be calculated fairly accurately, but it may be assumed that the mineral reserves currently proven may be substantially increased through future exploration and new discoveries, while at the same time the existing reserves are being used up at varying rates. In addition, there is no objective way of working out the comparative value of two different types of natural resource. How, for example, does 1 million tonnes of iron ore compare with 1 million hectares of forest?

The data in Table 3.3 have been gathered from a variety of sources to produce a comparison of the natural resource endowments of China and the USSR. Although economic achievement is measured at any given time by what is produced, not according to the resources a country has, the availability of particular natural resources or their absence influences the potential for and constraints on production and development. Compared with the former USSR, for example, China is very poorly endowed with forests and with natural gas. Room for manoeuvre in economic planning in China is, therefore, far more restricted with regard to these two items than in the former USSR.

While the inventory of natural resources included in Table 3.3 is far from exhaustive, it is reasonably broad and representative to cover all major types of natural resource. The material in the table will be explained column by column. Each natural resource considered is listed, and the measure used to quantify it is indicated. Column (1) gives the estimated total amount in the world (in the case of the mineral reserves, the commercially extractable quantities). Column (2) itemizes the quantities attributed to China. Column (3) lists the quantities attributed to the USSR. Column (4) gives the ratio of the quantity attributed to the Chinese to the Soviet quantity, with China's value expressed as per 1000 (mil) of the Soviet value. For example, the Soviet area of forest, 9 450 000 km^2 against that for China of 1 171 000 km^2, gives a score of 124, calculated by dividing 11 71 000 by 9 450 000 and multiplying by 1000.

In column (5), since China had almost four times as many inhabitants as the USSR around 1990 a further adjustment has been made to scale down the values in column (4) to take this fact into account. Thus each value in column (4) is divided by 3.941, the ratio of the population of China to that of the USSR.

The data in column (5) of Table 3.3 show that of all the items listed, China exceeds the USSR only with regard to two relatively unimportant non-fuel minerals. In the important areas of bioclimatic resources, including water supply, fossil fuels and major non-fuel minerals, the former USSR is much more generously endowed than China. Unfortunately, there is no straightforward objective way of determining the relative importance of different natural resources to the economy of a country. For example, bauxite reserves were of no significance a century ago whereas now the value of the world production of aluminium puts this metal among the top three in the world, together with iron and copper.

In order to give a broad if oversimplified comparison of the natural resources of China and the former USSR, an arbitrary weighting has been given to a number of groups of natural resources. The following weights have been given, one unit being allowed for area *per se*, the remaining nine units for various resources as follows:

Total area	1 unit
Water	1 unit
Cropland	2 units

Table 3.3 A comparison of the natural resource endowments of China and the former USSR

Population and natural resources	Measured in millions	(1) World absolute	(2) China	(3) USSR	(4) China/USSR absolute (USSR=1000)	(5) China/USSR per capita (USSR=1000)
Population		5 384	1 151	292	3 941	1 000
Total area[1]	thous.sq.km	134 000	9 560	22 400	427	108
Water[1]	cu.km/annum discharge	37 700	2 880	4 350	662	168
HEP potential	million terajoules	105.0	21.3	14.2	1 500	381
Arable	thous.sq.km	14 754	966	2 324	415	105
Effect of double cropping in China						
Forest	thous.sq.km	40 490	1 500	2 324[6]	645	164
Permanent pasture	thous.sq.km	32 120	1 171	9 450	124	32
Coal[2]	billion tonnes	637	3 191	3 718	858	218
Lignite[3]	billion tonnes	442	153	102	1 500	381
Oil	billion tonnes	136.5	13	137	95	24
Gas	trillion cu.m	119.4	3.2	7.8	410	104
Bauxite	million tonnes	21 000	150	300	500	127
Chromite	million tonnes	1 165	negl.	142	—	—
Copper	million tonnes	340	5[4]	36[4]	139	35
Diamonds	million carats	980	10	80	125	32
Gold	million troy oz	1 280	negl.	200	—	—
Iron ore[5]	million tonnes	72 000	3 500	25 000	140	36
Lead[5]	million tonnes	95	2	12	167	42
Manganese[5]	million tonnes	1 000	15	365	41	10
Nickel	thous.tonnes	58 000	800	7 300	110	28
Phosphate	million tonnes	14 000	210	1 300	161	41
Silver	million troy oz	7 830	50[4]	1 400	36	9
Tin[5]	thous.tonnes	3 060	680	80	8 500	2 157
Tungsten	thous.tonnes	2 800	1 200	280	4 290	1 089
Zinc[5]	million tonnes	170	5	11	455	115

Sources: For minerals, Bureau of Mines 1985. For land use, FAO 1990 (Table 1.)

Notes:

1. Excluding Antarctica
2. Anthracite and bituminous.
— Spurious calculation.
3. Sub-bituminous and lignite.
4. Author's estimate.
5. Metal content.
6. Negligible area double cropped in the USSR.

Forest and pasture	1 unit
Fossil fuels	3 units
Non-fuel minerals	2 units

The above weightings have been applied to the data in column(5) of Table 3.3, to the scores of single items or the average scores of groups of items, to give new values for China in relation to a standard value of 1000 for the USSR. For simplicity, chromite and gold have been omitted because a numerical score in column (5) for these resources would be spurious. Table 3.4 shows the results of multiplying the resources or groups of resources by the weightings indicated. Thus, for example, the score of 125 against forest and pasture is arrived at by adding 32 and 218 in column (5) of Table 3.3 and dividing the total (250) by two. In view of its great importance, the area cropped (allowing for double-cropping) has been counted twice. When all the scores in Table 3.4 are added and the total averaged, it emerges that China's natural resource endowment per inhabitant is 150 compared with 1000 for the former USSR.

Table 3.4 Natural resources in China per inhabitant (USSR = 1000)

Non-fuel minerals except three (see below)	391
Coal and lignite	203
Water	168
Cropland (counted twice)	164 + 164
Forest and pasture	125
Total area	108
Oil	104
Bauxite, copper, iron	66
Natural gas	6
Average	150

(*Source*: Derived from Table 3.3.)

Whatever reasonable criteria are used for making the above kind of assessment the answer is likely to come somewhere between 100 and 200, indicating that per inhabitant the former USSR has somewhere between 5 and 10 times the natural resource base that China has. It emerges clearly from the calculations, however, that in comparison with the former USSR, China is better endowed with some resources than with others.

The USSR has about 200 times as much natural gas per inhabitant as China but only about 10 times as much oil and 5 times as much coal. In both countries, the oil reserves have only a short life at present rates of production whereas coal (and lignite) reserves would last many decades at current rates of extraction. The largest remaining proved reserves of oil in the Russian Republic are in West Siberia, where particularly difficult environmental conditions make extraction difficult and costly, while movement to markets is over great distances. Natural gas is a great asset in the former USSR since it is cheap to extract and to transport, and relatively clean, although less versatile in its uses than oil. In contrast, China's fuel base has to be coal unless very large oil or natural gas deposits are discovered and successfully exploited.

With regard to bioclimatic resources, the former USSR is far more generously endowed with forest than China. Even when allowance is made for double-cropping on about half of the arable land of China, the former USSR also has much more land to cultivate. Climatic conditions in the main areas of farming are, however, not so favourable as in China, as a comparison of yields in many crops shows. In both countries, cereals are by far the most extensively grown crop. The following figures (FAO 1990, Table 15) show that cereal yields in China are about twice as high as in the former USSR thanks mainly to the contribution of rice in China. Thus in kilograms per hectare the average yield in 1979–81 was 3030 in China, 1410 in the former USSR, while the 1987–89 average was 3980 in China but only 1820 in the former USSR. Continental fresh water was given by Liu Zheng (1981) as the ultimate limit to the total population that China should hold, hopefully to be reached in the year 2080, of between 650 and 700 million.

If China is to modernize further, and industrialize as intensively as Japan or the former USSR, it will have to consume far more fuel and raw materials than it does now. Its inventory is far from adequate, so it would have to draw increasingly on other parts of the world for primary products, a prospect facing many other developing countries if they aspire to industrialize. In the case of China, geographical commonsense suggests that it could start by looking to Russia for the satisfaction of some of its needs of primary products. Many of the mineral reserves of Russia are, however, in areas far from the nearest railway and with harsh environmental conditions. The cost of their extraction in the foreseeable future could be very high, whatever type of economy prevails in Russia in the decades to come.

The above comparison of the natural resource endowments of China and the former USSR may to some extent explain why under Soviet control a great increase in industrial output was achieved there between 1930 and the mid-1970s. With hindsight it can be seen that for a state in which much publicity was given to improving the material conditions of its inhabitants under a socialist system, industrial development was excessively weighted towards heavy industry and the production of military equipment, while lavish and wasteful use was made of fossil fuels, land was excessively ploughed in marginal areas and the environment damaged in many different ways. Chinese planners do not have the same room for manoeuvre with regard to natural resources. They face the prospect at least for several decades of having to increase coal output and consumption, perpetuating undesirably polluted conditions in industrial areas, and of having to import many raw materials if they are to follow the pattern of industrialization of Japan and the Republic of Korea.

As Yuan Tian et al. (1992, p. 4) point out, 'the global significance of China's demographics is enormous . . . China's industrialization, modernization, expanding use of natural resources, and rising consumption will increasingly disrupt the earth's ecosystem'. Of a total world primary energy consumption of just over 8 billion tonnes of oil equivalent in 1990 China only accounted for 0.68 billion (8.5 per cent) compared with some 4 billion tonnes by OECD countries (BP 1991). It is perhaps unfair, there-fore, to put too much blame on China, but between 1980 and 1990 it did account for about two-thirds of the world's increase in coal consumption.

Production of goods and services

An accurate comparison of the total value of goods and services produced in China and the former USSR is not possible because neither country assesses its gross national (or domestic) product in the same way as Western market economy countries do, while conversion of the yuan and the rouble to US dollars, even in 1989, was virtually meaningless. In an assessment of the level of 'human development' for the countries of the world, UNDP (the United Nations Development Programme) gives an index in its *Human Development Report 1992*. Three measures are used to produce a human development index: life expectancy at birth, educational attainment and 'real GDP per capita'. The last of the three measures adjusts the official GDP to avoid distortions by exchange rate conversions and to give parity purchasing power per inhabitant in US dollars. Table 3.5 shows the values for a selection of countries in 1989, including China and the USSR.

Table 3.5 Real GDP per capita in ppp dollars, 1989

USA	21 000
Hong Kong	15 180
Japan	14 310
UK	13 730
USSR	6 270
Republic of Korea	6 120
China	2 660
India	910
Zaire	380

(*Source*: UNDP 1992, Table 1.)

With regard to the comparison of China and the former USSR, China's 'real' GDP per capita is far higher than its conventional or official GDP per capita of a mere US$350, whereas the estimate for the former USSR is around US$6000, although since 1989 the value of the rouble in relation to the dollar has dropped many times. If the real per capita values are compared, in the late 1980s, the production of goods and services per capita in the USSR was 2.5 times as high as that in China, whereas the official GDP per capita gave a gap of about 1 to 15.

As well as comparing China and the former USSR with regard to the global production of goods and services, it is of interest to compare their performance in various sectors of the economy, although here also there are problems of definition. Fourteen products and services in China and the USSR in 1989 are compared in Table 3.6. The absolute quantities of the items listed are shown in columns (1) and (2). In column (3) the Chinese value is expressed as per 1000 of the Soviet value, while in column (4) the Chinese score in column (3) is divided by 3.94 (the ratio of the two populations) to allow a comparison in per capita terms. While China lags far behind the former USSR in most products, as with natural resource endowment, the disparity varies enormously from one item to another. In the industrial sector, China is further below the Soviet level in the production of most heavy industrial items than in the production of consumer goods. Natural gas and brown coal production are so small in China that a comparison is not realistic. Even in the production of tractors, and of passenger cars, for which the former USSR is hardly distinguished, the gap is enormous. A more comprehensive list is provided by Cole (1987, p. 463).

Table 3.6 A comparison of production of selected goods and services in China and the USSR

	(1) China total	(2) USSR total	(3) USSR= 1000	(4) USSR= 1000, per capita
1 Sewing machines (thous.)	7 100	1 553	4 572	1 160
2 Television sets (thous.)	21 700	9 938	2 183	554
3 Grain (million tonnes)	407.6	196.7	2 027	514
4 Coal[1] (million tonnes)	1 054	577	1 557	395
5 Cement (million tonnes)	210.3	140.4	1 498	380
6 Oil seeds (million tonnes)	12.95	8.72	1 485	377
7 Cotton (million tonnes)	3.79	2.69	1 408	357
8 Doctors (thous.)	1 718	1 278	1 344	341
9 Hospital beds (thous.)	2 568	3 822	672	171
10 Students in higher education (thous.)	2 082	5 178	402	102
11 Steel (million tonnes)	61.6	160	385	98
12 Electricity (billion kWh)	585	1 722	340	86
13 Rail goods (billion tonne/km)	1 039	3 852	270	69
14 Oil (million tonnes)	137.6	607	227	58

(*Sources*: CSY 1990, various tables; *Narodnoye khozyaystvo SSSR v 1989 godu*, Moscow 1991; Goskomstat SSSR, various tables.)
Note:
1. Hard coal (USSR also produces 166 million tonnes of brown coal).

In spite of its low level of material production compared with the former USSR and, even more so, with North America, Western Europe and Japan, China achieves a surprisingly high score on the UNDP human development index referred to above. A combination of scores for life expectancy, educational attainment and adjusted real GDP per inhabitant give it an overall score of 0.612 out of a possible maximum of 1.000. In Table 3.7 China is compared with a selection of countries of the world including the former USSR. Space does not allow a full description of the method used to make the calculation but it should be appreciated that any GDP (real) over approximately 5000 parity purchasing power* (ppp) dollars per capita is ignored, thus keeping the range on this variable between 5074 for the USA and 380 for Zaíre.

Table 3.7 Human development index (maximum 1.000)

Canada (highest)	0.982
Japan	0.981
USA	0.976
UK	0.962
Hong Kong	0.913
USSR	0.873
Republic of Korea	0.871
China	0.612
India	0.297
Guinea (lowest)	0.052

(*Source*: UNDP 1992, Table 1.)

The above human development index, first published in 1990 in the *Human Development Report* of that year, and subsequently slightly modified, may perhaps be seen as an attempt to present the world 'development gap' as less marked than it appears when measured exclusively in terms of GDP in US dollars at official exchange rates. What the index does imply is that whatever the shortcomings of China's economy, it falls in the group of countries with 'medium human development', comfortably among the top half of the less developed countries, whereas the former USSR comes low in the group of countries with 'high human development'. In spite of its superior natural resource endowment and a start of several decades on China with regard to the development of modern industry and transport, the former USSR failed to achieve living standards comparable with those in the West. With its increasing population, dependence on a limited quantity of natural resources and the need to trade more in an increasingly competitive and congested world, China may not be able to extend the modest affluence now enjoyed by a small part of its total population, particularly that living in coastal provinces, to replace the shared austerity of the mass of the population.

Spatial aspects of the comparison

The distribution of population in both China and the former USSR is very uneven, but no more so than in Canada, Australia and Brazil, all comparable in size to China. While the relative increase in population in the last four decades has tended to be higher in the thinly peopled areas,

*Parity purchasing power is the purchasing power of given amounts of different currencies, removing exchange rate bias.

the absolute gain has been far greater in the more densely peopled areas. In both China and the former USSR the role of the state and of central planners in determining where new developments occur and where new activities and jobs are placed has probably resulted in a greater increase of population in the more empty regions than would have occurred in a market economy situation. In the former USSR the power to move considerable numbers of Ukrainians and other non-Russians into Siberia, the Far East and northern Kazakhstan has now diminished, if not disappeared. Economic growth in the 'empty half' of Russia could slow down or cease entirely as people move or return westwards. In China the 'empty half' is still populated mainly by non-Han peoples. The natural resources of Xinjiang, Tibet and Inner Mongolia are far more modest than those of Siberia and Kazakhstan, and relative to the great size of the population of China are not capable of usefully absorbing as many people

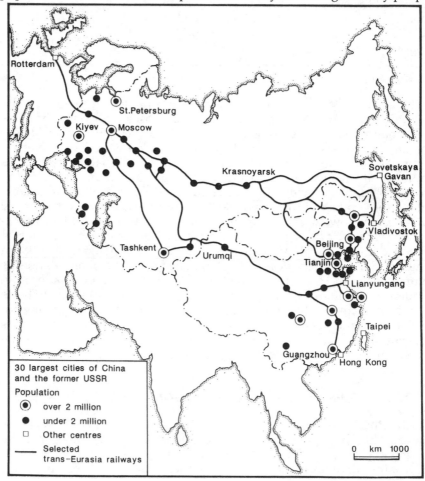

Fig. 3.3 The location of the 30 largest cities of China and the former USSR and selected trans-Eurasian railways.

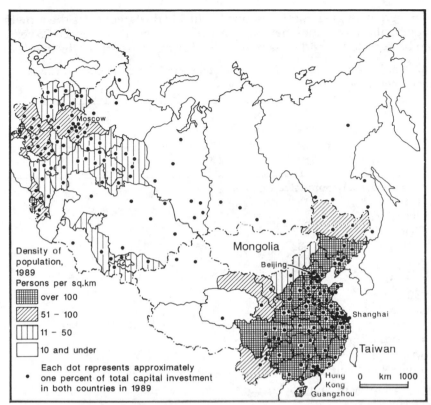

Fig. 3.4 The density of population and location of investment in 1989 in China and the USSR.

as the eastern regions of the USSR.

The distribution of population in China and the former USSR is shown in Figs 3.3 and 3.4. The location is shown of the 30 largest cities in each country. As shown graphically by Cole (1990), these cities are broadly comparable in size, but apart from Moscow and St Petersburg there is a conspicuous lack of very large cities in the former USSR. Only three out of the 30 in the former USSR (Omsk, Novosibirsk and Krasnoyarsk) are located in the eastern part of the country (Siberia). In China, only two of the 30 largest cities are in the equivalent thinly peopled western part of China (Urumqi and Lanzhou). In the more densely populated parts of the two countries, only three of the thirty Soviet cities, St Petersburg, Riga and Odessa, are ports, only the first of which is actually in Russia. In China, seven are on the coast and several others are close to the coast.

The density of population in major regions and provinces of China and the former USSR is shown in Fig. 3.4 and selected divisions in each country are ranked in descending order of density of population in Table 3.8. Since the average density of population is about nine times as high in China as in the former USSR, the outstanding contrast is in the sheer mass of population concentrated in about half of the area of China, although even here with great local variations. Outside the larger cities the growth of population continues inexorably in China, which in the next 20–25 years can be expected to add to its present total as many people as the whole of

Table 3.8 Population and capital investment in selected regions of China and the former USSR in 1989

	Density of population (persons per sq.km)	Investment (%)	Population (%)	Investment rate
Four most densely populated regions				
China				
Jiangsu (includes Shanghai)	718	14.29	7.03	203
Shandong	533	8.46	7.34	115
Henan	493	4.71	7.40	64
Zhejiang	413	5.34	3.79	141
USSR				
Moldova	129.4	1.1	1.51	73
Armenia	110.5	1.7	1.14	149
Donets-Pridnepr (Ukraine)	98.8	6.4	7.56	85
Southwest (Ukraine)	82.7	5.0	7.72	65
Four least densely populated regions				
China				
Inner Mongolia	18	1.40	1.91	73
Xinjiang	9	1.98	1.78	111
Qinghai	6	0.51	0.40	128
Tibet	2	0.18	0.20	90
USSR				
Kazakhstan	6.1	5.9	5.78	102
North (Russian Rep.)	4.2	3.8	2.13	178
East Siberia (Russian Rep.)	2.2	4.7	3.19	147
Far East (Russian Rep.)	1.3	5.3	2.77	191

(*Sources*: CSY 1990, p. 144; *Narodnoye khozyaystvo SSSR v 1989 godu*, Moscow 1990; Goskomstat SSSR 1990 p. 535.)

the population of the former USSR. A very large investment in new infrastructure and jobs would be needed, either in the comparatively empty western and northern regions of China or in the coastal provinces, to produce a marked shift in the present distribution. Otherwise future growth will produce more of the same.

The paths of China and the former USSR are likely to diverge greatly in the future unless China breaks up in some way. Great readjustments can be expected in the former USSR, whatever economic system prevails in the future. There could be considerable migration, as people from the different nationalities return to their 'homelands' (e.g. Ukrainians from Siberia, Russians from Uzbekistan). Much investment will be needed, as it is in the former German Democratic Republic, simply to rehabilitate run-down industries and transport links. In China such drastic changes seem unlikely at present.

The distribution of the allocation of capital investment in China and in the USSR in 1989 is shown in Fig. 3.4 by dots, each dot representing approximately 1 per cent of the total. In both countries it is evident that investment does not closely match the distribution of population. In China, the highest per capita levels of investment are in and around the municipality of Shanghai and in the provinces of Jiangsu and Zhejiang, where almost 20 per cent of the total was placed, in Hebei (including Beijing and Tianjin) with over 10 per cent, and in Guangdong (including Guangzhou), also with about 10 per cent. These three areas therefore have 40 per cent of all investment but only 25 per cent of the total population of China. None of these provinces and municipalities has natural resources of outstanding importance nationally. In contrast, the least densely pop-ulated six divisions of China account for little more than 5 per cent of all investment, but occupy almost half of the territory. In the former USSR, on the other hand, the four large, thinly populated and broadly compara-ble regions of West and East Siberia, the Far East, and northern Kazakh-stan, had some 20 per cent of all investment. Indeed, the policy of Soviet planners differs from that in China in that much investment has been placed in territorial production complexes away from the coast or the international boundary of the country, in regions such as the Volga, Ural, northern Kazakhstan and Siberia, none of them particularly attractive to foreign investors or well located to export to foreign markets.

In the decades to come, some of the smaller newly independent repub-lics of the former USSR, comparatively poor in natural resources, will probably develop light industries and services, whereas Russia and Kazakhstan will continue to be net exporters of fuel and of mineral raw materials. If reorganization is successful, they could also become net exporters of agricultural products to a much greater extent than now. In contrast, given its limited natural resource endowment and its growing population, China's future lies in the further development of branches of industry that use limited quantities of fuel and raw materials, and add much value to these ingredients.

Whatever path China follows, further industrialization will require larger imports of primary products, and competitive industries to provide exports to pay for these. Coal and oil will still come from places some distance inland from the coast, but the concentration of investment in China in places on or close to the coast reflects both the need to develop an interface with the rest of the world and the poor condition of transport links even to the second and third tiers of provinces, such as Hunan and Sichuan.

Recent changes in socialist and formerly socialist countries of Central and Eastern Europe have shown that ethnic contradictions of various kinds have not been eradicated by socialism but have remained dormant.

It is conceivable, therefore, that some concessions may be made by the Han leadership of China to non-Han minorities based on greater autonomy if not complete sovereignty. The break-up of the former USSR left the very large Russian republic with only about half of the total population but over three-quarters of the area. A break-up of China on similar lines would leave over 90 per cent of the population in a completely Han China. Soviet experience has shown that as the economy became more sophisticated and the planning process more complex, central planning became increasingly difficult. The fragmentation of the USSR has, however, given rise to a new set of problems. Political unity has been lost but economic interdependence remains. It is not clear at the time of writing what compromise will be worked out, but it is not unreasonable to anticipate the formation of a number of loosely associated economically based regions, with parts of Russia associated with some of the former republics and possibly an eastern region with growing links with the Pacific. The impossibly large population of China, even ignoring the non-Han minorities, could similarly be managed more viably.

According to Zou Jiahua (1992), it is planned to establish seven economic regions as part of China's new economic structure. Three of these (1–3), centred on Shanghai, Guangzhou and Beijing, occupy the coastal provinces, while the remaining four (4–7) are Southwest China, Northwest China, Central China and Northeast China. In the view of the author, such a distribution of regions would penalize the four interior ones, if only because their access to the coast would be by means of transport links already heavily used to serve the 'internal' needs of the three coastal regions. This arrangement could perpetuate or even increase the existing differences between coastal and interior regions in the same way that the emergence of the new independent states along the western and southern borders of the Russian Republic could impede its access to the coast, a prospect of much more significance in the future as the former USSR trades more heavily with the rest of the world than during the Soviet period, when self-sufficiency dominated policy.

A possible way of improving the territorial management of China, with some decentralization of political and economic power, is proposed in Fig 3.5. The coastal zone is divided into seven sectors. Each would be explicitly concerned with its own economic development as well as that of its hinterland. The configuration of the coast of China and the present concentration of much economic activity in a few small areas means that these seven sectors differ in both population size and level of sophistication. The weakest sectors are those opposite Taiwan and the newly created province of Hainan. While the inclusion of Hong Kong in the People's Republic will clearly have an enormous impact on Guangdong, a closer relationship with Taiwan could similarly boost the economic life of Fujian and Jiangxi. Under the system of regions proposed here, a vital advantage would be the fact that it would be in the interest of the planners of each region to ensure that the more interior parts should be developed appropriately and should have good links to the coast.

One further prospect for China is closer links with the former USSR. The transcontinental rail links between Europe and the Far East are shown in

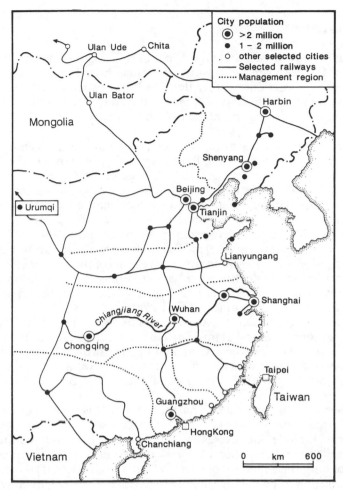

Fig. 3.5 Seven possible management regions of China, each designed with a coastal area and hinterland.

Fig. 3.3. The dead-end nature of the interior of China could be reduced by these links, especially the newly completed missing link between Kazakhstan and Xinjiang. To the east of the Mongolian People's Republic China faces the thinly populated, mainly Russian, regions of East Siberia and the Far East, rich in many of the primary products China is likely to need in future. To the west of the Mongolian People's Republic it shares a boundary with three newly independent republics, Kazakhstan, Kirghizstan and Tadzhikistan. In all three a considerable number of Russians are settled close to the Chinese boundary, but in the future many of these may move out, leaving China to form new relations with peoples similar in many respects to non-Han groups in this western part of China.

Conclusion

A number of aspects of the former USSR and China have been compared in this chapter. Both similarities and differences have been shown to exist. Can the Soviet experience throw light on the prospects for China in the next two to three decades? Five issues will be referred to briefly. They have been arranged in decreasing order of 'predictability'.

- *Territory and natural resources* It is unlikely that the cultivated area in China can be extended more than marginally. New mineral reserves may be discovered. In general, however, the natural resource constraints will remain high, with the prospect that, unlike the former USSR, China will be a net importer rather than exporter of primary products.
- *Population* Through its present momentum the population of China is set to increase by another 200 to 300 million, whatever family planning policy is adopted, whereas in the Slav regions of the former USSR little change is expected. On the other hand, China's national minorities are not likely to be as influential or disruptive in shaping future changes in China as those of the former USSR have been.
- *Production of goods and services* A comparison of trends since the establishment of central planning in the two countries points to a very marked time-lag between China and the former USSR with the prospect that in many sectors of the economy it could be some decades before Chinese production per inhabitant reaches Soviet levels of the 1980s.
- *Management of the economy* The former USSR is far more 'farflung' than China. The Russians in Kaliningrad and Vladivostok are over 7000 great circle kilometres apart whereas the Han Chinese in Heilongjiang and Hainan are only 3000 kilometres apart. The problem of managing the economy of eastern China is characterized by a large concentration of people in a small area. Much of Russia, even without the other republics, is difficult to manage on account of a low density of population and lack of communications.
- *Leadership* Most difficult to anticipate are the policies that may be adopted by the Communist Party of China with regard to the features and issues summarized above. As in the former USSR it is difficult to see what could replace the Communist Party if it 'resigns' from power in China. More likely, it seems, is a continuation of a 'two steps forward, one step back' process, from the Great Leap Forward through the Cultural Revolution, the death of Mao and Tiananmen Square to 1997, when the handing over of Hong Kong will no doubt produce some kind of crisis.

Chinese leaders renounced Soviet assistance and the Soviet model of development in the late 1950s but in practice they have still used many of the means used by Soviet politicans and planners up to the present. Only the extreme conservatism of China's present leaders can stop them from appreciating that they may face in their own country some of the problems and dilemmas that led to *glasnost* and *perestroyka* in the USSR in the late 1980s, not least a highly authoritarian political and economic system, with little regard either for public opinion, the natural environment or the need to modernize and innovate in the economic sphere. They would do well to recognize that while China and the former USSR are now very different in the early 1990s, the Soviet model still deserves their attention.

References

BP (British Petroleum) (1991) *BP Statistical Review of World Energy*, London.

Bureau of Mines (1985) *Mineral Facts and Problems*, US Department of the Interior, US Government Printing Office, Washington.

CSY (*China Statistical Yearbook 1990*) (1990) State Statistical Bureau of the People's Republic of China, Beijing.

Cole J P (1957) 'China surmounting a late start' *The Times Review of Industry*, January, pp. 80–2.

Cole J P (1987) 'China and the Soviet Union: worlds apart', *Soviet Geography* **XXVIII**, No. 7, 459–84.

Cole J P (1990) 'The cities of the USSR and China. Streets apart', *Cities* May, 159–68.

FAO (1990) *Food and Agriculture Production Yearbook*, United Nations, Rome, Tables 3 and 15.

Goskomstat (1990) *Demograficheskiy yezhegodnik SSSR 1990*, Moscow, 'Finansy i Statistika', pp. 149–54.

Goskomstat (1991) *Natsional'nyy sostav naseleniya SSSR*, Vsesoyuznaya perepis' naseleniya 1989, Moscow, 'Finansy i Statistika', p. 5.

Goskomstat SSSR (1990) *Narodnoye khozyaystro SSSR v 1989 godu*, Moscow.

Goskomstat SSSR (1991) *Narodnoye khozyaystro SSSR v 1990 godu*, Moscow.

Liu Zheng, Song Jian et al. (1981) *China's Population: problems and prospects*, New World Press, Beijing, p. 29.

Maddison A (1969) *Economic Growth in Japan and the USSR*, George Allen and Unwin, London.

Mitchell B R (1981) *European Historical Statistics 1750–1975*, Macmillan, London.

PRB (Population Reference Bureau) (1992) *World Population Data Sheet 1992*, Washington, DC.

SYC (*Statistical Yearbook of China 1985*) (1985) State Statistical Bureau, PRC, English edn, Oxford University Press, pp. 195–6.

UNDP (United Nations Development Programme) (1992) *Human Development Report 1992*, Oxford University Press, New York.

Yuan Tian H, Zhang Tianlu, Ping Yu, Li Jingneng and **Liang Zhongtang** (1992) 'China's demographic dilemmas, *Population Bulletin* **47**, No. 1, June.

Zhou Jiahua (1992) 'Plans for regional economy', *Beijing Review*, August, 14–18.

CHAPTER 4

China's population: prospects and policies*

Sarah Harper

'No government, no invader, no colonial power ever planned for China to have over 1 billion people. . . . Even a few decades ago leaders could hardly imagine that one billion people would so soon be living on the areas that had so often failed to produce sufficient food for half or a quarter of that size . . . demographic record speaks of the success of the government in pushing China through the demographic transition at a remarkable rate.'

(Hull and Yang 1991, pp. 11–13).

To a large extent the extraordinary demographic transition of the Peoples' Republic of China is the result of successful socio-economic planning: planning, however, which has produced a population that is both growing rapidly and ageing rapidly. These are possibly the two most pronounced dimensions of China's current population – dimensions that are inextricably united, for ironically it has been controlling the first that has over-encouraged the second. Furthermore, the People's Republic is perhaps unique among lesser developed nations in its awareness that social policy decisions regarding the aged cannot be made in isolation from policy decisions concerning the rest of the population, in particular family planning policy (Sankar 1989). Similarly, family planning policy decisions are increasingly integrating guarantees of future state welfare support in old age (Hull and Yang, 1991). China recognizes that family decisions about the number of children are intimately linked to family perceptions of security in old age.

*The author would like to acknowledge the British Society of Gerontology and the Pantyfedwyn Committee for their support of the research on which this chapter has been based.

Demographic change

Early figures from the 1990 census indicate that China's population stands at 1.13 billion, suggesting that the People's Republic has increased more than two-fold since its formation in 1949. Indeed, as will be discussed later, errors in population collection and accounting may well have led to a substantial underestimate of China's current population.

Birth, death and growth rates

At the time of its formation in 1949, the People's Republic was experiencing high fertility and mortality and low growth (Table 4.1). While the crude death rate (CDR) fell in the early years of the People's Republic, the birth rate remained high, a reflection of the country's young age structure and thus large number of fecund women, and the encouragement of high fertility by some members of the Communist Party, in particular by the powerful anti-Malthusians.

Table 4.1   Birth, death and growth rates, People's Republic of China

Year	CBR	CDR	NGR
1949	36.00	20.00	16.00
1953	37.00	14.00	23.00
1956	31.90	11.40	20.50
1959	24.78	14.59	10.19
1960	20.86	25.43	−4.57
1961	18.02	14.24	3.78
1962	37.01	10.02	26.99
1963	43.37	10.04	33.33
1970	33.43	7.60	25.83
1975	23.01	7.32	15.69
1980	18.21	6.34	11.87
1982	21.09	6.60	14.49
1985	17.80	6.57	11.23
1990	20.98	6.28	14.70

Source: State Statistical Bureau of China, *Statistical Yearbook of China 1986*, Chinese Statistical Publishing House, 1986.
State Statistical Bureau of China, Preliminary results from 1990 census.
CBR, crude birth rate.
CDR, crude death rate.
NGR, national growth rate.

The famine years of 1959–62, arising from a combination of natural disasters and the mismanagement of agricultural production and distribution, had a dramatic impact on growth rates. The growth rate descended as low as − 9.23 per 1000 in rural areas in 1960, with the crude death rate rising nationally to 25.43 per 1000 (28.58 per 1000 in rural areas) in that year. Though crude birth rate (CBR) remained low during the famine years of 1960 and 1961, forced below 2 per cent in rural areas, it rose dramatically in the immediate subsequent years, partly in response to the high infant mortality rates during the famine years. In 1963, the CBR reached an historic peak of 43.4, with total fertility rate (TFR) (births per fecund women) touching an unprecedented modern high of 7.5. The chaos of the Cultural Revolution prevented any long-term planning in response to this sharp increase in fertility, and the population again began to rise dramatically with an annual increase of some 2.5 per cent.

The increasing efforts at family planning during the mid- to late 1970s had an impact on the total fertility rate which fell to 2.5 in 1982, the initial year of the national One Child Policy, reaching 2.4 in 1986. As will be discussed later, however, there is considerable urban–rural variation, from a low of 1.1 in Shanghai, to nearly 3 in some western rural zones. Nationally, the crude birth and death rates have similarly fallen. This dramatic fall in fertility over the past two decades has been heralded as the world's single most outstanding example of success in reducing fertility levels (Hull and Yang 1991). The recent slight increase in crude birth rate (Table 4.1) can be accounted for by the currently large cohort of fecund women arising from high fertility of the early 1960s; an effect which will inflate crude birth rate for several years. Total fertility rate, however, appears to have remained stable.

Inaccuracies

It is worth briefly highlighting some of the concerns with the quality of China's demographic data. In addition to the general acknowledgement that, as in many underdeveloped countries, the actual collection methods of population data can lead to a variety of inaccuracies and mis-reporting of figures, China has specific problems. In particular, as Hull and Yang (1991) have pointed out, the consistently uneven sex ratio at birth indicates either widespread female infanticide or the non-registration of female babies. Ethnographic evidence would suggest a combination of the two (Croll 1985; Kane 1985), in which case both the CDR and the CBR are inaccurate. In 1986, for example, there were 100 female to 110 male births (1 per cent Sample Population Survey); the 1986 crude birth rate could be as high as 21.1 per 1000 and the crude death rate 7.3 per 1000. Furthermore, if the female babies were killed, the population growth rate in 1986 was 1.4; if female births were concealed, it was 1.46. This has tremendous implications for population predictions, as a mere 0.6 per cent difference in growth rate constitutes over half a million children (Hull and Yang 1991). This is of particular significance for future population growth given that the missing children are female.

China's demographic profile

The early 1960s saw a dramatic increase in the percentage of younger age groups – those under 15 comprising 40 per cent of the population by 1964. However, since then there has been a a slight shift towards the older ages, with the percentage of elderly (60+) increasing slightly, from 6.1 per cent in 1964 to 7.6 per cent in 1982 and 8.6 per cent by 1990s. As we discuss later, this percentage is forecast to increase substantially over the next few decades. Of greater significance, however, is the rate of increase of elderly people which has more than doubled since 1952. The gentle growth of the numbers over age 60 between 1953 and 1964, 1.7 per cent compared with an overall 22.4 per cent growth in population, was followed by dramatic expansion between 1964 and 1982: while the population grew by 44.5 per cent, those over 60 increased by 81.4 per cent (*RMRB* 26/1/56). As a result, the actual number of older people has increased significantly.

There is, however, considerable regional and rural–urban imbalance in this demographic profile. The cities to the east are ageing rapidly. In 1987 9.5 per cent of Tianjin's population and 10.4 per cent of Beijing's population were over 60. Shanghai has 13.5 per cent of the population over 60, with projections estimating that within 10 years the proportion of elderly in urban Shanghai will have reached 20.7 per cent. In contrast, rural areas, in particular those to the north and west, have far younger age profiles. The provinces of Guizhou, Qinghai and Ningxai for example, all have over 40 per cent of their population under 14. These figures become of particular significance in such provinces as Henan and Guangxi with a higher than average percentage of elderly people and of children, thus experiencing particularly high dependency ratios. Over 40 per cent of the population of these provinces are already dependants; as will be seen later, this figure is forecast to rise throughout China.

Future trends

To a limited extent it is possible to predict future demographic developments using our knowledge of past trends. For example, the level of the CBR during the late 1970s and early 1980s may have been kept artificially low due to the high rate of infant mortality which existed when the current group of fecund women was born, particularly during the famine years, and the resultant reduction in numbers of this cohort. Thus the CBR of 2 per cent of recent years may be the more natural rate of the past decade. The high fertility of the 1960s is of particular significance, producing a large cohort of women now of prime reproducing age. While this will keep the birth rate high for the next decade, it will also provide a large number of elderly people in the second and third decades of next century. In addition, the percentage of elderly people may have been reduced during the 1960s and 1970s due to the specific vulnerability of this group during the famine years. It is thus only now that the impact of high fertility in the early decades of the century and subsequent low mortality is being felt. Of particular interest are those elderly born during the early years of the People's Republic, a time when infant mortality was falling, who were sufficiently mature to avoid mass death during the famine years, and who will thus be entering old age in the early years of the new millenium.

More formal, less suppositive, predictions have been made by various bodies. The rest of the section will draw on two such sets of statistical data

– by the Sino-Japanese Population Ageing Research Group, and the United Nations Population Division – to examine future demographic scenarios. Both types of predictive material – suppositive and statistical – stress two significant future demographic trends for the People's Republic: population expansion and population ageing.

Statistical predictions

The Sino-Japanese Population Ageing Group based their predictions on the 1982 census. Using estimated fertility rates and life expectancy rates they have compiled predictions until the year 2050. The low variant predictions presume a high degree of success both in health delivery services, resulting in low mortality rates and thus long life expectancy, and in family planning with strong emphasis on fertility control and a high acceptance of the One Child Policy. The high variant option takes the other extreme and foresees high mortality rates and low life expectancy due to limited health service delivery in many parts of rural China, and limited success with family planning. Under this scenario two-child families are the norm (Table 4.2).

Table 4.2 Sino-Japanese Population Ageing Group: components of predictions

Low variant: Life expectancy at birth			Male	Female
		1981	66.43	69.35
		2000	69.93	74.03
		2050	77.45	82.94
	TFR	1982	2.63	
		2000–2050	1.8	
High variant: Life expectancy at birth			Male	Female
		1981	66.43	69.35
		2000	69.10	72.70
		2050	71.80	75.50
	TFR	1982	2.63	
		2000–2050	2.1	

The mean variant is the mean value of the two predictions

(*Source*: Sino-Japanese Population Ageing Research Group (1985) *Population Projection for China*.)
TFR, total fertility rate.

The United Nations' predictions follow similar scenarios (Table 4.3). As with the Sino-Japanese low variant predictions, the United Nations's low population assumes significant control of fertility and mortality, thus high life expectancy and low fertility figures. The medium population is similar to the Sino-Japanese high variant predictions, with high mortality, thus low life expectancy and medium–high fertility. The United Nations high population predictions stress medium–high fertility and low mortality, the latter resulting in a rapid increase in life expectancy. In addition, the United Nations produces a constant forecast in which the momentum of health promotion and thus falling mortality rates are continued, yet the fertility rate remains the constant with the 1980 figure. While this is an unlikely scenario, it is difficult to predict which of the many combinations are likely. Indeed such predictions can only be a guide as they inevitably fail to include the unexpected.

Table 4.3 United Nations: components of predictions

			Male	Female
Low populations: Life expectancy at birth			Male	Female
		1980–85	66.8	69.0
		2020–25	76.8	78.6
	TFR	1980–85	2.30	
		2020–25	1.70	
Medium population: Life expectancy at birth			Male	Female
		1980–85	66.7	69.0
		2020–25	73.0	78.6
	TFR	1980–85	2.37	
		2020–25	2.11	
High population: Life expectancy at birth			Male	Female
		1980–85	66.8	69.0
		2020–25	76.8	78.6
	TFR	1980–85	2.37	
		2020–25	2.11	

(*Source*: United Nations Population Division (1985) *Projections for China.*)
TFR, total fertility rate.

Population expansion

The different scenarios predict varied total population figures (Table 4.4). At the one extreme the high variant of the Sino-Japanese Group and the

Table 4.4 Predicted population growth of China (in millions)

Year	High	Mean	Low
A. Sino-Japanese Population Ageing Group			
1985		1 049	
1990	1 118	1 117	1 116
2000	1 270	1 259	1 249
2010	1 373	1 353	1 332
2020	1 459	1 428	1 397
2025	1 498	1 461	1 423
2030	1 525	1 481	1 437
2040	1 544	1 488	1 433
2050	1 547	1 473	1 399
B. United Nations			
2025	1 492	1 475	1 318

(*Sources*: Sino-Japanese Population Ageing Research Group (1985) *Population Projection for China.* United Nations Population Division (1985) *Projections for China.*)

high population of the United Nations both predict a population of nearly 1.5 billion by the year 2025. The lowest figure provided is that by the United Nations low population scenario of 1.3 billion (2025). If the United Nations constant predictions are also to be included in this analysis, China's population in 2025 would be approaching 1.7 billion.

Population ageing

Given generally more consistent trends in decline in mortality rate, and the more accurate knowledge about the numbers of living population than of future populations, the prediction of the demographic structure of China's population is likely to be more accurate. Indeed, even if unforecast fertility changes alter the percentage rates of population age groups, they will have limited effect on the numbers within these groupings. Thus, regardless of their percentage contribution, the People's Republic will have, in absolute numbers, the largest population of people over 60 in the world. By 2008 one-quarter of all the world's elderly people will live in China.

Using the population projections of the Sino-Japanese Population Ageing Research Group (Table 4.5), the China National Committee on Ageing has identified three phases of demographic development. The United Nations predictions fit in well with these scenarios.

Table 4.5   Predicted demographic structure of China: Sino-Japanese Population Ageing Group

Year	High %			Mean %			Low %		
	0–14	15–59	60+	0–14	15–59	60+	0–14	15–59	60+
1985				29	63	8			
1990	26	65	9	26	65	9	25	65	9
2000	26	64	10	25	64	10	24	65	11
2010	23	65	12	22	65	13	19	67	13
2020	21	64	15	19	64	16	18	64	18
2030	21	59	20	19	58	23	17	58	25
2040	20	58	22	17	57	25	16	55	28
2050	20	59	21	18	57	25	16	54	30

(*Source*: Sino-Japanese Population Ageing Research Group (1985) *Population Projection for China*.)

1982–2000 will see a *moderate ageing phase* from intermediate to young-old society, with an increase in the proportion of older people from 7.7 to 10.5 per cent. Within this older age group, the proportion aged 60–69 will actually decrease, while those over 70 will rise from 36 to 42 per cent. At the same time the percentage of children, those under 14, will fall from 33 to 25 per cent, thus seeing an increase in the percentage of workers, and an overall decrease in dependants. United Nations projected dependency ratios suggest a decline from 67 dependants per 100 workers to around 45 per 100. The effects on the economy are thus predicted to be small. The median age of the population will rise from around 22 years to 31 years of age.

Between 2000 and 2025, however, there will be rapid ageing of the population – the *quickening ageing phase* – as society moves from young-old to old-old, with the percentage of elderly almost doubling to reach 19.4 per cent. During this time the proportion of workers will peak at around 65 per cent before declining from thence forth. The median population age will have risen to around 40.

The *super ageing phase*, from old-old to super-aged, 2025–2050, sees an increase in the percentage of elderly to 25 per cent, and a decrease in those under 14 to 18 per cent. The percentage of elderly over 70 will reach 60 per cent (indeed one out of every eight Chinese will be over 70). Just under 50 per cent of the population as a whole will be dependants, with significant implications for the economy as a whole, and for the care of these dependants, particularly the elderly who will comprise over 60 per cent of the dependent group.

Two of the policy issues which have arisen out of China's particular demographic structure and change, commencing with a review of China's family planning policy, will be considered below. Throughout, the emphasis will be laid upon the social, cultural and political–economic aspects of the individual programmes.

China's family planning policy

It has been suggested by Hull and Yang (1991) that the development of China's fertility policy has comprised five campaigns: 1956–59; 1962–66; 1971–79; 1979–84 and 1984 90. They argue that these are not *stages* in the development of family planning programmes but different *styles* of family planning based on the different stages of the development of governmental structures. This distinction is important because it shifts the analysis away from the family planning debate *per se*, and instead lays emphasis on the fragility of family planning policy in the face of wider socio-political change. Reinstating these campaigns within their socio-political context we can identify three stages of demographic change, and within these, seven stages of population fertility planning which supported the various family planning policies.

1. Natural fertility decrease: little formal family planning (1954–66)

Party debate and fertility planning (1954–58)

The views of Chairman Mao and that of the Chinese Communist Party on controlling population growth during the early days of the People's Republic, are unclear. Stacey (1983), for example, strongly opposes the generally accepted view, advocated by Kane (1987) and Sidel and Sidel (1982) among others, that the Chinese Communists actively pursued a pro-natalist policy. Rather, she argues, it was the anti-Malthusian element of the Communist Party who kept a strong check on population planning and control, particularly in these early years.

In this Stacey is supported by Wang Hong (1991) who argues that, with Mao's encouragement, the Ministry of Health's regulations on family planning, which comprised part of a general push for improved maternal health and welfare, were integrated into the Party ideology on population control from 1954. In that year the Central Committee declared:

'Birth control is a significant policy issue which is associated with the life of the broad masses. Under current historical conditions, and for the benefit of the country, the family and the new-born generation, our Party agrees to suitable birth control measures.' (Population Research Centre 1986, p. 1265; Wang Hong 1991)

Party cadres were instructed to disseminate this message to the people throughout the People's Republic, with the exception of the minorities. Concentrating initially on urban and other densely populated areas (Chen, Pi-chao 1985), the programmes primarily comprised information campaigns as to the availability of contraceptives and were still heavily linked to maternal health and welfare provisions. In addition, the emphasis was on *fertility planning*, rather than on *fertility reduction*.

Over the next three years the Party emphasized the need for planned births. Both in the Programme of Agricultural Development of the Country (1956), and in the Recommendations of the Second Five Year Plan of National Economy (1956), planned births were encouraged (Wang Hong 1991), and in 1957 at the Third Plenary Session of the Eighth Central Committee of the Party, Chairman Mao laid out a 'ten year plan for birth control . . . there should be three years of publicity and education and tests at selected points, three years of spreading the program and four years of popularization and implementation' (quoted in Wang Hong 1991).

Such campaigns, however, cannot be considered in isolation from other aspects of the social and economic transformation of China as it prepared for the Great Leap Forward. Of particular importance was the desire to increase the number and status of female workers as part of the economic expansion programme. With the emphasis on industrial growth in the First Five Year Plan (1953–57), women workers became a valued commodity (Kane 1985), and loss to the labour market through childbearing an economic consideration. The introduction of paid maternity leave and state child care during this period (Kane 1976), brought the debate of birth control and child spacing further into the broad economic agenda.

This period was thus characterized by ideological acceptance of planned births, within the rationale of female health and status, and economic growth. The move to population and fertility reduction was yet to make the agenda.

Famine and the 'anti-rightist' struggle (1958–62)

Such family planning programmes, however, were brought abruptly to a halt in 1958 as the 'leftist' elements within the Communist Party came into ascendancy. The subsequent 'anti-rightist' campaigns rejected any form of population control, openly attacking those advocating family planning. Early in 1958, Chairman Mao, signifying the commencement of the Great Leap Forward, denounced population control and, in a swift reversal of position, actually advocated an increase in population. The dramatic fall in production which resulted from this transformation of rural China was partly responsible for the Great Famine which was to follow (Kane 1988). 1958–61 saw an estimated 30 million additional deaths, with the growth rate plummeting to − 4.57 per 1000 in 1960. Jowett (1990) has further suggested that 25–30 million births were lost or postponed during these years. As a consequence, attention was refocused on increasing, rather than planning, the population (Kane 1988).

Fertility reduction and maternal health campaigns (1962–66)

Hull and Yang (1991) identify these campaigns as an attempt to rekindle the effort of the previous family planning programmes. The economic measures of the post-famine years supported the natural desire of the population ravaged by horrendous mortality, in particular infant mortality. The birth rate rose from 18.02 per 1000 in 1961 to 43.4 per 1000 in 1963, producing a growth rate of 2.7 per cent in 1962, and over 3.3 per cent the following year. The government responded with 'The Instruction on Serious Advocacy of Family Planning' advocating family planning to 'appropriately control the natural increase rate and to gradually change the blind reproduction to planned reproduction'. And significantly adding 'this is a fixed policy in the socialist construction of our country' (quoted in Wang Hong 1991).

The following year the CPC and State Council issued a directive that family planning centres should be re-established at both central and local levels. Wang Hong has recently contradicted Croll's (1985) declaration that the government did not explicitly aim to reduce family size until the early 1970s. Croll suggests that the family planning attempts of the first two decades were simply directed towards assisting the control of *unwanted fertility*. In contrast, Wang Hong (1991) identifies Zhou Enlai's announcement at the National Planning Conference in September 1965 that net population growth rate should be reduced to within 1 per cent per annum, as heralding the first explicit national target in population control. The 1964 census had revealed China's population to have reached 700 million.

Thus family planning tentatively entered the realms of family reduction. The results were significant. Family planning work was more vigorously promoted in densely populated rural and urban areas, and within two years the birth rate had fallen to 35.1 per 1000, and the growth rate to 26.2 per 1000. It is inevitably difficult, however, to separate out the various contributory factors: family planning clinics; education, economic and social variables; the natural decline in reproductive behaviour following an artificial boom. Myrdal (1967) suggests that the family planning cadres actually possessed very limited power and influence at this time. Similarly, improved maternal and child health and obstetric care led to a higher percentage of live births and infant survival rate (Sidel and Sidel 1982) – a natural precursor of independent family limitation. Clearly, however, the mechanisms of national structured fertility control had entered the Chinese experience.

2. Population disruption (1966–70)

The cultural revolution and population disruption (1966–70)

During the confusion of the Cultural Revolution, the crude birth rate remained around 34 per 1000 with an average growth rate of 2.6 per cent per year. However, while this period certainly did see discontinuation of a specific population policy and the paralysis of family planning organizations (Wang Hong 1991), the limited data from this period suggest that desire for family planning did continue. In addition, the increased pressures of economic employment, education and correction classes, domestic and community tasks, coupled with the general disruption of the population, led to exhausted, spatially separated couples, deterred by the current climate from bringing a child into such an uncertain world: a form of contraception in itself. There was a steady decline in total fertility rate throughout this period, from 6.3 per 1000 in 1966 to 5.8 by 1970, with a dramatic fall in 1967 to 5.3 per 1000, possibly due to the intense population disruption of this time. As has been previously stressed, there were significant regional and rural–urban differences with a TFR of 7.0 in rural areas in 1966, and a low of 2.9 in urban areas in 1967 (Chen, Pi-chao 1985).

3. Planned fertility decrease: various degrees of enforcement

Two Child Policy (1971–79): 'Late, spaced, few'

Wang Hong (1991) identifies three important stages in the recommencement of China's family planning programme. The first was in 1969 when Zhou Enlai warned of the impending 800 million population and the need to promote birth control; he suggests that this was ratified by the Central Committee of the CPC in 1970, and by the State Council the following year, when they distributed the Report on Intensive Implementation of Family Programs, which formally proposed that the optimum number of children per family was two. This heralded the era of family restriction through the mechanisms of late marriage and spaced births. Mirroring this specific move towards family planning was the incorporation of key population growth targets into the economic development plans. The Fourth Five Year Plan in 1971 contained a population target, while the Fifth Five Year Plan, 1976, had an actual population plan (Wang Hong 1991).

This was implemented at the local level through the establishment of birth control committees under the direct supervision of Party members. These were charged with establishing local population growth targets in association with national and local economic plans (Stacey 1983). While the earlier campaigns had emphasized commitment to the Party and the state, the government now began to impose material sanctions against excessive family growth. Additional children, for example, no longer automatically qualified for additional rations, and parents' wages might be reduced (Aird 1978).

Despite the emphasis that is given publicly to the One Child Policy (Goodstadt 1982), substantial fertility control was effected during the decade before. Crude birth rate fell consistently throughout this period, from 30.7 per 1000 in 1971 to 18.25 in 1978. Of more significance, TFR almost halved during this period, falling from 5.75 in 1970 to just under 3 by 1978. Stacey (1983) accounts for this as much in terms of structural change as in actual population campaigning, arguing that it was due to 'a shift in the balance of considerations that structure peasant reproductive decisions' (Stacey 1983, p. 234). Under collectivization sons now provided less access to accumulating family wealth. Similarly, the increased participation of women in the labour market both increased the perceived merits of daughters and relatively reduced women's childbearing role. Ironically, such structural changes were to be fundamentally reversed over the next decade with the introduction of the production responsibility system and associated moves towards family private production; structural changes which were to coincide with the introduction of the severest family planning campaign to date: the One Child Policy.

One child policy (1979–84)

1978 saw the shift in party policy from emphasis on ideology to determined economic modernization. This transformed the family planning programmes, shifting the emphasis from family spacing to strict control of family numbers.

Demographers had presented various scenarios of China's population, focusing on potential populations of 1.4, 1.2 and 1.1 billion by the year 2000, depending on family sizes of 3, 2, 1 respectively. The latter, the 'zero growth option', was reliant on one child per family for 25 years or one generation (Kane 1987).

The 1979 National Report Conference of Family Planning suggested that 'awards should be given to those who have one child, disincentives to be made to those who give birth to a second child and punishment be inflicted upon those who have a third child' (Wang Hong 1991, p. 49). In June 1979 at the Second Session of the Fifth National People's Congress, there was a public call on couples to have only one child. Following this, an open letter laying down the goal of one child per couple was distributed to Party members, promising advantages in schooling, housing and employment for only children (Hull and Yang 1991). The One Child Policy had been launched.

65

These early stages combined socialist ideology, stressing the political and economic rewards of planned births both for the family and the state, with family-reform programmes and feminist values. The Report Concerning the Arrangements of the National Economy in 1980, for example, stated that 'As far as family planning is concerned, it is mandatory to take legal, administrative and economic measures to encourage [couples] to have only one child' (Wang Hong 1991, p. 49). At the same time a massive education campaign commenced, and Party officials were dispatched to spread the message, attacking patrilocal marriage practices and the preference for sons (Stacey 1983).

This initial stage of the policy relied on the persuasive method of financial incentives and fines. Though there was considerable variation between rural and urban zones, and indeed within counties and provinces, the government issued a set of official incentives and disincentives. Those signing the One Child pledge received a cash incentive, up to 10 per cent of the monthly income, priority on housing lists, additional maternity leave, increased pension on retirement, and free education, health care and priority job placement for the one child. These were all removed on the birth of any subsequent children, and in addition financial penalties were imposed on the parents to compensate the state for the burden of an additional person (Croll, 1985). However, higher quality schooling, free health care and priority access to jobs were meaningless in the rural context, as was increased living space. The introduction of a new system of production responsibility in 1981 removed economic penalties and further encouraged high parity births due to the seeming advantage that large peasant families had under the new production system (Croll 1983b).

In addition, two highly sensitive practices were encouraged to limit excess children: abortion and sterilization. There was increased use of abortion from 1981. This procedure has a long history in Chinese society and does not appear to carry with it the moral stigma found in Western society (Potter and Potter 1990). Rather, it is indicative of a system in which birth is the concern of the family and the state (Potter and Potter 1990), women having no exclusive rights over their reproductive system (Stacey 1983; Kristeva 1986). The degree of general acceptance of mass abortion by the peasants is, however, unclear (Wolf 1985).

The concentration on abortion was short-lived. The financial cost was high and there was no guarantee that the women would not become immediately pregnant again. In addition, there was growing concern as to the health of women undergoing repeated abortions (Sidel and Sidel 1982). From 1983, therefore, the state introduced a policy of sterilization for those with two children. At this stage it was not mandatory (Potter and Potter 1990), rather the provinces were to report back on their experiences and a future mandatory policy would then be considered.

Unlike the previous emphasis on abortion, sterilization strongly violated cultural norms (Potter and Potter 1990). In a society which defines a person through their means of production and reproduction, sterilization significantly reduces the social worth of the individual. This is made even more so by the belief that sterilization, particularly male sterilization, reduces the ability to work. Thus the three facets of life – work, reproduction and family life – are damaged by this process. Ethnographic evidence from the period suggests that in practice, despite government policy, at the local level couples were not required to consider sterilization until after the birth of their second child, regardless of the sex of their first: 'Central policy is that, if you have a son first, you have to stop, but our county lets the peasants have a second child, even if the first is a son' (Family-planning official, Guangdong Province. Quoted in Potter and Potter 1990, p. 258).

Such local interpretation of state policy had important implications for variations in fertility control. Potter and Potter suggest, for example, that while the policy was interpreted in urban areas as a One Child Policy, this was far from the practice in their rural case area in Chansen district, Guangdong. Filtered through a complex bureaucratic process, specific local regulations were formulated. Strict emphasis was given in the first place to the Marriage Law and late marriages (25 for men; 23 for women) and the role these played as a form of natural birth control. However, the clauses allowing local conditions to be taken into account were interpreted in the context of strong local familialism and couples were allowed four births in an attempt to produce at least one son before penalties were exacted. Numerous other local interpretations have been reported by Croll (1983a, 1985), Davin (1985), Kane (1985) and Stacey (1983), etc.

Modified One Child Policy (1984) and future policies and programmes

Hull and Wang regard the initial One Child Policy 'an aberration out of context with regard to the post-1978 reform' period (Hull and Wang 1991, p. 181). The moves in 1984 were thus a partial correction of that deviation of style. They argue that it was acknowledged in the early stages that one child was an ideal, which would be achieved by around one-third of the couples. However, 'the simplified rhetoric of the campaign, overly enthusiastic calls from the leadership and misunderstandings by local cadres' led to widespread enforcement of the one child policy regardless of individual situations and desires. Hull thus argues that in 1984 the government acknowledged that this rigid enforcement had created a 'big hole' which they wished to be replaced with a 'small hole' in that there would be a range of exceptions, but only on the understanding that there would be no third or subsequent children allowed.

As a result, the use of contraception fell and the range of exceptional cases increased dramatically. Zhao Ziyang's declaration in December 1986 that one child was ideal, but a planned second child was possible for those with real practical difficulties, did little to help the work of family policy officers, who were increasingly turning their attention away from the prevention of second births in order to concentrate on third and higher orders of parity (Hull and Yang 1991).

It is clear that the success of the One Child Policy and other future population programmes is reliant on a mesh of social, cultural and economic factors. Recent changes in production and relations of production (Kane 1987; Croll 1983b); China's fundamentally patriarchal society with its inherent structural emphasis on male children (Stacey 1983; Arnold and Xhao Xiang 1986) and patrilocal residence (Wolf 1985); cultural emphasis on pronatalism and familialism (Potter and Potter 1990); and reliance on the inter-generational support for care in illness and old age (Davis–Friedmann 1985; Harper 1992) all provide strong forces encouraging the procreation of children. However, it can be argued that the overriding theme which binds these factors into a powerful pronatal force is the continuation of patrilocal residence supported by the over-elevation of familialism.

As Potter and Potter (1990 p. 230) have argued, the Chinese concept of familialism exalts the family and the procreation of new family

'marriage is to create family continuity, and the explicit purpose of marriage is to have children: this is the pattern of human existence. When a child is born, its importance lies in its social relationships. It exists in relation to the family, as one who is carrying on the line, if male, or as one who will help carry on the line of another family, if female.'

Children are thus the means of the family continuity, the basis of its prosperity, and the only valid source of personal help and security. However, due to the continuation of traditional patrilocal marriage patterns, this source of family continuation and support is primarily vested in the son. Despite government intervention, daughters still leave the parental home on marriage and accept responsibility for and obligation to their husband's parents. Daughters thus do not continue the lineage, they do not provide security in old age and their labour is not defined as valuable as that of their brothers:

'A woman with sons not only has an old-age pension, she also has a hold on her husband and his relatives through that son. Many things in China have changed, but women are still outsiders in their husband's communities until they are mothers in their son's communities'

(Wolf 1985, p.258)

Patrilocal residence has remained a fundamental barrier to the One Child Policy. The government has attempted to restrict such practices, with limited success. The 1981 Marriage Law, for example, attempts to extend to women the rights, privileges and obligations formerly accruing to men and their families: spouses should make their own decision about which family home to join; daughters as well as sons have an obligation to support their ageing parents.

There is some evidence that deep cultural and structural changes are occurring in urban China; changes which are reducing the priority for sons. Overcrowding, and the success of economic rewards and disincentives, have already created a strong peer precedent for one child regardless of sex. The extra provision for old age security, through pension provision and increased community-based health and welfare programmes, has only served to emphasize the trend away from strict patrilocal practices.

In rural areas, however, the One Child Policy has, if anything, further reinforced the value of the male child. For with only one son, which parents are going to jeopardize *their* future security by allowing him to move into his wife's family? Economic advantage for the household and security in old age remain strongly vested in the possession of a male child. Unless the problem of patrilocal residence is tackled, it can be argued that future population programmes based on the restriction of family size are bound to fail.

Health and welfare programmes for the elderly population

The situation of the elderly population is meshed with China's population planning in a complex web of interlinking frameworks. Of particular importance is the influence that the perception of old age places upon family reproductive decisions. In addition, such decisions have had a significant impact on the current cohort of elderly people: fertility control has increased their percentage within the total population, particuarly in urban areas, and has started to undermine the traditional source of support in old age. This latter factor is discussed below together with the programmes the government is seeking to implement to supplement potentially dwindling family support.

Health and social welfare (1949–78)

In general, there were no policy statements concerning elderly Chinese during these years. In a deliberate move by the Chinese Communist Party away from traditional Confucian forms of hierarchy, power and respect based on seniority, the elderly were deliberately not singled out for special attention. In rural areas families were still expected to care for their elderly, at least in the early days of the People's Republic, and childless elderly peasants came under the rural reform programmes by virtue of their poverty. General welfare provision was thus provided under the auspices of social reform, rather than any recognition of the specific requirements of this age group. Many elderly people benefited, for example, from the tremendous progress in general health care during this period (Lampton 1974; Sidel and Sidel 1976, 1982), with a corresponding rise in life expectancy at birth from 55 years to 70 years between 1949 and 1974 (Sanders 1985). Similarly, during the collectivization programmes of the 1950s, the law requiring collectives to support those who could not work and who had no kin (*RMRB* 26/1/56) was particularly beneficial to the rural, childless elderly. Many were provided with housing under the qualification of poor and destitute members of the collective, often becoming 'five guarantee households' (*wu bao hu*), and guaranteed food, fuel, clothing, education and burial fees.

While the segregation of old people in homes for the aged was thus rare during this first decade, the Great Leap Forward heralded a sudden and short-lived change in policy. In 1958 the scheme of integrating elderly five-guarantee households into the community was abruptly replaced by the establishment of a variety of collective homes for the aged (*RMRB* 10/6/58). This move appears partly in sympathy with the general trend towards collective living for all the population, but was also an attempt to reduce the growing expense of supporting large numbers of elderly five-guarantee houses. Some 2 million old people were reportedly housed in 100 000 rural old people's homes between June and November 1958. The urban areas mirrored these moves towards institutionalization, though on a far smaller scale, with a maximum of 65 000 urban institutionalized elderly being recorded at the peak of the programme (*RMRB* 15/1/59). Yet far from reducing welfare costs, the scheme proved expensive and administratively cumbersome to operate; in addition it required large numbers of trained personnel, which the country as a whole lacked. By early 1960 most elderly had been rehoused in the community (*RMRB* 12/2/61).

It is evident that this move towards age segregation was based on economic criteria rather than a specific health and welfare policy for the care of the elderly. In the spirit of the other communal, communist, living arrangements being encouraged at that time, it found few supporters after its collapse. From 1958 onwards any perceived need for special policies towards the elderly further diminished as those elderly parents who had lost their children, and thus their support in old age, during the struggles of the civil war, themselves died. By 1970 the relatively few childless elderly households were receiving the sixth and seventh guarantees of housing and medical care, and little attention appeared to be shown to the elderly as a specific group.

Health and social welfare (1978–90)

During this post-Mao period, health and social welfare provision for China's elderly population has fallen into three main streams of delivery: domiciliary and community care; residential homes; and medical services. Each stream operates independently, typically resulting in fragmented and uncoordinated service delivery. In addition, the programmes lack an overseeing body able to advise on legislation or make recommendations concerning policy for the elderly: civil administration departments provide resources for the needy elderly; public health departments provide medical care; insurance policies, including pensions, are implemented by individual labour departments. Since 1982 veteran cadre administrations have controlled services for retired cadres. Alongside this, the committees on ageing are introducing their own mass activities and services. Despite declarations in China's Seventh Five Year Plan (1986–90) that a social security system is to be established and social welfare services further developed, the National Committee on Ageing (1989) has reported that there are no plans to provide a central welfare body, or indeed to train professionals in geriatrics, geriatric nursing, service provision, or geriatric and gerontological research.

Domiciliary and associated community care

Most elderly Chinese people live with their families (Gui *et al*. 1987; Zhang 1987; Chen, 1988; Gui, 1988; Jai, 1988;). Given the widespread community infrastructure encouraged throughout China by the Communist Party, domiciliary care and associated community care services are particuarly poor. Such provision tends to be local, uncoordinated between the various governmental and non-governmental organizations supplying such services, and severely limited. In a survey carried out by the National Committee on Ageing, under 4 per cent of elderly households had received any assistance from welfare services, or expected to do so in the future (China National Committee on Ageing 1989).

Limited evidence suggests four main types of domiciliary and community provision. 'Home help provision', to assist the resident primary care givers, typically children, is divided into public provision and a growing privately operated sector. A very few, typically urban elderly, have access to 'day care nursing stations' and to 'service stations', providing daily living care. Under the 'service group for fixed households', volunteers adopt a childless elderly household and provide primary care.

Residential homes for the aged

The mutations of the collective system during the post-Mao period removed those care structures which were alternative to sole reliance on the family. There was thus an attempt in the early post-Mao period to formalize an alternative policy of housing and financial assistance for needy elderly, centred around a system of homes for the aged. Although some of the larger metropolitan homes may provide medical care, the service in general, officially at least, is aimed at providing daily living facilities for those unable to live independently within the community.

By 1981 the brigades and communes had established 8262 homes for elderly people without children, caring for some 111 600 old people. These were typically dual financed, with the state paying for their construction, 9.2 million yuan being allocated in 1980, and the communes financing their daily running, setting aside 17.8 million yuan in 1980 alone. This growth in homes for the aged continued throughout the 1980s, increasing rapidly in the mid-years of the decade to reach over 32 000 by 1987, accommodating over 300 000 elderly residents.

The priorities behind the establishment of homes for the aged

An examination of the current growth of residential care, suggests that there is a hidden agenda (Harper 1992). Firstly, homes for the aged are clearly being established to reduce concerns of those following the One Child Policy. Homes for the aged throughout China are currently receiving a high press profile, and are an overt sign to the younger population that they will be well cared for in *their own* old age. There is also genuine concern about the growing number of childless, and sonless, elderly people.

However, the client group being addressed by residential provision is not necessarily the frail, who typically appear to remain in their own homes under the care of kin. These homes for the aged are also serving a hidden client group – the elite. China operates a strong reward system, with the high officials, cadres and those who have served the Party expecting recognition. While these individuals remain within the labour market, this reward can take the form of promotion, or special acknowledgement. Large numbers of those who served the Party in the Revolution and before, however, have now reached retirement age, and expect this recognition to continue. They are being rewarded through preferential allocation in high prestige homes, which will waive the qualification of no children if required. In addition, those elite members with ageing parents are also being rewarded, not only through increased allocation of housing space (Sankar 1989) but also through the opportunity to obtain free space for the placement of the parent(s) in a home for the aged.

The residential programme in China appears set to continue, with a call in September 1988 for every township to build a home for the aged by the end of the century. While the criteria behind the selection of various care strategies are complex, it is evident that the system of homes for the aged is one way in which the Party can continue to reward its faithful and maintain its strong elitist society.

Medical service provision for the elderly

Post-Revolution China has seen tremendous progress in general medical care, successfully integrating traditional Chinese medicine into Western hospital-based structures (Henderson and Cohen 1984), while still retaining emphasis on community health workers and primary health carers, in particular the 'barefoot doctors' (Sanders 1985).

Geriatrics and associated medical services was identified by the government as a key component of future health care strategies. The National Geriatrics Society was formed in 1981; its sister body, the China Gerontological Society, in 1986. A Division of Elderly Health Care and Rehabilitation was established under the Ministry of Health in 1984, followed by the opening of health care centres for the elderly in most provinces by the end of the decade (National Committee on Ageing 1989). The Ministry of Health has also called for the institution of departments of geriatrics in all general hospitals throughout the country, providing both clinical and rehabilitation services.

As with domiciliary and community care, however, elderly health care is fragmented. Local and regional services operate in an uncoordinated manner, with little exchange of information, personnel or resources between the levels. The government has acknowledged this and the need for a multi-level health care delivery system, which also includes geriatric research institutions and domiciliary support services (Huang *et al*. 1991).

The post-Mao period has thus seen two fundamental shifts in policy towards elderly people. The late 1970s and early 1980s saw the development of a problem-orientated approach, directed at the childless, potentially homeless elderly, which found manifestation in the construction of homes for the aged. With the establishment of the National Ageing Committee in 1982, there was a fundamental change in elderly policy, from identifying the childless as a problem group, towards recognizing that the whole elderly age group had certain needs and requirements with which society should be concerned. Zhao Ziyang's report to the Thirteenth National Congress of the Communist Party of China, declared 'attention must be paid to the trend of rapid ageing of the population, and correct policy should be adopted' (China National Committee on Ageing 1989). We shall consider separately these two issues: that of perceiving the childless elderly as a problem group; and that of recognizing the ageing of the population as a whole.

Reflections on future policy for China's ageing population

The National Committee on Ageing in 1988 identified a variety of problems forecast to arise as China's population ages:

- China's increasing dependency ratio will be made more severe by the general low productivity of the population.
- The traditional ability of the family to care for its elderly has been weakened, particularly by changes in female employment practices and the One Child Policy.
- Existing welfare provision is underdeveloped and cannot meet the needs of the elderly.
- China lacks a coherent pension policy and any social insurance system for its rural elderly population.
- Geriatric medicine is poorly equipped and lacks specialist medical workers.
- There exists no specialist organization which can provide advice on gerontology and geriatric legislation and policy.

The Committee thus proposed potential policy directives aimed at ameliorating the situation. These include further population control aimed at preventing the 'over-ageing' of the population, whereby population planning allows gradual transition to a stationary population. Both health care and pension provision, the Committee argues, should become socialized. Pension policy should develop an insurance fund for the elderly, supported by contributions from the individual, the employer and the state, and pension provision should be based on labour market principles. Government expenditure on health care should be increased, allowing a social security system of coherent health care provision including a high allowance for free medical treatment. Education, training and research, including educating elderly people in good health care practices, should be expanded. Retraining and encouragement of elderly workers to return to or remain within the workplace should be given priority.

Of most interest, however, are the Committee recommendations for family care. Acknowledging that family care practices are altering, it proposes a service industry for the elderly which will work alongside the family, supporting not only the elderly person but also the primary family carers themselves. However, in order to pay for this increased family support, it argues that current free services provided in the community should become fee charging.

It is clear that the government has chosen to rely heavily on kin to provide mass care for its potentially large elderly population: its residential care policy is limited and multi-faceted in its *raison d'être*. Ironically, given the Party's overall ethos towards traditional norms, the People's Republic still relies on the system of life-long reciprocity and moral obligations between parent and child, established under Confucianism, to create the structure of care for its elderly population.

What is clearly of most concern is whether the main agencies selected for care of the mass elderly, namely kin, will be capable of carrying out their task. Throughout the Western world there is growing acknowledgement of the need for the wider community to support not only the elderly but also their primary care-givers. The provision of a community care service which has this as one of its fundamentals would be of significant conceptual advancement. If welfare provision for the elderly is to be rationalized and consolidated, then emphasis needs to be placed on services that can support both the elderly and their primary carers – their kin – *in situ*. Furthermore, if such provision is to operate on market terms, then a sound system of social security and pension provision must be implemented for all elderly people, particularly in rural areas.

As the National Committee on Ageing has stated, if China is to deal with its potential problem of ageing, it is of urgent necessity to approach the issue in a planned and regulated way. Unless the government turns away from a policy that currently serves to reward through welfare provision those elderly who are still able to care for themselves, and turns towards establishing programmes directed at supporting the frail elderly, it is not clear that China will be in a position to cope with its ageing population.

References

Unless otherwise stated, the statistics in the text have been taken from the State Statistical Bureau of China, *Statistical Year book of China 1988*, China Statistical Publishing House, Beijing, 1988.

Aird J (1978) 'Fertility decline and birth control in the People's Republic of China', *Population and Development Review* **4** (2) 225–53.

Arnold, F and **Xhao Xiang** (1986) 'Sex preference and fertility in China', *Population and Development Review* **12** (1) 221–46.

Chen Hunchang (1988) *Survey of Old People in Beijing Xicheng District*, Beijing University of Medical Science.

Chen, Pi-chao (1985) 'Birth control methods and organization in China', in Croll E, Davin D and Kane P (eds). *China's one-Child Family Policy*,

Macmillan, London.

China National Committee on Ageing (1989) *Population Aging in China,* Asian Population Studies series: 95 ESCAP Bangkok. United Nations, New York.

Croll E (1983a) *Chinese Women since Mao,* Zed Press, London.

Croll E (1983b) 'Production versus reproduction', *World Development* **11** 467–81.

Croll E (1985) 'Fertility norms and family size in China', in Croll E, Davin D and Kane P (eds) *China's one-Child Family Policy,* Macmillan London.

Davin D (1985) 'The single child policy in the countryside', in Croll E, Davin D and Kane P. (eds) *China's one-Child Family Policy,* Macmillan, London.

Davis-Friedmann D (1983) *Long Lives: Chinese elderly and the communist revolution,* Harvard University Press, Cambridge, Mass.

Davis-Friedmann D (1985), 'Intergenerational inequalities and the Chinese revolution', *Modern China* **11** (2) 177–201.

Goodstadt L (1982) 'China's one-child family: policy and public response', *Population and Development Review* **8** (1), 37–58.

Gui Shi-Xun (1988) 'A report from mainland China', *Journal of Cross-Cultural Gerontology* **3**, 149–67.

Gui Shi-Xun, Li-Kui Li, Zhe-Ning Shen, Jue-Xin Di, Quan-Zhong Gu, Yang-Ming Chen and **Fang Qian** (1987) 'Status and needs of the elderly in urban Shanghai', *Journal of Cross Cultural Gerontology,* **2** 171–86

Harper S (1992) 'Caring for China's ageing population. The residential option – a case study of Shanghai,' *Ageing and Society* **12**, 157–84.

Henderson G and **Cohen M** (1984) *The Chinese Hospital,* Yale University Press.

Huang Y, Wang X and **Yue X** (1991) Medical and Health Care Problems of the Rural Elderly. Paper presented to the Workshop on Population Ageing, ESCAP Bangkok, July 1991.

Hull T and **Quanhe Yang** (1991) 'Fertility and family planning in Wang Jiye and Hull T (eds). *Population and Development Planning in China,* Allen and Unwin, Sydney.

Jai Aimei (1988) 'New experiments with elderly care in China', *Journal of Cross-Cultural Gerontology* **3**, 139–48.

Jowett J (1990) 'People: demographic patterns and policies', in Cannon T and Jenkins A *The Geography of Contemporary China,* Routledge, London.

Kane P (1976) 'How women hold up half the sky', *People* **3**, 3.

Kane P (1985) 'The single child policy in the cities', in Croll E, Davin D and Kane P (eds) *China's one-Child Family Policy,* Macmillan, London

Kane P (1987) *The second Billion: Population and family planning in China,* Penguin, Ringwood, Victoria.

Kane P (1988) *Famine in China: 1959–61: Demographic and social implications,* Macmillan, London.

Kristeva J (1986) *About Chinese Women,* Marion Boyars, London.

Lampton D (1974) 'Health conflict and the Chinese political system. *Michigan Papers in Chinese Studies.* No. 18

Myrdal J (1967) *Report from a Chinese Village,* Penguin Books, Harmondsworth.

National Committee on Ageing (1988) 'China's ageing population' Paper presented to Australian Association of Gerontology Conference, Brisbane, September 1988.

Potter S and **Potter J** (1990) *China's Peasants: the anthropology of a revolution*, CUP, Cambridge.

Rang Zhigang and **Cheng Liankang** (1991) 'Population aging and social security', in Wang Jiye and Hull T (eds). *Population and Development Planning in China*, Allen and Unwin, Sydney.

Sanders D (1985) *The Struggle for Health: Medicine and the politics of underdevelopment*, Macmillan, London.

Sankar A (1989) 'Gerontological research in China: the role of anthropological enquiry', *Journal of Cross-Cultural Gerontology*, **4**, 199–224.

Sidel V W and **Sidel R** (1976) 'The health care delivery system of the People's Republic of China', in Newll K (ed). *Health by the People*, WHO Geneva.

Sidel V W and **Sidel R** (1982) *The Health of China*, Zed Press

Stacey J (1983) *Patriarchy and Socialist Revolution in China*, University of California Press, Berkeley.

Wang Hong (1991) 'The population policy of China', in Wang Jiye and Hull T (eds). *Population and Development Planning in China*, Allen and Unwin, Sydney.

Wolf M (1985) *Revolution Postponed: Women in contemporary China*. Stanford University Press, Stanford.

Zhang Kai-Ming (1987) *Report of the elderly in Shangai 1986*; China Population Science, August 1987.

CHAPTER 5

Necessity, policy and opportunity in the Chinese countryside

Frank Leeming

The golden age

The countryside was for a few years the great success story of the Third Plenum reforms of 1978 onwards. The centrepiece of this success was the introduction of the responsibility and contract systems, which in effect awarded the status of family farmer to rural households which had previously been much more like employees of the brigades. This change in status, with its accompanying changes in the practical experience of the working day, capacity to take decisions, opportunities for diversification of production and so forth, was accompanied by farm price increases and, for some years, rising incomes for farmers (CSY 1990, p. 274). It also heralded a variety of other changes in the countryside, mostly very popular, such as the dissolution of the commune system with its union of economic management with administrative authority, the relaxation of planning control of cropping schemes year by year, and the abandonment of the principle of official compulsion to particular courses of action by farmers. Enrichment of the working people was now a proclaimed aim of the system. Most of these provisions now seem self-evidently rational, but most had been anathema to the operators of the previous Maoist systems.

The reforms in the countryside were broadly successful. Obligations such as the delivery of grain supplies to the state continued, but against higher prices and a much better-motivated peasant workforce. Various features of change previously introduced during the 1970s, particularly greatly improved supplies of fertilizers and various rational cultivation practices associated with learning from Dazhai and other agricultural 'models', helped to support greatly increased outputs of grain. Grain outputs rose from 305 million tonnes in 1978 to 407 million tonnes in 1984 (CSY 1990, p. 349). The former was the first such figure in Chinese history to rise above 300 million tonnes; the latter was a record figure not exceeded until 1990. In 1984 cotton output also reached a peak, still not exceeded, of 6.3 million tonnes (CSY 1990, p. 349). Yields per unit area greatly increased

– of grain as a whole by 45 per cent between 1978 and 1984; of wheat, by 61 per cent (CSY 1990, p. 355). Much of this improvement was said to depend upon improved motivation, and that apparently depended partly upon the peasant farmers' new sense of independence, with increased participation in farm work by young and old family members, partly upon the new capacity of the family to keep the fruits of its own hard work, rather than sharing them with others whose work might be thought less effective. The same rationales applied to household pig and poultry keeping. Outputs of pigs rose rapidly after 1978, by some 7 per cent per year in the period up to 1985 (CSY 1990, p. 360). One writer says that it was 'erroneously believed that the grain problem had been solved' (Zhang Gengsheng 1990, p. 66).

In fact, 1984 was a turning point. The bumper harvest of that year led to official anxiety about grain storage and more ambitious uses for grain. As a result the state, anxious to save money as always, especially in a year of tight credit, reversed the payment priorities in the official grain purchase system – henceforth, a higher price was to be paid for the first 70 per cent of purchases, and a lower basic price for the remaining 30 per cent (CCP 1985, p. K2; Oi 1986a, p. 281). At the same time, the state gave up its monopoly of trade in grain. Grain quotas were now converted to contracts, with a clear undertaking (not always honoured by the state) that henceforth they were wholly voluntary. Quotas for pigs, fish and vegetables were also abolished. 'No units whatsoever may set mandatory production plans for the peasants' (CCP 1985, p. K2).

The new rural concept

The specific motivation of the Communist Party in making these changes cannot be known, but there is evidence that they form part of a wider body of change promoted at that time, and hence were perhaps not simply a response to perceived over-production of grain in 1984. Other changes in the rural system in 1984–85 included a fresh approach to rural industries, both collective and individual, now to be called 'township enterprises' and much more wholeheartedly encouraged, and notice of implicit toleration of migration of rural labour to local towns, and by implication further afield as well. There was also an indication by the central authorities of adoption of a new concept for the rural economy itself – 'larger-scale commodity production' (CCP 1984, p. K1), and 'rural production . . . transformed into a commodity economy' (CCP 1985, p. K1). To further this objective, 'the gradual concentration of land among efficient families should be encouraged', and land contract periods should generally be longer – typically more than 15 years (CCP 1984, p. K1). Other official documents of the same phase proposed more liberal regimes for employment of workers, for industrial, commercial and transportation enterprises and for households specializing in various kinds of production, including grain. At the same time the state started the policy of transferring the administration of rural counties from prefectures to cities, with the proclaimed aim of stimulating rural change and development. Clearly, there was a rational policy underlying all these proposals – a policy for a countryside much less self-sufficient locally, much more commercialized, much less ordered by the officials, and much more sympathetic to economic growth, and perhaps economic adventure, than that of the first phase of reform.

On the basis of experience in the countryside up to that time, the Communist Party might reasonably have expected favourable peasant responses to most of the proposed changes, particularly since they proposed the lifting of restrictions rather than fresh obligations. But from 1985 onwards the previous rapid growth in grain and cotton outputs came to an end. These outputs have since fluctuated below or close to the high figures for 1984. Outputs of other kinds, such as pigs, have continued to increase, but at quite moderate rates. Meanwhile demand for rural produce has increased rapidly, not least because population has increased by some 90 million since 1984 and the labour force by nearly as many. A distinctly sour note has intruded into media discussions of rural development, and no less into comments by peasants and their spokespeople on the same issues. All is not well in the Chinese countryside.

Rural dissatisfaction

Problems in the grain system

The heart of the present rural malaise is a group of problems involved in grain production, especially state grain procurement. For these problems, there are several heads of discussion. It is worth noting at the outset that the state's 'take' of grain is some 125 million tonnes all told (Grain Studies Group 1990, p. 38). This is only about 31 per cent of total output but it dominates the commercial market in grain. Most of the rest of Chinese grain is used by those who grow it.

One problem arises directly from the reversal of the state's payment system in 1985. It is argued that the result of this was to reduce farmers' incomes on average by about 10 per cent (Hou Zhemin and Zhang Qiguang 1989, p. 38). The market price has tended since that time to rise against the state's fixed price – from 30 per cent higher in 1985 to figures close to double in 1988 (Wen Guifang 1990, p. 50). This is no doubt one reason (some people argue, the main reason) for the subsequent failure of grain output to rise further until 1990, and then only under exceptional official and media pressure, and with the help of an exceptional price rise; but it is not the only one.

Grain is cheap – 100 kg of grain is cheaper than a bottle of good wine (Mao Yangqing and Tang Jianzhong 1987, p. 24). Official grain prices are now nearly three times those of 1978, but many other prices, including other farm prices, have risen much more in the same period. Cheap grain is an aspect of national policy designed to help support the cities at the expense of the countryside; it is difficult to defend, but so far impossible to reform. Official price subsidies for the cities have risen from 1 billion yuan in 1978 to 37 billion in 1989 (CSY 1990, p. 224). A province such as Heilongjiang, with a high proportion of urban consumers, finds this system difficult to tolerate (Wu Yunbo *et al*. 1990). However, the official subsidy system is additional to the 'subsidy' which low procurement prices squeeze out of the countryside. It is also on top of the use of outputs from rural township enterprises to subsidise grain-growing families in prosperous parts of the country such as south Jiangsu. This last is an important practice, called by the Communist Party 'industry subsidizing agriculture', but more accurately 'rural subsidizing urban'. It is interesting that details of this practice in local cases are no longer readily found in the literature – perhaps because the real form of this subsidy is now generally understood. However, it remains commonplace, and has even suggested an adaptation at province level, that Guangdong, with its exceptional prosperity, but in recent years in deficit for grain, should invest money in low-yield farmland in hard-up Jiangxi, which would then be able to supply Guangdong with grain – of course at low prices (Huang Bingxin 1989).

Prices, costs and deliveries

Grain is cheap, but the inputs which are necessary to produce it are not, or not perceived as such. The 'scissors' of rural output prices versus manufactured input prices, having closed for some years in the early 1980s to the advantage of the countryside, are said now to have opened again to its disadvantage (Kong Xiangliang 1990). The expense of farming is a constantly repeated complaint in surveys of peasant opinion. In addition, supplies are often difficult to obtain. In the majority of provinces in 1989, supplies of chemical fertilizer, other chemicals and plastic sheeting, fine-strain seeds, diesel and farm tools were all in deficit, often to the extent of 20 or even 30 per cent (Beijing broadcast, 6 March 1989, translated in FBIS *Daily Report*, 13 March 1989). Assumption of general state control over these supplies has not been able to guarantee supplies. Oi (1986b) shows that local officials retain a great deal of discretionary control over rural supplies, and also that they can easily manipulate supplies to take advantage of 'double-tracking' in prices – differences in price between official sales (cheap) and unofficial (dear). This kind of corrupt practice exists among local officials and their agents; and it is also said to exist at provincial level in around half the provinces (Li Delai 1989). Other practices of which officials are accused in this field are less corrupt but even more offensive. Stories have appeared in the Chinese press about officials collecting grain for 'contracts' by force from peasants' homes, or seizing pigs, cash and savings bonds from households where grain deliveries were in default (Lin Zifu and Wang Man 1989, p. 59). Stories of this kind appear to come mainly from southern provinces, especially the group of inland provinces (Anhui, Jiangxi, Hunan, Hubei, Sichuan) which are expected to supply grain to more advanced and richer coastal provinces. It is true that peasants who do not deliver their contract grain may be selling the same grain for a higher price on the market, though not necessarily so. There is also the problem (from the grain agencies' point of view) that the province is bound to deliver a specified quantity of grain; if it cannot produce this from its own production, it must buy up grain from other sources in order to do so. But understandably this kind of manoeuvre is not favoured by the state, and cannot be considered valid except in the short term. Nor can it be welcome to Jiangxi to be committed to low-return grain production when the authorities there know that industrial crops would pay much better, and that in Guangdong grain is scarce because Guangdong land resources are being used for such things as local factories which pay much better than grain.

However, the state itself, or rather its agencies the banks, is not innocent of exploitation in this field. Some purchasing agencies are accused of grading peasants' grain low at time of purchase, but higher at the time of delivery to the state, and pocketing the cash difference. When grain purchasing agencies have been short of cash they have 'paid' for contract grain in the form of IOUs, in some places (centre and centre-west again), sometimes to the extent of 50 per cent. Needless to say this practice is greatly resented by peasants. It is also said that when purchasing agencies are short of cash this sometimes results from the previous misappropriation of grain-purchasing funds by the banks, for instance lending out these funds for profit.

Survey data put some of this material into perspective (Wang Qiang *et al.* 1989). In 1987 the gross income per working day for cereal cultivation was 6.5 yuan; for business and service industries it was 8.9 yuan; for industry 16.5 yuan; and for transportation 20.5 yuan. At the same time there was a tendency for these ratios to develop to the disadvantage of agriculture (Wang Qiang *et al.* Part 1, p. 51). The net output value of grain crops per hectare and net income after taxes for grain cultivation around 1989 were 1230 and 773 yuan respectively, but for economic crops on average 4665 and 3480 yuan (Wen Guifang 1990). It is argued that where prices of inputs are moving upwards further and faster than those for outputs, partly because of the failure of the price control systems, peasants have found in recent years that incomes per unit of grainland have actually fallen.

State purchases of grain

The state has long supplied cheap rationed grain to the cities. Both the 'cheap' and the 'rationed' status of this grain are under criticism. Against 'cheap', it is argued that common sense requires that urban populations pay more realistic prices for grain, if necessary with continued specific subsidy for the poor and very poor. It is argued that a range of ways exists in which prices can be gradually raised – for example, by making a special case for high-quality grains. Against 'rationed', it is argued that the present allowances of grain per person in the cities are now unrealistic, because other kinds of food are now common. According to survey evidence, official grain is available at an average rate of 48 kg per month, but actual consumption is substantially less – only 42 kg per month. In fact, grain purchase accounts for only around 6 per cent of household expenses, suggesting that to allow the price of official grain to rise to the market price would not represent a great burden to urban households.* It is already the case that many households (23 per cent in the survey) trade in state grain for grain of higher quality at grain shops, and a much larger proportion (44 per cent) buy higher quality grain as well as state grain (Deng Yiming 1991).

Investment

At the same time, official investment in agriculture is exceptionally low, and understandably the peasants are in no mood to pay for any substantial investment themselves. The state's investment in agriculture fell from 11.1 per cent in 1979 to 2.9 per cent in 1988, in spite of much talk to the contrary (Zhang Gengsheng 1990, p. 66). Bank lending meanwhile was prone to channel more savings into urban construction, because the latter yields higher dividends. In Hubei, banks have set up more than 600 new rural branches since 1987 but less than 10 per cent of the rural funds collected have returned to agriculture (He Shaozi 1990). Voices are from time to time raised to suggest that banks should finance agricultural improvements more freely, but even in the countryside the banks are more interested in local factories than farming. No doubt farmers as individuals are reluctant to take on debts, even for purposes of production – there is a good deal of anecdotal evidence that peasant communities are still unhappy with activities which may rank as business, rather than simple cultivation. Meanwhile, collective investment in the countryside has weakened sharply in the 1980s, and very little local money goes to support agricultural production, even from township industries. According to some writers, agriculture is being run into the ground. Financial investment remains scanty but management and labour investment have also been quite limited; many peasants' management style is one of 'plunderer' (Liang Xiufeng 1989, p. 34). The irrigated area actually fell between 1980 and 1985 by nearly 2 per cent, and has still not regained its peak figure (Zhang Liuzheng 1989). Either because they depend on 'quick-fix' cultivation methods or under an impression that 'modern' methods are always superior, peasants in recent years have relied unduly upon chemical fertilizers rather than organics; in this and other ways the land is being stripped of fertility (Huang Bingxin 1989).

Population and land resource

Enough has been said in the foregoing pages to demonstrate that all is not well with the institutions of the Chinese countryside, and that difficulties in the supply of food are due partly to man-made problems such as the low price of grain. There are, however, more far-reaching problems afoot, and these have to begin with the well-known condition of Chinese agriculture: that it maintains about 22 per cent of world population from around 7 per cent of the world's arable land.

---

*The state price for grain in 1988 was 0.504 yuan per kilogram; the market price of 1.112 yuan was about 2.2 times the state price (Deng Yiming 1991, p. 61).

Both halves of this forbidding equation are tending to deteriorate. In spite of the efforts of the central authorities, working very much against the grain of popular thinking, population in China continues to increase by about 16 million a year. The relevant indicators have now been stable for several years, but they are stable at levels which still generate a population increase at a level which is difficult to handle. In addition, at the present time population increase has an aspect which is particularly important – the effects on the labour supply of the long phase of birth rates above 30 per 1000, from 1962 to 1971. These babies are now young adults, looking for jobs and planning to marry. In both capacities they are hard to assimilate.

Meanwhile, the extent of Chinese arable land is falling, due to occupation by suburban housing and industrial development, rural house-building and township enterprises, excavation for coal and building materials, burials (increasingly), new transportation links like roads, bridges and airports, soil erosion and (on the Great Wall frontier) desertification. From a maximum of around 112 million hectares in 1957, the arable total has now fallen (1989) to around 96 million hectares (*People's Daily* 31 July 1989).* Although there is increasing official effort to protect arable land, it is obvious that this will be very difficult to do effectively. When farmland is converted to other uses, such as local industry, a tax is charged, and local regulations may also require payments which represent the grain lost to the local unit. Local industry, which if successful can be very profitable, simply pays these charges if it must; this will satisfy the bureaucracy but will not protect good farmland from development.

The ratios between population and arable land figures are discouraging in the extreme. In the 1950s arable was around 1800 square metres per person; around 1400 m^2 in the 1960s; 1100 m^2 in the 1970s; and 1000 m^2 in the 1980s. It is now around 900 m^2 (Mao Yangqing and Tang Jianzhong 1989). Even on very favourable assumptions, the figure for year 2000 is bound to be lower than 800 m^2; some writers argue for a figure nearer to 650 m^2 (Zhang Gengsheng 1989, p. 39). Some of the arable lost to cultivation, in provinces like Jiangsu and Guangdong and near the cities, is of the highest quality but of course some (in Shaanxi or Guizhou, for example) is very poor land indeed.

There is one special feature of the land problem which is a natural 'bug' in the rural system. This is the problem of land contract distribution among families, when after 11 years of rapid change there are both national demographic development and changing household circumstances to evaluate. One important survey (Sun Zhonghua 1990, p. 78) shows that since 1985, 65 per cent of villages have readjusted contracted landholdings, but that in these villages grain output had typically fallen some 3 per cent more than in villages where landholding

*Figures in discussion of the arable area are open to challenge. Both total arable area and losses of arable due to local building are now said (as a result of special surveys and studies of satellite data) to be greater than recorded, as a result of peasant and local official concealment in the official record.

had not been readjusted. There is real conflict between the interest of long-term landholding families in nurturing the soil and improving installations, and the need of new potential tenants for land. Typically, farming families who take up other activities, for instance local industry, do not part with their land, but farm it minimally or through family members who may well have no labour to spare – in this way good land goes effectively out of cultivation. Various surveys agree that families are reluctant to give up their land rights, whatever their practical circumstances, because these rights are regarded as a fundamental security.

Levels of consumption

Finally, where grain is directly involved, consumption itself is at fault. The standards for urban grain consumption were set in 1955, but great changes have taken place in eating habits since that time, with much greater consumption of meat, eggs and so forth. The standard grain allowances are now generally more than are needed. As a result grain is often consumed without need, or wasted. At the same time some people use grain coupons corruptly; for instance restaurateurs illegally buy up fixed-price grain to process into high-price items such as pastries (Chen Xiaoping 1990).

Some authors (Mao Yangqing and Tang Jianzhong 1989) particularly criticize wasteful use of grain – too much eating, too many banquets; too much conversion to grain spirit – as in 1988, for 5 million tonnes of spirit, 12 million tonnes of grain; and spirit output is growing at around 10 per cent per annum. Beer output, 6.4 million tonnes in 1989, was only 0.4 million tonnes in 1978 (CSY 1990 p. 434). In addition, some writers criticize the use of good arable land for tobacco – around 1.5 million hectares (Zhao Guangyao 1989). Strength is lent to alcohol and tobacco outputs by the practice of taxation of them by local governments, giving the latter a vested interest in them.

Diversification

To what extent have farmers who are discouraged by the low prices and high costs of grain turned to diversified outputs such as poultry, cash crops, pork and so forth? These kinds of production are not officially regulated nor their prices controlled; they would appear to be obvious places for farmers to put their operational capital and their labour.

Official information on these kinds of production is not abundant, and they have not attracted much commentary in the journals, but it is possible to put some materials together. 'Sidelines' are treated as part of 'agriculture', but they are differently defined for different purposes; if all kinds of 'sideline' are considered, including 'sideline' grain crops, the national average figure for these outputs comes to 60 per cent of agricultural gross output. This classification includes the four main kinds of non-farming production (forestry, fisheries, animals and 'sidelines' so called – collecting, hunting and household-run industry) plus vegetables, orchards and plantations and green fertilizer or forage, plus 'sideline products' under both 'grain' and 'industrial crops'. Total gross value in 1989 is given as 392 billion yuan. Table 5.1 gives the breakdown of this figure in terms of percentages of gross agricultural output (653 billion yuan). (In terms of percentages of all gross rural outputs, including local industry, building, transportation and commerce – in all, 1448 billion yuan (*CSY* 1990 p. 317), the proportion for sidelines is of course much smaller at 26.9 per cent.)

Table 5.1 *'Sidelines' of various kinds in Chinese agriculture, 1989*

	Percentages of gross agricultural output
Animal husbandry	27.6
Vegetables, melons; orchards (tea, mulberry, fruits); forage and green manure; others	12.7
Collecting, hunting, household industry	5.4
Fisheries	5.4
Grain and other crop 'sidelines'	4.7
Forestry	4.3
TOTAL	60.1

(*Source*: CSY 1990, 319. For total rural outputs, *ibid*, p. 317.)

It is possible to investigate some of these kinds of production a little further. Table 5.2 gives figures for growth in several important kinds of output for 1983–89, with 1978 figures added for the sake of comparison.

Table 5.2 *'Sideline' outputs in rural China, 1978; 1983–89*

	1978	1983	1984	1985	1986	1987	1988	1989
Pigs (millions)	2	14	19	36	44	48	47	49
Fowls (millions)	40	225	305	400	484	516	588	581
Eggs (thous tonnes)	45	330	445	900	1 220	1 250	1 500	1 446
Vegetables (sown area mill. *mu**)	56		65	71	80	84	90	94

(*Sources*: Pigs, fowls, eggs: 1978 and 1983, *SYC* 1985, p.476; 1984 and 1985, *SYC* 1986, p.471; 1986, 1987, *CSY* 1988, p.636; 1988, 1989, *CSY 1990*, p.598.

  Vegetables: 1984 and 1985, *CSY* 1986, p.142; 1986 and 1987, *CSY* 1988, p.211; 1988 and 1989, *CSY* 1990, p.348.)

* mu=one-fifteenth of a hectare (667 square metres)

The broad implications of the figures in Table 5.2 are clear: that expansion of outputs of pigs, fowls and eggs was much more rapid in the phase

1983 to 1985 than since 1985 – for pigs in 1983–85, 79 per cent per year as against 9 per cent per year in 1985–89. For pigs and eggs the year of maximum percentage increase was 1985; for fowls, 1984; for vegetables in terms of sown area, 1986.* It appears that the general wisdom on the subject of sideline outputs is not mistaken: since 1985, these have increased only gradually and sometimes fitfully. For whatever reason, not only grain outputs, but these alternative and much more profitable outputs have also faltered since 1985.

The reasons for this weakness appear to be very mixed. Pork production has experienced a series of crises since 1985 whose origins are in part interference with demand and supply by the authorities, particularly provincial authorities, and in part difficulties with supplies and prices of feed grains (Aubert 1990, 25). Pigs, like grain, may now cost more to bring to market than the market price. It is argued that the heart of these difficulties is the supply and price of grain, which brings the story back to the problems of grain output. More generally, it is argued that although sale prices of 'sideline' outputs have risen in the past few years, net incomes have increased only marginally because prices of inputs have increased still more. It is particularly interesting that sales of sideline products per peasant household increased only marginally between 1984 and 1989 – pork hardly at all; poultry by around 13 per cent; silkworm cocoons around 16 per cent; eggs registered a slight fall. Fish and milk sales more than doubled, but in five years even that growth is not strong (CSY 1990, p. 369; SYC 1986 p. 165). This suggests what some authors have commented upon: the persistence of small-scale sideline production (as in traditional times) against large-scale demand (as in modern times in the world at large). Conformably with this, slaughter rates in China are much more akin to those in traditional times, than to those adopted by modern battery farmers. It is argued that mass demand must be catered for by mass supply (Xia Jinhu and Wu Jianmin, 1987). But this argument is bound to run up against the peasant prejudice against 'business' farming, at least in the short run, as well as the possibility of producing, no doubt, outputs of inferior quality. It is perhaps revealing that the argument was produced, in the article mentioned, from as untraditional a place as Harbin in the north-east, where modern methods were said to have resolved persistent shortages of eggs.

Township enterprises

Diversified outputs were worth 392 billion yuan to the Chinese countryside in 1989, but local industries and businesses – township enterprises as they are now called – were worth much more at 482 billion yuan. Meanwhile, grain outputs were worth only 220 billion yuan (CSY 1990, p. 319).

---

*Figures exist for values of vegetable outputs but not for quantities. By value, 1985 was the year of maximum growth in vegetable production. Figures of sown area have been preferred to those for value because of the effects of inflation, especially in 1988 and 1989.

'Township enterprises' include individually owned or cooperatively owned businesses of all kinds, together with businesses (usually but not necessarily factories) owned collectively by towns or villages. The latter are particularly important as on the one hand they enjoy the stability, privilege and relative invulnerability of the collective sector, and on the other hand the flexibility and capacity to do the unorthodox deals of the private sector. Typically, these enterprises are factories which employ local labour which is surplus to need on the land – this is their main function in official thinking. They enjoy local official support which is fortified by payment of fees of various kinds into official kitties by the enterprises. In 1989, after some contraction, there were 1.5 million such collective enterprises in villages and towns, mostly factories, employing 47 million people with gross output value 482 billion yuan (CSY 1990 p. 382). Factory work in these conditions is preferred by many country people, especially women, to work on the land. There is evidence of constructive relationships (not always in orthodox forms) between local factory managements and state industry, for instance for supplies of fuel, materials or parts. Even more important, these enterprises are often able to take root in crevices in the industrial system which are overlooked by the state factories and the state planning organization which governs them. Industrial incomes, even in rural factories, are typically at least double those which can be made on the land; and in addition, as explained earlier, the official grain system is now deeply dependent upon rural industry to subsidize grain outputs at source.

In spite of occasional dog-fights with left-wing reactionaries (who dislike the 'village capitalist' ethos of the enterprises) or with right-wing innovators (who dislike their collective base) and state industries (which dislike competition for supplies and markets), local industrial enterprises are now deeply dug into the rural systems, especially in prosperous provinces; indeed it is not too much to say that the present rural systems could in many cases not survive without them. They are capitalism, so to speak, with a Communist Party face. They must be reckoned the most powerful of the new waves of opportunity now sweeping through rural China, and as the figures given earlier in this section suggest, they are significant competitors with both grain farming and the diversified farm sector.

Surplus labour and the move to town

From 1956 until 1978, the problem of surplus labour was little discussed in the Chinese media. Maoist thinking did not willingly recognize the possibility of this category in a planned economy. But by 1991 it was officially recognized that between one-third and one-half of rural labour was surplus to rural need in many – perhaps most – areas, and schemes of diversification of the rural production systems were being proposed as the most important solution to these difficulties. By 1984 this thinking had deepened to the point of identifying rural industry as the most promising form of diversification, and widened to the point of proposing radical changes in the rural production and social systems:

'As the theme of dividing labour among the people of different trades continues to develop in the rural areas, more and more people will give up farming and take up forestry, animal husbandry and fishing production instead; a still greater number of people will become the workers of small industrial plants or join the service trades in small towns.'

(CCP 1984 p. K7)

The same circular also provides for migration to towns:

'In 1984 all provinces . . . may carry out pilot projects in certain towns where peasants who are engaged in industrial production, commercial work and service trades are allowed to settle, as long as they can take care of their grain ration.'

(CCP 1984 p. K8)

For all its cautious wording, it is this text which represented the new possibility of rural-to-urban migration.

The orthodox and approved model for re-engagement of surplus labour is *li tu bu li xiang* – to leave the land but not the countryside; and some tens of millions of workers have done just that since 1984. In that year around 6 million township enterprises employed some 52 million people; in 1989 around 19 million rural enterprises of all kinds (including individual businesses) employed around 94 million people (*CSY* 1990 pp. 386, 387). About half of these are in village or town-owned enterprises; the rest in *getihu* (individual) enterprises. But a similar number of rural workers have left the countryside as well as the land, and migrated in search of work either to towns beyond commuting distance, or to places, including the great cities, which are distant from their places of origin in the countryside. In 1989 a writer in the *People's Daily* considered that this migration involved more than 50 million people (Shu Yu 1989).

Where labour is surplus on the land, it may be thought helpful that so many workers are leaving it, whether for local jobs or not. But this is not necessarily the case. In a survey of 1989, covering rural units in 23 counties in 10 provinces and relating to various years during the past decade, about one-quarter of migrants fell within the 35–49 age-group, in which rural men are almost bound to be heads of households (Wu Huailian 1989). This cannot help with agricultural production. In prosperous provinces like Jiangsu, hundreds of thousands of peasants are leaving the land to take industrial jobs – one writer complains that agriculture is becoming an occupation of the aged. This is one obvious cause for the fall in sown area in many provinces in recent years and the national fall in sown area of 3.5 per cent from 1978 to 1988 (of grain, 8.7 per cent) (*CSY* 1990 p. 342). Indeed labour may be less 'surplus' on Chinese farms than statistics suggest; the characteristic farming system, developed not only under the Maoists but during at least the past 400 years in which population has been growing towards present densities, is essentially an intensive one which uses labour virtually as a free good, and which is likely to need reconstruction if labour becomes scarce in the household.

Motives for migration

A number of analyses of the motives for leaving the land have been published in China; it is worth reviewing one of the most revealing.

Jie and Chen (1990) propose several 'direct' causes. One is the scarcity of arable land and the extent of concealed unemployment in the rural communities: the average agricultural worker, they say, is employed less than 100 days out of the year. The township enterprises, say these authors, are no longer able to absorb all the rural labour which is seeking alternative employment. A second cause is the social rigidity which results from the allocation of contracts, especially for 15 or more years. A third reason is said to be the operation of the 'scissors' – the high costs and low returns in agriculture. These authors explain in this way the disappearance of the 'grain specialist households' which were a prominent feature of media accounts of the countryside in 1984 and 1985. Able households now can find better things to do than grow grain. A fourth argument takes its origin from low investment and the sense of indifference to the future of agriculture and rural resource.

Jie and Chen (1990) also make allowance for more general moves towards urbanization of the rural population. The facts are that until the 1980s, migration to town had been practically impossible since 1958; but meanwhile, Chinese individuals and families have been no less interested in this kind of migration than those elsewhere in the Third World – and indeed in Europe. In the wide-ranging survey reported by Wu Huailian (1989) which has already been quoted, favoured motives for migration were: first, that farm incomes were too low; and secondly, a group of motives some of which also depended on poor returns from farming 'costs of farming too high', but others of which related to inclination ('do not wish to farm', 'lacking skill for farming', 'wish to see the world').

The 'new countryside' – losses and gains

The directives of 1984 and 1985, which have been quoted, envisaged countrysides tied closely to local towns and cities both by administrative bonds and through business links. Rural production systems were to be enlarged, stabilized, professionalized and commercialized; the self-sufficient small farm was to be marginalized, and the intensification model which had provided for the continuing increases in Chinese population since Ming times was to give way to a scheme of rural management tailored not to an ever-growing rural labour supply but to the relatively finite data of resource, informed increasingly by science.

What is gained and what lost, in these formulations? On the side of loss, it seems more than likely that the new rural policy contributed to the failure of agricultural output to grow after 1985, partly by inviting intelligent and enterprising farmers to leave the land, partly by loss of arable land to other activities such as rural industry and partly by promoting the notion that other kinds of livelihood could easily be substituted for farming, even in the countryside. Labour was certainly very much in surplus in the countryside of the early years of reform, and becoming more so as the 1962–71 cohort reached working age. However, the customary farm practices are based on a dense labour supply and it is not clear that they can yield equally well without it. Withdrawal of labour from farming in 1958 was one of the things which led the Great Leap into disaster. According to this argument, the Chinese countryside cannot afford so extensive and abrupt a relocation of surplus labour as that of the past five or six years. It would seem rational to make a parallel case for the problems of creating jobs for so many people so suddenly in either the small towns or the cities.

It is tempting to say that what has been gained in the same phase and within the same policy has been most of all the township enterprises. It has already been shown that apart from households (703 billion yuan in 1989), township and village enterprises produce the highest proportion of total income in the countryside (482 billion yuan in 1989 – CSY 1990 p. 379). But per person (CSY 1990 p. 107), rural secondary industry produces around 10 100 yuan gross per person employed, rural primary industry only around 2200 yuan (CSY 1990 pp. 379, 107). 'By 1989 the development of township enterprise had absorbed 92 million surplus rural workers, and the gross value of township enterprise output had increased to 60 per cent of the gross value of output in rural society – up from 31 per cent in 1978' (Chen Yaobang and Mu Gongqian 1990, p. 74). The township enterprises (whether collectively owned and managed or individual businesses) are by any standards the great success story of the 'second phase of reform' – whether by successful calculation in the Communist Party, or by happy accident of policy.

Opportunity, policy and necessity

In terms of the language introduced in the title of this chapter, the policy of the new rural concept has introduced a group of major new opportunities in the form of rural industry, and has contributed to depression in the farm economy which surely represents bungled opportunity.

Much of the current Chinese analysis of the problems of the countryside centres around this bungle, and particularly around the cheap and rationed supplies for the cities, whose cost (as has been shown) is a serious burden on public revenue, and whose administration is a major cause of general disaffection and indifference to production in the countryside.

Total demand for grain, it is clear, exceeds total supply. In recent years, demand has been increasing by 10–15 million tonnes per year; net imports are now around 8 million tonnes annually. Peasants lack motivation for producing grain for sale, and most of this lack of motivation relates to high costs or low returns or both. The 'scissors' are unfavourable, and in addition peasants' social burdens (taxes and various charges) are too high – around 15 per cent of income. Chinese peasants are still poor. It is now argued that cheap rationed grain for the urban consumer has become an anachronism, except for limited social groups (Grain Studies Group 1990).

Even without price reform in urban grain, it is argued, the state's 'take' of Chinese grain could be reduced by the 12 or 13 per cent – realistically possibly as much as 20 per cent – which represents state grain entitlements not consumed by ordinary families (Deng Yiming 1991); but this would be only around 25 million tonnes annually, a useful saving but not one which would transform the system. It must be remembered that some four-fifths of the state's 'take' of grain (around 100 million tonnes) will be consumed in the cities in one way or another, whether the supplies are cheap or dear, rationed or unrationed. It seems evident that reform of the state's procurement system (or even its virtual abolition) would be a sensible move in social and economic policy – perhaps one which is already overdue, given its role in creating disaffection in the countryside – but not a solution to the chronic problem of mismatch between grain demand and supply. The scale of these problems, and the tendency of demand to grow quite steadily, at a rate of about 3.7 per cent annually, demand stronger measures. Here is the long arm of necessity – the provision of day-to-day food for the vast and still growing population, plus clothing, housing and jobs. By international standards, China is not initially poor in resource; in arable land and coal (both central to most resource inventories) it is very rich in absolute terms. Poverty results from the disproportion of excessive demand to reasonable supply in China's resource experience. In recognizing the hard constraints imposed by population and population growth, thinking about the countryside must applaud the present regime's good intentions, and even its flawed performance, in the field of birth control. Understandably, most of the discussions in the Chinese literature are now adopting a very gloomy view of the population's relations with its resource base – whether arable land, energy or even water.

Can grain output be raised, perhaps within the forthcoming decade, to 500 million tonnes? This figure would correspond to a population total close to 1300 million, which is now being foreshadowed by some writers. To do so must involve changes in the production systems which are much more wide-ranging and much more long term than changes to the distribution system. Discussion along these lines is now appearing in the Chinese literature. One writer (Zhou Yixing 1991) proposes four central inputs which relate to bigger grain outputs – fixed investments, financial support for costs, payments, and fertilizer supplies. Arguing from long-term trends in the production system, he believes that the output of 500 million tonnes of grain will require (compared with the 400 million tonnes of the present), 92 per cent more fixed investments, 276 per cent more financial support, 325 per cent more in payments, and 78 per cent more fertilizer. He does not discuss either his categories of input or his figures in detail, but these seem to be possible orders of magnitude for a 25 per cent increase in grain output during the forthcoming decade, which is what has to be aimed for. Zhou's largest estimated increase is that for payments, which must relate directly to incentives. It must also relate to prices, though these are not discussed. Other authors lay much more stress on fixed investment, both for irrigation and drainage and for manufacture of fertilizer, pesticide, plastic film and so forth. (Study Group on Inputs for

Food Production 1990). The achievements of the past 40 years, in raising grain output from 200 million tonnes to 300 million tonnes between 1958 and 1978, and from 300 million tonnes to 400 million tonnes between 1979 and 1984, were made with depressingly low inputs from the state or other public bodies. What is argued for here, in effect, is a radical restructuring of Chinese finance to the advantage of the countryside. This might almost be called the last opportunity to do this and make a success of it; it might also be called the final necessity.

References

Aubert Claude (1990) 'The agricultural crisis in China at the end of the 1980s', in Delman, Jørgen *et al.* (eds). *Remaking Peasant China*, Aarhus University Press, Aarhus, pp. 16–37.

CCP (1984) 'The CCP Central Committee's Circular on Rural Work in 1984' (1 January 1984). Translated in FBIS *Daily Report*, 13 June 1984, pp. K1–K11.

CCP (1985) 'Ten policies of the CCP Central Committee and the State Council for further invigorating the rural economy' (1 January 1985). Translated in FBIS *Daily Report*, 25 March 1985, pp. K1–K9.

Chen Xiaoping (1990) 'Shaanxi province's excess urban grain rations', *Shaanxi Ribao (Shaanxi Daily)*, 18 April 1990. Translated in JPRS *China Report*, 26 June 1990.

Chen Yaobang and **Mu Gongqian** (1990) 'The strategic significance of developing township enterprises', *Zhongguo Keji Luntan (Forum in Science and Technology in China*, 1990/2, pp. 1–4). Translated in JPRS *China Report*, 11 July 1990, pp. 73–76.

CSY* *(China Statistical Yearbook), (1990)*, (1990) prepared by the PRC State Statistical Bureau. English edn. China Statistical Information and Consultancy Service Centre and University of Illinois, Chicago, 1990. Also earlier years.

Delman Jørgen, Christiansen Flemming and **Østergaard Clemens Stubbe,** (1990) *Remaking Peasant China*, Aarhus University Press, Aarhus.

Deng Yiming (1991) 'A tentative plan for the reform of the grain marketing system and the analysis of the investigation of citizens' support', *Zhongguo nongcun jingji (China's rural economy)*, 1991/4, pp. 10–15. Translated in JPRS *China Report*, 23 August 1991, pp. 59–65.

Grain Studies Group (1990) Grain Studies Group of the Ministry of Agriculture's Economic Policy Research Centre. 'Prices and the purchase system for grain', *Nongye jingji wenti (Problems of agricultural economy)*, 1990/2, pp. 7–11, 37. Translated in JPRS *China Report*, 13 April 1990, pp. 38–42.

He Shaozi (1990) 'Thoughts about the problem of increasing financial

*SCY is *Statistical Yearbook of China*, an earlier title in the same series.

investment in agriculture', *Hubei Ribao*, 24 January 1990. Translated in JPRS *China Report*, 20 March 1990, pp. 64–5.

Hou Zhemin and **Zhang Qiguang** (1989) 'Peasants – government – agricultural problems', *Jingji Zhoubao (Economic Weekly)*, 21 May 1989. Translated in JPRS *China Report*, 19 July 1989, pp. 37–40.

Huang Bingxin (1989) 'Analysis of current grain supply and demand', *Zhougguo nongcun jingji (China's rural economy)*, 1989/12, pp. 22–6. Translated in JPRS *China Report*, 9 April 1990, pp. 58–61.

Jie Shusen and **Chen Bing** (1990) 'Exploring the crux of the problem and solutions to the rural population flow', *Renkou Yanjiu (Population Research)*, 1990/5, pp. 7–13. Translated in JPRS *China Report*, 16 January 1991, pp. 54–60.

Kong Xiangliang (1990) 'Barriers to increased agricultural investment', *Nongye jingji wenti (Problems of agricultural economy)*, 1990/12, pp. 8–11. Translated in JPRS *China Report*, 3 March 1990, pp. 37–40.

Li Delai (1989) 'Where has the chemical fertiliser gone?', *Jingji Ribao (Economic Daily)*, 22 February 1989. Translated in FBIS *Daily Report*, 6 March 1989, pp. 48–9.

Liang Xiufeng (1989) 'Reconsidering China's agricultural problems', *Zhonggue nongcun jingji (Chinese rural economy)*, 21 April 1989, pp. 3–10. Translated in JPRS *China Report*, 8 August 1989, pp. 31–8.

Lin Zifu and **Wang Man** (1989) 'Some thoughts following the completion of the 1978 grain procurement task', *Nongmin Ribao (Peasants' Daily)*, 31 March 1989. Translated in FBIS *Daily Report*, 17 April 1989, pp. 58–61.

Mao Yangqing and **Tang Jianzhong** (1989) 'Anxiety over grain', *Jingji Guanli (Economic Management)* 1989/7, pp. 22–6.

Oi Jean C (1986a) 'Peasant grain marketing and state procurement: China's grain contracting system', *China Quarterly* **106**, pp. 272–90.

Oi Jean C (1986b) 'Peasant households between plan and market', *Modern China* **12**(2), pp. 230–51.

Shu Yu (1989) 'One in 20 of China's people is on the move', *People's Daily*, 26 February 1989.

Study Group on Inputs for Food Production (1990) 'Research on material inputs for food production', *Nongye jingji wenti (Problems of agricultural economy)*, 1990/12, pp. 43–6. Translated in JPRS *China Report*, 15 May 1991, pp. 58–63.

Sun Zhonghua (1990) 'A glimpse of grain production from 1984 to 1988 – A survey of the grain output of 13 000 peasant households in 155 villages', *Zhongguo nongcun jingji (Chinese rural economy)* 1990/3, pp. 16–24. Translated in JPRS *China Report*, 26 June 1990, pp. 73–9.

SYC – see *CSY* (1990) and footnote thereto.

Wang Qiang et al. (1989) 'Rural reform and development – Report on analysis of data for the 1987 National Rural Survey', Part 1, *Nongye jingji wenti (Problems of agricultural economy)*, 1989/3, pp. 52–7, 42; translated in JPRS *China Report*, 26 June 1989, pp. 48–55: Part 2, *Nongye jingji wenti*, 1989/4, pp. 40–5; translated in *ibid*, 31 July 1989, pp. 46–53.

Wen Guifang (1990) 'Fundamental ways for solving the grain problem', *Nongye jingji wenti (Problems of agricultural economy)*, 1989/12, 13–17. Translated in JPRS *China Report*, 9 April 1990, pp. 49–53

Wu Huailian (1989) 'The tidal wave of peasants leaving the land in the 1980s', *Renkou xuekan (Demography)*, 1989/5, pp. 41–9; reprinted in People's University Materials Centre, *Renkouxue (Demography)*, 1989/6, pp. 71–9.

Wu Yunbo *et al.* (1990) 'Study of remedies to reduce grain business losses in Heilongjiang province', *Zhongguo nongcun jingji (China's rural economy)*, 1990/5, pp. 20–7: Translated in JPRS *China Report*, 17 August 1990, pp. 46–53.

Xia Jinhu and **Wu Jianmin** (1987) 'The root cause of pork shortage lies in the incompatibility between small-scale production and large demand', Beijing broadcast, 16 December 1987; translated in FBIS *Daily Report*, 18 December 1987, pp. 16–18.

Zhang Gengsheng (1989) 'Vigorously increase overall agricultural production capacity', *Jingji Ribao (Economic Daily)*, 30 November 1988: Translated in JPRS *China Report*, 23 February 1989, pp. 39–40.

Zhang Gengsheng (1990) 'Views on making a breakthrough in agricultural stagnation', *Nongmin Ribao (Peasant's Daily)*, 24 January 1990. Translated in JPRS *China Report*, 20 March 1990, pp. 65–9.

Zhang Liuzheng (1989) 'How to deal with the food problem under inflation', *Zhongguo jingji tizhi gaige (China's economic structure reform)*, 1989/3, pp. 29–32. Translated in JPRS *China Report*, 26 June 1989, pp. 56–60.

Zhao Guangyao (1989) 'Defects of overproduction of cigarettes and wines', *Jingji Ribao (Economic Daily)*, 6 May 1989; translated in JPRS *China Report*, 26 June 1989, pp. 59–60.

Zhou Yixing (1991) 'Increase of grain output in the forthcoming decade, and investment in agriculture', *Nongye jingji wenti (Problems of agricultural economy)*, 1991/1, pp. 15–18.

CHAPTER 6

Rural health care in China: past, present and future

Sheila Hillier and Xiang Zheng

The popular image of health care in China was created 20 years ago, when China's relations with the United States began to develop. Through the 'open door' came a trickle, and later a flood of visitors from the United States and Europe. Their numbers included radical health professionals, and a number of medical delegations. The World Health Organization also took an interest, and there were a number of publications on health and health care. There were specialist works on cancer, medical education, surgery, population and health care organization, as well as the changes in the health of the Chinese people wrought under the Communist government.

To the Western reader, whose own health care systems were beset by rising costs without corresponding improvements in mortality and morbidity, and to health planners in low income countries faced with solving the terrible burdens of disease with little money and ramshackle structures of health care, what China had achieved in its first 20 years since the Revolution seemed like a beacon of hope. China represented accessible affordable health care for all its people; prevention was high on its agenda, compared with the marginal nature of such interventions elsewhere; medical dominance of the health care system was controlled, traditional medicine was incorporated into the mainstream of care; above all, there was a strong emphasis on citizen participation in health, epitomized by the 'barefoot doctors' – part peasant, part health worker – who carried low cost medical care to the villages of China and enabled places previously without any facility, access to basic medical care.

Later assessments (Lampton 1979; Hillier and Jewell 1983) provided a more sober picture, and while not denigrating what had actually been achieved, attempted to provide a more dynamic picture of China's health care system, as a structure which was evolving in response to political processes. Some policies followed were incremental, others innovative, but all had to confront the practical material realities of a large, poor, populous country, wherein a particular type of political control, by the Communist Party, was itself subject to ideological change, and policy oscillation.

It is, therefore, of fundamental importance to thaw the picture frozen in many people's minds of the health care system in China as a fixed and taken-for-granted structure, for it is not. Nowhere is this more evident than in the changes that have taken place since the early 1980s and are still continuing. These changes mirror the important and radical transformations in industry and agriculture, are politically directed and have had a huge impact on all spheres of Chinese life. The search for new organizational forms in response to the rhetoric of 'the four modernizations' has had a powerful effect on the structure and delivery of health care in China. The attempt to provide a solution to some problems has been matched by the re-emergence of long-standing difficulties in the provision of health care, which, in their turn now become an important focus for policy. Put simply, there has been an attempt to introduce market forces into health care to combat what was regarded as the inadequacy, low quality and waste which characterized attempts at broadly accessible low cost provision. It was also hoped that health services could be provided without increasing costs to central government. These reforms in the supply and financing of health care have produced a number of consequences, including some reduction of access, stagnation of preventive services and an increasing gap between urban and rural provision. The reforms have also done little towards confronting the real health problems of China and have been largely concerned to reflect, in close political parallel, the large-scale attempts to reform the economy of China as a whole. Below, the situation prior to the changes of the 1980s will be considered, the changes themselves described and analysed, and the implications of these for the future of health care in China assessed.

The evolution of health care policy

In 1948, China was described as having the greatest and most intractable health problems of any country in the world. The extent of morbidity and mortality from infectious and parasitic disease was enormous. It was estimated that there were upwards of 10 million cases of schistosomiasis (Cheng 1971) and 50 million cases of hookworm (Qian 1958) alone. Filiariasis, leishmaniasis, trachoma, tuberculosis, leprosy, as well as measles, polio, diphtheria and dysentery produced enormous morbidity. There was a tiny Ministry of Public Health and approximately 20 000 trained doctors for a population of 500 million. There were about 430 hospitals (the majority of which were run privately, or were missionary hospitals), although most of China's 2000 counties had a small health clinic (Lampton 1979). Into this situation came a government whose health experience was moulded from three widely different sources. The officials who ran the Ministry of Public Health were trained in the Soviet Union, those who ran the professional societies and dominated the few medical colleges were trained in the US and Europe; the ex-guerrilla fighters (Mao Zedong among them) had learnt their approach to health care in the 'Red bases', which had provided a training ground for many experiments in preventive health care, including mass health and sanitation campaigns. Where there were few professional doctors, public health was maintained by the participation of all the inhabitants of the base areas – villagers, soldiers and party cadres – in regular campaigns for sanitary improvement (Hillier 1984).

The structure of the health care system was pyramidal, with the Ministry in Beijing at the apex down through provincial and county bureaux of public health with a three-level network at the base linking the village to the township and county hospital. This model of health service delivery was similar to that designed by the League of Nations Health Organization experts (LONHO) in the 1930s (Lucas 1982), and has proved to be remarkably robust.

Immediate action was taken – centrally controlled and directed – towards the eradication of parasitic and infectious disease. Mass environmental 'clean-ups', and inoculation campaigns using mobile medical teams, who toured remote areas, all signalled a thoroughgoing assault on China's disease burden. Campaigns continued throughout the 1950s, supported by a growing number of epidemic prevention stations. Prodigious gains were claimed at both the beginning and the end of the decade (*China Reconstructs* 1953; Hou 1958). Towards the end of the 1950s during the Great Leap Forward, when the commune became the fundamental economic unit, and the basis of agricultural production, free health care, based on commune and village clinics was introduced.

There were conflicts between the politically motivated health cadres who sought to make improvements in health part of an overall economic and social transformation, and professionals who sought what they believed were more technically effective approaches to prevention and health care organization (*JRB* 1958).

Flood, drought and widespread famine resulting in about 20 million deaths (World Bank 1984a), now generally attributed to the disastrous agricultural policies of the Great Leap (Eckstein 1973), wiped out many of the developments in health care organization and left the rural areas of China severely disadvantaged relative to the cities (Hillier and Jewell 1983; World Bank 1984a). Free, commune-based health care ceased, and treatment was to be obtained only after a journey of several days and long queuing at the county hospital. Maternal and child health stations, whose functions had been taken over by the communes, declined by one-third (*SYC* 1983); 82 per cent of hospital beds were concentrated at city and county level (*CWD* 1968; *SYC* 1983) which showed that policies to deal with rural–urban inequalities, both in terms of the burden of disease and the availability of health care, were inadequate.

The Great Leap Forward – Mao's great experiment in speeding up economic growth – had failed both to transform the economy and to reduce social tensions of imbalance and inequality in China (MacFarquhar 1981). The widening of the private sector's scope in the countryside (which included health care) coupled with a greater use of the market and wage and price mechanisms produced a split in the Communist Party about the path of China's economic development. Health questions – which were about how the health care delivery system should be organized and paid for, and how disease eradication should be planned – were defined as essentially political questions by Mao Zedong, when in 1965 he attacked the Ministry of Public Health (MOPH) for its 'urban bias': . . . 'it only works for 15 per cent of the total population of the country . . . the broad masses don't get any treatment. First, they don't have any doctors, second they don't have any medicine'. (*Current Background* **892**, 21/10/65).

The ensuing Cultural Revolution produced a bitter period of struggle throughout China as Mao Zedong sought to consolidate his power. In the health care system radical changes were proposed by a political commitment to 'putting the stress on rural areas'. This generalized directive undermined the detailed planning which the MOPH favoured. As part of the assault the MOPH was closed, as were most medical schools, their staffs criticized and sometimes killed. At the same time the cities were required to send teams of doctors and students to work in the countryside, as part of mobile medical teams. The basic three-level network of rural health care was revived, with the major emphasis on supporting and staffing the village clinics and expanding their numbers.

Throughout the period of the Cultural Revolution (1965–68) until Mao's death in 1976, per capita state expenditure on health doubled (World Bank 1984b). Central government support for rural hospitals and clinics increased, and whereas in 1965 only 18 per cent of hospital beds were in small towns, and rural clinics and hospitals, by 1971 this had reached 41 per cent (*SYC* 1983).

The production brigade (usually comprising a number of villages) became the focus of two important developments: the barefoot doctor and the Cooperative medical system. Although medical auxiliaries and village health workers had existed since even before the Revolution, they now became a key focus for solving problems of rural health care. Young peasants were selected by their village and given a short practical training in all aspects of primary care, both preventive and curative. This enabled appropriate staffing levels for the expanding rural services to be achieved in a short space of time. The peasants worked about one-third of their time in the fields, and attended to health work for the rest. It was claimed that they treated 80 per cent of illnesses in the villages, limiting expensive hospital referrals. By 1972, there were about 2 million barefoot doctors, a figure which has never been matched since.

The Cooperative Medical System was to generate a major part of funding for rural health care. Unlike schemes operating during the Great Leap, the CMS was based on the brigade rather than the commune and required a relatively substantial financial input from brigade members. The price was fixed at about 2 yuan per head. This money was then pooled and out of the amount, plus a matching sum from the brigade's welfare fund, medicines, a portion of hospital costs, clinic equipment and barefoot remuneration were paid for (*People's Daily* 1968).

Each area or unit was designed to be self-financing and responsible for its own needs. In this way, it was thought, the incentives for improvement were strong and the control of waste and mismanagement easier. Risks were shared and the scheme represented a redistribution of resources within the brigade. The CMS can be seen as an effective method of providing low cost services for millions of people. Some 85 per cent of brigades were in the scheme by 1975 (World Bank 1984c) covering 650 million people, about 76 per cent of China's rural population.

These developments were consolidated in the years following the Cultural Revolution. An infrastructure of basic level health care existed, with a referral system upwards for serious illness. There was decentralized responsibility for provision and financing, low cost care and deprofessionalized health workers. Preventive health care was organized at grassroots level, carried out locally rather than by the chain of epidemic prevention stations and maternal and child health centres. It was this picture that foreign visitors saw and liked, either for its novelty, its effectiveness or (according to some) its moral superiority as a system of organization, since its attempts to achieve equity between town and countryside were supported by a clear political commitment.

Two distinct strategies of economic development have been observed in China's development. The first of these, the centralized command economy of the early 1950s, gave way to the mass mobilization strategies of the Cultural Revolution. The basic weakness of the command strategy, which was otherwise successful as a design for achieving modernization and economic growth, was its high rate of accumulation. It brought prosperity to the economy as a whole, but sectoral and geographical inequalities were increased (Sweezy and Bettelheim 1971). The mass mobilization strategy on the other hand involved politically directed rapid decentralized self-development based on the commune. Mass support was lacking and this led during the Cultural Revolution to the authoritarian implementation of apparently 'socialist' policies like redistribution and egalitarianism. Most writers agree that the economic strategies pursued towards the end of Mao's life had no clear policy to balance growth and distribution at the local level, which led to widespread frustration and stagnation in the rural sector (World Bank 1981; Feuchtwang and Hussein 1982).

Despite the drawbacks of both strategies, it was generally agreed by observers outside China that the rate of economic growth compared well with other developing countries. Whilst other economies like those of Korea or Brazil were growing faster, China differed from other countries in that the basic needs of its people for food, shelter and health care were met reasonably well (World Bank 1981). This view was not shared internally, however.

The climate of reform

In 1976, Mao Zedong died. Although expected, his demise had far-reaching political effects. The factional struggles which had been increasing in intensity in the early 1970s as to the nature of China's economic and political development reached a climax in the overthrow of the Gang of Four less than a month later. Mao's widow Jiang Qing, Wang Hung Wen, Yao Wenyuan, a leading ideologue of Maoist policies, and Zhang Chung Quo, an economist and leading exponent of the Shanghai school of radical socialist theory, were arrested, tried and given suspended death sentences.

The true political force to emerge without a doubt was Deng Xiaoping, a man completely opposed to Cultural Revolution policies. He was deeply committed to the view that China's eventual strength in economic development depended upon modernization in industry, agriculture and technology. In 1979, new policies began which were designed to stimulate the economy and overcome the low levels of productivity in industry and agriculture, particularly the latter, to reduce unemployment and inflation and improve living standards. These policies were a hybrid attempt to combine socialist planning with a competitive market system. Collective agriculture, based on the team and commune system was abolished. Instead, individual household production of grain and a diversification of rural enterprises were encouraged. This in turn led to increases in agricultural production, and a rapid rise in living standards (Xinhua 1984). Essentially growth was seen as more important than redistribution, and it was to be achieved by the operation of the market rather than within the restraints of a command economy.

The difficulties encountered in the late 1970s, before the economic reforms, were already undermining the rural health care system. Although some degree of redistribution had been achieved, overall investment by localities was low. In addition, health care facilities nationally, both in town and countryside, were failing to keep pace with population growth and with the changing pattern of disease. While parasitic and infectious diseases still took their toll, morbidity and mortality from chronic complaints like heart disease and cancer were also increasing. Cancer is the leading cause of death in the 35–54 age group (Li and Li 1981). The localization of primary health care tasks at village level, although admirable in promoting horizontal and grassroots integration placed a huge burden on the primary care health workers – the barefoot doctors.

The barefoot doctors epitomized many of the problems as well as the successes of China's health care policies. There were problems relating to their level of skill, and in 1976, despite leftist opposition, a small number of barefoot doctor colleges were set up. Local commune and village health services could not pay the costs of training, and barefoot doctors themselves lost money if they spent time in further training. They often did not earn sufficient from their health work, and rather than stemming the flow of referrals to hospitals, were often bypassed by peasants who preferred treatment at county hospitals. Their numbers were declining by the late 1970s; they were down from 2 million in 1975 to 1.8 million by 1978. This was still, however, an average of over two per village.

Similar problems had hit the cooperative medical service after its inception. In 1975, 85 per cent of brigades (as villages or a collection of them were called) had instituted the service (World Bank 1984c). Each village was planned to be self-financing and responsible for meeting its own needs. The scheme varied from place to place in its details. It was by no means cheap – it depended upon an improving economic situation, and families were spending between 1.5 and 3 per cent of disposable income (Hillier 1978) – but it should be remembered that the costs for medical care to individual households prior to the introduction of the scheme were extremely heavy.

There were, however, a number of disadvantages. Richer peasants were sometimes reluctant to pay for poorer ones and the healthier might think the investment not worth while. Richer villages could afford a cooperative medical system whereas poorer ones were less likely to and within villages, the older, poorer and sicker would have fewer funds to pay into the service. Trust among villagers was an important factor in keeping the system going. Parish and Whyte (1978) in their study in Guangdong province noted that small villages with a single lineage system where peasants were kin-related were able to provide cheaper and more extensive coverage.

A particular problem occurred when villages had insufficient funds to cope with the demands made upon them. The production 'brigades' surplus was heavily dependent upon local agricultural conditions, and when the cooperative production of grain was low or stagnant, there was a decreasing amount of money available. Even in well-off Shanghai county combined prepayments and small fees by village members were inadequate to cover all expenses and the county government had to make up the deficit of 100 000 yuan for the whole county (Chao *et al.* 1982). By 1981 only 58 per cent of villages were covered by the scheme (World Bank 1984c).

It was, therefore, inevitable that changes affecting the agricultural sector, as proposed under the reforms in agriculture, would have a profound effect on the delivery and financing of health care. In particular the demise of the collectivist system and abolition of the communes and their subsidiary organizations, the production brigades and teams, removed the organizational basis for collective health care in the villages.

The Ministry of Public Health is one of the smallest and weakest ministries of government. The latitude which it enjoys in independent policy making is small indeed. It had to approach problems in a way which reflected the broader political changes occurring in China in the early 1980s. The problems which it faced at the time were serious. Despite measures to slow down growth, the population of China continued to rise, to just over 1 billion according to the 1982 census (*Beijing Review* 1982) with a natural increase rate of 14.54 per cent 1000 (Wu 1983). The majority (86 per cent) of people (and the highest growth rates) were in the countryside. At the same time a strong disparity existed (despite the efforts of the 1970s) between the health care facilities available to those living in the countryside compared with those in the cities and large towns. Even so, city facilities were also under strain, run down, overcrowded and usually in debt. There were only 1.8 million hospital beds. There were not enough health workers. At the same time, for the rural clinics the political trend towards 'modernization' enjoined the

Ministry to promote advances in science, technology and organization relating to health. All these problems had to be tackled on a budget of 2.02 per cent of state expenditure in 1978.

Reform in health care

The immediate actions taken were to 'open up' the rural areas to a 'multitype' health system which would allow for all types of health enterprise, with a variety of forms of ownership, to flourish. A major landmark was a report from the Ministry of Public Health which recommended that private doctors should be encouraged to practise, and this was approved by the State Council in 1980 (SCPRC 1980). This document gave legal status to private practitioners. When they had passed an examination they would receive a licence to practise from the country or city bureau of public health. By 1983 there were 50 560 registered private doctors (Fu 1986).

By 1982, the idea of the pluralistic health care system was being established in the rural areas. This allowed for a mixture of health care delivery systems including private clinics and hospitals and privately run or group or solo practices in villages. The MOPH was allowing the old system of collective health care to break up and be replaced by a freer, more market-oriented system of provision. The stated objective was to improve the volume and quality of rural health services available to rural residents in a way compatible with the more general administrative and economic changes in rural areas. At first, the changes proceeded slowly, since localities were cautious in undertaking new health care ventures, or giving up the old forms of organization.

There also appeared to be resistance from the MOPH to undergo a thoroughgoing change in its traditional structures of health care. At first, only 'collectively run' clinics, administered and financed by the village or township but charging fees to patients, were allowed, although the ban on private practice had been lifted (Xinhua 1989). In 1983, 60 per cent of China's 620 000 village clinics were run by the 'collective', which still resembled the 1970s system of provision, and only 10 per cent by private doctors (CMJ 1984a). In all cases, the clinics' doctors were contracted with the village to provide medical services and a degree of control by the locality remained. This change was not rapid enough to satisfy those who felt that a more thoroughgoing reform was necessary to produce enough medical services for rural areas and release the money that the peasants, richer through economic reforms, now had available to spend. Fees themselves were raised, as it was argued that the reduction in medical prices in the 1970s had been a major factor in producing lack of investment in the rural health care system (MOPH 1985). Those private doctors who existed in the countryside – about 80 000 by this time (Beijing Review 1985) – now formed a quarter of the rural medical force, which is indicative that attempts to keep the existing structure of collectively run clinics were collapsing (CMJ 1984b). The question was seen as crucial because 'Our 800 million peasants have an increasingly greater demand for disease prevention and medical treatment service, but it is impossible for a large number to go to the cities for treatment' (MOPH 1985). After 1985, however, Document 62 of the State Council confirmed the pluralistic 'multitype' rural health system as a major policy to be implemented. The document stressed the new relaxed policies, new methods of collecting payment, controls on building, decentralization of rural hospital finance, and the status of private doctors (SCPRC 1985).

The economic reforms exacerbated the difficulties which have been recounted in rural health care above, and paved the way for the changes which the State Council ratified. The introduction of the production responsibility system, and the alteration of the administrative basis of finance in the villages made collection of CMS fees almost impossible. Since the villages no longer administered collective revenue, and peasants now earned income on the basis of their individual household's economic activity, the CMS system of funding health virtually ceased throughout China, remaining in less than 10 per cent of villages by the early 1980s (Ding 1980) and 5.4 per cent by 1986 (ZGWSTJ 1987). Free health care had become a thing of the distant past, and the majority of the population (about 90 per cent) were paying a fee for treatment (Shao 1988).

The decline in the numbers of barefoot doctors, rural midwives and other part-time village health workers accelerated as a result of the changes – by the early 1980s 3.7 million of these had left their jobs. Although barefoot doctors had been allowed to charge small fees, or even earn salaries under contract, villages could not pay them enough compared with the opportunities offered in agricultural work. Early drives to improve their quality had weeded out some 100 000 barefoot doctors, and the numbers fell between 1981 and 1982 (SYC 1983) and went down to 1.2 million (SWB 1984). From 1985 onwards the title itself was dropped in favour of 'rural doctors' for those who had passed particular examinations. These formed over 60 per cent of the remaining 'barefoot doctors', while the remainder are classified as health workers. Although there were fewer rural medical personnel by the mid-1980s they were better trained. There were about 1.6 million in 1984 (SYC 1984) and there were constant calls by the MOPH for their training to be improved (CMJ 1984b) and their numbers expanded.

However, without a specific organization responsible for paying for their training, upgrading their skills becomes difficult. This matter is particularly urgent when the issue of preventive health is considered, for primary health care in the rural areas is not simply a matter of providing curative treatment. The health worker in the village should ideally be the key worker in maternal and child health, immunization and environmental sanitation. There is little doubt that even before the economic reforms, barefoot doctors were struggling with conflicting work demands. Afterwards, village preventive health work suffered. Emphasis on preventive programmes was inevitably going to decrease because these were not as profitable on a fee-for-service basis as medical treatment.

By the late 1980s the number of clinics run by villagers as 'collective' clinics had become progressively smaller. Almost half of all clinics were privately owned, 11 per cent were run under contract to rural industry, the same amount were owned by township hospitals. About 28 per cent were owned by village committees (Aldis 1989) – a decline of over 50 per cent since 1985. Whatever the type of ownership, treatment was on a fee-for-service basis. A modified form of the cooperative medical system existed, at most in about 5 per cent of China's villages, and in a modified form known as RPV (reduced payment for villages), financed by payments from rural industry's welfare funds. Therefore, the most dramatic changes in rural health care were not simply in the change in ownership, but in the methods of payment as well.

The Jiangxi study

Our own researches during 1988–89 in three counties of Jiangxi province and one in Zhejiang province covered 725 households, 30 villages and 3489 people which were typical of middle income rural China (Hillier and Xiang 1991). By investigating health expenditure, household income and health need, we sought to establish the extent to which the reforms had impacted on health care in the villages. In Jiangxi province, 21 health stations run privately and collectively were also investigated, and their staff and village leaders were interviewed. Compared with general surveys of China carried out by the MOPH, per capita income was about average (600 yuan), the prevalence rate of chronic disease somewhat lower 75 per 1000, compared with 86 per 1000 nationally. The health care delivery system retained its three-tier referral structure. At the apex was the county hospital, below that the township hospital with the village clinics forming the base. Before health reforms, referrals were controlled from the village, but since that time people could refer themselves to any level of hospital if they were prepared to pay for it.

The majority of people (89 per cent) were paying for their own health care. Only 5 per cent were covered by the cooperative medical service and a further 6 per cent had self-insurance coverage from their factories. Utilization was higher in the CMS group. The percentage visiting their clinic in a two-week period was 15.9 per cent, compared with 7.9 per cent in the self-financing group. Their per capita medical expenses annually were lower, 15.3 yuan compared with 25 yuan. However, people in the CMS group tended to be more sick. Over double the amount of people reported suffering illness in a two-week period – 19 per cent compared with 9 per cent in the self-financing group. They also reported twice the number of illness episodes annually. After health reform, joining the CMS was no longer compulsory, therefore it is likely that the system – which was in effect a form of insurance – could have attracted a disproportionate number of elderly, chronically sick and those with small children. A study by Zhu (1988), where the at risk groups were equally distributed among both cooperative and self-financing groups, none the less shower higher utilization among the cooperative group.

One factor behind the MOPH's reforms was the belief that peasants were now rich enough to afford a better health service, and in this they were supported by a World Bank report which showed that 32 per cent of total health expenditure in China was personal payment (World Bank 1984d). The Banks study did not take into account the fact that the changing rural health system necessitated personal health expenditure from 1980 onwards. Nor did it ascertain what proportion of the 32 per cent was derived from richer urban rather than poorer rural residents.

The survey showed that high income families had a lower per capita expenditure on health, and an only average rate of utilization, whereas low income families had the highest rate of utilization and were spending about 10 per cent of their annual income on medical care. People who were self-financing were more likely to use the county and township hospitals than village clinics, but they did not regard it as an important freedom. They were particularly critical of the county hospital, where they criticized the service attitudes of staff. Just under half were very dissatisfied with having to pay for health services, because it was a serious and unpredictable drain on family resources. Most (68 per cent) peasants were prepared to take out a health insurance, and the premiums they considered were 2 per cent of annual income, less than the average 3.3 per cent which they were spending on medical expenses at the time.

The survey was unable to identify anything more than a small number of people (26) who were unable to afford hospital admission, but other surveys have identified more problems among people paying for their own health care. The MOPH's own survey showed that shortage of money was the cause of non-hospitalization for those who needed it in 58 per cent of cases (MOPH 1988). A survey of hospital patients in Jiangsu reported that 64 per cent left hospital early for financial reasons (JKB 1988a). An early study showed that per capita health expenditure increased 10-fold when the cooperative medical service was abolished (I Iu et al. 1988).

All of this points to a miscalculation on the part of policy makers hoping to transform the value and quality of health services by the introduction of a market system. They overlooked the fact that hospitals, which had been responsible for their own profits and losses, would in the absence of government subsidy also increase their prices and increase the number of specialist items for which fees could be charged. They also underestimated the popularity of free health care, especially for hospitalization. (JKB 1988b).

By the time of the survey of village health stations, private doctors and clinics were well established in China. There were over 166 000 licensed private doctors but many more were unlicensed. Reports of overcharging, quackery and incompetence had been dogging their reputation throughout the decade (China Daily 1988a). In fairness, doctors who worked for government hospitals were also subject to criticism even if it was not so harsh or prolonged (Yan 1989).

The Jiangxi survey (Hillier and Xiang 1991) showed a distribution of ownership similar to that found in China as a whole. We studied 21 village health stations of which 49 per cent were run as solo private practices, 41 per cent were group private practices and the remaining 10 per cent were collectively owned. About half the doctors working in the clinics had a middle school level education, less than half had sufficient preventive health training necessary for a primary health worker, and less than 9 per cent had received any further training in the two previous years.

Doctors working for the collective spent 90 per cent of their-time in health work compared with the 75 per cent spent by private doctors, 25 per cent of whose time was taken up with other sidelines. Collective doctors were more likely to carry out a range of preventive health tasks – for example 75 per cent undertook maternal and child health care and the same applied to family planning. For private doctors, the average was 45 per cent, with solo private practitioners doing the least preventive work.

Collective doctors complained about their low level of income, although they apparently earned slightly more than private doctors. Private doctors were concerned about patients' confidence in them. Village leaders were generally of the opinion that the rural health service quality needed to be improved, but stated that there was insufficient health investment or help to the rural sector to produce improvements in the salaries of those doctors working for the collective. Services provided by the collective clinics were approximately two and a half times cheaper than those of private doctors.

Difficulties with the reforms

The findings above, coupled with many press reports of disquiet in the MOPH point towards an uncertain future for rural health care, and a growing recognition that the reforms had not produced the hoped for benefits for the rural areas that had been envisaged. The decline of the CMS has not produced a corresponding volume of privately run services. As the Ministry of Health in its own newspaper *Jiankang Bao* reported in 1990: 'Health reform produced benefits at the level of county and city hospitals, but below this level the township hospitals in the rural areas had a negative outcome' (*JKB* 1990a).

Township hospitals (the old commune hospitals) had declined in number from 55 000 in 1983 to 45 000 in 1990, thus reducing the number of hospital beds available to rural dwellers (JKB 1990b). Their main problem was that, despite managerial reforms which removed them from the control of the county health bureau and placed them under township government, the investment was not forthcoming from the township, and most of them found it difficult to balance their books without raising prices (Hillier and Xiang 1991). Privately leased hospitals produced instances of overcharging and excessive and inappropriate prescribing (*China Daily* 1988a). Overall in China, hospital beds have increased from 1.8 million in 1978 to 2.8 million in 1988, but most of this increase has benefited city dwellers.

Hospitals generally were in the invidious situation of opening their doors to more patients to make more money, but because the cost of treatments borne by the hospital could not be reflected in the price structure, the more patients they saw the more money they lost. The Minister was unable to provide a way out: 'The government cannot give more funds to the health service . . . for the time being the medical institutions have to rely on themselves' (*China Daily* 1988c).

These problems afflicted all hospitals, but the township hospitals were hardest hit, their staff poorly paid and their situation parlous (Xiang Zheng 1992). Their development depends upon the willingness of townships to aid survival by, for example, paying staff salaries. But township governments have shown reluctance to commit themselves in this way (*JKB* 1990a).

Although nearly half of village clinics are now privately run (*JKB* 1990b), the growth of the private sector has not accelerated as much as might have been hoped. Our own researches have shown that privately owned clinics charge higher fees, and that in itself has proved to be a disadvantage as far as peasants are concerned. Despite political pressures to increase privately run organizations, support from the Ministry of Public Health was weak. The loosening of government controls over rural health organization in itself deprived the Ministry of Public Health of an important sphere of influence. Speaking at his frankest, the Vice-Minister Chen Minzhang spoke about failures and future directions:

'At the beginning of reform, rural doctors abandoned medicine for agriculture, industry or trade in some rural areas and as a result health organs at village level and the cooperative medical service were in a state of disintegration . . . the smooth development of health work was covered with a dense layer of fog. After 1986 . . . the situation gradually changed . . . in 1987, directors of Public Health Bureau emphasised the principle of giving first place to collective medical cooperation. Further, in 1989 the system of running a medical service in a collective way and accumulating funds for medical and health care in the rural areas had been listed as an important goal . . . in some areas health service at township and village level is still in a very difficult situation . . . we must pay attention to investment for peoples health . . . health work *must be under the guidance of government at all levels*'

(*JKB* 1989)

The Minister mentioned a number of objectives for health care: to follow WHO objectives of 'Health for all by the year 2000'; to set minimum standards for health service development in preventive and curative services; to put developments under technical leadership whose cadres are enjoined to 'work selflessly'.

What power does the MOPH have to enforce its goals? The answer is: on its own, very little. The MOPH is a small, weak ministry, near the bottom of the ministry hierarchy. It does not control the manufacture of products, its plans are regarded as producing greater consumption of national resources (as an aspect of social welfare) rather than contributing to national wealth. The ministry has always found it difficult to withstand political pressures and maintain its own power base (Lampton 1979). Despite this, its achievements were considerable up to the reforms, when the relaxation of governmental control over health work left the ministry unable to plan its health service without taking into account the nature of the health market.

While making health enterprise responsible for its own finances reduced some of the drain on the ministry budget, it also removed a means by which planning objectives could be enforced. Further, the market introduced an element of unpredictability into the development of health services – an element which has made the reforms largely unworkable in the rural areas. It was believed that rising peasant incomes would create increased demand for health care and the means of paying for it. To some extent this happened but peasants are not in the habit of spending on health and medicines, nor in coping with unpredictable demands of sudden illness or the drain of long-long term chronic illness. The agricultural reforms since 1978 have enabled peasants to be much freer in their relationships with the state, and to make their own decisions about agricultural production. A similar freedom has applied to patterns of consumption, and as peasant incomes have boomed their expenditure on consumer goods – bicycles, television sets, refrigerators, extensions to their houses – has increased substantially. They cannot, as in the old days, be forced to join a cooperative medical service.

Return to the CMS

In its strongest proposal to date, the MOPH now seeks to return to what it still calls the cooperative medical service as a 'public benefit in which government society and all the people should work together' (JKB 1990c). However, there are important differences from the old system. Rural industry is being strongly urged to contribute to a health fund, as well as village committees and individuals. One early example is the system adopted by Pingdu city, Shandong province, where peasants pay a couple of yuan a year to a fund which is managed at township level. The fund pays for doctors' salaries, future training of rural doctors and preventive health (JKB 1990d). In this scheme (one of several), however, peasants still pay fees for treatment but prices are controlled and the doctors are a licensed part of an organized health system. Another variation was in Pengan county, Sichuan province, which provided free consultation, inpatient treatment and tests, but charged for medicines (JKB 1990e).

Essentially, the government has not committed itself to any clear pattern of investment from the centre. Its budget has fluctuated between 2.5 and 3 per cent of state expenditure over the decade and there was a small budgetary increase in 1989 (China Quarterly 1989). Therefore, pronouncements from the MOPH have tended to emphasize that developments in producing funds for rural health care 'must be in accordance with social and economic conditions' but that localities should target 8 per cent of financial expenditure on health services (JKB 1991).

Nevertheless, the MOPH is now committed to the return of the cooperative medical system in 70 per cent of China's rural areas by the year 2000, and the latest experiments show that where the scheme is in operation, average health costs to peasants have been halved, from 29 to 12 yuan per annum (China Daily 1991a). It is estimated that between 30 and 40 per cent of villages are already using the system, and in the more forward-looking provinces and municipalities the figure is much higher – 92 per cent in Shanghai, 95 per cent in Shandong, 70 per cent in Jiangsu.

CMS is more prevalent in the rich and developed eastern provinces than in the western regions where only 10 per cent of villages have introduced it (*JKB* 1990f).

The expansion of the CMS depends to a very large extent upon the degree to which localities can afford the 8 per cent health investment proposed by the MOPH (JKB 1991). The Minister for the health care of rural areas, Fang Suzhen, has stressed that MOPH plans for the widespread readoption of the CMS 'will be put into practice in 1992 after revision' (*China Daily* 1991a) which suggests a cautious approach taking into account the competing demands on investment in the rural sector, and the degree of stagnation that has recently beset economic reforms, which, in the words of Liu Zhaongyi, Minister of Agriculture 'allow no room for optimism' (*China Quarterly* 1991). Rural health investment has been described by the MOPH as an 'aspect of agriculture'. While this analysis is in the long term correct, it is a fragile argument when the rural economy is weak. The real hope must be that the rural industries, perhaps coupled with rising rural incomes, will form the basis for investment in rural health. Rural industries have been a very successful aspect of the economic reforms, contributing 30 per cent of national industrial gross value output and 60 per cent of rural social value output in 1990 (*China Quarterly* 1991).

Outstanding problems – training and prevention

Besides the provision of basic level services, there are two outstanding issues in rural health care towards which the maintenance of the CMS is seen as the basic key. If basic level services in the villages can be supported, then the issue of training rural doctors and the promotion of preventive health can be expanded.

The issue of training expansion must be set against the rather slow development of the training of doctors in higher education. Although the modernising trend of the early reforms led to an expansion, the proportion of new medical students enrolling in universities fell from 11.1 per cent of all students in 1980 to 6.4 per cent in 1987(Cui 1987). In the mid-1980s there were 2.4 per 1000 university trained doctors in the cities, compared with 0.5 per 1000 in rural areas, and planned expansion throughout the decade has barely kept pace with population growth. Middle-level assistant doctors and nurses were also in short supply, and the number of rural health workers had been seriously depleted.

During the Cultural Revolution, medical students were sent to work in rural areas. This was a very unpopular move and did not provide a long-term solution to shortages. Nevertheless, the issue was floated again during 1990, to be rapidly squashed by the Minister Chen Minzhang:

'It is not a good method to send students to the rural areas. First, there are not enough students, second they don't like it. The best way is to train health personnel for the rural areas – the quality of these doctors is *not superior* to those in urban hospitals, but they will solve the problem and their training is simple and quick. This way, we'll get the benefit within 5.5 years' [present writer's italics].

(*JKB* 1990h)

The Minister went on to outline special arrangements that linked the promotion of urban doctors to their willingness to spend some time in the rural areas, and even hinted that this might become a rule of employment. However, the main source of personnel is to be rural health workers, trained at the expense of their localities. It is for that reason that the continued vitality of rural industry, the increased managerial strength of the local government and the peasants own financial contribution must be effectively combined to support the CMS. It is a complex set of arrangements which cannot be forced upon localities.

The years of reform have also produced a serious reversal in preventive health work – an essential ingredient of primary health care and of any development strategy which seeks to link agricultural production and health. The government-run epidemic prevention stations had their subsidies cut and they were required to make up the difference from the money they earned in preventive work. This was difficult since their activities did not involve curative work, and they were often required to play a policing role, for example fining factories for industrial pollution or inspecting food. The stations ran into severe financial problems. Now the majority are back under the control of county health departments, although some independent ones remain (*JKB* 1990g).

Equally problematic was the fact that, with dissolution of the CMS and the demise of the barefoot doctors, the means of vaccination and inoculation as well as the reporting of infectious diseases from the village level were severely affected. Staffing and money were inadequate to run a proper preventive service and epidemiological knowledge on the rate of spread of infectious disease was lacking: 60 million rural Chinese were suffering from endemic diseases like leprosy, goitre, plague, malaria and schistosomiasis. The last, which had been the subject of huge labour-intensive long-term campaigns to wipe out the snail vector in the first three decades of communism, reappeared (*China Daily* 1989). Snail infested fields increased from 2.5 billion square metres in 1980 to 3.7 billion square metres in 1988. An epidemic of hepatitis in Shanghai in 1989 affected 300 000 people. Cases of plague increased by 61 per cent between 1986 and 1990, and the incidence of diphtheria, polio, B-encephalitis and, most alarmingly AIDS, went up in 1990 (*China Daily* 1991b). A MOPH estimate suggested an under-reporting rate of up to 200 per cent (*JKB* 1990h).

One innovation during health reform had been an 'immunization insurance' for children. The proposal was that children under seven years old paid 7–10 yuan to epidemic prevention stations for immunization against the major childhood diseases. If they subsequently developed the disease, they would be paid compensation. This was one method of ensuring income for epidemic prevention stations. One survey by the Deputy Director of MOPH's Preventive Department (Dai, 1988) showed that 40 per cent of EPS directors found themselves unable to implement the insurance. The vaccines were of poor quality and erratically supplied. Some children did not take up the insurance. In Beijing, where there had not been a case of polio for four years, two cases were found in June 1989. These children were not insured. Because public health doctors were only paying attention to children on the programme, they were reluctant to supply free services or simply overlooked children who did not have the insurance. This contradicted the MOPH's policy on inoculation which was to make it available to all children, whether insured or not. The idea of compensation contained in the insurance proposal was to act as a 'carrot' to persuade people to become inoculated, but it seems an ill-conceived piece of doctrinaire thinking, where political free market objectives were set against the long-term preventive policies of the ministry.

The situation in rural health is now back on the agenda of central government. In January 1991 the 7th Plenary Session of the 11th CCCP Central Committee emphasized the necessity to develop rural health work as an important part of the Ten Year Economic Plan (1991–2000) and eighth five year plan 1991–1995. Of particular importance was the strengthening of the three-level network (*People's Daily* 1991). State Council Document No. 4, *The Report on the Reform of Strengthening the Rural Health Work*, said in its preamble:

'During health reform we ignored the management and support of rural health work. Investment for rural health care was reduced; the lower levels of the health care system in townships and villages were severely hit. The CMS was dissolved. Medical prices increased without regulation and we could not control private doctors. Rural residents could not afford medical care and diseases which had disappeared, appeared again and the gap between rural and urban areas increased.'

(SCPRC 1991)

The preamble says everything about the drawbacks of the previous decade. It goes on to place the seal of five ministries – Agriculture, Public Health, Planning, Education and Personnel – on the proposals worked for since 1990 by the MOPH. These include supporting the expansion of the CMS, and strengthening MOPH control of health services by stressing the importance of the three-tier linked system (county–township–village) 'which has fitted the condition of China through many years of practice'. Finally, training is to be expanded.

The State Council Document carries much more force than MOPH reports and means that 'putting the stress on the rural areas' is a real policy, as real as that embodied in the State Council Documents 10 of 1980 and 62 of 1985 which had confirmed the reforms in health care and led to such wholesale changes in the structure. However, the new phase of health policy is not simply a copy of the rural health system 30 years ago.

The degree to which China is able to maintain economic growth will have implications for the future success of health policy in the rural areas. If, as the MOPH maintains, the village clinics are to be the key to the health of China's population, these clinics will have to be supported by the prosperity of the locality. The State Council has been careful not to set an absolute standard of investment, but has suggested that each area should provide a certain percentage of its budget. This suggests a more limited redistributive goal, which has implications for raising standards overall, since poorer areas will have to be as self-sufficient as rich ones, and wide disparities will remain. As well as the large-scale rural–urban inequalities in health care facilities, intra-rural inequalities are likely to continue.

The MOPH continues to make policy, and has re-established a degree of administrative control over health services, especially preventive services, which it had lost in the previous decade. However, it does so without the authority to command resources for health care from regions, localities, townships and villages. The overall responsibility for the provision of health services lies, more than it ever did, in the hands of the people themselves, who must finally decide what they wish to spend. This suggests that the goal of uniform provision for China's rural areas is still a long way away.

References

Aldis W (1989) 'Changing structure of China's health care', *Lancet* 16 December, 1457.

Beijing Review (1982) 'Results of the census' **48**, 22 November p. 13.

Beijing Review (1985) 'Government gives private doctors the OK', **20** 20 May, 9.

Chao Limin, Gong Fu and **Gu Shuiji** (1982) Financing the cooperative medical system *Am. J. Publ. Hlth,*. **72**, Suppl., 78.

Cheng, T. (1971) Schistosomiasis in mainland China, *Am. J. Trop. Med. & Hygiene* **20**(1), 27–53.

China Daily (1988a) 'Check on private hospitals', 4 November.

China Daily (1988b) 'Ailing medical service needs private hospitals', 29 December.

China Daily (1988c) 'Hospital reforms face difficulty', 1 November.

China Daily (1989) 'Jiang vows every effort to wipe out snail fever', 15 December.

China Daily (1991a) 'Rural areas plan group health care', 10 July.

China Daily (1991b) 'Epidemics kill fewer people', 3 May.

CMJ (1984a) 'Health Minister on 1984's tasks', *Chinese Medical Journal* **97**(3) 205.

CMJ (1984b) 'China's attempts to improve health work in the countryside', *Chinese Medical Journal* **97**(11), 794.

China Quarterly (1989) 'Quarterly chronicle and documentation,' *China Quarterly* **118**, 395.

China Quarterly (1991) 'Quarterly chronicle and documentation', *China Quarterly* **127**, September, 664.

China Reconstructs (1953) 'Battle for health', *China Reconstructs* March/April.

Cui Yueli (1987) Speech to Directors of Central and Local Health Services, 9 January, Weishengbu, Beijing.

CWD Chuan Wu ti (Invincible Fist) 1968, No. 17 Suppl. SCMP 209.

Dai, Z. (1988) Study the present conditions and future trends of Epidemic Stations in China. *Chinese Rural Health Services Administration*, No. 11.

Ding You He (1980) An investigation of the current state of the cooperative medical system, *MOPH*, Document July 1980, Beijing, China.

Eckstein, A (1973) Economic growth change in China – a 20 year perspective, *China Quarterly* **54**, 215.

Feuchtwang S and **Hussein A** (1982) *The Chinese Economic Reforms* Croom Helm, London.

Fu Xing-Zhi (1986) Report of an investigation into private doctors conducting their own businesses. *Ministry of Public Health Document* April 1986, Beijing, China.

Hillier S M (1978) Unpublished field notes from Renho People's Commune. Guangzhou. March 1978.

Hillier S M and **Jewell JA** (1983) *Health Care and Traditional Medicine in China 1800–1982* Routledge, London.

Hillier S M (1984) Forty years of primary care in China, an interview with Ma Haide, *China Now* **111** (4) 10–13.

Hillier S M and **Xiang Z** (1991) Township hospitals and village clinics in China, *China Information*, **VI** (2) 51–61.

Hou Tsung Ching *et al.* (1958) Achievements in the fight against parasitic diseases in China, *Chinese Medical Journal* **97** (12) 493–520.

Howe C (1988) *China's Economy*, Paul Elek, London Granada, London, p. 72, Table 19.

Hu S Zhu N, Lin Z and **Jie S** (1988) The present system of cooperative medical service in China. *Proceedings of 4th Conference of ISSSHC. Les Sciences des Systems dans la domaine de la santé.* Collection de Médecine Légale et Toxicologie Médicale No. 139, Massow, Lyon.

JKB *(Jiankang Bao)* (1988a) 'Examination and eradication of unreasonable medical fees', 1st December; 'Building a rational expenditure structure' 4 December.

JKB (1988b) 'The implementation of different levels of medical fee collecting in Ben Bu city', 17 December.

JKB (1989), 'Several opinions concerning the overall plan for experimental primary health care', 13 August.

JKB (1990a) 'Basic level hospitals' conditions are poor, and their development difficult', 21 April.

JKB (1990b) 'The Statistical Bulletin of health care in China' 10 April.

JKB (1990c) 'Developing a health prospect for people's health', 22 April.

JKB (1990d) 'Pingdu city builds a rural health fund', 29 May.

JKB (1990e) 'A new rural health insurance system: doctors fees are insured, but not medicines', 17 May.

JKB (1990f) 'Health reform is the only way to develop Chinese rural health care', 22 March.

JKB (1990g) 'It is very serious to fail to make the legally required report of infectious disease', 1 May.

JKB (1990h) 'How to perfect Chinese rural areas', Preventive Health Organisation, 13 May.

JKB (1991) 'Stress should be put on the rural areas in medicine and health care', 22 January.

JRB (1959), *Jilin Ribao*, JPRS 544D 17 February 1959, p. 73. Intensive programme to prevent 3 endemic diseases in Kilin Province.

Lampton, D. (1979) *The Politics of Medicine in China*, Dawson Press, Folkestone.

Li Ping and **Li Junyao** (1981) National survey of cancer mortality in China, in Marks P (ed.). *Cancer Research in the PRC* Grune and Stratton, New York,

Lucas (1982) *Chinese Medical Modernisation*, Praeger New York.

MacFarquhar, R. (1981) *The Origins of the Cultural Revolution II*. Stevens London.

Mao Zedong (1965) 'On the 10 major relationships'. Speech of 25 April 1965 in Schram, S. (ed.) 1974 *Mao Tse-tung Unrehearsed*, Penguin, Harmondsworth, 1974; 81. 75–83.

MOPH (1985) Report on certain policies concerning the work of reform in rural health, 29 March 1985. *State Council Bulletin*, 20 May 1985, Weishengbu, Beijing.

MOPH (1988) December 1986 Survey of the reasons why patients are not admitted to hospital. *Chinese Health Statistical Digest*, MOPH, Beijing, China.

Parish W and **Whyte M** (1978) *Village and Family Life in Contemporary China*, University of Chicago Press, Chicago, pp. 90–1.

People's Daily (1968) 19 December.

People's Daily (1991) 29 January.

Qian Xinzhong (1958) Summing up mass technical experiences with a view to eradicating the five major diseases, *Chinese Medical Journal* **77** (12) 521–32.

SCPRC (1980) 'A report of the Ministry of Public Health concerning permission for doctors to undertake private practice', State Council of the PRC, August, People's Publishing House, Beijing.

SCPRC (1985) 'Some policies of health work reform', State Council of the PRC Document No. 62, 25 April, State Council Beijing.

SCPRC (1991) 'Report on the reform and strengthening of rural health work'. State Council of the PRC Document No. 4, 17 January, State Council, Beijing, China.

Shao Y (1988) *Health Care in China*, Office of Health Economics, London, p. 9.

SWB Summary of World Broadcasts (Far East) FE W1303/A/1, Improvements in health and medicine, 5 September, BBC Monitoring Service, Caversham.

Sweezy P M and **Bettelheim** C (1971) *On the Transition of Socialism*, Monthly Review Press, New York.

SYC *(Statistical Yearbook of China 1983)* (1983) Economic and Social Agency, Hong Kong, pp. 540–2.

SYC *(Statistical Yearbook of China 1984)* (1984) New Economic Agency, Hong Kong.

World Bank (1981) *China: Socialist Economic Development*. Report 3391 CHA. Washington. World Bank, p. 73.

World Bank (1984a) *China: The Health Sector*, World Bank, Washington DC, p. 45.

World Bank (1984b) *China: The Health Sector*, World Bank, Washington DC, p. 182.

World Bank (1984c), *China: The Health Sector*, World Bank, Washington DC, pp. 155–6, Tables C14, C15.

World Bank (1984d), *China: The Health Sector*, World Bank, Washington DC, p. 63, Figure 33.

Wu Canping (1983) Some population problems that must be discussed at an early date *Shijie Jingjie Baobu* (Population Affairs), 12 December.

Xiang Zhang (1992) *The transformation of the three tier rural health network in the Peoples Republic of China (Mimco)*, Department of Human Science and Medical Ethics, The London Hospital Medical College, London.

Xinhua (1984) *Planning Ministers Report on 1984 Social and Development Plan*, 1 June. SWB FE7661 C/1, 5 June.

Xinhua (1989) 'Private doctors cure for medical service problems', *SWB FE* 0349 B2/9, 4 January, BBC Monitoring Service, Caversham.

Yan Hui-Zhong (1989) An analysis of the crisis of hospital health services. *Chinese Hospital Management* No. 7, p. 9–11.

ZGWSTJ (1987) *Zhonguo Weisheng Tongji*, Weishengbu, Beijing, China.

Zhu A *et al* (1988) Report of a survey of the co-operative medical service, *Chin. J. Hlth Econ* **4**, 13–19.

CHAPTER 7

State, collective and private industry in China's evolving economy

Rupert Hodder

In recent years a body of important work on industrial development has appeared in the literature on China. Much of this information deals with changes in industrial policy during the Maoist period; the effects of the reforms since 1978; the changing balance between industry and other sectors of the economy; and the spatial patterns of industrial activity in the country. There has also been some significant work on regional development and urban planning; on the special economic zones and open coastal cities; and on the implications for China's industry of the open-door policy – especially foreign investment, technology transfer and the shift from import substitution to export-oriented industrialization (Goodman 1989; Howard 1990; Lin 1990).

This chapter, however, is concerned solely with the nature and implications of the three forms of industrial ownership in China: state industry; 'collectively owned' industry, commonly located in rural areas; and private (or 'individual') industry. There is in the literature some discussion over the distinction between these three types of industry, especially as regards what some authors regard as the ambiguous position of collectively owned industry, variously described by different sources as 'cooperative', 'non-state', 'neither wholly state nor wholly private', or 'more-or-less-private' industry. This ambiguity is indicative of the way in which the balance between these three types is shifting; and this shifting balance has important implications for China's future industrial and economic growth over the next few decades.

In the period between the Communist takeover of 1949 and 1956 almost all of China's modern industry was effectively placed in the hands of the state, capitalist industrial enterprises being taken over under 'joint state–private ownership' (Howard 1990, p.170). This was not as catastrophic a move as is sometimes implied, for 35 per cent of China's industry was already state-controlled when the Communists took over power in 1949. Moreover, living standards more than doubled and industrial progress was by no means negligible between 1956 and 1978. Indeed, as several authors have emphasized, China could have continued with a steady, if slow, rate of progress in industrial output of some 2 to 3 per cent a year without the need for any significant structural readjustments in 1978 (Perkins 1989, pp.54–5). But in the post-Mao period it was recognized that by the end of the century this would still have left China as a predominantly peasant economy in a region – East Asia – which already contains many examples of comparatively very rapid industrialization and enviable economic prosperity. The reforms demanded much faster industrial growth and greater all-round efficiency.

The reforms

After 1978 numerous specific reforms dealing with China's industry were implemented. Their main thrust – and this is the crucial point – has been to allow a distinction to emerge between, on the one hand, the state's administrative organs and, on the other hand, the industrial enterprises. The only proviso was that this distinction should emerge within the existing structure of ownership, except in the case of a few joint ventures and for a number of small firms in the countryside.

This emergence of a distinction between state administrative organs and individual enterprises was very much a precondition for tackling one of the main practical aims of the industrial reforms – that of developing horizontal linkages (Hodder 1990). These linkages were to replace the vertical channels of command which had coordinated administrative units; horizontal linkages would thereby enable the unrestricted flow of raw materials, funds, equipment, labour and goods. Each industrial enterprise would be connected to the rest through these linkages, allowing each settlement and region to be integrated into a national whole.

In this way it was hoped that some cohesion would be brought to fragmented areal administrative units and that the regional specialization of industrial activities would be effected. For instance, in Shanghai, China's foremost industrial city, it was argued that the development of horizontal linkages would facilitate the spread of industry from the narrow corridor which centred on a few major urban centres and transport routes through Ningbo and Hangzhou to Shanghai and thence to Nanjing. The wasteful duplication of industrial activities by separate administrative units at provincial and sub-provincial levels would thereby be rationalized.

In attempting to achieve an effective distinction between the state's administrative organs and industrial enterprises, several other important measures were introduced. One was to draw a clear distinction between profits and taxes. Rather than handing nearly all profits over to the state, state-run enterprises were to pay a series of taxes at rates stipulated before production began. In practice, an enterprise could now retain anything up to 40 per cent or more of its profits. Although a stipulated proportion had to be used for establishing reserve funds, depreciation funds, funds for the development of production, for the trial manufacture of new products, for repairs, and to meet the enterprises's commitment to the welfare of its employees, the enterprise now had control over the management of these funds. The remainder of its profits could be used as the enterprise so wished.

Another important measure was to grant to some industrial enterprises and factories the right to distribute wages and bonuses to their workers; instead of each worker receiving a fixed wage direct from the state administrative organs, the enterprise or factory received a total wage fund. Part of this fund could not be increased or lowered, irrespective of changes made in the number of employees; and part floated with the economic performance of the enterprise or factory, according to an agreed scale. The enterprise or factory was, therefore, able to select a remuneration system that would reflect the economic performance of individual workers and of the organization itself. Many industrial enterprises were also allowed greater control over their employees: for example, the introduction of the responsibility system for factory directors in Shanghai gave directors the authority to dismiss and to appoint certain grades of cadres, and enabled the management of a factory to become more and more dissociated from the Party Committee (SSKY 1986).

Yet another important change was to give to industrial enterprises the authority to set ex-factory prices for certain commodities whose prices were previously fixed by the administration. Investment decisions could also be made at lower levels, including the enterprise, rather than in Beijing. And the practice of setting planning quotas for industrial enterprises was on occasions discontinued, thereby allowing profit to play its part in decision-making at the enterprise level.

However, although these and other measures allowed industrial enterprises greater independence from state administration, interference in the affairs of industrial enterprises has remained commonplace. For instance, the higher administrative levels can renege on any contract or agreement stipulating the share of the profits an enterprise can retain, or the percentage of commodities produced by that enterprise which the enterprise itself can market. Furthermore, despite a reduction in pre-tax profits caused by an increase in price for raw materials and processed goods and a fall in price for some manufactured items, taxes levied on some enterprises remain so heavy that enterprises are unable to pay for necessary technological improvements. Profits on some goods, such as engines for agricultural purposes, have been severely restricted; and for some items applications to raise prices have been turned down, even though prices were set so low that factories were losing money.

The final arbiter on such matters is in most cases the industrial bureau or some other higher administrative organ of the state, though the responsibility for any shortcomings is commonly laid at the door of industrial enterprises and companies. However, it is perhaps more accurate to direct these strictures at an administrative and legal system which, while allowing industrial enterprises more independence, interpreted any matters not specifically attended to in the regulations and commissioned to the industrial enterprise as being properly under administrative control; in practice, therefore, such matters were handled according to established administrative procedures.

Clearly, an important aim of the reforms since 1978 has been to increase the decision-making powers of industrial enterprises and to introduce a greater market element into the decision-making process. But success has been limited: the reforms in industry seem so often to be aimed at trying to imitate the superficial characteristics of private enterprises without providing the basic ownership structures and market freedoms without which no industrial enterprise can hope to be entirely successful.

The industrial economy is still very much dominated by state-owned enterprises. Accurate data are hard to come by, but one source suggests that in 1989 there were over 100 000 state-owned enterprises in China – most of them in urban areas, and accounting for 77 per cent of national industrial output by value. A further 22 per cent of industrial output in 1989 was accounted for by over 300 000 collective or cooperative enterprises, most of them in rural areas (Yahuda 1990, p.55). Another source gives rather different figures which suggest that in 1987 state-controlled industrial enterprises accounted for 60 per cent, collectives for 26 per cent, and private industry for 14 per cent of total national industrial output (Xie Yichun and Costa 1991) (Table 7.1). The state's share of industrial output declined from 81 per cent in 1978 as against private industry's share, which increased from zero to 14 per cent over the same period. Rural industrialization (collectives) also increased its share of industrial output (from 19 to 26 per cent), supporting the government's aims of spreading the benefits of industrial growth into the countryside. A similar trend occurred in Shanghai municipality where private industry's percentage share of industrial output rose from zero in 1978 to almost 9 per cent in 1986, and the collective sector's share from just over 8 per cent to over 23 per cent. Over the same period, the state sector's share fell from over 91 per cent to under 68 per cent.

Table 7.1 Distribution of national industrial output

1978 % of industrial output		1987 % of industrial output	
State	81	State	60
Collectives	19	Collectives	26
Individual (Private)	0	Individual (Private)	14

(*Source*: Xie Yichun and Costa 1991, p. 321.)

A common view is that the collective or rural industrialization – as the fastest-growing category of industry, with an industrial growth rate over twice that of industry in the country as a whole – will become increasingly important. Other writers, however, see rural industrialization in practice as simply an extension of the country's urban industrial programme:

Factories in the large cities increasingly sub-contract activities to neighbouring rural areas as a way around restrictions on their ability to hire more labour or to acquire more land for expansion. This is urban – industrial expansion rather than dispersed rural industrialization' (Perkins 1989, pp. 78–9).

Whichever figures or categories one accepts, there is little doubt that private industrial enterprises – controlled though many of them have been in the extent and nature of their operations – have already made a real, if limited, contribution to industrial development since 1978. It is not easy to be precise about the extent of this contribution because of the way in which data are presented by the authorities in China. In Shanghai, for instance, official figures for the number of private industrial enterprises are listed only when they are joint-managed with enterprises run by collectives or the state. Thus, in 1985 the official list of some 80 000 private industrial enterprises, employing between them a combined workforce of 110 000, referred to industrial and commercial households engaged mainly in handicrafts, repairs and construction. This contribution of private industrial enterprises to Shanghai's total industrial output value was little more than 1 per cent in 1980 and only 2.7 per cent in 1985 (SSTJ 1986).

Private industrial enterprises throughout China have benefited from a number of government measures. One of these was the explicit move away from the formerly rigid centrally planned economy, enabling private enterprises to operate more freely. The government also decontrolled prices of many 'small commodities' (household items) in which private industrial enterprises have been most active: in Shanghai, for instance, 510 items were decontrolled as early as 1982/83 (SSTJ 1986). Moreover, private enterprises have been allowed and encouraged to develop in many rural areas in order to allow room for commodity producers to expand their operations. This move, together with the decontrolling of prices, was directly linked with market demand, as a result of which the production of many consumer goods rapidly increased. Much of this increase was in the light industrial sector, and output value of light industry grew at an average annual rate of 12.6 per cent between 1979 and 1985. Between 1978 and 1988 the percentage of total industrial output value rose from 43.1 per cent to 49.3 per cent for light industry and fell from 56.9 per cent to 50.7 per cent for heavy industry (Lin 1990).

The government's efforts to improve the industrial performance since 1978 by liberalizing many of its operations have certainly had some effect. By the mid-1980s growth was averaging around 10 per cent per annum and is predicted to be around 7 per cent in the early 1990s, in spite of the overheating of the economy and rising inflation which caused some concern in the late 1980s and led to some retrenchment and an attempt to reduce growth rates. Nevertheless, both in state industry and in domestic private industrial enterprises, progress has been slower and less effective than was anticipated at the beginning of the reforms. Administrative interference and bureaucratic inefficiences still riddle the industrial system, and many problems remain to be solved. In particular, the matter of prices has still to be successfully tackled. The prices of some basic commodities are still completely state controlled, others are subject to varying degrees of central or local control, while yet others are entirely free to float in the market (Yahuda 1990, p. 55).

Another important problem is subsidies – paid to protect inefficient enterprises and to some urban workers, and eating up almost one-third of the annual national budget. There is still the sense that much of China's industrial potential is being frustrated by being neither properly and confidently controlled from the centre nor entirely free to find its feet in the market place. As Yahuda (1990, p. 55) puts it: 'the nub of the problem is that while many of the administrative controls from the centre have been undermined, there are not yet effective mechanisms to take their place . . . China is a half-way house between a communal Stalinist economy and a reformed market one: the country suffers the worst of both worlds.'

The main reason for China's recent success in her industrialization programme has been, not the improvements in state and domestic private industry discussed earlier, but the large degree of foreign investment which followed the introduction of the country's 'open-door policy' and the setting up of the five special economic zones and the 14 'open coastal cities'. Apart from the many attractions these locations had for foreign investors, they also forced the authorities in China to take a more pragmatic attitude to their own philosophy of development. Inevitably, the emphasis now is neither on the social dimensions of economic policy nor on the need to ensure regional equality: the emphasis now is much more on regional comparative advantage, on the regional division of labour and on the critical importance of foreign trade. It is accepted that successful industrialization will, initially at least, increase regional income differentials. But it is argued that the wealth attracted by and developed in the coastal areas will eventually 'trickle down' into other parts of China. In other words, there has been a switch from a regional balance approach to a growth pole strategy. The March 1989 State Council 'Decision on the Current Industrial Structure Readjustment' was unequivocal about this. It dealt with the need for credit and investment and with the need to control inefficiencies and waste. It also emphasized the need to speed up the market system and to promote the assimilation of produce factors so as to facilitate optimization of the industrial structures. Perhaps most significantly, it was concerned to control the scale of capital: 'to turn industrial enterprises into genuine commodity producers, we can even consider using foreign funds for technology transformation, so as to accelerate the process of intensive management' (Lin 1990, p. 9).

The future

Looking to the future, it is impossible to ignore what is happening in the southern coastal provinces of Guangdong and Fukien. Here, according to many observers, a 'miracle' similar to that which has already occurred in the four newly industrialized countries (NICs) of East Asia is now taking place. There has been a dramatic transformation in the industrialization of these provinces – and not only in the special economic zones (SEZs). During the 1980s, according to one source, output in Guangdong grew at an average rate of 13 per cent a year in real terms: in Shenzhen SEZ the population grew to over 2 million and its output by 47 per cent a year during the 1980s. Guangdong has its advantages – the trading tradition of the Cantonese; its distance from Beijing, which has always considered the south to be of peripheral interest and importance; and its nearness to the successful NIC and port of Hong Kong with its largely Cantonese population. But here again the main factor in Guangdong's boom economy has been foreign investment, particularly from Hong Kong, but also from Japan and the United States. Encouraged by the low cost of land and labour, Hong Kong companies have moved many of their operations out from Hong Kong and into Guangdong. Indeed, while manufacturing employment in Hong Kong has fallen from 900 000 jobs in the early 1980s to 720 000 today, Hong Kong companies have created over 2 million new jobs in Guangdong (*Economist*) 1991a, p. 17).

The same kind of dramatic growth is beginning to occur in Fukien, especially in the Xiamen SEZ. Taiwan, Japan and the United States are now investing heavily in Fujian, and Taiwan is transferring many of its industrial operations across the straits to the mainland opposite. Whether this kind of rapid growth will occur in the traditionally major industrial areas around Shanghai (Shanghai, Jiangsu and Zhejiang provinces) or in the north-east (Liaoning, Jilin and Heilongjiang provinces), it is as yet too early to say.

It is tempting to speculate about the possible future political as well as economic implications of these developments in southern China. To quote from one recent survey: 'Imagine that the Chinese empire run from Beijing were to disintegrate – Guangdong, Fujian, Taiwan and Hong Kong could form the Republic of Southern China. This new country would have a population of 120 million and a combined GDP of roughly $310 billion, which would put it on a par with Brazil' (*Economist* 1991a, p. 17). This may be a quite unreal scenario, but certainly the pattern of industrial development and the differential growth rates of productivity and prosperity seem likely to create increasing stresses on the unity of the state.

More prosaically, many observers see no reason to doubt that China, with its vast natural resources and population, has the potential to become another, and possibly the greatest, NIC in East Asia; indeed, it could well become within the next three decades what Perkins (1989) has called Asia's next economic giant.

What are the main obstacles China faces in its progress towards this vision of massive industrialization and economic growth? They are clearly numerous and include such problems as the population growth problem, the faltering agricultural sector, environmental degradation, and low levels of education and technology (Dwyer, 1992). For the purposes of this chapter, however, three matters seem to demand particular attention.

First, some writers seem to believe, or at least to imply, that the problem lies with the *dirigiste* nature of government in China – that unless China embraces democracy then it cannot prosper. But this ignores the fact that all the governments of the East Asian NICs, with the possible exception of Hong Kong, have had or still have strong and authoritarian governments.

Rapid and successful industrialization in the NICs is not and cannot be correlated with non-interventionist governments. As Wade (1990) has pointed out, state direction and control has been a critical factor in the industrial growth of Taiwan, Singapore and South Korea. The problem is whether the government is prepared to adapt the nature, degree and style of its intervention so that it guides rather than rigidly controls the economy. There is plenty of evidence that economic imperatives as well as current theoretical and ideological arguments in China are being used to justify this kind of change or adaptation. The Chinese no longer argue that Communism and capitalism are logically incompatible. In 1990 Li Peng argued that planned and market economies each have their own strengths and weaknesses and that China needs to draw upon the strengths of both in order to build an integrated mixed economy (*Economist* 1991b, p. 67). However, even if the government is not prepared or able to change the emphasis of its control in this way, there seems little doubt that the demonstration effect of successful foreign firms and businesses operating in China will in the end force the government to go along with the principle of the 'guided' or 'governed' market – the mixed economy referred to by Li Peng. Industrial change, in other words, may well come as much from pressure from below as from changing policies at the top.

There is already plenty of evidence in China that academics and officials are well aware of the specific problems that have to be addressed if industrialization is to proceed successfully and more rapidly. One is what Lin (1990) has called 'the hot topic' of the moment – the need to deal with the uneconomic small size of state industrial enterprises. In China's iron and steel industry, for instance, the 38 largest enterprises account for less than 50 per cent of total production; in Japan the 20 largest enterprises account for 84 per cent of production; and in the United States the seven largest iron and steel enterprises account for 83.7 per cent of production (Table 7.2). Clearly there is an urgent need in China for a firm policy to encourage mergers, consolidation and concentration, whatever the type of industrial ownership.

Table 7.2 Industrial concentration by major industrial sectors in China, USA and Japan

Sector	China		USA		Japan	
	Largest enterprises	Sales (%)	Largest enterprises	Sales (%)	Largest enterprises	Sales (%)
Iron and steel	38	46.5	7	83.7	20	84
Automobiles	7	35.6	13	94.6	10	74.1
Chemicals	7	10.2	1.9	84.9	15	48
Engineering	6	2.9	9	58.4	10	53.9
Textiles	2	1.5	5	40.7	10	68.4

(*Source*: Lin, 1990.)

Another problem is the present worrying shortage of energy and raw materials for industry. This reflects an imbalance in investment and productivity between the various industrial sectors: between 1984 and 1988 manufacturing industry grew by some 18 per cent a year, mining grew by only 7 per cent and raw material production by less than 12 per cent. The result is that resource-rich China is already having to import some of its raw material requirements, and this is particularly the case in the industrial areas of southern China.

A third problem derives from the pre-reform legacy of local and regional self-sufficiency. Leading industries are often the same or very similar in different regions, a fact which makes it difficult to achieve the expressed aim of unifying the market, developing a nationwide commodity exchange relationship, and coordinating the division of labour between regions. But if this is to occur, then horizontal economic networks will have to develop. Commerce, completely socialized in the pre-reform period, needs to be allowed much greater freedom from government restrictions. As White (1988, p.186) notes: 'if the logic of the reforms is to be pursued consistently and if reform policies are to achieve their desired effects across the board, comprehensive changes in commodity circulation and exchange are necessary.' Yet state trade (or, more accurately, the state system of procurement and distribution) is still so rigid, bureaucratic and administratively overburdened, that it cannot hope to cope with the problem by itself. It is here, especially, that private trade – now growing rapidly and creating its own flexible networks – has a crucial role to play in China's future economic growth.

Conclusions

In spite of the problems facing China in its efforts to become an urban-industrial, commercially integrated economy along the lines of its most successful neighbours – Japan, Hong Kong, Taiwan, South Korea and Singapore – there are firm grounds for taking an optimistic view of China's industrial future over the next few decades. Foreign trade, foreign investment and imported technology are already providing the catalyst, as they did in those countries China is now trying to emulate. China's resources – both physical and human – are potentially far greater than those of her neighbours, and there can be no doubting China's determination to achieve economic success and global economic power.

While political imperatives may reduce the speed at which industrial development occurs, there is no reason to believe that the dead hand of the state will continue to be anything like as damaging as some writers suggest. Even if one assumes the continuance of the present government, it is clear that this need not be a barrier to growth. State industry is being reformed from within, albeit in a way and at a pace determined by political considerations. Domestic private industrial enterprises are beginning to develop and the country's economy has been boosted by the inflow of investment, firms and technology from abroad.

At the same time it is clear that the Chinese government has by no means entirely given up its faith in state-controlled industry or in the principles of regional industrial balance. Shanghai, China's largest industrial city and responsible for some 7 per cent of China's industrial output, is now being encouraged to develop its industries as a means of counterbalancing the rapid growth of the south (Guangdong). The new national party head in Beijing, Jiang Zemin – who was previously head of the Party in Shanghai – is attempting to re-establish Shanghai as China's premier international financial and business centre. The Pudong Development Project just east of Shanghai is planned to become an important industrial, commercial and financial zone, shifting policy emphasis away from the south and acting as a catalyst for the economic advancement of the Yangtze River Region. But, unlike in the south, the project at Pudong is not planned to depend on foreign capitalist centres of investment (*Far Eastern Economic Review* 1990).

Indications of China's future industrial strategy over the next few decades are by no means gloomy, even though that strategy may be forced on the government by irresistible economic imperatives rather than by choice. The Chinese authorities can claim some dramatic successes in the economic sphere. In the first three-quarters of 1991, for instance, industrial output in China was 14 per cent higher than in the same period for 1990. But the government is well aware that this improvement owed nothing to the state industrial sector. For during this period the industrial output of foreign and private businesses rose by 45 per cent; that of 'collectively' owned businesses by 25 per cent; and that of state industrial enterprises by only 11 per cent. To make the point even more sharply, the most dynamic industrial region of China – Guangdong – now has over two-thirds of its industrial production accounted for by non-state industrial enterprises, many of them originating from and linked to the wealthy, capitalist colony of Hong Kong, due to be taken over by China in 1997. As a report in the *Economist* (1991b, p.67) reveals, the difference between state and non-state industrial enterprises in Guangdong is such that: 'people are buying the output of non-state companies, while the shoddy goods from the state factories are piling up in warehouses'.

On a recent visit to Guangdong, Li Peng suggested that the province's successful experience should be used as an example in the reform of state industrial enterprises. Holding companies for state enterprises are to be created; and shares in these holding companies will then be sold or given away, first to employees and then to the public at large. Whatever the government's rhetoric may suggest, it seems likely that the next few decades will see an increasing acceptance by the Chinese authorities that industrial growth throughout the country demands a fundamental change in the balance between state and non-state industrial enterprises.

There is at the moment a great deal of interest in the economic problems of countries which in one way or another are attempting to liberalize their economies, releasing state control and embracing the market. Most of these, like the former USSR and the countries of Eastern Europe, are trying to cope with economies now seriously damaged by loss of political control and by political fragmentation. The transition from a Communist command economy to a free market economy is proving both difficult and painful. There is indeed no certainty that the transition will be accomplished successfully. This is well understood in China, where there is a clear determination to avoid the mistakes of its former great Communist neighbour to the west. There are as yet no signs that political freedoms will be allowed either before, during or after economic liberalization. Under the present government, certainly, there is to be some *perestroika* but no *glasnost*.

The question now being asked outside China is how far the necessary economic freedoms can flourish effectively within a tightly controlled and repressive political system. Much of the literature in the West suggests that greater economic freedom and continued political repression are mutually incompatible. But in China there are those who see no logical reason why this should be so. Perhaps the worst-case scenario for China in the next few decades is not that Communist control will continue, but that a precipitate clamour for political freedom will ignore and then destroy, as it has in the former Soviet Union, the industrial progress on which the prosperity as well as the stability of the Chinese state must ultimately depend.

References

Dwyer D J (1992) 'Doubts surround China's economic future', *Independent*, 8 February.

Economist (1991a) 'Asia's emerging economies', 16 November, 5–24.

Economist (1991b) 30 November, 67.

Far Eastern Economic Review (1989) 14 September, 61–4. *Far Eastern Economic Review* (1990) 31 May, 57–8.

Goodman DSG (ed.) (1989) *China's Regional Development*, **RIIA**, Routledge, London.

Hodder RNW (1990) 'China's industry – horizontal linkages in Shanghai', *Transactions, Institute of British Geographers*, **15**, 487–503.

Howard M (1990) 'Industry, energy and transport', in Cannon T and Jenkins A (eds), *The Geography of Contemporary China: the impact of Deng Xiaoping's decade*, Routledge, London, pp. 168–202.

Lin Shuiyan (1990) *China's Industrial Structure and the Present Industrial Adjustment*, Institute of World Economics and Politics, Chinese Academy of Social Sciences, Beijing, 25 June.

Perkins D H (1989) *China: Asia's Next Economic Giant*? University of Washington, Seattle.

SSKY (Shanghai Shehui Kexue Yuan) (1986) Shanghai Academy of Social Sciences, *Shanghai's Economy, 1983–85*, Shanghai People's Publishing House, Shanghai, pp. 135–9.

SSTJ (Shanghai Shi Tonggi Ju) (1986) Shanghai Statistical Bureau, *Shanghai's Industrial Structure: its historical evolution and present condition*, Shanghai Statistical Publishing House, Shanghai.

Wade R (1990) *Governing the Market: Economic theory and the role of government in East Asian industrialization*, Princeton University Press, Princeton.

White G (1988) 'State and market in China's socialist industrialization', in

White G. (ed.), *Developmental States in East Asia*, IDS, Macmillan, London, pp. 153–88.

Xie Yichun and **Costa F J** (1991) 'The impact of economic reforms on the urban economy of The People's Republic of China', *The Professional Geographer*, **43**, 318–34.

Yahuda M B (1990) 'China', *The Asia and Pacific Review*, 53–62.

CHAPTER 8

Dilemmas of urbanization: review and prospects

R.J.R. Kirkby

The Chinese Communist Party in power has never wavered far from its grand design – the industrialization of the nation. For this, the modernization of agriculture, and thus the guaranteeing of the required rural surpluses, has always been a precondition. The periodic convulsions within the Party are rooted in these fundamental questions, turning not upon whether super-industrialization is desirable, but how best to realize it.

The relation between agricultural and industrial spheres provides the dynamic of the urbanization process. In the Mao period, however, the term urbanization was rarely articulated. This changed greatly under the post-Mao regime, and a considerable and often sharp discourse now surrounds the complex question of appropriate urbanization strategy. In contrast to the pre-1978 situation, all parties concur that urbanization is an inevitable feature of China's further development; many even assert that it is in itself a desirable phenomenon, betokening a 'modern' society. But the main issues of contention concern the pace of transformation to an urban society, the regional distribution of urban growth, and above all the appropriate settlement hierarchy. To some, the only option is that presented by a small and intermediate settlements strategy. For others, urban agglomeration on an unprecedented scale is demanded by present trends in population growth and agricultural capacity. The purpose here is to examine the issues surrounding urbanization policy since the late 1970s, the debates which they have provoked, and the constraints on future options which suggest the makings of a growing crisis of urbanization.

Urban population increase 1978–90

Since the publication in 1991 of the preliminary 1990 census results, a new urban population series has been accorded primary status in China, and applied retrospectively to the 1982–89 period. It is this series which informs statements regarding urban population changes in the present discussion. Prior to the 1990 census redefinition, China's urban population data had become increasingly confused and often contradictory. Unravelling the urban figures of recent years, and attributing growth to differing factors, is a complex matter. As well as natural increase and migration, administrative adjustments to the urban system were a key cause of formal urban population growth.

Natural increase

Natural increase accounted for a greater proportion of overall growth than might be expected, given the rigorous application of state family planning programmes in the urban areas. For structural reasons, China's crude birth rate climbed somewhat after 1979; perversely, the urban rate rose more markedly than did the rural rate. Between 1979 and 1982, the municipal crude birth rate (CBR) climbed from 13.89 to 18.24 per 1000. A contributory factor was the return of up to 13 million as yet unmarried young people to their native cities following periods in the countryside during the Cultural Revolution. While the 1982 municipal CBR was not exceeded over subsequent years, it remained both unstable year to year, and relatively high compared with the figure for China as a whole (in 1989, 15.98 per 1000, against 21.97) (*RKNJ* 1990, pp.612–15).

In terms of the new (1990 census) criteria, total urban population rose by almost 130 million between 1978 and 1990 (Table 8.1). Application of annual rates of natural increase for China's municipal population (a process which underestimates due to higher rates in designated towns) suggests that one-quarter (32 million) of overall urban increase was caused by natural growth rates (*RKNJ* 1990, pp. 592–3, 612, 616).

Migration

Inconsistencies in data, changes in the household registration system and the enormous fluidity of population after the abolition of collective farming render the estimation of migration's contribution to overall urban growth an even more difficult matter. Several field surveys provide some indication of the magnitudes involved. A fuller picture regarding the impact of youth returnees (estimated at 23 million) is provided in a UN-supported study: real transfers from the rural to urban spheres between 1978 and 1982 amounted to almost one-third of the entire net rural–urban migration after 1949 (Ma 1987; Ma and Wang 1989). Migration slowed during the following five year period: a 10 per cent sample survey by the State Statistical Bureau concluded that between mid-1982 and 1987, there were 13 million full transfers of household registration from rural to urban (*CD* 17.8.1988). Research covering eight provinces conducted in 1987–88 confirms the volume of movement in the first years of the economic reform: 52 per cent of all permanent migration into towns between 1949 and 1986 occurred after 1979 (Taubmann 1992, p.279). These figures are somewhat at odds with the other survey findings cited, the probable reason being a more liberal basis for counting movements to towns after the household registration system changes of 1984. If, however, the order of findings in the first two studies is correct, and if we assume that migration continued at about the same pace after 1987, the total net figure for the period 1978–90 would be in the region of 45 million – around 35 per cent of the overall urban population increase.

Administrative adjustments

On the basis of the above estimates of the impacts of natural growth and migration, we can conclude that some 40 per cent of China's total urban increase in the post-1978 period was due to various alterations to the urban administrative system. Firstly, after 1978 there was a huge increase in the number of settlements with the formal designation of town (*zhen*) – the basic 'building block' in Chinese urban population statistics. In 1963, *zhen* designation criteria had been tightened, leading to a steady reduction in numbers over the ensuing 15 years (Ma and Cui 1987, Table 2, p.377; Middelhoek 1992, App. Table 1, p.262). This reflected the declining political and economic status of China's rural townships. The new rural policies post-1979 arrested this decline, the *zhen* designations increasing as a consequence. Table 1 shows a more than doubling of *zhen* numbers in 1984. This followed a revision in the conditions of eligibility, though the new non-agricultural population (NAP) requirements were not greatly changed; it is likely that the leap in *zhen* numbers arose in part from the scramble for a new role and status by the cadres of the just-disbanded people's communes.

For most areas of the country, the 1963 rules had stipulated a minimum permanent population of 3000, in which 70 per cent were NAP. Smaller places (2500–3000) could also be considered, provided their NAP proportion reached 85 per cent. After 1984, all county-level seats of government were now automatically eligible for *zhen* status. In the rural administrative units which officially replaced the people's commune in 1984 (the *xiang*), a *zhen* could be established where the *xiang's* population was under 20 000 and the NAP of the seat of *xiang* government (comparable to the former commune centre) exceeded 2000. Further, in *xiang* of over 20 000, *zhen* could be established provided the *xiang* seat had a NAP of over 10 per cent. In the latter two cases the location of the *zhen* would be the *xiang* seat itself. The constraints and incentives concerning the acquisition of *zhen* status, and the economic and administrative regime of the designated urban places in general, are an important but little understood aspect of China's urbanization policies.

The second adjustment of an administrative nature underlying urban population increase in the 1980s was in the number of designated municipalities (*shi* – Table 8.1). Prior to the economic reform period, this had only once exceeded 200. After 1978, however, the swelling in *zhen* populations, along with relaxation of designation criteria, brought a more than doubling in *shi* numbers. The increase by one-fifth in 1983 was due to the adoption by the Ministry of Civil Affairs of lower population thresholds: while the previous rules had generally specified a minimum urban population of 100 000, the 1983 changes introduced considerations of employment structure and level of economic development. Now a *zhen* could seek upgrading if its NAP exceeded 60 000, provided its annual gross product was over 200 million yuan. This new ruling was formalized in 1986 (Yeh and Xu 1989 p.6).

Table 8.1 Growth in numbers of designated municipalities and towns 1978–1990.

	Towns (*zhen*)	Municipalities
1978	2176	193
1979	2851	216
1980	2874	223
1981	2843	233
1982	2819	245
1983	2781	289
1984	**6211**	300
1985	7511	324
1986	9755	353
1987	9121	381
1988	11481	434
1989	11295	446
1990	11622	464
1990 census	11937	449

(*Sources*: Designated municipalities: From the annual reports issued by the Civil Affairs Ministry, *Zhonghua Renmin Gongheguo xingzheng quhua jiance* [The Administrative Divisions of the People's Republic of China], 1979–88: Cartographic Publishers, Beijing; 1989, 1990: Surveying and Mapping Publishers, Beijing. The 1990 figure is from *TJNJ* 1991, p. 3.)

Designated towns:
1978:	Zou Deci 1990, p. 1
1979–82:	see Kirkby 1985, Table 3.5, p. 85
1983:	Ma and Cui 1987, Table 2, p. 377
1984:	Ministry of Public Security (Third Bureau), 1985, p.1
1985–86:	*TJNJ* 1987, pp. 23, 137
1987:	Middelhoek 1992, App. Table 1, p. 262
1988:	Ministry of Construction, Urban Planning Division 1990: footnote, p. 124
1989–90:	*TJNJ* 1991, p. 311
1990 census:	*RKNJ* 1991, p. 709; note reduction in *shi* numbers, which may have arisen because of scrutiny of census planners.

Shi numbers were also inflated by a departure in administrative proce- dure which has proved as controversial as it is novel. Now, rural counties were to be permitted to transmute in their entirety into muncipalities. Again, criteria for eligibility concerned non-agricultural population and economic output. A county of under 500 000 population having an NAP of more than 100 000 in the county seat, less than 40 per cent of its entire population in agriculture, and an annual gross product of 300 million yuan would meet the conditions for *shi* status. Counties of greater population were not entirely excluded from this unorthodox means of municipal- ization. In 1978 China had 193 *shi*; by the end of 1990 the figure stood at

464, 60 per cent being lower order (county level) centres which had acceded to municipal status after 1980. The blurring of the distinction between rural and urban spheres wrought by these developments is a matter of some concern to academics and policy makers.

The growing distortion in China's urban population data

The urban population figures issued annually by China's State Statistical Bureau spiralled inexorably upwards during the 1980s. For the period between the 1964 and the 1982 censuses, the official measure of urban scale was 'city and town population' (*chengzhen renkou*) – this being the aggregate of all non-agricultural population in the designation urban places, the *shi* and the *zhen*.

In order to reflect the growing complexity of employment and spatial interaction arising from liberalization of the rural economy and migration rules, the 1982 census introduced a quite different measure, the 'total population of municipalities and towns' (*shizhen zongrenkou*). At the time, the core distinction appeared to lie in the fact that all non-county population in all the districts of the *shi*, irrespective of agricultural or non-agricultural status, was now included. Even more significant in view of later changes in the *zhen* designation criteria, all the population within *zhen* were to be counted as urban. This new basis was then applied retrospectively to the series from 1964 onwards. The initial disjunction between the two series is illustrated by the 1981 year-end situation: according to the first, China's urban population was 138.7 million – 13.9 per cent of national population. By the new standards, the total stood at 201.716 million or 20.2 per cent (Table 8.2).

Throughout the 1980s, both the huge numbers of designations of urban places, and in particular the changes in criteria for their designation, rendered the new official definition ever more implausible. Table 8.2 illustrates the spiral in the official urban total: 382 million (36.6 per cent) by 1985, 504 million (47.7 per cent) by 1987, and by 1989, 571 million – or more than half the Chinese nation. There was growing concern at the large proportion of non-agricultural population entering the urban count: of the 212 million urban total of 1982, almost one-third was comprised of registered farm persons. By the end of the 1980s, two-thirds of China's supposed urban dwellers lived in small settlements of a predominantly agricultural character. Under the new 'town control of villages' (*zhen dai cun*) slogan, many *zhen* were designated covering the entire area previously administered by the rural tier which they displaced, the *xiang*. By 1989, over three-quarters of *zhen* population contributing to the urban total was registered as agricultural (*RKNJ* 1991, pp. 592–3). Similarly for the municipalities, in which the agricultural population comprised one-third in 1982, and over a half in 1989 (Table 8.2). Here, the distorting influence was the growing weight of non-agricultural population in suburban districts or, in the case of lower order *shi*, within the peri-urban band.

Table 8.2 China's urban population 1978–90 according to the 1982 and and 1990 census criteria

| | CHINA (m.) | Urban: 1990 basis | | Urban: 1982 basis | | | | | | | | | |
		Total (m.)	%	Total	%	NAP (m.)	%NAP	*shi* Aggreg. (m.)	NAP (m.)	%NAP	*zhen* Aggreg. (m.)	NAP (m.)	%NAP
1978	962.59	172.45	17.9	172.452	17.9	124.44	72.2	119.29	84.05	70.5	53.16	40.39	76.0
1979	975.43	184.96	19.0	184.96	19.0	133.12	72.0	129.40	90.37	69.8	55.56	42.75	77.0
1980	987.06	191.41	19.4	191.41	19.4	138.63	72.4	134.47	94.48	70.3	56.93	44.15	77.5
1981	1000.72	201.72	20.2	201.72	20.2	143.20	71.0	143.32	98.28	68.6	58.40	44.92	76.9
1982	1015.41	214.80	21.1	211.59	20.8	147.15	69.6	149.40	101.36	67.8	62.16	45.79	73.7
1983	1024.95	222.74	21.6	241.23	23.5	152.34	63.2	178.95	107.52	60.1	62.28	44.83	72.0
1984	1034.75	240.17	23.0	330.06	31.9	166.89	50.6	195.59	114.61	58.6	134.47	52.28	38.9
1985	1045.32	250.94	23.7	382.44	36.6	179.71	47.0	216.11	122.50	56.7	166.33	57.21	34.4
1986	1057.21	263.66	24.5	437.53	41.4	185.15	42.3	233.84	125.52	53.7	203.69	59.63	29.3
1987	1072.40	276.74	25.3	503.62	47.7	194.41	38.8	264.35	132.98	50.3	236.66	61.43	26.0
1988	1089.78	286.61	25.8	542.45	49.8	204.06	37.6	304.05	143.73	47.3	238.45	60.33	25.3
1989	1103.56	295.40	26.2	570.63	51.7	208.50	36.5	315.70	146.14	46.3	254.93	62.36	24.5
1990	1143.33	301.91	26.4										

(*Sources: TJNJ* 1991, p. 79; *RKNJ* 1990 pp. 5923.)
Note: The 1982 census-based data include all permanent residents within the districts/boundaries of designated urban places (*shi* and *zhen*). The 1990 census-based data include all those in the districts of higher order *shi* (*shequ de shi*), and restricted categories in both lower order *shi* (*bushequ de shi*) and *zhen* (see text).

The basic rule for the 'cities control counties' (*shi dai xian*) system which was extended in 1983 to many parts of the country was that the core city should contain a NAP of 250 000 (Peng Qing 1990). Yet the new county-to-municipality conversion method suddenly allowed very modest settlements both to upgrade to *shi* and to incorporate a high proportion of NAP. Zhou and Shi (1991) compare eight well-established cities (ranging in size from 0.5 to 1.3 million according to the 1982 census standard) with eight typical 'upstarts' with very similar total populations. In the former group, the proportion of NAP is on average 75.4 per cent. For the newly designated *shi*, it is a derisory 6.9 per cent.

The 1990 census: a new approach to the urban population data

In their design of the 1990 census, the State Council Census Office initially defined two aims with regard to the enumeration of urban population. The first was to include all the population in the districts of *shi* and *zhen*, in order to ensure comparability with the situation at the time of the 1982 census. The second was to introduce new criteria 'in order to truly reflect the urban population of *shi*, *zhen*, and counties' (Qiao and Li 1991, p.22).

In pursuit of these aims, the authorities sought a 'rational' (*helide*) total urban figure which was seen to be both in line with the 1982 count (206.588 million, 20.6 per cent) and somehow appropriate to China's current level of economic and social development. This approach, with its *a priori* foundation, had none the less to be operationalized according to a highly specific, justifiable and replicable methodology. Stated baldly, the whole procedure can be characterized as a mixture of pragmatism, guile and good sense. The 'appropriate' urban total was an essential requirement, and that was achieved: 296.518 million, being 26.3 per cent of the national figure. Common sense demanded the exclusion of excessive concentrations of non-agricultural persons: that too was realized.

The methodology adduced to distinguish rural from urban population in the 1990 census is complex (Fig. 8.1). A brief description follows. *Shi* fall into two categories: those with districts (*shequ de shi*) and those without (*bushequ de shi*). Basically, the former are the higher order (i.e. sub-provincial level) ones, while the latter are lower order (sub-prefectural or county level). All the population within the former group is counted as urban; in the latter, only that under the lowest form of state administration, the *jiedao* (street) committees, is incorporated. For the *zhen* falling within counties, and for those within the boundaries of lower order *shi*, all population within the jurisdiction of *jumin* (residents') committees is counted as urban. Detailed clarification of the part of the total urban count comprised by each component of the administrative system is offered in Fig. 8.1.

The 1990 census approach to the question of China's urban population statistics represents a significant improvement – theoretically, practically and aesthetically. The urbanization impulses pressing on China are

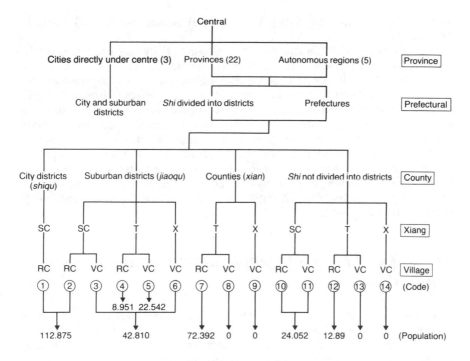

Fig 8.1 Urban population in the 1990 census: simplified diagram. (*Source:* Qiao and Li 1991, p. 26; *RKNJ* 1991, pp.74–7)

mediated through an administrative and morphological matrix which is becoming ever more complex. Doubtless the changing objective situation will bring demands for further adjustments in the formal urban system. The 1990 census interpretation of urbanness has already met some criticism, but it will most likely be retained until the next full census. Its chief shortcoming lies in the scope for widespread misapplication of present *shi* and *zhen* designation rules. In order to guard against this, some analysts have already recommended a refinement of the 1990 criteria in order to excise almost all cohorts of non-agricultural population. Referring again to Fig. 8.1, the suggestion is that population under codes 3, 6 and 11 be excluded.

At each level of the administrative system, differing branches of the bureaucracy have data requirements particular to their functions. Suppliers of staple foodstuffs to the registered urban population, for example, will need to use data sets which differ from those of public transport planners who must take into account often very large volumes of temporary visitors. Efforts to determine a single definitive urban population series are therefore increasingly academic; they should perhaps be abandoned in favour of a pragmatism which acknowledges an array of differing series. The formative criteria of any such functional series must, however, be entirely explicit; further, they should be capable of adaptation to the fast changing and ever more complex process of urbanization in China.

The quest for a manageable distribution of urban population

The image of China in the 1980s was one of dynamic expansion of urban-centred functions and activities, embracing settlements of every scale and almost every sub-region. And yet there have been explicit contradictions in official policy regarding the distribution of growth.

The official line laid down in the early 1980s has become a familiar refrain: strict control of the growth of large cities (over 0.5 million in core populations), 'rational' development of medium-sized cities (0.2 – 0.5 million) and active promotion of the small cities (under 0.2 million) and the sub-municipal towns (*RMRB* 16. 10. 1980). Despite a barrage of criticism from the academic community, in formal terms the government has held the line on this guiding policy. Eleven years after it was first enunciated, a conference on urban development received an address by Vice-Premier Zou Jiahua which restated it in precisely the same terms (*JJRB* 12.9.1991).

Yet throughout the 1980s there were countervailing policies, promoting the growth (economically, at least) of the larger centres. These were, briefly, the restoration of the key-point city concept, the currency given to the 'central city' (*zhongxin chengshi*) or growth pole idea, and the promotion of large-scale municipal annexations of surrounding regions – systematically throughout the country through the 'city control of counties' (*shi dai xian*) administrative reform, and erratically through the paper designation of super-city regions such as those centred on Shanghai and Chongqing. From the mid-1980s on, regional metropolitanization was encouraged in the Lower Yangtze and Pearl River Deltas, in the Beijing–Tianjin–Tangshan belt, and in central Liaoning. Here the explicit aim was 'concentrated urbanized areas' (*JJRB* 12.9.1991).

An evaluation of the record with regard to restraint of further population growth of the 'large' cities (those over 500 000 in NAP) shows that their aggregated population increase between 1980 and 1989 was 27.6 per cent (Table 8.3). This is only half the rate for all urban population increase over the same period (54.3 per cent) – broadly showing the inverse relationship between city size and rate of growth in the 1980s. None the less, a remarkable feature of China's changing urban profile is indicated by the fact that in 1980 there were 45 cities with core populations of over 0.5 million; a decade later there were 58. During the same period, 'million' cities doubled in number to 30.

Population counts for metropolitan centres underestimate the true numbers having *de facto* residence. China's economic reforms have created a growing pool of mobile labour, as well as the means by which they can

Table 8.3   Cities of over 0.5 million in 1980 – overall growth by size class 1980–89

Size class (millions)	No. of *shi*	Aggregate population (millions)		Change 1980–1989 (%)
		1980	1989	
0.05–0.75	13	7.70	10.00	29.8
0.75–1.00	17	14.66	18.75	27.9
1.00–1.50	5	6.02	7.70	28.0
1.50–2.00	3	5.05	6.23	23.6
2.00+	7	24.05	29.75	23.7
TOTAL/AVERAGE	45	57.47	72.44	26.0

(*Source*: RKNJ, pp. 6027; *TJNJ* 1990, p. 92.)

Note:
1. Figures are based on classification of major cities according to non-agricultural population.
2. The table shows an average of 26 per cent growth of population of the 45 cities during the period. Compare with the much higher rate for urban population as a whole 1980–89 of 54 per cent (based on the 1990 restricted series: see Table 8.1).

exist as unregistered residents. Estimates of the 'mobile population' (*liu-dong renkou*) or temporary population (*linshi renkou*) are by their nature fraught (*CCPR* 1988, **4**, 2). It is generally agreed that the larger the city, the greater the proportion of unregistered persons in comparison with the core city population. Ma and Cui (1987) suggest an inflation of official figures for large cities of at least 7.5 per cent. A 1988 Public Security survey in 23 of the then 26 'million' cities put the average number of unregistered persons at over 0.5 million in each. For certain cities the situation was severe: since 1984, Beijing had consistently reported the presence of over 1 million temporary residents and transients. In Shanghai, the average for 1986 was around 1.6 million, climbing to almost 2 million in late 1988 and giving rise to public security concerns (*CCPR* 1988, **2**, 77; *CD* 12.8.1988). The pressures on public infrastructure, most visibly transport, were manifest.

The appearance of a transient population in China's large cities, particularly in provincial capitals, was a response to developments in both urban and rural labour markets. At the same time, the household registration and associated rationing system had become far less effectual in controlling movement. A nationwide survey of 1988, involving 10 million respondents, showed that for the great majority of rural–urban migrants the question of transfer of household registration (*hukou*) had been no deterrent to movement. Four out of five respondents who had moved during the 1982–90 period had failed to effect a transfer of their registrations (*LW* 16.8.1988, p. 6). None the less, throughout the 1980s, permanent transfers of registration from the rural areas to the municipal sector was only permitted in any volume in the smaller *shi* of under 200 000 in population.

The pull of metropolitan centres was greatly reduced as a result of the economic retrenchment experienced between 1988 and 1990. Huge numbers of temporary workers (and especially those in the construction trades) were no longer able to maintain their urban niches. This demonstrated the continued impact of the household registration system in the largest cities. The strategic objective of limiting further metropolitan growth was, therefore, largely met in the 1990s. But the aim was never to impose constraints on the concentration and development of modern sector industry and commerce within the large cities. Their continued importance in this respect is given detailed consideration by Kim (1991).

Urbanization and food security

From the mid-1950s, and particularly after the Great Leap Forward, official determination of sustainable rates of rural–urban migration was largely based upon agricultural performance and the consequent size of the mobilizable grain surplus. In the early years, the agricultural sector was cast as the main source of capital accumulation for China's industrial revolution. The establishment of the people's communes in 1958 was in great part aimed at exerting state direction over the farm surplus. By denying any free urban market in food, and through the stern application of the household registration system, the state was able to regulate closely any changes of domicile. This was a factor crucial to the suppression of urbanization rates after 1960.

The economic reforms brought a remarkable diversification in agriculture, with grain's contribution to rural income much reduced. At the same time, in the cities there was a discernible trend away from reliance on traditional staples, apparently marking the beginnings of a historic shift away from a grain-dependent culture. The Maoist exhortation to 'take grain as the key link' appeared to have little relevance to post-commune China. Partly at the urging of the World Bank, over the 1980s a number of measures were introduced aimed at liberalizing the internal grain market. In 1984, China's total grain harvest was officially registered at an all-time high of over 400 million tonnes. The ensuing flush of optimism brought a lifting of the mandatory grain procurements in place since the early 1950s. But at the same time, oversupply meant farm-gate price reductions of 9 per cent. In fact, it is likely that the 1984 harvest figures had been greatly exaggerated: the formal abolition of collective farming in that year released large quantities of grain which had previously been held in reserve by communes and production brigades

(Hinton 1991, p.139). The 1985 harvest was found to be some 30 million tonnes less than that of the previous year; when the veteran economic planner Chen Yun addressed the question of grain security in 1985, he evoked old fears of shortage, instability and even famine. As a result, by the end of 1986 grain procurement contracts had been reimposed (*FEER* 10.10.1985, p.36).

The concerns of the traditionalist faction in the Party were heightened by an increasing engagement in the world grain market. Whereas in the early 1970s, China's grain self-sufficiency stood at 102 per cent, by the mid-1980s it was down to 94 per cent (World Bank 1991, p.1). China had become a major net exporter of grain-derived products; but the nation was now the world's largest net grain importer. The 1986 reimposition of grain procurement quotas did not bring the intended reassertion of control over the grain sector. Indeed, where urban grain rationing had been lifted, in 1989 it was reintroduced because of continual supply problems. Surveys showed that many traditional grain surplus areas were now in deficit, with farmers reluctant to produce because of low prices, rising input costs and frequent inability of the state to honour purchasing contracts (*FEER* 2.3.1989, pp.51–2).

Subsidization of urban grain consumption was a cornerstone of the Maoist industrialisation model. Even after a decade of economic reform, in the late 1980s grain support still accounted for over 10 per cent of central government expenditure, raising average per capita urban incomes by almost one tenth. On the other hand, the state purchasing system prevented producers from achieving market-influenced prices, thereby depressing average per capita rural income by an estimated 4 per cent annually. Here was a process of redistribution which remained 'unambiguously regressive' (World Bank 1991, p.147).

In the early years of the economic reform, grain supply models were still being used as the basis for projections of future sustainable urbanization (Kirkby 1985, pp.204–5). There was less of a retreat from this perspective during the 1980s than might have been expected. The dissolution of the communes, and the need for a diversified rural sector, brought irresistible pressures to expand the off-farm sector by allowing movement from the villages to the rural townships. It was well understood that such unprecedented pressures for urbanization could not be matched by an enlargement of the mobilizable grain supply. The outcome was a historical break with the principle that China's non-farm labour was guaranteed its staple grains by the state. Many rural dwellers, especially in well-developed areas, had already in the early 1980s effected the transition to non-agricultural employment. Initially, transfers were mainly of the *yigong yinong* ('both peasant and worker') type, in which 'leave the land but not the native place' (*li tu bu li xiang*) was the watchword. But the household registration (*hukou*) system (basically discriminating between agricultural and non-agricultural persons) had not kept pace. Only limited categories of persons could gain urban *hukou*: children inheriting fathers' jobs, children under 16 whose mothers had acquired urban *hukou*, recruits to leading positions in *xiang* and *zhen* administrations, some peasants displaced by non-agricultural developments, and so forth (Christiansen

1990, pp.38–9).

In April 1983, the State Council issued a circular legitimizing domiciliary transfer of many millions of new employees in small rural towns. The proviso was that they maintained rural *hukou*, and hence responsibility for their food grains. Following the apparently excellent harvest of 1984, a further circular consolidated the new arrangment, permitting farmers who had moved to nearby rural townships to become 'permanent residents with personal responsibility for grain' (*zili kouliang de changzhu jumin*) (Taylor 1988, p.759). Middelhoek (1989) describes the orderly mass transfer which these important changes allowed. Intending migrants to a Zhejiang *zhen* were required to prove that they had access to accommodation, they were not reneging on farm contracts under the household responsibility system, and that at least one member of the household would be engaged in non-agricultural employment in the *zhen*. Under the new arrangement, the peasant migrant retained responsibility for his own grain supply, securing it from his village, from the local free market, or from state suppliers at the 'negotiated' rather than the subsidized price. The local labour administration authorities would now have certain key responsibilities towards him, including support in the event of job loss, and provision of jobs for offspring entering working age. Further relaxation of the *hukou* system came in 1985. Peasants wishing to enter larger urban places in order to run businesses or for long-term contracted employment could now apply for a 'lodging card' (*jizhuzheng*). This represented a more stable status than the normal temporary urban registration (Ma and Noble 1986, p.284).

The overall impact of these *hukou* adjustments remains unclear. One estimate suggested that by 1988, the national total of *zili kouliang* migrants was only 4.6 million, most being concentrated in five provinces (Christiansen 1992, p.243). On the other hand, Taubmann (1992) cites an official figure of 7.6 per cent of all non-agricultural population of China's *zhen* – giving a total of almost 15 million. In certain areas, such as the Pearl River Delta, there is evidence of very heavy utilization of the new means of official transfer from the rural to urban spheres. Thus while the close relationship between grain harvests and the permissible urbanization rate had been loosened during the period of the economic reforms, the link has by no means been broken. China is unlikely in the foreseeable future to become structurally dependent on the world market for its grain shortfalls. Indeed, since 1989 there has been a withdrawal towards greater self-reliance. That being the case, a single poor harvest would bring into focus the question of the appropriate scale of China's non-agricultural population, and the suitability of the present *hukou* rules. The parameters for urbanization policy would, therefore, also be subject to re-evaluation.

The push from the land

The 1980s was a period of unprecedented transfer of China's farm population away from traditional agricultural pursuits. The proliferation of the rural enterprise sector (owned collectively at township and village levels, and after 1984 complemented by millions of small privately run operations) has been the cornerstone of an urbanization policy emphasizing small and intermediate settlements. While the creation of China's off-farm sector in the 1980s has been spectacular, the nation still faces a scenario of further urbanization of staggering proportions. The grand questions for the present are as follows:

- how firm a foundation has been established in the expanded rural township sector, in terms both of employment and infrastructural provision?
- can the rate of future expansion of the sector meet the projected need?

The dimensions of the rural industrialization and urbanization questions are now laid out.

The paucity of basic land resources possessed by the world's most populous nation is familiar: China supports over 20 per cent of global population on 7 per cent of global cropland. Both quality and absolute quantity of land have declined since 1949. The nature of these problems is addressed by growing numbers of environmental specialists in China (e.g. Guo *et al*, 1989; Han 1989). They are also dealt with by Edmonds in Chapter 9 of this volume. The figures which most starkly illustrate the overall problem compare changes in cultivable land availability with population. Between 1949 and 1982, there was a halving of per capita arable land (0.19 to 0.10 ha). More alarmingly, a further loss of one-fifth occurred during the 1982–90 period. Much of the latter was due to the redivision of previously collective land, to rural housing construction and the development of rural enterprises. In the two decades preceding reform, the net annual reduction to China's cropland was around 0.5 per cent; in the 1980s, the rate was 1 per cent. Provinces most in deficit were all in eastern China, where population concentrations in general are great, and rural densities often exceed 2000 persons per square kilometre. Further intensification of cropping is constrained by resource and land degradation factors (World Bank 1991, p.100).

Already by the early 1980s, the oft-repeated official view held that one-third of the rural workforce was surplus to the needs of traditional crop cultivation. This bald figure masks the complexity of the rural labour surplus, its characteristics being mediated by time (seasonally) and space (regionally). There are many regions of the more developed provinces where the rush to enterprise employment has left a marked labour shortage. Here, diminishing returns have begun to assert themselves, with farming left to women and children, the elderly and the infirm. In the vicinity of large centres, where off-farm work opportunities are great, farm work has often been sub-contracted to incomers, including migrants from distant provinces.

Survey evidence of the first decades of the century shows that, discounting the winter slack season, in many areas only one rural labourer in three was in full-time work. After 1949, increased labour utilization was a key objective, and multiple cropping, regular application of fertilizer, intensive weeding and deep ploughing were emphasized.

Collectivization was the institutional means of intensifying labour input. Consequently, between 1953 and 1978 there was a dramatic increase in labour application per crop; there was also a change in the crop mix, towards those requiring greater labour intensity (Taylor 1988, p. 740, Fig. 1).

Rural over-population was relieved during the Mao era through a variety of means. One such was the mobilization of mass labour for land improvement and infrastructural projects, the fruits of which often increased overall demand for labour. The household registration system was designed essentially to shackle the rural population to the countryside. Yet there was some leakage – China's burgeoning urban industrial sector recruited perhaps 60 million peasants during the first three decades of the People's Republic. Additionally, by the end of the Mao era, over 20 million peasants had been taken out of the rural workforce by the rural industries programme.

The *de facto* enlargement of the rural workforce through the incorporation of the young and elderly, the accelerated loss of agricultural land, and new policies allowing mobility of labour have all brought the surplus question to the fore. The underlying pressure of population growth is an obvious cause: in the early to mid-1970s, the annual increase in the officially counted rural workforce ranged between 2 and 4 million. In the late 1970s the figure was depressed by the mass return to the cities. But between 1979 and 1988, the annual increment was never less than 8 million, while in some years it reached 12 million (*TJNJ* 1989, p.120). Far more important as a force impelling the surplus has been the fact that the new responsibility system places a premium on household labour efficiency. The data for 1978–85 demonstrate an extraordinary decline in the average number of labour days required by almost every crop (Taylor 1988, p.748, Fig. 3). Though the surplus problem has received much official attention, estimation of its scale remains an imprecise art. The reformist Rural Development Research Centre put the 1984 figure at over half of the total rural workforce of 330 million (*BR* 20.3.1989, p.7). Deng (1988) arrives at a more modest figure of 22.8 per cent, with the average for 12 most developed provinces at 40.5 per cent. A further study of the anticipated situation in AD 2000 concluded that, were there to be no further expansion of the rural enterprise sector, the surplus labour force would rise to 225 million in a total projected workforce of 520 million (*CD* 3.6.1991).

Most analyses of the surplus rural labour force question choose to ignore the additional factor of family dependants. While not all would be shifted away from agricultural pursuits and village residence, the dependent rural population none the less magnifies the redeployment problem facing China's planners. It is thus easy to see why, for the early 1990s, a 'surplus' figure of over 100 million is often cited. It is small wonder that scholars such as Pannell (1986, p. 309) anticipate a scale of urbanization unprecedented in human history.

The rise of the off-farm sector

The history of the rural enterprise phenomenon over the past decade is obscured by conflicting official accounts and an ever-shifting morass of dubious data (Wong 1988). Initially, much of the evidence came from the group of rural anthropologists around the veteran scholar Fei Xiaotong; it was overlaid with somewhat romantic notions concerning the restoration of a golden age in the Chinese countryside (Fei 1986). By the mid-1980s, rural enterprise development had become the focus of sharper study by China's policy-making and academic community. In the late 1980s, foreign studies added some important insights, the most comprehensive being that undertaken by the World Bank (Byrd and Lin 1990). A perspective incorporating social, economic, administrative and spatial issues as they relate to the rural enterprise sector can be found in Vermeer (1992).

The formidable scale of the resource and employment situation deriving from a youthful age structure is illustrated by some figures for the 1978–90 period. While China's total population rose by 181 million (18.8 per cent) Chinese registered labour force went up by 165 million or 41.2 per cent. Significantly, of all China's workforce increase for the period, over two-thirds was accounted for by expansion in the rural labour force (113.72 million). A diversifying agricultural sector has itself been able to absorb less than half of the increment in the rural labour pool (*TJNJ* 1991, pp. 79, 96, 113).

With the state sector unable to greatly expand its traditional urban base, it is these pressures which underlie the spectacular rise of China's rural enterprise sector. There had, of course, been significant growth of rural industries during the Mao era, dating as far back as the Great Leap Forward (1958–59) and boosted in the later stages of the Cultural Revolution. But by the beginning of the reform period, only one-tenth of the rural workforce was employed outside agriculture (Perkins *et al.* 1977; Sigurdson 1977). Initially, during the phase of dissolution of the people's communes, non-farm activities grew within the interstices of the partly formed new rural system. A crucial source of capital was the sharp increase in agricultural procurement prices introduced in 1979: by 1983, purchase prices for principal agricultural products had risen between 50 and 100 per cent, which was reflected in a more than doubling of per capita rural income between 1979 and 1983 (Byrd and Lin 1990, p.51; World Bank 1991, p.4). By 1983, a far greater proportion of farm and sideline production came under local control and could be processed locally. Other fortuitous developments aided the fledgling sector: Wong (1988, p.6) notes that reforms in the key First Ministry of Machine Building meant that peasants could get their hands on production equipment which had previously been confined to the state sector.

Gradually a policy of benign neglect of rural enterprise gave way to more explicitly supportive measures. These included tax holidays, higher tax thresholds, and a range of incentives tailored to sector and region. In the past, rural manufacturing had been restricted to low profit areas such as farm tools; when most restrictions were lifted, lucrative opportunities were opened up such as tobacco processing. By 1984, formal credit facilities had been considerably enlarged, the State Council encouraging rural managers to seek funds from a range of financial institutions (Wong 1988, p.11). But the most crucial innovation came in 1984, when the government sanctioned almost unrestricted private operation of non-agricultural enterprises. This move, identified closely with Zhao Ziyang, represented the reforming regime's most dramatic rejection of Maoist orthodoxy.

Between 1983 and 1986, the number of rural enterprises increased by a factor of ten, to over 15 million (Table 8.4). Some 90 per cent were privately owned, accounting for 43 per cent of the rural non-agricultural workforce. By 1988, the rural enterprise sector employed 95.45 million, representing almost a quarter of the official rural workforce (TJNJ 1991, p.113). Further, in many industrial sectors such as garments and building materials, it now accounted for over half of national output. By the mid-1980s, even one-third of China's massive coal output came from the rural sector (BR 8.6.1987, pp.20–3). For manufacturing, output grew four times faster than in state industry between 1983 and 1987. In economically advanced areas such as Jiangsu, rural industries overtook the state sector in their total contribution to provincial output. By 1987, total value of rural enterprise output exceeded that of China's agricultural sector (FEER 24.3.1988, 2.3.1989). By the end of the 1980s rural enterprises provided up to 25 per cent of China's export earnings (Zweig 1991). It had thus attained a status in the economy of national strategic significance.

The growth of rural enterprises in the 1980s shows considerable regional variation. There is a clear negative relationship between land availability per rural household and level of development of non-agricultural activities in general, and rural industry in particular. Among the coastal provinces, Jiangsu, Zhejiang and Guangdong/Hainan stand out: in 1990 the parts of their agricultural workforce outside crop cultivation are, respectively, 38.5, 34.3 and 32.3 per cent. On the other hand, more inaccessible and mountainous provinces such as Guangxi and Fujian were marked by far lower levels of off-farm employment. Despite both the low ratios of land to rural population and relatively advanced state of development of the inland provinces, few have a well-developed rural enterprise sector. For instance, Hunan, Sichuan and Guizhou stand at far below the national mean in terms of land availability, yet they await significant transfers out of agriculture. Shanxi, with its dispersed coal reserves, is exceptional in having over one-fifth of its rural workforce outside farming. As for the great reaches of China's north-west and borders, here off-farm enterprise has barely made a showing (TJNJ 1991, pp. 312, 338).

Table 8.4 Rural enterprises: number of units and workforce, 1978–90 (selected years)

	Number of units (millions)					Workforce (millions)					
	Total	Township	Village	Private	Industrial only	Total off-farm	As % of all rural	Township	Village	Private	Industrial only
1978	1.5242	0.3197	1.2045	—	0.7940	28.2656	9.2	12.5762	15.6894	—	17.3436
1980	1.4246	0.3374	1.0822	0.0050	0.7578	29.9967	9.4	13.9381	16.0586	—	19.4200
1982	1.3617	0.3379	1.0238	—	0.7492	31.1291[1]	9.2	14.9500	16.7910	—	20.7281
1984	6.0652	0.4015	1.4615	4.2022	4.1822	52.0811	14.5	18.7917	21.0300	12.2594	36.5607
1986	15.1530	0.4255	1.3022	13.4253	6.3550	79.3714	20.9	22.7488	22.6640	33.9586	47.6196
1988	18.8816	0.4235	1.1665	17.2916	7.7352	95.4545	23.8	24.9042	24.0352	46.5151	57.0339
1990	18.5040	0.3878	1.0661	17.0501	7.2200	92.6475	22.1	23.3324	22.5921	46.7230	55.7169

(*Source:* TJNJ 1991, pp. 95, 377.)
Note:
1. Due to entry error, Township and Village enterprise employment numbers exceed total given.

145

Tensions and conflicts in the rural township economy

Conflicting policy measures and unsettling fluctuations in the overall economy during the 1980s prevented the consolidation of a stable environment for the rural enterprise sector. A *laissez-faire* approach to township planning and development brought additional problems which exposed the fragility of small settlements as the prime absorbers of an expanding surplus farm population. Enthusiasts of the township, village and private enterprises (TVPs) emphasize their ability to adapt to a rapidly changing market and utilize a mix of technologies. Many relatively inefficient rural producers were able to thrive due to state industry's lethargy and the confusion caused by the post-1984 'urban reform' movement. Earlier efforts at massive rural industrialization, such as that of the Great Leap, had ended in chaos; even in 1978, a state-inspired push to industrialize the countryside had left a litter of unfinished projects. As the leading agricultural reformer Du Runsheng observed in 1984, the well-known pitfalls were 'rash efforts, duplication of projects, minor units squeezing out major units, and squandering of natural resources'. The lessons were now two-fold: small industries should wherever possible be highly specialized, and linked as component suppliers to large urban units; to avoid extravagant mistakes, rural industry should be developed firmly on the basis of local resources (Du 1989, p. 56).

Regardless of the number of state directives against 'blind development' of TVPs, the sheer volume and pace of their expansion guaranteed a high degree of irrationality and dislocation. The Chinese press of the early 1980s echoed a litany of complaints: they commandeered local raw materials, processed them at high cost, and turned out inferior products. Meanwhile, the more technologically advanced plants in the large cities were denied their inputs and suffered from energy shortages. One analysis claimed that in terms of yuan turnover, the township and village units used 60 per cent more coal, 270 per cent more coke, 105 per cent more gasoline, and 270 per cent more electricity than the average for all industry (Vermeer 1992, p.11). The state from time to time responded by imposing summary injunctions upon certain types of rural manufacturing. These were usually in high value-added or strategic sectors – cigarette manufacture, cotton textiles and processing of steel products being typical.

While state regulation had limited impact, the market was often more effectual in weeding out those units considered weak or undesirable. Even in 1985, when new start-ups were at their peak, almost one TVP in ten was obliged to close due to cash flow, raw material or energy problems; in prime areas such as Zhejiang and Jiangsu, up to 30 per cent of units went bankrupt (*BR* 8.6.1987, p.21; Furusawa 1990, p.12). These difficulties did stimulate some effort to rationalize and technically upgrade the rural enterprise sector. Late 1985 saw the introduction of the Science and Technology Commission's Spark Plan (*xinghuo jihua*), its object being the improvement of expertise in rural activities ranging from agriculture to township management. The publicity surrounding this initiative served to highlight the extremely low level of skills: it was found that on average there was one technically qualified person for every 160 rural enterprises (*CD* 14.5.1987). Despite the glowing progress reports on the Spark Plan, clearly its resources were lacking and its impact limited to a few model cases.

It was the economic downturn of late 1988, followed by the intense political struggles of the post-Tiananmen period, which brought the conflicts within the TVP sector into sharper focus. Of enterprises in the manufacturing sector, a high proportion produced light industrial goods which could no longer find an urban market. Public praise of TVPs was replaced by a catalogue of criticism and failure. Some estimates put the number who lost their jobs in 1989 alone at 5 million (Vermeer 1992, p.11); start-ups gave a net reduction in the TVP workforce of 3 million in 1989–90 (*TJNJ* 1991, p.377). At the same time, the urban state labour force was also enduring severe cutbacks, the total estimated at 7 million. More crucial for the rural non-agricultural employment sector was the fact that, of the 30 million peasants engaged in temporary or contract work in urban China in 1989, one-third was forced out by the retrenchment (*JJRB* 5.2.1990). Yet at a time when the number of under- or unemployed rural labourers was put at over 150 million, official advice to both redundant rural enterprise workers and sacked migrant labour in the cities was to return to agricultural production (*CD*9.1.1990). In some areas, the authorities attempted to mobilize returnees in public works such as water conservancy, road building and tree planting. Elsewhere, county labour administrations set up labour export agreements with areas less afflicted by over-population. But with both the apparatus and the will for collective rural mobilization now largely absent, such schemes could only scratch the surface.

Those around Zhao Ziyang had long been vocal advocates of TVP expansion. They were now accused of 'rampant exaggeration' of rural enterprises' place in China's development strategy (RMRB 27.10.1989). Opponents of further market liberalization considered it essential to reconsolidate central planning, without which the CPC's continued hegemony would be in doubt. As a matter of priority, the rural enterprise sector had to be reined in, and the principal means of so doing was to be economic rather than political. From 1981 to 1987, the average annual expansion of credit to the TVPs by the Agricultural Bank and the rural credit cooperatives was around 40 per cent. In 1988, this rate was halved; by March 1989, the Agricultural Bank announced plans to reduce lending to rural enterprises by over 50 per cent (*FEER* 2.3.1989; 2.10.1989). No area of the country was exempt. Even Jiangsu, with its importance as a TVP foreign exchange earner, was instructed by the Minister of Agriculture to raise further capital from the enterprises' employees – through pay cuts or enforced sale of bonds (*FEER* 14.9.1989; *BR* 22.1.1990, pp. 28–9). The attitude towards TVPs is evident from the remarks of a vice-premier who advanced the classic criticisms: '. . . they vie with large enterprises for raw material and energy, seriously pollute the environment, and consume a lot of resources yet produce low quality products' (*BR* 4.1.1990, p. 19).

Again, such views were heard at a key national conference on rural enterprises in early 1990: TVPs were charged with both ideological impurity and a disdainful attitude to the agricultural sector which had bred them. Furusawa (1990, pp. 13–14) suggests that this accusation has some basis.

In spite of the harsher political climate for TVPs, the reality facing the CPC leadership remained one of unrelieved pressure on land resources and a vast pool of potentially surplus rural labour. A year after the Tiananmen debacle, more moderate attitudes began to reassert themselves. Rural enterprises were considered capable of an important role provided that rationalization and partial integration into the central planning system occurred (*BR* 14.5.1990, p. 19). To mark their rehabilitation, in early 1990 a Rural Industry Association was founded, with long-time advocates as well as sceptics (such as the Minister of Agriculture) as its official backers. The declared intention was to single out the most efficient enterprises for credit support – those processing local raw materials, producing export goods, and sub-contracting to large factories. Polluting industries were to be specifically excluded (Christiansen 1992, p. 33). Later in 1990, the 'Regulations for Rural Collective Enterprises in the PRC' reasserted the validity of TVPs; but henceforth there had to be a rationalization towards economies of scale, environmental control and 'local recentralization'. Significantly, the new laws asserted that TVP property rights were to be guaranteed, as was their access to energy and raw materials, and a specific part of after-tax profits (Furusawa 1990, p. 14; Schädler 1992, 165. Pragmatic compromise had once again triumphed. But the underlying contradictions of the TVP sector, especially that part engaged in industrial processes, had only been temporarily relieved.

Economic and technical rationalization of TVPs has always been a stated policy, and never more so than in the period after the 1988–90 crisis. Even in Wuxi's suburban factories – a model for rural enterprises nationwide – seven out of ten products were deemed sub-standard. Imperfect market knowledge and local rivalry also meant much wasteful duplication: seven separate township-owned plants within Wuxi county specialized in the rolling of steel, and no fewer than 16 enterprises in the aluminium extrusion and processing sector. Most proved unable to sustain operations at full capacity, their continued existence due only to the web of special relationships and favours giving access to scarce inputs and protected markets (Byrd and Lin 1990, pp. 239–41).

Long-term trends in overall efficiency and profitability of the rural enterprise sector provide further evidence of the fragility of the small towns urbanization strategy. Labour productivity had indeed risen throughout the 1980s, but other key indicators provided a less happy picture. Between 1978 and 1990, there were large reductions in profits against fixed assets, new capital and turnover (*TJNJ* 1991, 379). A major cause was debt burden, with increased competition from a more efficient state sector also a consideration.

Many Chinese specialists engaged in the on-going debate on appropriate urbanization strategy oppose the further reliance upon the rural TVP sector. Their first recourse in support of this position is to data on economic performance and urban scale (Table 8.5). A less extreme position holds that the success of rural industries over the long term rests on their ability to integrate with larger and more advanced enterprises located in the cities. This option is constrained by communications, and is generally limited to the areas around major cities. Taubmann's investigations in Wujiang county, Jiangsu, indicate that linkage through sub-contracting arrangements is one key to success (Taubmann 1992, p. 276). The implications for less developed areas, especially those of western China, are obvious. This has led to suggestions by Chinese specialists that the rural industries/small towns approach should be geographically differentiated, with areas of high urbanization and high population density (typically, Beijing-Tianjin, the Pearl River and Yangzi deltas) basically relying upon it. In regions with a less developed urban network – essentially the inland and mid-western provinces – surplus labour may be a serious problem: it should be absorbed by medium, and even large-sized cities. As for the remoter peripheries, here further economic development must be awaited before a strategy is clarified (Middelhoek 1992, p. 251).

Table 8.5 Some per capita urban scale economy indicators, 467 municipalities (1990)

	Size class of municipality (*shi*) (millions)				
	over 2.0	1.0–2.0	0.5–1.0	0.2–0.5	under 0.2
Gross product (yuan per capita)	5113	3856	3949	2751	1600
Gross income (yuan per capita)	3733	2934	3125	2239	1384
Labour prod.rate (yuan per capita)	8434	6331	6600	4932	3113

(*Source: TJNJ* 1991, p. 656.)

Notes:
1. Gross product per capita – on revised Chinese basis, approximating to GDP (*guo nei shengchan zongzhi*).
2. Gross income per capita – newly added value in given period (*guomin shouru*).
For full description of these standard categories, see *TJNJ*, p. 72

Problems of rural settlement development

As a strategy, the revitalization of China's small towns has generally received the unqualified support of outside observers (Tan 1986; Lee 1989). However, in addition to the key issue of economic and employment viability, there are indications of grave problems regarding the physical planning, infrastructure and overall management of the burgeoning rural township sector. With the loosening of migration controls, an urbanization policy based on the lowest tier of settlements must create an environment which can compete with the larger centres, thus dimming their bright lights. In a situation of frenetic industrial expansion, regulation of the potential threat to the fragile rural ecosystem is also a clear requirement.

Reports suggest that the expansion and diversification of economic activities in small towns present difficulties for which there is currently an inadequate managerial and technical response. The planning and provision of sewerage, road construction, educational and cultural services, and housing is as haphazard as it is varied from town to town. Financial arrangements for non-productive developments have been *ad hoc*: Beijing has always taken the view that while it is prepared to provide incentives for enterprise development, finance for rural township governmental functions must be locally generated. Apart from the obvious logistical obstacles, the central government's endemic state budget deficit is the decisive factor here.

There are many well-advertised cases in which private entrepreneurs have shared the costs of township construction (Zong 1988, p. 21). The formal position with regard to the raising of public revenues for this purpose was set out in the 1985 *Urban Construction and Maintenance Tax Regulations*: enterprises in designated and non-designated towns should pay, respectively, 5 and 1 per cent of profits to the local authority, this to be used exclusively for public utilities and development. But the misuse of such funds, or their purloining by county authorities, is widespread (Middelhoek 1992, pp. 256–7). Local authorities are often tempted to reinvest tax revenues in the enterprises which they own and control (Byrd and Lin 1990, pp. 342–87). 'First production, then livelihood' (*xian shengchan hou shenghuo*) still lives on from Maoist days, but now for different reasons. Many small town governments, in their quest for self-aggrandisement, have squandered large sums which could otherwise have been used for various public facilities. They boast extravagant public edifices – theatres, large department stores and the all important multi-storey hotel in which to accommodate visiting dignitaries and members of the new entrepreneurial class. But beyond the main street, reliable water supply, sewerage and any sense of planned layout are absent.

As for direction of overall planning, it is the sheer scale of developments which impedes action by central ministries and provincial bureaux. With almost 12 000 *zhen*, 2000 county towns, and over 44 000 *xiang* seats, the resource and skills implications are dire, and cannot be met by the present under-resourced planning bodies set up by provinces and municipalities (*CD* 25.2.1987). Nationwide, fewer than half of *zhen* and *xiang* administrations had personnel specifically responsible for overseeing general urban development (Middelhoek 1992, p. 255).

Pollution, land loss and energy misuse are also factors which jeopardize the success of the small towns' urbanization strategy. The many directives of the State Land Administration and the National Environmental Protection Agency have little impact at the grassroots. Often the most productive land has been lost to the new enterprises which extend ribbon-like along rural highways (*CD* 13.12.1985; *JJDL* Vol. 9, No. 3, 1989, p. 195). Prompted by the exceptionally large land losses which followed the legalization of private enterprise, in 1987 the State Land Administration introduced a modest levy on land taken out of agricultural use. Further, by 1988, some three-quarters of all counties, municipalities and prefectures had set up agencies to deal with the 'illegal occupation' of farmland. In spite of these regulatory efforts, it is clear from national land loss figures that the problem did not diminish.

An array of national and local environmental protection legislation, including the revised statute of 1989, has had little impact due to inadequate monitoring and enforcement. According to a 1986 survey of townships, fewer than one-third had any means of coping with industrial wastes. In five counties of Jiangsu known for their development of industries, only 10 per cent of the waste water from 80 000 industrial units was treated in any way. The rudimentary efforts to tackle China's environmental problems were almost all directed to the more intrusive problems of the large cities (CD 7.1.1987). Indeed, their problems are frequently solved at the expense of the rural centres, through the 'export' of dirty processes. Khakee (1989 p. 257) reported that 40 per cent of the 6000 enterprises in the suburban counties of Shanghai manifest severe pollution problems.

Finally, from 1988 on, the news media regularly highlighted a phenomenon which had not been seen since the immediate post-liberation period. Between 50 and 80 million people were said to have left their native places and to be wandering the land. This new development caused considerable alarm, and the designers of the 1990 census were instructed to attempt to capture its true scale. While the greater part was concealed within the countryside (for example, mass rural–rural migration to the Pearl River Delta or Hainan), on occasions it erupted in the great cities. In a single month in early 1990, for example, 1 million migrants descended on Guangzhou (Hong Kong Monitor, June 1990, p. 12). A good part of this wandering population may consist of peasants exercising their new found rights to travel the country on private trading missions. But it is doubtless the inability of the TVP sector to provide employment opportunities in sufficient numbers which is the underlying cause.

China already faces, in the early 1990s, an enormous task in absorbing the existing surplus rural population. The crisis of 1988–90 exposed the limitations of the TVP sector, and the potentially massive shortfall in the employment base. Serious deficiencies in physical planning, infrastructure and environmental regulation add drastically to the overall constraints upon an urbanization strategy which seeks to further expand the sub-municipal rural settlements by absorbing hundreds of millions in the coming years.

Afterword

Tens of millions of China's villagers have made the transition to a new life in the rural-based enterprise sector. A significant part of national productive capacity is now provided by township and village industry;

further, state authorities at various levels have been relieved of the costs of redeployment and redundancy. China's 'rural urbanization' strategy has in these respects been extraordinarily successful. None the less, experience has shown that economic, social and environmental contradictions present a serious threat to the continued viability of this 'Chinese road' to urbanization. If official rural surplus labour projections are anywhere near accurate, a huge measure of state intervention and regulation will be demanded to sustain the current path.

This fact has driven analysts to seek alternatives to the urbanization strategy developed in the 1980s. Transmigration to less densely populated regions is one option: past experience has proved, however, that it is prohibitively costly, and politically unenforceable on the scale required. A more extreme option would be to coalesce the surplus rural propulation into urban agglomerations. Lai (1987) suggests that the most suitable size of settlement would be in the 0.5–1 million range, reaping all the economic advantages of the million cities but fewer of their problems of congestion and pollution. Others seek a far more radical concentration. In a wide-ranging futurological essay, an analyst at the Academy of Social Sciences considered the implications of agricultural mechanization upon farm labour. If in five decades time, China's population peaks at 1.5 billion, and agricultural productivity could be raised to just half the present levels of Canada or Australia, the number of persons supported by the labour of one agricultural worker would rise from the present 3.8 to 25. In this scenario, China would require only 60 million agricultural labourers.

The result of redeploying the very large numbers of surplus labourers in expanded rural townships would be a loss of cropland equivalent to one-quarter of the present stock. Without fundamental reform of the rural enterprise sector, its economy would remain highly unstable, with environmental problems ever more serious. The only solution lies in a strategy of super-agglomeration. In a population of 1.5 billion in AD 2040, two-thirds would be concentrated in several hundred large, medium and small cities, straddling eastern, southern and north-eastern China in contiguous linear belts (Zhang 1989).

Currently such radical scenarios remain marginalized, the government asserting the small and intermediate settlements solution as the only appropriate response to the nation's urbanisation conundrum. The achievements in terms of surplus labour absorption and development of the off-farm sector are, to date, undeniably impressive. Yet enthusiasts should be reminded that the starting point was the 'vacuum' created by the Mao years. Such conditions cannot be reproduced. But China is poised on the brink of a historic transformation to a post-agrarian society. This demands a new vision, and the articulation of urbanization strategies which are sensitive both regionally and temporally, yet on the grand scale.

References

Byrd W and **Lin Qingsong** (eds) (1990) *China's rural industry – structure, development and reform*, Oxford University Press (for the World Bank),

Oxford.

Christiansen F (1990) 'Social division and peasant mobility in mainland China: the implications of the hu'kou system', *Issues and Studies* **26**, 23–42.

Christiansen F (1992) 'Stability first: Chinese rural policy issues, 1987–1990', in Vermeer *From peasant to entrepreneur: growth and change in rural China*, Pudoc, Wageningen, (ed.). pp. 21–40.

Civil Affairs Ministry (1989) *Zhonghua Renmin Gongheguo xingzheng quhua jiance (The Administrative divisions of the People's Republic of China)*, Surveying and Mapping Publishers, Beijing.

Deng Yiming (1988) 'Shilun woguo bu fada diqu nongye laodongli de zhuanyi' ('The question of transfer of rural labour in less developed regions of China'), *Zhongguo renkou kexue (Population Science of China)* **3**, 35–6.

Du Runsheng (1989) *China's Rural Economic Reform*, Foreign Languages Press, Beijing.

Fei Xiaotong (ed.) (1986) *Small Towns in China – Functions, Problems and Prospects*, New World Press, Beijing.

Furusawa K (1990) 'Rural enterprises under reevaluation', *JETRO China Newsletter* **88**, 10–15.

Guo Hancheng, Wu Dengru and **Zhu Hongxiang** (1989) 'Land restoration in China', *Journal of Applied Ecology* **26**, 787–92.

Han Chunru (1989), 'Recent changes in the rural environment in China', *Journal of Applied Ecology* **26**, 803–12.

Hinton W (1991) *The Privatization of China: the great reversal*, Earthscan, London.

Khakee A (1989) 'China's thrust toward rapid urbanization', *Finisterra* **48**, 279–90.

Kim Won Bae (1991) 'The role and structure of metropolises in China's urban economy', *Third World Planning Review* **13**(2) 155–78.

Kirkby R (1985) *Urbanisation in China: town and country in a developing economy 1949–2000 AD*, Croom Helm/Columbia University Press, London and New York.

Lai Zengmu (1987) 'Economic benefits of urban agglomeration and institutional reform in China', *CCPR* **3**(3), 1–8.

Lee Y F (1989) 'Small towns and China's urbanization level', *China Quarterly* **120**, 771–87.

Liu Ming *et al.* (1989) 'Gengdi jianshao shi ge bu rong hushi de yanzhong wenti' ['Farmland loss is a serious problem which it is not easy to overlook'], *Jingji dili (Economic Geography)* **9**(3), 194–9.

Ma J C and **Cui Gonghao** (1987) 'Administrative changes and urban population in China', *Annals of the Association of American Geographers* **77**(3) 373–95.

Ma J C and **Noble A G** (1986) 'Chinese cities: a research agenda', *Urban Geography* **7**(4) 279–90.

Ma Xia (1987) 'Dangdai Zhongguo nongcun renkou xiang chengzhen de da qianyi' ('Large scale movement of the rural population to the small towns in contemporary China'), *Zhongguo renkou kexue (Population Science of China)* **3**, 7–8.

Ma Xia and Wang Weizhi (1989) 'A study of population movement and urbanization of China's towns and cities', *China City Planning Review* 5(2), 48–63.

Middelhoek J (1989) 'Spatial aspects of absorbing China's rural labour surplus – policy outlines and a case study', *China Information* III(4) 36–55.

Middelhoek J (1992) 'Recent development of small towns in China', in Vermeer (ed.). *From peasant to entrepreneur: growth and change in rural China* Pudoc, Wageningen, pp. 241–72.

Ministry of Construction, Urban Planning Division (1990) *Zhonghua Renmin Gongheguo chengshi guihua fa: jieshuo (Urban Planning Law of the People's Republic of China: commentary*, Masses Publishers, Beijing.

Ministry of Public Security (Third Bureau) (1985) *Zhongguo chengzhen renkou ziliao shouce (Handbook of China's urban population)*, Cartographic Publishers, Beijing.

Pannell C (1986) 'Recent increase in Chinese urbanization', *Urban Geography* 7 (4), 291–310.

Peng Qing (1990) 'Xianxing sheshi biaozhun de pingjia yu jianyi' ('Proposals regarding the currently applicable criteria for designated municipalities'), *Jingji dili (Economic Geography)* 4, 7–10.

Perkins D et al. (1977) *Rural small-scale Industry in the People's Republic of China*, University of California Press, Berkeley.

Qiao Shaochun and Li Jingwu (1991) 'Dui disici renkou pucha shizhen renkou huafen koujing de tantao' ('An exploration of the urban population criteria of the 4th census'), *Renkou yanjiu (Population Research)* 3, 22–8.

RKNJ *Zhongguo renkou tongji nianjian – Yearbook of Population Statistics*, published annually by the Division of Population Statistics, State Statistical Bureau (Science and Technology Documentary Publishers, Beijing).

Schädler M (1992) 'Rural non-agricultural activities in the period of stagnation and prospects for further development', in Vermeer (ed.). *From peasant to entrepreneur: growth and change in rural China*, Pudoc Wageningen, pp. 157–68.

Sigurdson J (1977) *Rural Industrialization in China*, Harvard University Press, Cambridge, Mass.

Tan K C (1986) 'Small towns in Chinese urbanization', *Geographical Review* 76 (3) 265–75.

Taubmann W (1992) 'The growth of rural towns in China's urban regions', in Vermeer (ed.). *From peasant to entrepreneur: growth and change in rural China*, Pudoc, Wageningen, pp. 273–91.

Taylor J (1988) 'Rural employment trends and the legacy of surplus labour, 1978–86', *China Quarterly* 116, 736–66.

TJNJ *Zhongguo tongji nianjian – Statistical Yearbook of China*, published annually by the State Statistical Bureau of China (China Statistical Publishers, Beijing).

Vermeer E (ed.) (1992) *From peasant to entrepreneur: growth and change in rural China*, Pudoc, Wageningen.

Wong C (1988) 'Interpreting rural industrial growth in the post-Mao period', *Modern China* **14** (1), 3–30.

World Bank (1991) *China: options for reform in the grain sector*, World Bank, Washington.

Yeh A G-O and **Xu Xueqiang** (1989) City system development in China 1953–86, Working Paper No 41, Centre for Urban Studies and Urban Planning, University of Hong Kong.

Zhang Jianxiong (1989) 'Lun wo guo de shengtai huanjing zhanlue he chengshihua daolu' ('on China's ecological and environmental strategy, and path to urbanisation'), *Guanli shijie (Administration World)* **2**, 4–26.

Zhou Yixing and **Shi Yulong** (1991) on China's urban population, *China City Planning Review* **7** (3), 12–19.

Zong Lin (1988) 'On scale, structure and development strategy', *CCPR* **4** (4), 13–21.

Zou Deci (1990) Guanyu bashi niandai Zhongguo chengshi guihua de huigu he dui jiushi niandai de tantao (A review of China's urban planning in the 1980s and a probe forward into the 1990s), Working Paper, China Academy of Urban Planning and Design, Beijing.

Zweig D (1991) 'Internationalizing China's countryside: the political economy of exports from rural industry', *China Quarterly* **128**, 716–41.

Journals and newspapers

Published in China:	*BR*	*Beijing Review*
	CD	*China Daily*
	CCPR	*China City Planning Review*
	JJRB	*Jingji ribao – Economy Daily*
	JJDL	*Jingji dili – Economic Geography*
	LW	*Liaowang – Outlook*
	RMRB	*Renmin ribao – People's Daily*
Published outside China:	*FEER*	*Far Eastern Economic Review*

CHAPTER 9

China's environment: problems and prospects

Richard Louis Edmonds

China experiences virtually every type of environmental degradation and the situation is worsening. As a poor and populous country undergoing rapid economic changes China's environment is facing a double threat. On the one hand, problems commonly found in an underdeveloped agricultural society such as soil erosion, deforestation and desertification are becoming increasingly critical; on the other, industrial growth has led to severe pollution. Recent analysis suggests that China can support 950 million people at a good standard of living based on the country's land resources, a figure already exceeded by about 200 million.*Predictions are that population will peak at 1500 million or 1600 million between AD 2020 and 2030 if strict population controls are enforced (Zhongguo Kexue Bao She, 1989, pp. 9, 17). If China pushes its resource base to the limit it is thought that the country can feed and keep warm 1500 million to 1600 million people at a low standard of living. Without stringent population control measures China could well reach this theoretical saturation point prior to AD 2015.

The per capita level of natural resources is already quite low. China's per capita levels of land, forest cover and water resources are only 36 per cent, 13 per cent and 25 per cent, respectively, of the estimated world per capita levels (Wang X *et al*. 1989, p. 1). Cropland accounts for only 10 per cent of China's total area and both the per capita level and the total quantity of arable land is decreasing. As of 1991, it is estimated that arable land is being reduced by approximately 366 666 hectares per annum (Chen 1991, p. 4). Even though the pace of arable area reduction appears to be slowing down, the population to arable land ratio is likely to rise at a faster rate than the world average for some time to come.

There are also problems of insufficient energy and mineral resources.

---

*This analysis was undertaken under the auspices of the State Science and Technology Commission and the State Natural Science Foundation Commission.

China's reserves of coal are less than half of the world average in terms of immediately exploitable coal reserves on a per capita basis. Oil and natural gas are even less and while there is hydroelectric potential, it is generally found far away from population centres. Moreover, the country's fuel conversion efficiency is quite low at 28 per cent when compared with levels such as 40 to 55 per cent in North America and 60 per cent in Japan. Even India is 1.8 times more energy efficient in terms of the ratio of GDP to energy use (Lees 1991, p. 5).

Poverty and the lack of education among the peasant population contribute directly to China's environmental problems. Half of China's counties still do not have rural extension services. Combined with high illiteracy rates the lack of extension services means that it is difficult to disseminate ecologically sound techniques.

In mainland China, environmental policy was reborn out of the ashes of the Cultural Revolution around 1972. From 1980 heavy industry, manufacturing and infrastructural projects have had environmental impact statements written for them. In a centrally planned totalitarian system, however, such impact statements did not necessarily stop pet projects. Degradation in the countryside increased in percentage during the early 1980s as many of the rural reforms encouraged practices which were not of a sustainable nature. Although the full Environmental Protection Law was adopted in 1989, China has yet to implement efficiently all its environmental policies. Policy decisions are slowed by attempts on the part of the central government to produce a consensus among various factions. The uneven distribution of natural resources and population further complicates attempts to formulate policies at the national level.

The purpose of this chapter will be to review the various types of environmental degradation found in China and to evaluate the country's environmental prospects for the coming decades.

Resource degradation

Water shortages

China is feeding 22 per cent of the world's population with 8 per cent of the world's water resources. Many rivers, lakes and reservoirs are shrinking and in some cases have even dried up in the last two decades. China has not been able to expand its irrigated area since the beginning of the 1980s owing to a shortage of water. The ground water table in north China has been decreasing and funnels extending thousands of square kilometres at the earth's surface now exist. Lowering of the water table around pumping centres has reached levels of 10 to 70 metres below that of the 1950s (Han 1989, p. 806). Cities such as Shanghai and Tianjin face serious subsidence problems. By AD 2000, China could be short of water anywhere from 48 000 million to 106 000 million m^3 per annum.

The water supply problem is most extreme in north China around big cities where major efforts to recycle and to save water really only began in the 1980s. Many water diversion projects were also completed. More local projects are planned for the 1990s. The large-scale answer to water shortages on the north China plain is major inter-basin water transfer from south China to the north via the Grand Canal. It is possible that waters from the Chang (Yangtze) River may be pumped to the banks of the Huang (Yellow) River by AD 2000. The water shortage problem in north China could get worse before many of these projects are completed. Water shortage problems are also increasing in south China and even on the Qinghai-Tibetan Plateau.

No matter what public works solutions the Chinese attempt to solve their water problems, basic essential measures include conservation of existing water resources. The shortage problem is compounded by inefficiency of water use in agriculture and industry. Water quotas have already been applied to industries which have resulted in some savings. Increased recycling of wastewater in industry will help.

One method in use in Beijing since 1988 has been a policy of rewarding savers and fining units which do not make good use of water. While the Chinese suggest that such a policy has been effective, better results could be achieved by metering all users and raising the cost for water. In 1991 the Chinese planned to more than double the charge for irrigation water and to suspend supply to users who refuse to pay.

Household use has so far not been very wasteful. However, public facilities have been extremely wasteful with an estimated 20 million tonnes of water leaking annually from toilets and public washing facilities in Beijing alone (Ling and Bai 1990, p. 14). As more people move from traditional housing into modern plumbed homes water consumption will increase.

Vegetation loss

Although many suggest that a figure of 8 or 9 per cent is more accurate (Wang X et al. 1989, p. 1), official statistics indicate that China has forest cover equal to 12.98 per cent of the country's total area (Guojia Tongjiju 1991, p. 4). In any case, China is far below the world average forest cover of 31 per cent and vegetation cover has generally been decreasing since 1949. Although one planning report suggests that usable grassland will increase by up to 50 per cent in AD 2000 (Zhongguo Kexue Bao She 1989, pp. 18, 20), the per capita amount of grassland over the same period will decrease. Yet, it is hard to imagine any increase in usable grassland since degradation of grassland is continuing at a rate of over 1.3 million hectares per year.

Afforestation efforts since the 1950s have not been very successful and overall survival rates still average no more than 30 to 40 per cent. In primary non-production forests management is still only token and what natural forests remain today have been saved largely by inaccessibility. Forestry responsibility systems, which arose in the early 1980s, are crucial for the success of afforestation and have been quite complex with individuals or households contracting either for individual activities or for management of a portion of forest. Over 30 million hectares of mountainous land were reportedly allocated for forest management on 30 to 50-year renewable leases as of mid-1986 (Richardson 1990, p. 98). The Chinese have been quick to point out examples where the system has led to increased incomes. However, it is too early to say if contract and semi-privatization policies have been successful.

In 1986 the Basic Forest Law was ratified. However, such basic laws still read much like wish lists with the actual concrete regulations a matter of speculation. In recent years planned cutting levels have been 40 million m^3 while the actual cutting levels appear to have been five times more (Wang X *et al.* 1989, p. 1). In some remote areas lack of state control rules out enforcement of laws. Illegal logging activities have been widespread, even with government organizations involved. Estimates suggest that illegal felling, fire, and disease loss accounted for 100 million m^3 of wood per annum during the 1980s (Richardson 1990, pp. 104–5).

In poorer areas of the country, there is likely to continue to be a considerable amount of illegal cutting by peasants, especially as the market economy makes it easy to sell timber. The state wood supply system has been excessively wasteful due to a lack of realistic pricing mechanisms. However, higher prices for timber, retention of earnings, tax exemptions and encouragement of mergers with commercial organizations have appeared since the mid-1980s.

The continued opening of new lands for agriculture is another cause of deforestation. The Chinese say that as of 1982, one-third of the cultivated steep slopes had been taken out of cultivation, but in 1986 slopes which should not be cultivated still totalled 8 million hectares and the pace of conversion of slope lands out of agriculture was slowing down (*Zhongguo linye nianjian* 1987, pp. 123–4).

Major afforestation programmes now under way include the Obligatory Tree Planting Programme, the Great Plains Project, the Greening of the Taihang Mountains Project, the Three Norths Shelter Project, and the Coastal Protective Forest Project. A new shelter belt project of 20 million hectares along the middle and upper reaches of the Chang River was in full operation in 145 counties by the end of 1990 but is not due to be completed until AD 2030 (*China Today*, August 1990, p. 5).

The Three Norths Shelter project (*sanbei fanghulin*) which began in 1978 is the major project for north China. This 200 000 km^2 shelter belt is a mammoth undertaking which includes small tree belts, shrub plantings, grasslands, fuelwood forests, timber forest and plantations of 'economic' trees. Halting soil erosion in Shaanxi, slowing of desertification in eastern Inner Mongolia and protection of Beijing appear to have been the major goals. The second phase is due to be completed in 1996. Hopefully, this phase will increase vegetation cover in the area from 5.9 per cent to 7.7 per cent in 466 county-level administrative units. Initial reports of the Three Norths project are optimistic. However, it will be necessary to wait for several decades to judge just how successful this project has been.

The Obligatory Tree Planting Programme, adopted in 1981, requires all Chinese citizens above 11 years old to plant three to five trees each year or do other relevant afforestation work. Most Chinese cities show the benefits of urban tree planting programmes, many of which are obligatory.

China hopes current reforestation efforts will make the country self-sufficient in timber by AD 2040 (Richardson 1990, pp. 99, 111). The current plan is to increase forested areas by 20 per cent or to create 66 million hectares of new forest in China by 2000. If this plan is successful, China will be able to supply only two-thirds of its own wood demands by AD 2000. However, the country could be out of wood by AD 2000 if its forests continue to be depleted at the same rate as occurred during the 1980s (Zhongguo Kexueyuan Shengtaihuanjing Yanjiu Zhongxin 1989, p. 17).

Soil quality and salinization/alkalization

The soil nutritional base upon which Chinese agricultural development is to take place is not strong. The organic matter content of soil averages less than 1.5 per cent. It has been estimated that if China adds no fertilizer to its soils, nitrogen will be exhausted in 20 to 40 years, phosphorus in 10 to 20 years and potassium in 80 to 130 years (Zhao 1990, p. 155).

Moreover, the second national soil survey found that overall soil fertility is dropping. In some cases the drop in soil fertility has been accompanied by severe secondary salinization and waterlogging. In part the drop in fertility is due to reductions of fallow times. The increase in triple cropping and rice monoculture on paddy soils since the 1950s combined with poor drainage systems has led to gleization or the formation of 'secondary gleyed' paddy soils. Gleization lowers the growth potential in the paddy. Approximately one-sixth of China's paddy lands suffers from secondary gleization. Although the soils north of the Qin Ling range are generally alkaline, the majority of soils in the populous south-east are acidic with one-third of the total agriculture land in the south having a pH value below 5 which renders the crops susceptible to acid pollution.

Although China has improved an estimated 4 million hectares of salinized/alkalized land since 1949, problems of salinization and alkalization due to inefficient and excessive irrigation have increased. Various estimates indicate that the amount of salinized cropland throughout China is nearly one-fifth of all of China's irrigated cropland. Half the land once cultivated in the Hetao region of Inner Mongolia, one-third of the land in the Ningxia irrigated region, and about one-third of the cultivated land in Xinjiang have been abandoned since 1949 due to salinization or alkalization (Qu 1986, p. 3).

Beside salinization and alkalization of the topsoil, over-pumping of ground water in coastal areas has led to salinization of ground water. In Shandong this has affected ground water in an area of nearly 1000 km^2 since 1975 (Zhongguo Kexueyuan Shengtaihuanjing Yanjiu Zhongxin 1989, p. 10).

Soil erosion

China has one of the most serious soil erosion problems in the world. Different Chinese sources state that between one-sixth and one-third of the nation's arable land is seriously affected by soil erosion (Table 9.1).

Annual soil losses are estimated at between 5000 and 10 000 million tonne with a loss of fertility equal to about 40 million tonnes of chemical fertilizers, close to China's annual fertilizer production (Wang X *et al*. 1989, preface p. 2). These figures for the late 1980s represent a 30 per cent increase on the area affected in the 1950s (Han 1989, p. 804). Although such figures can be debated, there is little doubt that one of the most serious degradation problems which China faces is soil erosion. The urgent question this raises is whether China's topsoil will be so depleted as to cause severe food shortages in the near future.

The most severe erosion occurs on the semi-arid Loess Plateau which is reportedly losing one centimetre of topsoil per annum. Sediment yields on the Plateau above Sanmenxia are said to have increased by 32.9 per cent between the early 1950s and the early 1980s (Chen and Jing 1983, p. 1).

Between 1957 and 1986 the area in the Chang River valley affected by soil erosion more than doubled (Chang 1990, p. 5). In Sichuan erosion is now four times what it was in the 1950s. There has been serious soil erosion in recent years in areas of the far south where there formerly was little erosion as in Yunnan, Hainan and Fujian. In the far north the Nonni (Nen) River Plain of Heilongjiang and extreme eastern Inner Mongolia have soil erosion problems existing on over half of the cultivated land with one-quarter of the cultivated area so seriously eroded that over half of the thick black soil layer was washed away by the 1980s.

Rapid soil erosion has contributed to China's overall environmental degradation in several ways. The loss of good quality topsoil has reduced arable land. Siltation of river beds, lakes and reservoirs has reduced their flood control, hydroelectric capacity and storage capacity. China has made considerable efforts to stem the flow of topsoil. Over half of the eroded land which has been improved since the mid-1950s has been afforested with almost another one-fifth terraced. There are plans to improve 3400 eroded small basins (Guo *et al.* 1989, p. 790). Methods of erosion improvement have shifted from a plot-by-plot basis to a more systemic basin-by-basin approach. Both mechanical engineering solutions and vegetation solutions have been employed – often together. The problem with soil erosion control is the massive scale of the effort required. Despite claims of improving eroded land and the building of 30 000 check dams, the area suffering from soil erosion has increased between 1950 and the 1980s (Table 9.1). As the problem is being addressed in one area the pace of erosion is picking up in other places.

Control of soil erosion will require regulations keeping farmers off steep slopes as well as introducing new farming conservation techniques. The 1985 State Council document 'Ten Policy Points for Progress to Enlivening the Agricultural Economy' noted that: 'Cultivated land in mountainous districts with slopes over twenty-five degrees will have to be planned to be progressively taken out of cultivation and returned to forests or to animal husbandry, in order to derive maximum benefit from the land. If this results in a lack of food, the state will sell it or supply it on credit' (*Zhongguo linye nianjian* 1987, p. 123). Policies employed to get farming off the slope lands and to replace it with privately managed forests or herding centre around the contract responsibility system. However, the areas in which

161

Table 9.1 Eroded and rectified areas in China

Category	Area (km²)	Percentage
All China in 1950	1 160 000	12.1
All China in mid-1980s (estimate)	1 603 150	16.7
All China 1990 official (estimate)	1 500 000	15.6
Minor erosion (mid-1980s)	803 970	8.4
Largely caused by soil movement (mid-1980s)	259 680	2.7
Light erosion (mid-1980s)	689 150	7.2
Moderate erosion (mid-1980s)	318 750	3.3
Moderately heavy erosion (mid-1980s)	187 770	2.0
Heavy erosion (mid-1980s)	75 950	0.8
Extremely heavy erosion (mid-1980s)	61 390	0.6
Excessively heavy erosion (mid-1980s)	10 460	0.1
Rectified Areas		
Area 'controlled' by conservation 1955–90	530 000	5.5
Area 'controlled' on Loess Plateau 1955–85	75 000	0.8
Area expected to be 'controlled' by 2000	660 000	6.9

(*Sources*: Zhao 1990, p. 156: Guo *et al*. 1989. p. 790; Zhongguo Kexueyuan Shengtaihuanjing Yanjiu Zhongxin 1989, pp. 12–13.)

the policy needs to be carried out are generally poor, peripheral and difficult for the local government to supply with cheap good grain. The peasants can neither afford the risks nor tide themselves over during the transition from agriculture to forestry or herding.

International involvement in soil erosion control in China is increasing. Work has included terracing and the construction of check dams while grain subsidies are given to peasants. Whether such efforts can produce long-term results remains to be seen.

Desertification

Chinese scientists estimate from aerial photographs that between 1975 and 1986, 2100 km² of 'desertified land' were created each year which represents an increase over the pace of desertification between 1958 and 1975.* By 1991 the State Council felt that desertification, particularly in the zone where pastoralism and agriculture meet in north China, was serious enough to call for the setting up of a National Sand Control Aid Group and for the Ministry of Forestry to establish a National Sand Control Ten Year

*(Zhu Zhenda and Wang Tao 1990, pp. 431–3). As Andrew Warren and Clive Agnew (1988, pp. 10–11) note, percentage of sand cover and dune types, while significant indicators for a desertification typology, do not tell us about the productivity of a particular area. Vegetation may have decreased within an area, but desirable grazing grasses or economic crops may actually have increased and the environment may not be under such severe stress. Therefore, it is significant that Zhu and Wang tell us that the indicators for the 1975–86 air photograph analysis included the lowering of agricultural yields as well as the creation of sand dunes.

Plan. If lands where there is significant potential for desertification as well as lands undergoing wind-blown sand dune encroachment are excluded, 1.7 per cent of China's area can be actually considered human-induced desertified land.

An almost continuous belt of degraded land stretches for 5500 km from the north-west to north-east China. Zhu and Wang (1990, p. 433) point out that the greatest increases in desertified area between 1975 and 1986 were in the semi-arid and sub-humid regions with the north-west arid region showing a more modest increase. Zhu and Wang consider that the character of this recent desertification differs from that between 1950 and 1970 since the desertification from 1975 to 1986 is more often a degradation of agricultural land which can be restored rather than complete desertification with loss of all productivity. Desertification already affects nearly 55 million people and 10 million hectares of pasturage while threatening 3.9 million hectares of cropland, 4.9 million hectares of range land and 2000 km of railway lines (Guo et al. 1989, p. 790; Han 1989, p. 805). In recent years there has even been much discussion as to whether the area around Beijing is becoming desertified.

The open policy which has led to greater integration of all China into the world economy created new problems for China's dry lands. The impact of the international liquorice market on certain areas in Xinjiang has been described by Hoppe (1987, pp. 65–8). In their race to catch up with the eastern coastal region and to generate foreign exchange it is possible that China's dry lands will become further degraded.

Plans for rapid economic development of the eastern coast region and statements from party leaders that some areas must get rich first so that others can benefit are indications that the authorities are giving low development priority to the dry lands. Within the dry lands, recent policies encourage development of more humid and already better developed regions. A recent study of Shaanxi province economic regionalization suggested that the more developed and more humid central portions of the province be given priority over the northern and southern economic regions (Chen, Tang and Liu 1988, pp. 14–19).

Individual ownership of herds is now back in vogue in China. The land, however, still belongs to the state and China must work out a new method to ensure that herders will protect the range. The local people must be given control over their land as well as their herds, but they must also be persuaded that sustainable land use practices are for their own benefit.

Finally, water is the key to arid land development. Up to now irrigation in China's arid and semi-arid lands has been operating at 30 per cent or 40 per cent of maximum efficiency (Qu 1986, p. 5). Better use of water will reduce desertification, as well as salinization, alkalization, soil erosion and the need for expensive water transfers and land improvement measures.

Natural disasters

Table 9.2 gives some idea of the type and location of some natural disasters which China experiences. It should be noted that these so-called natural disasters are often closely linked to human activities. For example, deforestation has meant that drought and flooding are now annual occurrences in all major river basins and the average area affected by such disasters in the 1980s was 68 per cent more than in the 1950s (Han 1989, pp. 804–5). The most recent case in point was the flooding along the Chang and Huai Rivers during the summer of 1991.

Table 9.2 Geographical distribution of some natural disasters in China

Natural disaster type	Regions of major occurrence	Regions of secondary occurrence
Drought	North China Plain Dongbei (north-east) Plain Sichuan Basin	Central and east. Mongolian Plateau Loess Plateau. Chang River Valley South Guangxi, west Hainan
Flooding	Chang River Valley North China Plain	Dongbei (Northeast) Plain Zhu (Pearl) River Valley South-east coast
Earthquakes	Taiwan, Bejing–Tianjin South Ningxia West Sichuan South Tian Shan range Xinjiang	Shandong-Anhui, Taihang Mts. Lanzhou-Tianshui, Hexi Corridor South Tarim Basin of Xinjiang Himalaya Mountains
Flash rains	South-east coast West Sichuan	Chang River Valley Sichuan Basin, east central coast South-east hilly uplands
Strong winds	Xinjiang Inner Mongolian Plateau South-east coast	Qaidam Basin of Qinghai Ordos Plateau Qinghai-Tibetan Plateau
Excessive cold temperatures	Plains of the north-east Qinghai-Tibetan Plateau	Huai River Valley

(*Source*: Zhang P *et al*. 1991, p. 25.)

Although the floods of 1991 were in part caused by nature, there is no doubt that the level of water conservancy protection in China was inadequate and that increasing deforestation has helped to weaken flood defences. The damage from the floods will be felt for years as the quality of cropland in China's major grain producing areas could well be seriously damaged leading to poorer harvests for several years. It has been suggested that Anhui will need four or five years for its agricultural production to recover. The floods have also brought into focus the question of whether the Sanxia (Three Gorges) Dam in western Hubei should or should not be constructed. It looks likely that the dam will be formally approved. However, to this author the Sanxia Dam looks like another grandiose Chinese government project which attempts to solve immediate problems at the expense of sustainable development.

Pollution

Water pollution

Studies from the mid-1980s suggest that about 25 per cent of China's fresh water is polluted to some degree (Boxer 1989, p. 677) with the proportion in rivers and lakes near to industrial areas far worse. A survey of 94 rivers undertaken in 1990 stated that 65 were polluted (Guojia Huanjing Baohuju 1991, p. 2). Moreover, pollution levels in rivers could double between 1990 and 2000 (Wang J 1989, p. 852). Some rivers, such as Shanghai's Huangpu River, are getting warmer from all the warm wastewater being dumped in it.

Table 9.3 shows that some progress has been made in the treatment of industrial water during the 1980s. However, official statistics are not likely to include wastewater from rural small-scale industries which proliferated during the 1980s and there are other surveys which suggest that industrial wastewater output is higher in total volume (1988 = 45 000 million tonnes) as well as proportion of wastewater (80 per cent) than the 70 per cent official statistics indicate (Gu [sic Qu] 1988, p. 17). In any case, the levels of cyanide and many bacteria are generally beyond standards set by the government (Zhu L 1990, p. 10).

Table 9.3 Enterprise wastewater in China (all figures rounded to million tonnes)

Year	Overall	Industrial				
	Total	Total	Achieving standard	Treated		
					Total	Achieving standard
1986	33 879	26 024	11 059		6 321	3 470
1987	34 861	26 375	12 072		6 784	4 042
1988	36 726	26 839	12 389		7 234	4 157
1989	35 345	25 209	12 033		7 539	4 348
1990	35 379	24 868	12 460		8 023	4 638
1991	33 620	23 566	11 820		15 588	4 233
1992	36 650	23 385	12 362		17 568	4 449
2000 est	77 600	56 100	n.a.		39 270	n.a.

(*Sources:* Guojia Tongjiju 1991, p. 797; 1992, p. 816; 1993, p. 824; Wang J 1989, p. 852.)

It has been estimated that 80 per cent of urban surface water is polluted with ammonia and nitrogen as the main pollutants (Zhu L 1990, p. 10). A survey in the late 1980s concluded that only 6 of 27 major cities can provide drinking water within the limits of the state standards (Han 1989, p. 806). Water pollution is more serious in populous eastern China than in the west. In general, only lakes and reservoirs which provide drinking water have been protected. About one-quarter of lakes surveyed have been assessed as seriously or moderately seriously polluted, and another one-quarter are considered 'lightly polluted'. There are many hyper-eutrophic lakes which have not supported fish for years and the number of such lakes is increasing. However, the Chinese do not regard the increased production of plankton by eutrophication as a major problem because this plankton can be used to feed certain kinds of aquatic seafood or to produce fertilizer.

There have been some alarming cases of pollution of the coastal seas in recent years. Serious pollution from organic chemicals and heavy metals has been found in the Bohai Bay and at the mouth of the Zhu (Pearl) River. Oil concentrations above fisheries standards have been found in coastal waters and are increasing. Red tides are on the increase having occurred 34 times in 1990 compared with only 12 times in 1989. The government of Shanghai and the World Bank are trying to cope with that city's horrific wastewater problem by flushing the sewage out of Shanghai to the East China Sea via a giant underground flow pipe with pumping stations. While this project will improve water quality for Shanghai, its impact on neighbouring portions of the East China Sea could be serious. As a result of recent increases in coastal pollution, the National Marine Ministry has begun to issue more regulations for oil exploration and dumping at sea.

An investigation in 1985 found phenols, cyanides and chromium in the ground water around some cities (Wang J 1989, p. 853). Wells have had to be shut down in some cases. Other major ground water pollutants include an increasing general degree of hardness, nitrates, sulphates and chlorides. In some cases the dropping water tables around coastal cities have led to salinization of ground water.

The water pollution problem is compounded by the protection which many industries receive, which allows them to operate inefficient equipment with little or no treatment facilities. For example, the paper making industry's average output of wastewater is 300 tonnes or six times the international average.

Water pollution problems are by no means confined to urban areas. Despite the limited information available, it is clear that there is an increasing number of nitrates in suburban areas where there are high animal stocking rates. Nowhere can this problem be so easily seen as in southern Jiangsu and northern Zhejiang provinces. Research in the late 1980s has shown that some rivers no longer contain dissolved oxygen or have levels below 1.0 mg per litre throughout the year and have average chemical oxygen demand (COD) levels below 45 mg per litre (Zhao and Dong 1990, p. 32). In the get-rich quick atmosphere of the 1980s many high polluting processes which faced difficulties locating in cities were farmed out to the Tai Lake area. As enterprises are often in small towns and villages roughly spaced at 12 km apart with rivers and canals connecting them, the water pollution from one town can affect the drinking supply in the next village, to say nothing of the water used by the farmers. Increasing concentration of rural population and water pollution around prosperous villages and towns has led to increases in diseases.

There have been some successes in the control of water pollution in rural towns in recent years. Many rural areas, particularly in Jiangsu and

Guangdong, have employed complex and intensive recycling of wastes to produce high value products such as silk and freshwater fish. Aquatic plants have been used to remove pollutants from water by leaving the wastewater in holding ponds full of plants for about two weeks. In some cases water pollution in rural areas has been reduced by consolidating small plants so that their wastewater can be treated and minerals recycled. However, for every such positive attempt there are still a growing number of serious cases of untreated rural wastewater being discharged that could be recycled or at least treated.

Table 9.4 Proportion of pollution control expenditure in the People's Republic of China for various types of pollution

	1986	1987	1988	1989	1990	1991	1992
Total (million yuan)	2877	3594	4241	4354	4545	5973	6466
Percentage spent on:							
Water pollution control	44.0	43.6	44.0	45.3	47.6	48.9	46.1
Air pollution control	33.3	34.5	36.0	36.2	32.6	33.0	33.3
Solid waste control	10.6	11.1	10.1	9.1	11.2	11.3	12.4
Noise control	3.2	3.1	2.9	3.0	2.6	3.1	2.7
Other	8.9	7.7	7.0	6.4	6.0	3.7	5.5

(*Source:* Guojia Tongjiju 1991, p. 795; 1992, p. 814; 1993, p. 822.)

While no one knows for sure the true cost of wastewater to China, Table 9.4 shows that control of water pollution has been taken most seriously of all pollution problems. While the worst of the heavy metal water pollution was reduced during the 1980s, the most pressing tasks for the 1990s will be control of phosphates, COD, nitrogen ammonia and dissolved oxygen.

Soil pollution and pest control

Although China has undertaken many efforts to improve soils in a wide range of environments, soil pollution has negated much of this effort. Industrially-polluted land in China is estimated by the Ministry of Agriculture to be about 6.67 million hectares and this is estimated to amount to grain losses of 5 million to 10 million tonnes per annum (Han 1989, p. 806; Yao 1991, p. 58). Such figures are obviously crude estimates as there were only 220 municipal sewage monitoring stations set up by the Ministry of Agriculture to check municipal sewage irrigation pollution levels as of the end of 1988 and the local industrial waste monitoring network was only completed in 1990 (Vermeer 1990, pp. 40–1). In addition to industrial pollution, pesticide-polluted arable land has been estimated at 13 million hectares (Han 1989, p. 806).

Chemical fertilizers introduced since the 1960s, coupled with increased livestock production, have increased the amount of pollution in rural areas and led to degradation of soil quality. Smil (1984, p. 143) notes that

167

much fertilizer was applied on the surface resulting in considerable quick losses. Moreover, poor packaging still is the cause of considerable wastage and pollution. China's average annual fertilizer usage is estimated to be 208 kg/ha (80 per cent of which is nitrogen) which is twice the world average (Han 1989, p. 806). Much of the pollution problem is actually due to the over-application of human and animal wastes rather than just chemical fertilizers, as some of the highest doses of nitrogen fertilizers are in areas which also have large human populations or high animal stocking rates. Research done in Guangdong during the 1980s has shown that in most soil types an increase in potassium and phosphorus fertilizer application could actually reduce the need for heavy application of nitrogen fertilizer as well as produce a more stable yield (Liang 1989, p. 254). In some cases over-application of chemical fertilizers is known to have resulted in soil caking. Consequently, farmers have been using more quantities of organic fertilizer since the mid-1980s.

Beginning in 1979 there was an upsurge in the use of organochlorine pesticides in the countryside. This was particularly serious in cotton growing areas. Smil (1984, p. 146) notes cases of pesticide poisoning reported during the early 1980s – sometimes caused by the use of pesticides in food preparation! The production of organochlorine pesticides, including benzene hexachloride (BHC) and dichlorodiphenyltrichloroethane (DDT), was banned by the government in 1983 and the percentage of cereal grains with residues exceeding permissible limits went down by the second half of the 1980s (Han 1989, p. 805). Although the situation relative to organochlorine pesticides has improved, overall pesticide use is still increasing. The extensive use of pesticides in the past also means that pests have developed resistance to chemicals formerly used.

Use of sewage water for irrigation was promoted during the 1960s because the water contained useful nutrients. Chang (1990, p. 6) states that official statistics indicate that 1 per cent of China's cropland was using wastewater for irrigation at that time and the percentage has been increasing ever since. However, at the same time as the use of sewage for irrigation has been increasing, the levels of industrial and organic toxic matter in wastewater have generally increased. How long soils can continue to absorb pollutants remains to be seen. In addition, there is serious concern about the increasing use of plastic sheeting in farming as much of this sheeting has simply been turned into the soil. However, there are now campaigns to urge farmers to recover plastic sheeting.

One way to control the introduction of pesticides into the soil and food chain with which the Chinese have had considerable success has been integrated pest management. In the early 1970s, integrated pest management developed as an alternative to pesticides. By 1979 the Chinese were using integrated pest management over a larger area of territory than any country in the world. However, with the rise of the reform movement and the return of the family farm, individual farmers have returned to the use of pesticides since integrated pest management can be successful only when applied over a wide area.

An increase in tree pests in recent years may be due in part to the very low bird populations found in China. The situation is now being partially corrected by encouraging households to raise insectivorous bird species that can be rented out to control pests (Richardson 1990, p. 222).

Research into pest control appears to be quite advanced and the Chinese have many clever solutions and can manage pest control to a high degree of excellence in a research environment. However, practice in the field trails behind the model research stations, with peasants and local bureaucrats using what means they have at hand. This can imply labour intensive techniques, which often are not necessarily the most appropriate. Integrated pest management could be far more effective in some of these situations.

Solid waste problems

Prior to 1978 manure and household organic waste was not much of a problem as it was utilized as fertilizer. With the increase of availability of chemical fertilizers since around 1980, 'night soil' collection has become more of a problem. There often was no one in the towns willing to undertake management of human wastes while the population continued to increase.

Use of manure and human wastes has increased since mid-1980s but there are continuing worries that rapid industrialization means that more industrial wastes and plastics are mixed in than previously was the case. Kinzelbach (quoted in Ross 1988, pp. 150–1) notes that the problem of industrial wastes and increased amounts of paper in urban sludge had already made farmers in the south reluctant to use it.

The residual sludge from the production of biogas in small reactors can be used as a pest free fertilizer and was viewed as a solution to rural waste pollution as well as energy shortages. In 1978 the Chinese said there were 7 million biogas reactors in use. However, estimates suggest that these reactors only produced 1.6 million tonnes of hard coal equivalent per annum or under 2 per cent of China's total energy supply (Glaeser 1990, p. 262). Most of these reactors were found in Sichuan province. North of the Chang River the reactors cannot be used in the winter when they are most needed. However, reports from the north-west plateaux (Ma 1989, p. 2) suggest higher incomes for biogas-using eco-farmers and indicate an increase in the use of biogas reactors. The transformation to the family farm has generally hurt the production of biogas. The communes provided a better scale operation for reactors and the labour force needed to clean them. Although biogas has made a small come-back, by 1990 the number of biogas reactors in use had dropped to a total of 4.7 million households generating 1000 million m^3 of biogas annually (Lees 1991, p. 12).

With the economic growth of the 1980s, the amount of household rubbish produced grew rapidly. Levels of heavy metals and other inorganic matter found in the rubbish of Shanghai are approaching levels found in developed countries. Mining tailings have been allowed to pile up, especially around mining sites in rural areas, and are creating tailing reservoirs of polluted water.

169

Table 9.5 suggests that the industrial solid waste levels stabilized during the second half of the 1980s and real progress has been made in controlling industrial solid waste from large and medium urban enterprises. As it is not clear whether rural industrial wastes are included in the statistics in Table 9.5, they may hide the removal of waste-producing industries to the countryside. Of the urban waste from large industry which is released, approximately one-fifth is dumped directly into rivers and streams.

Urban domestic waste grew at a rapid pace during the 1980s. For example, Tianjin's solid waste grew at a rate of 6 to 8 per cent per annum in the second half of the 1980s. By 1989 annual output of urban household rubbish was estimated to be about 0.6 kg per person per day. One prediction is that China's urban rubbish will have annual growth rates of 8 to 10 per cent between 1980 and 2000 (Xu 1987, p. 81). Chinese urban refuse contains a large amount of coal ash. A shift away from solid fuels to gas would reduce daily per capita rubbish output by an estimated 0.2 kg in southern cities and 0.4 kg in the north. However, natural gas production is stagnating.

Table 9.5 Industrial solid wastes in the People's Republic of China in million tonnes

Year	Total produced	Total emitted	Total accumulated[1]
1986	603.6	132.8	7415.4
1987	529.2	87.2	6079.7
1988	561.3	85.4	6586.5
1989	571.7	52.6	6748.9
1990	577.9	47.7	6481.7
1991	587.6	33.8	5962.5
1992	618.4	25.9	5916.1

(*Source:* Guojia Tongjiju 1990, p. 697; 1991, p. 799; 1992, pp. 822–23; 1993, pp. 829–30.)
Note:
1. The amount piled up in dump sites.

Kitchen wastes make up the vast majority of organic rubbish and about 31 per cent of China's total urban refuse. This means that urban refuse has a high humidity. In the early 1980s, 25 per cent of the vegetables sent to the urban markets ended up on the rubbish heap without being used due to inefficient marketing and management (Xu 1987, p. 82). Better marketing and transportation should help China to improve on this figure, although it is likely that more vegetables will be packed in plastic in the future adding another worry to China's refuse problem.

Certain cities have given rubbish disposal projects priority in order to improve their foreign exchange earnings from tourism. Most urban refuse is still removed from cities by lorry or boat to farms or rural dumping sites and very little of it is sorted. Throughout the 1980s the distance urban rubbish was moved increased (Xu 1987, p. 80). China has a serious shortage of incinerators and tip lining systems. The practice of tipping into unlined dumps has been known to cause water pollution. Research and experimentation into how to bury rubbish only began in 1986 in Tianjin (Yang C. 1991, p. 10). Although Ross (1988, pp. 150–1) argues convincingly that industrial recycling prior to the reforms of the late 1970s was not very successful, rural recycling was quite significant – not so much out of choice as of necessity. Today recycling of metal, scrap and other solid wastes can still be improved because pricing, marketing and technology are inadequate.

As of 1990 about 6.4 per cent of the total agricultural land was covered by industrial solid wastes. Figure 9.1 shows the amount of agricultural land used to store industrial waste in 1990 as a proportion of the total cultivated land area of 1988. There are problems with these data as the discrepancies from province to province vary greatly. However, we can see that the dumping problem is most serious in highly industrialized eastern provinces with good agricultural land.

China only recently began to set up toxic waste storage sites. In September 1991 the Standing Committee of the Seventh National People's Congress approved a motion to adopt the Basel Convention on Controlling Trans-boundary Dangerous Wastes and their Disposal. While laws and regulations are now being put into place, it could be some time before they actually take hold. A 1991 report suggests that people living within 150 km of a nuclear testing site in Xinjiang are showing symptoms of radiation pollution similar to those found among Japanese near Hiroshima and Nagasaki at the end of the Second World War ('Hece' 1991, p. 4). A nuclear power station became operational at Qinshan in Zhejiang province during December 1991 and another station at Daya Bay in Guangdong should be completed during the 1990s.

Control of solid wastes cost China over 672 million yuan in 1991 amounting to over 11 per cent of the funds spent on pollution control (Table 9.4). Central investment in urban waste control and other infrastructure is likely to decline throughout the 1990s as local government will be expected to come up with funds.

Air pollution

It is estimated that industry accounts for over 80 per cent of China's total waste gas emissions. In recent years some state controlled enterprises have improved their gas cleaning (Table 9.6). However, as the state sector is largely stagnant in terms of China's overall growth, such improvements do not necessarily indicate large reductions in air pollution.

Particulate levels in Chinese cities are far worse than in most cities in industrialized countries and Chinese threshold values are frequently exceeded. In the push for industrial development, China's coal consumption has continued to rise steadily throughout the 1980s. By the late 1980s over 76 per cent of China's energy was produced by burning coal. This ratio is not likely to go down much in the near future and coal 'will be the mainstay of China's economy until at least 2025' (Lees 1991, p. 13).

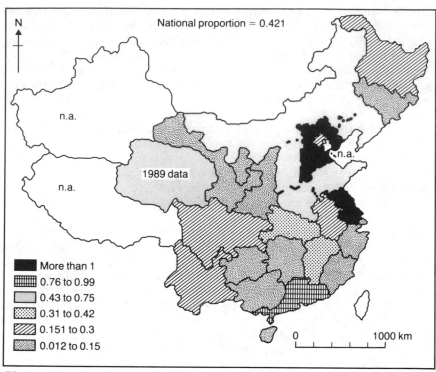

Fig. 9.1 Agricultural fields occupied by industrial waste 1990 as a proportion of cultivated area in 1988. (Source: Guojia Tongjiu 1991, p. 799; Zhongguo Nongye Bianji Weiyuanhui 1989, p. 238)

Table 9.6 Annual waste gas emissions from industrial enterprises

Year	Total (10⁹ standard m³)	Fuel burning (% of total)	(% treated[1])	Product production (% of total)	(% cleaned)
1986	6968	66.7	61.8	33.3	47.5
1987	7728	68.1	61.5	31.9	50.7
1988	8238	68.5	65.4	31.5	52.3
1989	8307	69.4	70.1	30.6	57.3
1990	8538	69.7	73.8	30.3	70.0
1991	8473	63.3	85.3	36.7	64.6
1992	8963	63.8	85.5	36.2	68.9

(*Sources:* Guojia Tongjiju 1990, p. 693; 1991, p. 798; 1992, pp. 818–19; 1993, p. 826.)
Note:
1. Smoke burned and dust removed.

The serious particulate pollution problem is in part due to the fact that only about 17 per cent of the coal is washed and most coal is burned in small to medium-sized furnaces. Official statistics suggest that particulate emissions began to decrease from 1988. Progress made in particulate control has been largely offset by increased consumption. Although under one-quarter of coal produced energy is converted into electricity the power industry is perhaps representative of what has been happening. Between 1985 and 1990 coal consumption for power generation rose from 150 million tonnes to 250 million tonnes while particulate emissions remained at roughly the same level.

The percentage of household particulate emissions recovered is much lower than in industry. Most homes in Chinese cities use coal as the sole fuel and coal combustion is responsible for 69 per cent of China's particulate emissions (Cao 1989, p. 763). The low smoke-stacks on household stoves further aggravate the particulate problem. Particulate levels are more serious in the cities of north China.* In 1990 the average daily particulate levels in northern Chinese cities were 475 μg/m^3 whereas in south China cities the levels were around 268 μg/m^3 which represents a significant improvement over the early 1980s (Guojia Huanjing Baohuju 1991, p. 1). There were cities in China with particulate levels of more than 1000 μg/m^3 during the 1980s whereas London normally has 48 μg/m^3 and the World Health Organization recommends 90 μg/m^3 as a safe high level.

As China continues to industrialize, various elements have been added to the particulate pollution. Particulates in cities have been found to contain things such as benzene-soluble matter, lead, zinc, copper, arsenic, manganese, iron, cadmium and molybdenum.

China is the third largest emitter of sulphur dioxide after the Soviet Union and the United States of America. Sulphur dioxide, like particulates, is closely connected with coal smoke. As with particulates, levels of sulphur dioxide are more severe during winter in the northern Chinese cities than in the south. Beijing, Xi'an and Shenyang are among the world's ten worst cities for sulphur dioxide concentrations (Chang 1990, p. 7). However, in the summer months certain southern cities such as Chongqing and Guiyang can have higher SO$_2$ levels than northern cities. Guo et al. (1990, p. 53) give north China SO$_2$ daily average levels of 250 μg/m^3, presumably from the late 1980s – well above the World Health Organization's safe level of 60 μg/m^3. All Chinese city centres have SO$_2$ emission levels which exceed the Chinese legal limits. Vermeer (1990, p. 43) notes that there are plans to bring SO$_2$ levels in all northern cities to below 130–150 μg/m^3 by AD 2000.

Coal combustion is also responsible for two-thirds of the nitrogen oxides emitted in China. Nitrogen oxide pollution is not yet serious when compared with particulates and sulphur dioxide. In 1990 the urban daily average nitrogen oxide level for a sample of northern cities was 47 μg/m^3 whereas southern cities had 38 μg/m^3. These statistics indicate some improvement over levels in the early 1980s. Such levels are well within Chinese safety standards. Research in the early 1980s into Lanzhou smog showed that the density of methyl hydrocarbons in the Xigu Industrial

---

*Wind-blown dust accounts for 60 per cent of suspended particulates in the summer time in the north and 40 per cent during the winter time. The contribution of wind-blown dust in the south is probably less than one-third of the particulate total.

District was 70 times that of nitrogen oxides which is quite dissimilar from American and Japanese automobile-induced smog. The increasing quantity of automobile and industrial petrol fumes suggests that carbon monoxide, hydrocarbon and nitrogen oxide problems will grow during the 1990s. Traffic congestion in cities has made for very high levels of NO_x at intersections which often exceed class III standards. In preparation for an increasing number of photochemical smog problems and ozone alerts, the National Environmental Protection Agency and the police put together regulations for managing the supervision of auto emissions in 1990.

China is one of the few areas in the developing world with a major acid pollution problem. Acid pollution in China is caused largely by high levels of domestic sulphur dioxide pollution. Acid pollution in south China is particularly serious as the high temperatures in the atmosphere help sulphur dioxide convert to acid faster than in most other places in the world with high levels of acid pollution (Fig. 9.2). Chang (1990, p. 7) says that over half of the rainfall in southern China is now overly acidic. Rainwater with annual average pH readings below 5.0 is concentrated in

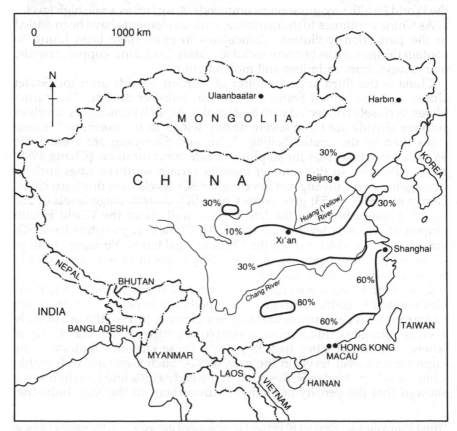

Fig. 9.2 Frequency of acid precipitation in eastern China (Source: Zhang, *et al.* 1989, p. 73)

the provinces of south-west China, south central China and a smaller area in eastern China including the cities of Shanghai and Hangzhou. As soil pH is generally more alkaline in the north (over pH 7) and the positive ion exchange rate, the levels of airborne ammonia and the rate of base absorption are generally higher, the north is better able to deal with higher levels of acids (Zhang and Tang 1990, p. 181).

Chlorine and hydrogen fluoride as well as sulphur dioxide have been found to be seriously affecting vegetation. It has been estimated in the second half of the 1980s that 2.66 million hectares of crops were annually polluted by sulphur dioxide and 1.33 million hectares were polluted by fluoride (Cao 1989, p. 772). Research on the effects of air pollution on crops has demonstrated that the ambient concentration of both sulphur dioxide and fluoride has been sufficient to reduce yields by 5 to 25 per cent in the Baotou, Chongqing, and Liuzhou areas (Cao 1989, p. 767). Serious corrosion of metal and damage to concrete has also been thought to be caused by acid pollution although it is often difficult to assign damage directly.

Since 1982, 296 acid precipitation monitoring stations have been established throughout China and the Chinese have tried to combat the impact of air pollution on vegetation. Plant varieties which have been tested and found to have a resistance to polluting compounds have been recommended. For example, Elsom and Haigh (1986, pp. 640–1) note the planting of 17 000 trees around the Guangzhou chemical works to combat air pollution in the mid-1980s which supposedly reduced chlorine concentrations around the plant by 20 per cent in two years.

Crop damage done by acid pollution was estimated at 1800 to 2000 million yuan (£300 million) a year by the late 1980s (Cao 1989, p. 772). Vermeer (1990, p. 13) feels that this is a huge underestimate with losses in Guangdong alone reported for the late 1980s as 2300 million yuan per annum. Losses from metal corrosion were estimated to be about US$11 000 million in 1988. Air pollution control efforts account for about one-third of total pollution control costs (Table 9.4). Clearly air pollution is costly to Chinese society.

With all the other pollution problems facing China, noise pollution has taken a back seat. Prior to 1975 China produced virtually no noise testing equipment and had no factories producing noise control facilities. Also prior to 1982 there were no standards for construction materials. Many buildings were constructed with steel reinforced concrete panels that were only three or four centimetres thick. When one walks on the stairs in these buildings the noise produced sounds like the pounding of drums.

In 1979 the Sanitation Ministry and the National Labour Bureau decided on 85 dBA (85 decibels on the A scale) as the work place standard with 90 dBA set as the absolute permissible high. Noise in most Chinese cities exceeds the suggested Chinese standards. A study of noise in 46 cities during the mid-1980s found an average noise value of 60 dBA (Li 1989, p. 197): 17 cities exceeded this average with Shanghai, Chengdu and Lanzhou having the highest values. The target for the mid-1990s is to get the most noisy cities to levels below 73 dBA.

By the 1980s some steel mills, chemical plants, electricity generating stations and textile mills were using Chinese manufactured noise controlling materials and some cities reduced noise levels within designated districts. For every such success story, new factories in newly urbanized districts are creating so many new noise problems that overall noise levels are remaining the same or continuing to rise. Lack of funds means that new buildings cannot be built up to the standards necessary to take full effect of noise reducing properties. For example, windows are often of poor quality and must be left open because of the lack of ventilating equipment. Today the differences in noise levels inside and outside of most rooms is only 10 dBA.

Fang Danqun (1989, p. 177) notes that machine sound levels in factories have often exceeded 90 dBA 30 per cent to 40 per cent of the time and an estimated 20 million workers were working under such conditions. Fang also notes that as of the mid-1980s an estimated 100 million people in China were living in environments which exceeded Chinese noise standards.

Nature conservation

The growth of the conservation movement and the establishment of nature reserves

China is known as a treasure house of many rare species of wildlife. The first nature reserve and laws directly dealing with nature conservation appeared in 1956. A few other nature reserves were founded in the following years up to 1965. It has been said that there were no guiding principles for the establishment of nature reserves nor any real plan for their distribution during these years (Zhu 1989, pp. 831–2). The height of the subsequent Cultural Revolution from 1966 to 1972 was a period of chaos and no new conservation policies were implemented.

Around 1975, the State Council set out documents to begin in earnest the establishment of nature reserves (Wang X et al. 1989, p. 4). However, substantial development did not begin until after 1979. In the early 1980s a wildlife protection bureau and an office to control import and export of endangered species were first set up under the Ministry of Forestry and the China Wildlife Conservation Association was founded. By 1987 the State Council was alarmed enough about the hunting and smuggling of wildlife to issue a directive to local governments to increase their surveillance and punishments. In 1988 the government promulgated China's first wildlife protection law which stipulated details on administration and punishments. Local governments followed suit with similar laws. Positive results are being seen as certain endangered species are recovering. However, many species continue to dwindle. The late 1980s has seen an increase in use of artificial breeding to save many endangered species.

By 1988, there were over 600 nature reserves in China covering about 3 per cent of China's national territory (*Zhongguo huanjing nianjian* 1990, p.

137). Although statistics from various sources are inconsistent, the approximate distribution of nature reserves can be seen from Fig. 9.3. One group of experts has singled out the reserves found in the temperate coniferous–deciduous mixed–forests of the north-east as the best managed (Wang X *et al*. 1989, p. 121). The reserves of north China were set up rather late and, along with the reserves of east China, are facing a lot of recreational pressure.

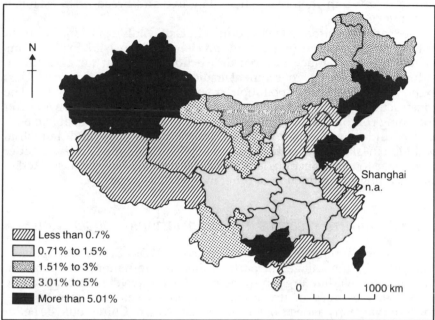

Fig. 9.3 Area of nature reserves as a percentage of local area, late 1980s. (Sources: Division of Natural Conservation National Environmental Protection Agency of China 1989; Wang X *et al*. 1989; Zhang R 1989, p. 58; and Chang *et al* 1986).

As of 1990, 61 of mainland China's nature reserves, including five coastal fish reserve zones, were approved by the national government and considered national nature preserves. The administration of nature reserves in China is not uniform, with different reserves administered by different organizations as well as at different government levels. On the whole, the forestry bureaux tend to dominate due to the fact that nature conservation work began in the Ministry of Forestry.

Classification of wildlife protection in the People's Republic

As of 1989, 379 vertebrate species were protected in the People's Republic and classified into first-class or second-class levels of protection (Zhu 1989, pp. 829–31). There were 389 species of plants, protected in three categories. Animals and plants receiving first-class protection are those which are endemic, rare, precious or threatened. Those accorded second-class protection are species whose numbers are declining or whose geographical distribution is becoming more restricted. The third-class species are plants of economic importance for which harvesting is to be limited. In general the method for preserving wildlife has been to establish nature reserves in the areas where they live and breed or to establish breeding centres.

The scarcity of birds as well as other kinds of wildlife in China has been noted by many authors (e.g. Elsom and Haigh 1986, p. 645). Explanations for their disappearance include: destruction of habitat for agriculture, industry and housing, government eradication policies for certain species, excessive hunting and pollution from pesticides and industry. The construction of dams and weirs, while helping to regulate flood water and spawning conditions for some fish, has led to an overall reduction in both finfish and crustaceans. Increased nutrient loadings and industrial pollution in lakes have led to reductions in fish yields and species. In order to increase food production, larvae of crabs and carp have been stocked in lakes leading to a reduction of other indigenous species.

China's nature reserves and international cooperation

Since the beginning of the open policy in 1979, China has come to recognize the advantages of participating in international cooperation. International wildlife organizations have been interested in cooperating with China because of its varied environments as well as increasing concern that many aspects of nature conservation in China could be better managed. China also plays a key role in the market for products from endangered species such as ivory.

In 1979 China became a member of the UNESCO Man and the Biosphere Programme. Eight Chinese nature preserves are now part of the Man and the Biosphere Programme Network. In 1981, China signed the Convention on International Trade in Endangered Species of Wild Fauna and Flora. Of the plant and animal species protected under this treaty, over 640 are found in China.

Many of the larger reserves have research organizations attached, sometimes with international cooperation. For example, in 1981 an agreement was signed with the International Wildlife Foundation to protect and study the giant panda with an initial project completed in 1988 (*Zhongguo linye nianjian* 1988, p. 82). Efforts at bird conservation in conjunction with the Japanese began in 1983.

Wang Xianpu *et al.* (1989, p. 193) have even pointed out the possibility that China could establish 'international parks' with Nepal or Pakistan. The Zhangmu Kouan Nature Reserve in the Xigaze area of Tibet borders with Nepal and it is less than 100 km from Kathmandu. On the Nepal side there is also a nature reserve. It is possible that tourism could be enhanced by getting tourists to enter an 'international park' from the Nepal side.

Problems with China's nature conservation

Most environmentalists would argue that China's efforts at nature conservation are too little too late. The total area for nature reserves is still not what it should be. Other types of nature reserves beside those already in existence are necessary. Also, the distribution of nature reserves is out of balance (Fig. 9.3). There are two areas that are critically short of nature reserves: one is the densely populated eastern portions of the country and the other is the Qinghai–Tibetan Plateau.

The Chinese admit that administration of their nature reserves is uneven with some being far more effective than others. There will be administrative problems for the nature reserve system as a whole so long as there is not a single government organization supervising. The various units which administer the nature reserves are still likely to look for some short-term economic advantages or to protect only those aspects of the environment which are beneficial to the bureau's interests. The Wolong Nature Reserve in Sichuan has established its own special district government and this has proved most helpful in facilitating management of the reserve (Wang X et al. 1989, p. 142). However, even in a showcase reserve such as Wolong, Richardson (1990, p. 107) found widespread evidence of illegal tree felling, which leaves one to wonder about the management of less famous and newer reserves.

The scale of some of China's nature reserves is too small to be effective. In many cases, state forests or forestry parks are located next to nature reserves which, if jointly managed, could bring increased conservation benefits. The problem of scale can be compounded by attempts to zone reserves for various uses. Once part of the reserve is zoned for productive or revenue generating activities its original preservation functions are compromised.

The lack of laws relating specifically to nature reserves prior to November 1988 meant there was a lot of confusion, especially as laws regarding possession of the means of production, land, etc., are also in flux. Laws should standardize procedures for establishing nature reserves, management procedures and penalties for violations. Now that such laws have appeared there is a need for clear enforcement of local versions pertinent to specific circumstances. In 1989 and 1990 there were still some serious cases of the killing and smuggling of endangered species.

For laws and their enforcement to be successful, the nature reserve managers must consider solving the economic and social problems of the local inhabitants. Attempts have been made in some of the nature reserves to compensate local inhabitants. At Wolong relocation of farmers to non-traditional village housing has been resisted. The government has been trying to solve employment problems for some local people by training them as forest rangers or nature reserve staff.

Enforcement problems are compounded by the low level of environmental education among the people living in surrounding areas. Low levels of education also mean that it is very difficult to find well-qualified staff to manage the reserves. Under such circumstances, some nature reserves are reserves in name only. In many cases logging and hunting are still going on in areas where such activities are prohibited by law.

Although nature reserves are now a part of China's annual plans, their overall planning and guaranteed budgeting are not part of the annual national or local budgets (Zhang R 1989, p. 59). Also very little has been done in terms of economic assessment of Chinese nature reserves (Wang X et al. 1989, p. 69). Therefore, plans to exploit renewable resources within reserves could easily become excessive.

The effects of tourism on China's nature reserves has rarely been positive. In some cases tourism has destroyed part of the resource which the reserves were meant to protect. Even some of the famous nature reserves which participate in the Man and Biosphere Programme are threatened by tourism. Problems in other designated scenic areas are equally bad. The opening of locations to foreign hunters during the mid-1980s gave officials the possibility to trade wildlife for cash. Officials are supposed to maximize income from all their lands, even though they are supposed to help preserve the nature reserve lands. Richardson (1990, p. 232) points out that the Ministry of Trade sets quotas of skins for trade even though China is a signatory to the CITES convention giving all wildcat species protected status.

Most Chinese environmentalists argue for improved management of nature conservation by pointing out the long-term economic value of such a policy. This is the only viewpoint they can stress when faced with a poor, inefficient and at times and in places, corrupt government. However, in the long term, policy makers will have to come to the realization that nature conservation is a necessity for long-term survival.

Conclusion

Improvement in China's environment will require internal political stability and international support and, even then, it would take a total optimist to predict that within the next couple of decades China will be able to halt the ecological degradation now occurring. While we can expect some progress in environmental control in certain places over the next decade, the overall trend will be for environmental conditions to continue to worsen. Despite the reappearance of some market mechanisms in the 1980s, political pressure from local governments is still the main driving force in encouraging investment in environmental control since many inputs, such as water, timber and coal, remain artificially underpriced. However, market mechanisms have helped to control some forms of degradation such as pollution in the state-run industries. If there is steady economic growth and little policy change over the next decade, China's urban pollution should be reduced and the pollution mix gradually come to resemble that found in Western developed cities.

However, market forces have engendered other environmental problems, particularly in the rural areas and the worst pollution in the next couple of decades will continue to be in eastern rural areas where small-scale industries proliferate. The potential for rural industrial pollution to increase can be seen from the rural enterprises' total output value which registered an annual average growth rate of 25.3 per cent between 1985 and 1990 and the fact that they now employ about one-quarter of the rural workforce. Rural enterprises often use outdated equipment and cannot afford to spend money on pollution abatement. The rural enterprises have been inefficient energy users and have reduced the incentive of peasants in wealthy areas to take care of their land.

Water quality degradation will continue to be the most serious pollution problem caused by the small-scale industries. For example in Jiangsu during 1984, damage from polluted wastewater accounted for over 94 per cent of the total losses from rural industrial pollution (Yang G. 1991, pp. 62, 64). The results of a 1989 Shandong rural industrial survey indicate that COD and suspended particles are the most serious forms of water pollution (Luan and Wu 1989, p. 1). However, the same survey also indicated that rural industries generate a considerable amount of air pollution, largely particulates and sulphur dioxide.

The government still can only guess about the seriousness of the total pollution caused by small-scale rural industries. It was not until August 1989 that any province had completed a basic survey of the levels of pollution from rural small-scale industries. To deal with the rural industry problem will require a tremendous investment by the Chinese government as well as strict enforcement of regulations for rural areas. Part of the solution lies with making agriculture more attractive which will require higher prices for agricultural products and a certain degree of land consolidation to maximize farm efficiency. The natural tendency will be for the government to move slowly on this high cost, relatively slow return investment.

Perhaps even more serious will be the continuing resource degradation, particularly in poor remote areas. At best the pace of water depletion, deforestation, soil erosion and desertification will slow down. Natural disasters will continue to be amplified by such resource degradation. If efforts at afforestation and population control during the 1980s prove to have been successful, we can expect to see a pay-off sometime after AD 2010. However, much depends on implementation of sound policies.

Many authors see improved economic efficiency – largely through the implementation of market mechanisms, as the ultimate key to improving China's environmental problems (Ross 1988, p. 132; Liu 1989, p. 354). As we have seen, market mechanisms help to solve some environmental problems while they create new ones. Although economic policy is important, the degradation problem cannot be solved solely through economics or politics. As the population increases, the ability to consume and pollute increases. Physical factors in China are constantly changing as is the technological ability of the Chinese to degrade their environment. Fragile transitional environments occupy almost 10 per cent of the total area. Ecosystems in the sparsely populated western and border areas are already under strain and cannot absorb surplus population from the east.

Management efficiency could help reduce environmental problems. It has been stated that industrial pollution in China could be reduced by 30 per cent simply by improving technology management in enterprises (Zhao and Dong 1990, p. 35). There are cases of plants using the same equipment but requiring twice as many raw materials to produce the same volume of product. Pollution abatement equipment is often not installed properly nor regularly maintained and pollution-related accidents are common. The Environmental Protection Law stipulates that environmental assessments are to be part of construction projects. However, assessments are rarely carried out for small-scale construction projects and often ignored in the case of large-scale pet projects. More funds and personnel are needed to carry out assessments for smaller projects and much more openness to assessment information will be necessary.

General education can be particularly useful in reducing certain forms of environmental degradation, such as noise pollution and littering. Within factories, staff training on various aspects of pollution control began in the early 1980s. The number of people being trained in environmental studies grew throughout the 1980s and is likely to continue to grow. Factories are still being encouraged to apply to receive 'clean factory' signs to be put up at the front gate if the factory meets environmental standards and peasants can be designated as model 'eco-farmers'. While this exhortation technique has limited effect, raising of general education levels will have more far-reaching consequences.

In a situation where the state controlled social organizations, the media and the factories there was little room for any check against state industry polluting the environment. This was the situation in the People's Republic of China prior to 1978. While the China of the 1980s was still far from being an open society, the open policy led to some loosening of state control. The opening of Chinese society could make it easier for people to form environmental pressure groups. While some authors have noted that well meaning but uninformed pressure groups can help create further environmental problems, the overall contribution of non-governmental watch-dog organizations is beneficial to the environment.

China's environmental degradation must be halted if the country is to feed and clothe all its people to a good standard of living in the next century. To tackle this gigantic problem, China needs strict population control, a rise in the education and consciousness level, an increase in wealth and infrastructural investment, stability and a more open society where information can be obtained and opinions freely expressed. To what degree these goals are met in the coming decade will have far-reaching implications not only for China but for the whole earth.

References

Boxer B (1989) 'China's environmental prospects', *Asian Survey* **29**(7), 669–86.

Cao H (1989) 'Air pollution and its effects on plants in China', *Journal of Applied Ecology* **26**, 763–73.

Chang Ch'ang-yi et al. (1986) *Taiwan yanhai diqu ziran huanjing baohu jihua*, Guoli Taiwan daxue dilixuexisuo yanjiu baogao 750329, [T'ai-pei].

Chang W Y B (1990) 'Human population, modernization, and the changing face of China's eastern Pacific lowlands', *China Exchange News* **18**(4), 3–8.

Chen Desheng (1991) 'Zhonggong nongye fazhan de wenti yu duice', *Zhongyang ribao: Guojiban* **22730**, 10 January, 4.

Chen Yongzong and **Jing Ke** (1983) 'The reality of soil and water loss in our country and some questions to be speedily studied', *Shuitu baochi tongbao* **4**, 1–6, (in Chinese with English title).

Chen Zongxing, Tang Haibin and **Liu Kewei** (1988) 'A preliminary study on comprehensive economic regionalization and strategic allocation in Shaanxi Province', *Jingji Dili* **8**(1), 14–19 (in Chinese with English title).

Division of Natural Conservation, National Environmental Protection Agency of China (ed.) (1989) *A list of the Nature Reserves in China*, Zhongguo Huanjing Kexue Chubanshe (China Environmental Science Press), Beijing (in Chinese and English).

Elsom D and **Haigh M** (1986) 'Progress and pollution', *Geographical Magazine* **58**(12), 640–5.

Fang Danqun (1989) 'Woguo zaosheng kongzhi jinzhan', in *Zhongguo Huanjing Kexue Nianjian*, Zhongguo Huanjing Kexue Chubanshe, Beijing, pp. 171–80.

Glaeser B (1990) 'The environmental impact of economic development: problems and policies', in Cannon, T. and Jenkins, A. (eds), *The Geography of Contemporary China: The Impact of Deng Xiaoping's Decade*, Routledge, London and New York, pp. 249–65.

Gu G [*sic.* **Qu G**]. (1988) 'China's industrial pollution survey', *China Reconstructs* **37**(8), 16–18.

Guo H, Wu D and **Zhu H** (1989) 'Land restoration in China', *Journal of Applied Ecology* **26**, 787–92.

Guo Xiaomin, Zhang Huiqin and **Li Ping** (1990) 'The calculation of economic losses from environmental pollution in China', *Zhongguo Huanjing Kexue* **6**(1), 51–9 (in Chinese with English abstract).

Guojia Huanjing Baohuju (comp) (1991) *Zhongguo huanjing zhuangkuang gongbao 1990*, Guojia Huanjing Baohuju: (Beijing).

Guojia Tongjiju (ed.) (various years) *Zhongguo tongji nianjian*, Zhongguo Tongji Chubashe (Beijing).

Han C (1989) 'Recent changes in the rural environment in China', *Journal of Applied Ecology* **26**, 803–12.

'Hece shichang de xishengpin?'. (1991) *Zhongyang ribao: Guojiban* **22025**, 6 November, 4.

Hoppe T (1987) 'An essay on reproduction: the example of Xinjiang Uighur Autonomous Region', in Bernhard Glaeser (ed.) *Learning from China?*, Allen & Unwin, London, pp. 56–84.

Lees R M (1991) 'China and the world in the nineties', summary report of the International Conference on Economic Development and Environment in China, 25 January.

Li Bingguang (1989) 'Woguo chengshi huanjing zaosheng diao yu yanjiu', in *Zhongguo huanjing kexue nianjian*, Zhongguo Huanjing Kexue

Chubanshe: Beijing, pp. 196–207.

Liang X (1989) 'Analysis of the stability of the NPK effects on rice in Guangdong Province', in E. Maltby and T. Wollersen (eds.) *Soils and their Management: a Sino-European Perspective*, Elsevier Applied Science, London, pp. 249–54.

Ling J and Bai L (1990) 'Beijing's water problems', *China Today*, August, 12–14.

Liu Tianqi (1989) 'Zhongguo huanjing guanli de fazhan licheng', in *Zhogguo huanjing kexue nianjian*, Zhongguo Huanjing Kexue Chubanshe, Beijing, pp. 351–8.

Luan Xuezhu and Wu Yanqiu (1989) 'Shandong Sheng xiangzhen gongye wuran zhi duoshao', *Zhongguo huanjing bao* **693**, 12 October 1.

Ma Xiaojun (1989) 'Xibu gaoyuan shengtai cun', *Zhongguo huanjing bao* **727**, 30 December, 2.

Qu Ningshu (1986) 'Land-use problem [sic]. in China's arid and semi-arid region', *Zhongguo shamo* 6(1), 1–5, 13 (in Chinese with English abstract).

Richardson S D (1990) *Forests and Forestry in China: Changing Patterns of Resource Development*, Island Press, Washington and Covelo, CA.

Ross L (1988) *Environmental Policy in China*, Indiana University Press, Bloomington and Indianapolis.

Smil V (1984) *The Bad Earth: Environmental Degradation in China*, ZED Press, London; M.E. Sharpe, Armonk, NY.

Vermeer E B (1990) 'Management of environmental pollution in China: problems and abatement policies', *China Information* 5(1), 34–65.

Wang J (1989) 'Water pollution and water shortage problems in China', *Journal of Applied Ecology*, **26**, 851–7.

Wang Xianpu, Jin Jianming, Wang Liqiang and Yang Jisheng (1989) *Ziran baohuqu de lilun yu shijian*, Zhongguo Huanjing Kexue Chubanshe, Beijing.

Warren A and Agnew C ([1988]) 'An assessment of desertification and land degradation in arid and semi-arid areas', unpublished paper, Ecology and Conservation Unit, University College, University of London, London.

Xu Zhuang (1987) 'Comprehensive evaluation on the characteristics and contaminated situation of municipal domestic refuse in China', *Huanjing Kexué*: 8(5), 80–4 (in Chinese with English title).

Yang Chunhua (1991) 'Yixiang chuli chengshi laji de shiyan- Tianjin de lajidui shan', *Dili zhishi* **2**, 10.

Yang Guishan (1991) 'Problems occured [sic] in the development of rural industries and the developmental trend of the future – take Jiangsu Province as an example', *Ziran Ziyuan* **1**, 61–5 (in Chinese with English title).

Yao Jicheng (1991) 'Impacts and countermeasures of the development of industries run by towns and communes on rural ecology and economy', *Ziran Ziyuan* **1**, 56–60 (in Chinese with English title).

Zhang Piyuan, Wang Fenghui, Jiang Hong and Ge Quansheng (1991) 'Zhongguo zhuyao ziran zaihai de dili fenbu', *Dili zhishi* **3**, 24–6.

Zhang Ruiling (1989) 'Establishment and estimation of nature area reserve [sic] in Loess Plateau, *Shaanxi linye keji* **8**, 57–9 (in Chinese with English abstract).

Zhang Shen and Tang Yijian (1990) 'Variational regulation of environmental pollution and control measures in China', *Dili xuebao* 45(2), 178–86 (in Chinese with English abstract).

Zhang Xiubao, Gao Weisheng and Ying Longgen (eds) (1989) *Daqi huanjing wuran gailun*, Zhongguo Huanjing Kexue Chubanshe, Beijing.

Zhao Qiguo (1990) 'Land resources of China', *Dili xuebao* 45(2), 154–62 (in Chinese with English abstract).

Zhao Yinwei and Dong Yawen (1990) 'On the discussion of the water pollution control and eco-environment construction in small size cities and towns of China', *Nongcun shengtai huanjing* 21, 31–35 (in Chinese with English abstract).

Zhongguo huanjing nianjian> Bianji Weyuanhui (ed.) (1990) *Zhongguo huanjing nianjian*, Zhongguo Huanjing Kexue Chubanshe, Beijing.

Zhongguo Kexue Bao She (ed.) (1989) 'Shengcun yu fazhan', unofficially published report printed by the printing factory of the Chinese Academy of Sciences, Beijing.

Zhongguo Kexueyuan Shengtaihuanjing Yanjiu Zhongxin Yujingxiaozu (ed.) (1989) *Shengtai chizi: weilai minzu shengcun de zuida weiji*. Report submitted to the National Scientific and Technical Standing Committee, 073, Beijing.

'Zhongguo linye nianjian' Bianji Weiyuanhui (ed.) (1987) *Zhongguo linye nianjian 1949–1986: China Forestry Yearbook 1949–1986*, Zhongguo Linye Chubanshe, Beijing (in Chinese with English title).

'Zhongguo linye nianjian' Bianji Weiyuanhui (ed.) (1988) *Zhongguo linye nianjian 1988: China Forestry Yearbook 1988*, Zhongguo Linye Chubanshe, Beijing (in Chinese with English title).

Zhu J (1989) 'Nature conservation in China', *Journal of Applied Ecology* 26, 825–33.

Zhu L (1990) 'Protecting water resources', *China Today* August, 10–12.

Zhu Zhenda and Wang Tao (1990) 'An analysis on the trend of land desertification in northern China during the last decade based on examples from some typical areas', *Dili xuebo* 45(4), 430–40 (in Chinese with English abstract).

CHAPTER 10

Water resources and environmental problems of China's great rivers

*Ian Douglas, Gu Hengyue and He Min**

To a geographer, China offers a great variety of landscapes from the humid tropical conditions of Hainan island to the alpine environments of the Xizang plateau and the periglacial landscapes of the far north-east. In terms of water resources, the fundamental contrast is between a relatively well-watered south and a water-deficient north. A second contrast is between mountainous and plateau country in the west, and low-lying plains in much of the eastern, coastal area of the country. The whole country experiences a remarkable seasonality of water availability, with summer rains and winter drought.

The overall land and water issue in China is that most of the cultivated land lies in the north, but most of the water is available in the south (Fig. 10.1), so that the overriding problem in the north is water deficiency, while in the south it is that of population pressure on the land and associated land degradation and erosion. The key water resource issues facing China are providing adequate water for the water-deficient areas in the north, especially the densely peopled Huang-Huai-Hai plain (Zuo and Zhang 1990) and coping with the hazards of floods in the summer and drought in the winter.

The pressure on the land is well described by Wu Chuan-Jun (1990):

> 'In China over a long period of time, land has been used gratis, occupied at will with destruction and waste, consequently intensifying the problem of land shortage. Whilst upholding the socialist public ownership of land, and adapting the law of socialist planned commodity economy, the system of paid utilization of land is to be implemented, both in urban and rural areas. Those lands already disturbed or left abandoned by extraction and mining are to be rehabilitated for appropriate use.'

*(All authors are working on a Manchester-based, Leverhulme Trust funded, project on the sediment problems of the Changjiang basin)

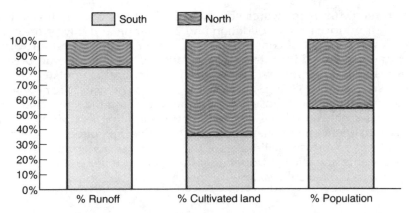

Fig. 10.1 Distribution of land, water and people between northern and southern China

To achieve the goal of quadrupling gross industrial and agricultural production by the year 2000, the emphasis of Chinese water resource development is on flood prevention and water supply. The immediate objectives are to consolidate, improve and appropriately expand water conservancy facilities and to minimize flood and drought problems as far as the national economy is able to support the necessary works (Gao Jiacai, 1989). The scale of works involved is huge: by 1985 there were:

- 170 000 km of levee banks;
- 83 000 reservoirs with a total storage capacity of 447 billion m^3;
- 2.43 million tubewells with a total installed capacity of 62.4 million kW;
- 48 million ha of irrigated land;
- hydroelectric power plants with a total installed capacity of 30.19 million kW capable of producing 20 per cent of the country's electricity.

The key tasks in water resources management are seen as follows:

- To consolidate and raise the capability of flood defence structures in major river basins and reinforce dams which are in poor condition.
- To seek every possible way to widen the sources of water supply, reduce consumption of water and to relieve water shortages in north China.
- To consolidate and develop farmland irrigation, improve and complete irrigation facilities and increase the irrigation area from 48 million ha to 53.3 million ha.
- To insist on the control of soil erosion.
- To control the worsening pollution of water supplies and to improve the quality of water in key river reaches.
- To strengthen the construction of hydropower projects.
- To speed up the development of inland navigation.

In developing policies to achieve these tasks, the emphasis in water resources development has shifted from construction to management.

Government funds for water supply activities have been redirected to give high priority for consolidation and renovation and low priority for new development and construction. The government has raised water rates and has started the integrated operation of agricultural enterprises. Water charges for both agriculture and industry are now related to the cost of supply (Tong Guang-gun 1989). Both land and water are now seen as commodities for whose use payment is required. By charging industrial users cost plus 4 or 5 per cent, water suppliers can build up reserves to finance new construction projects. The integrated operation of agricultural businesses will increase the revenue of water management agencies enabling them to operate and maintain engineering facilities properly and to raise the salaries of the agencies' personnel.

Ground water resources

Water needs are met from the surface waters in the great river basins and from the exploitation of aquifers carrying ground water: 85 per cent of the ground water currently exploited comes from the Quaternary sand and gravel aquifers beneath the north China plain (Anon. 1987). In the areas of karstic rocks, including the scenic limestone areas around Guilin, underground dams have been built and subterranean pumps lift water from cave systems to the surface. Springs are widely exploited, with their water often being carried in irrigation ditches around mountainsides to fields on the alluvial floors of karst poljes (Institute of Hydrogeology and Engineering Geology 1976). Some underground rivers in karst systems have been harnessed for hydroelectric power projects, such as at Shuanlung Cave in Chekiang province and Liulang Cave in Yunnan province.

Nevertheless, the Quaternary alluvial aquifers of the plains remain the most important source of ground water. Beijing relies heavily on the resources of the aquifer to the west of the city bounded on the west by the Western Mountain and to the north by Haidian. Here the buried alluvial fan is made up of a complex series of ancient river channels in which coarse-grained sediments were laid down. Although the reservoir was over-pumped for some years, it has a high annual recharge capacity, and takes in 0.1 billion m^3 of water in a normal year and 0.2 to 0.8 billion m^3 in wet years. To avoid depletion of the ground water resources, an artificial recharge project has been designed to divert river water in wells and so into the aquifer. At the same time steps should be taken to reduce the demand, especially through a decrease in industrial and agricultural abstraction (Liu and Cai 1988). Such careful management of ground water is essential. The west Beijing aquifer water table had dropped by 5 m as a result of excessive pumping, but the cost of implementing the ground water management scheme would be less than one-twentieth that of a new surface reservoir.

Elsewhere, over-pumping of ground water has caused more severe problems, particularly subsidence in coastal cities such as Tianjin, Ningpo and Shanghai, cumulative land subsidence in the latter city amounting to

2.63 m between 1921 and 1965. In Shanghai, the problem was alleviated by a combination of control of ground water consumption, readjustment of the way in which individual aquifers were exploited and artificial recharge. These remedial measures are now increasingly being augmented by stronger legislation and regulation to prevent over-use of ground water (Anon. 1987). Recharge during the summer wet season is the logical way to use the natural storage capacity of the aquifers, and such techniques are going to play an ever more important role in water management both in rural areas dependent on irrigation and in urban water supplies. Summer flooding provides the natural opportunity for aquifer recharge. Flood control, desirable for many other reasons, can be reducing overbank flows and by natural spreading of the water, reduce natural recharge. This then poses another dilemma for China's water planners.

The characteristics of the major river basins and their water resources

The arid and semi-arid nature of the west and north of the country means that, unlike many other continental river systems, the great rivers of China and South East Asia receive far less runoff from their upland and mountain headwaters than from their middle and lower course tributaries. However, both past and present tectonic and climatic geomorphic influences in the upland headwaters cause severe natural problems for river management and water resource use. The geologically rapid uplift of the plateau has created great gorge sections through unstable terrain on both the Huang He and Chang Jiang within which occur some of the most spectacular debris flows and rockslides experienced anywhere in the world (State Commission of Science and Technology 1988). In the north, the vast spreads of loess accumulated in every Pleistocene cold period provide depths of up to 400 m of highly erodible material which is eroded into some of the most elaborate ravine terrain to be found anywhere (Liu 1988). On to these naturally spectacular and unstable landscapes have moved people who use agricultural land more densely and intensively than most others. Population pressure on the land intensifies the erosion problem, but also creates new demands for water. Soil erosion is a major water resource management issue because it leads to deposition of sediment in reservoirs and loss of reservoir storage capacity. As the nature of the terrain leads to high erosion rates and reservoir siltation is such a major problem, Chinese scientists have made outstanding contributions to the study of erosion, sediment transport and soil conservation. Considerable attention is, therefore, given to the sediment problem in the remainder of this chapter.

In terms of relief and fluvial geomorphology, the eastern margin of the Tibetan plateau is one of the most fascinating regions of the world. The major rivers of East and South East Asia almost all arise here, converging in the region of Yunnan, then dispersing in different directions. The

Irrawaddy and the Salween rise near the centre of Tibet and flow south-eastwards to Yunnan, where they turn south to flow 1500 km to the Andaman Sea. The Mekong also rises in the centre of the Tibetan plateau but after passing through Yunnan flows south-eastwards to the southern part of the South China Sea. North of the Mekong, the Red River of Vietnam and the Zhu Jiang (Pearl River) of southern China, rise in Yunnan and flow south-eastwards and eastwards, respectively, to the South China Sea. The Yangtze (Chang Jiang) rises on the Tibetan plateau and flows south-eastwards to Yunnan, before turning north and then east to enter the East China Sea. Further north, the Huang He (Yellow River) rises on the eastern margin of the Qinghai plateau, north-east of Tibet, and flows through a series of angular reaches before discharging into the Gulf of Chihli.

The Huang He (Yellow River)

With a mean suspended sediment concentration of 37 600 mg l^{-1} and a sediment yield of 2480 t km^{-2} a^{-1}, the Huang He is rightly considered the world's muddiest river (Fig. 10.2, Table 10.1). Of this sediment load, 90 per cent comes from the loess plateau region in the middle course of the

Table 10.1 Characteristics of major Chinese rivers

River	Length km	Drainage area (10^3 km^2)	Average annual runoff (10^9 m^3)	Average annual sediment load (10^6 t)	Average sediment conc. (mg 1^{-1})	Average tidal range at mouth (m)
Chang Jiang	6300	1808.5	928	486	470	4.66
Huang He	5464	752.4	44	1120	25200	0.2
Zhu Jiang	2210	442.6	336	83	230	1.26
Liao	1390	219.0	14.5	18	6860	2.3
Hai	1090	263.0	23.3	38	1060	2.48
Huai	1000	261.0	45.9	14	460	—
Min	584	60.9	62.1	8	130	4.5
Qintang	410	49.9	38.2	7	200	5.45

(*Source*: After Yen *et al*. 1986.)

Note:
These data differ slightly from those used to compile Figure 10.2. The reliability of the two sources is difficult to ascertain.

river. Up to 25 per cent of the sediment delivered to the head of the alluvial fan at Xiaolangdi is subsequently deposited between the dikes restraining the river along its course across the north China plain. Deposition is rapid enough to raise the channel bed 10 cm a^{-1} and consequently the channel flow is now generally between 3 and 5 m, and in places 10 m, above the plain outside the dikes (Douglas 1989). Deposition in the delta adds some 23.5 km^2 of new land every year, with the delta growing seaward by about 0.42 km a^{-1} (Gao Jiacai, 1989).

The basin sediment system of the Huang He is at a critical stage where constant effort to evacuate peak water and sediment flows through the endiked channel across the alluvial fan depositional tract may be disrupted by any major natural or people-caused events upstream affecting peak discharges or sediment loads. Huang Bingwei (1988) has described the problem succinctly:

'Simply stated, embankment strengthening alone is doomed to failure in the race against channel siltation. Should the river break at its most dangerous locality, the resulting flood would directly affect an area with more than 150 million inhabitants. The only dependable remedy for this problem is soil conservation on the loess highlands, for if the lower Yellow River is not so heavily silt-laden, our engineers can easily grapple with the problem of river control.'

The key to silt reduction in the loess highlands is to protect the surface against raindrop impact and detachment. Active gully enlargement is almost ubiquitous on the loess plateau where sediment concentrations in runoff reach 100 000 mg l^{-1}. Erosion rates of 18 600 t km^{-2} a^{-1} have been recorded in parts of Shaanxi (Derbyshire 1990). Raindrop splash, rilling, gullying, slurry flow and sliding of loess blocks combine to produce persistently high sediment yield, that of the Dali River in Shaanxi averaging 19 600 t km^{-1} from 1959 to 1969. However, much of the actual soil loss occurs from within the gully systems; in the Wuding River system, 30 to 62 per cent of the erosion occurs on the interfluves between gullies, but 38 to 70 per cent within the gullies (Jiang et al. 1981). Determinations of caesium-137 levels in soils indicate similar proportions,

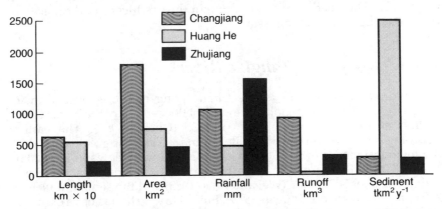

Fig. 10.2   Contrast in length, catchment size, rainfall depth, annual discharge volume and sediment yield of China's three major rivers (data from Pan Qingshen et al., 1983).

191

7 to 20 per cent of the eroded material coming from interfluves and 74 to 93 per cent from the gullies (Zhang *et al.* 1989). Although revegetation of actively eroding gullies is difficult, maintenance of a good plant cover on the interfluves not only reduces erosion there, but encourages infiltration and so lowers the runoff to gullies and thus the potential for erosion with gullies (Huang Bingwei 1988). Much of the eroded sediment is trapped behind dams or erosion control works with the catchment but nevertheless flood flows with extremely high sediment concentrations are carried into the endiked plains section of the river, where the coarse particles of more than 0.05 mm diameter account for more than half the accretion within the dikes (Zeng and Zhou 1989).

Despite the importance of watershed management and soil conservation, north China often is short of water and multipurpose reservoir construction has long been part of the strategy for managing the Huang He. The main stem of the river is regulated by a chain of eight reservoirs from the Longyang Gorge Dam upstream in Qinghai province to the Sanmenexia Dam, with a ninth at Lijia Gorge in Henan under construction and a tenth, the Xiaolangdi Dam, on the lower river, now under construction. The Yihe and Louhe tributaries in Henan, which at times contribute up to 50 per cent of the flow of the Huang He across the palin, are dammed, the Guxian reservoir on the Lohe being due for completion in 1992 (Yuan Jiang 1991). The variability of the sediment load in the endiked plains course of the Huang He is increased by the operation of regulating valves on the reservoir dams. In dry years the valves are closed and sediment is deposited in reservoirs, while in wet years, especially during flood flows with high sediment concentrations, gates are opened and sediment is scoured out of reservoirs adding to the load carried across the plains (Zuo Dakang and Zhang Peiyuan 1990). The operation of the Sanmenxia Reservoir is thus to minimize reservoir sedimentation and maximize water storage during dry periods (Gao Jiacai 1989). This means that during high water when sediment concentrations are also high, water is fed into the plains tract of the river and aggradation may occur. The need to alleviate drought thus reduces flood capacity of the endiked channel downstream.

The Chang Jiang (Yangtze River)

The hydrologic behaviour of the Chang Jiang has long been a major concern of the Chinese people. The earliest flood-mark of the Three Gorge section of the river dates from AD 1135 (Cheng 1989). The earliest hydrological station on the river dates from 1865 and the greatest floods in the historical record of the Three Gorge section were flows of 110 000 m^3 s^{-1} in 1870 and 1981 (Table 10.2), with the mean annual runoff at the mouth estimated at 29 300 m^3 s^{-1} (Wei and Zhao 1983) and the sediment yield as 280 t km^{-2} a^{-1} (Gu and Douglas 1989). Since 1135, 10 floods have exceeded 80 000 m^3 s^{-1}, , while in the last 100 years over 20 floods have exceeded 60 000 m^3 s^{-1}. . The main stem of the river, the Jingsha Jiang, rises in the dry eastern plateau of Tibet and has the lowest mean runoff per unit area of all the upper tributaries of 0.009 15 m^3 km^{-2} s^{-1}, compared to a mean flow of 0.021 m^3 km^{-2} s^{-1} in the Mian Jiang in western Sichuan. In a normal year, the flooding of the various tributaries and the main Chang Jiang do not coincide. However, in an abnormal year, if storms affect the southern tributaries later than usual, the flood peaks of the southern tributaries and that of the mainstream may combine to form an exceptional flood, such as the historic flood of 1931. If the flood on the mainstream comes earlier than usual it may combine with the peak wet season discharges of the southern tributaries to create a catastrophic event, such as the flood of 1935 (Cheng 1989).

Table 10.2 Historical floods at Yichang on the Chang Jiang

Year	Height (m)	Discharge (m^3s^{-1})
1870	59.14	110 000
1227	58.11	98 100
1560	58.09	98 000
1153	57.70	94 000
1860	57.96	92 500
1788	57.14	86 000
1796	56.45	84 000
1613	56.31	81 000
1896	56.56	71 100

Downstream of Yichang, at the downstream end of the Three Gorges, large areas are so low-lying that they have to be protected by 30 000 km of levees. Since 1949 some 30.065 $\times$ 10^9 m^3 of earth and rock have been moved to reinforce and extend the levees, the most critical of which is the 180 km long, 12 m high Jingjiang levee which protects some 18 000 km^2 of land, housing 7 $\times$ 10^6 people and providing 12 000 km^2 of farmland. The levee can withstand the 1 in 10 year flood, or if all existing flood diversion works are in operation the 1 in 20 to 1 in 50 year flood. However, operation of the Jingjiang flood diversion scheme means sending floodwaters over an area occupied by 700 000 people.

The multipurpose Three Gorge project is regarded as highly effective in bringing greater control of flooding in the lower reaches of the Chang-jiang. The flood storage capacity of the dam of 22.15 $\times$ 10^9 m^3 would be sufficient to reduce the 1 in 100 year flood downstream from around 105 000 m^3 s^{-1} to 80 000 m^3 s^{-1}. In addition, with an installed capacity of 17 680 MW, the hydroelectric station would generate the equivalent of a saving of 40 million tonnes of coal per year while navigation would be improved to permit larger vessels than at present to pass upstream to Chongging, creating a navigable waterway up to 700 km long, reducing transport costs by about 35 per cent.

The Three Gorge Dam project illustrates many of the ambivalences over water resources development in China. On the one hand, the growing shortage of power in the lower Changjiang and especially Shanghai, the need to reduce flood losses below Yichang and the conviction that Chinese engineers can tame nature as well as any other engineers are strong arguments to go ahead. On the other hand, the resettlement of between 700 000 and 1.2 million people, the loss of much of the scenic grandeur of the gorges, the need for an elaborate sediment flushing system and concerns about sedimentation at the upstream end of the reservoir and possible salinization downstream provide powerful arguments against the scheme. The debate about the proposal has been world-wide and long and detailed studies have been undertaken, with a wide range of international aid and expertise in China. In 1991 and 1992 the international press contained much comment on the likelihood of a start to the construction work. In April 1992, the National People's Congress saw deputies raising many questions about the project before it was eventually approved with 1767 votes in favour, 177 against and 664 abstentions. Although the start appeared to have been delayed by the debate in Congress, local reports said that much preliminary work, including preparations to move people out of the construction areas had begun before formal approval was obtained.

The impounded waters will stretch as far upstream as Chongging. It is probable that the contact between the swift flowing summer runoff and the still backwaters in the vicinity of Chongging will become a zone of sediment deposition as river velocities fall. The build-up of silt may have severe consequences for navigation and channel stability around the city (Yuan Meiqi *et al.* 1992). The benefits of the the Three Gorge Dam will largely be felt downstream, particularly through flood relief in Hubei province, while the majority of the costs will fall upstream in Sichuan (Macmillan 1989). However, lessons from other major dams on great rivers, such as the Nile and Colorado, suggest that modification of flood regime and trapping of silt could have major impacts on the delta, where gain of land has been significant over the last 100 years. The engineers and planners believe that an equilibrium condition between sediment inflow to reservoir, flushing of sediment out of the reservoir and downstream sediment transport can be achieved by releasing clay particles in suspension (sediment finer than 0.01 mm) from the reservoir from the very start of its operation so that impacts on coastlines and nutrient transport are minimized (Lin 1992).

However, many of the arguments about the Three Gorge project rely on comparisons with much-criticized major dam projects elsewhere. Yao Jianguo (1992) reports that investment in the project will account for 0.073 per cent of GNP and 0.123 per cent of China's national income, saying that both figures are lower than those required for the Aswan Dam on the Nile and the Itapua project on the Paraguay River built by Brazil and Paraguay.

The most daunting social aspect of the Three Gorge project is the resettlement of 1.13 million people. Their movement from the lower to higher parts of the valleys along the total 600 km length of the reservoirs is likely to introduce further risks of land instability. Official statements talk of converting 20 000 ha of wild mountain land to cash crop cultivation, mainly orange orchards, and of using 10 000 ha of hillside for cultivation of grain crops (Li Ping 1992). If the evidence of such activity around Chong-qing is typical, high rates of soil loss may ensue. Fear of missing out on new land allocations may be making peasants enthusiastic about volun-teering for trial resettlement schemes. They would probably prefer to have kept their original holdings.

The whole resettlement programme requires careful timing and fund-ing. Being so politically sensitive, the matter needs constant review by central government, but also needs effective management at the local level. Official statements about the agricultural possibilities read like plans for land development schemes in some other countries; plenty of informa-tion and ideas on what can be grown, and where, but little attention to where the crops can be sold, particularly in view of the slow transportation over the rugged terrain of the Three Gorge area, and even less to the training of the settlers in modern techniques of cultivation and soil conservation.

Flooding is not merely a problem in the lowland reaches downstream of Yichang. In the Sichuan part of the catchment from AD 1400 to 1950 extensive flooding produced by rains of 350 to 500 mm in ten days occurred 133 times, but in 1951 to 1980 they occurred 16 times, and in the 1981–90 decade, eight times, with especially disastrous impact in 1981. The greatest frequency of floods in Sichuan occurs in the area to the west and north of Chengdu where the mountain rivers debouch on to the plains. Although flood generation is closely related to rain-producing events, the increasing frequency of major floods since 1950 is thought to be linked to deforestation and growing cultivation on steep slopes.

Land degradation in the middle and upper portion of the Chang Jiang basin has led to a doubling of the river's sediment load since 1958 (Li and Cheng 1987). The 533 million tonnes total annual sediment transport at Yichang is about one-third that of the Huang He. Two areas and problems dominate the sediment supply: the severe debris flows, yielding up to 33 000 t km^{-2} a^{-1} of sediment, in the steep, rugged area along the Yunnan-Sichuan border; and severe agricultural soil erosion in eastern Sichuan, especially in the catchment of the Jialin River. Although the Jialin accounts for only 15.5 per cent of the catchment area and 15.9 per cent of the runoff above Yichang, it contributes 30.4 per cent of the total sediment discharge. The southern part of the upper catchment, north of Kunming, also con-tributes a large amount of sediment through debris flows (Gu and Douglas 1989).

Debris flows develop in terrain where there is a combination of abun-dant loose rock material, steep topography and the occurrence of high intensity, short duration rainfalls (Tang Bangxing and Liu Suqing 1984). Tectonic activity and abundant shales, mudstones and boulder beds favour the production of fragments which are easily transported down steep, 30 to 50 degree, slopes when lubricated by rainfalls of over 30 mm per day and intensities of over 60 mm per hour (Table 10.3). In the western Sichuan tributaries of the Changjiang, most debris flows occur in the summer months in the catchments of the Anning, Dadu, Heishui, Min and Nu Rivers. The frequency of debris flows has been accelerated by removal of vegetation on hillslopes and by construction activity related to mining, industrial and transportation developments.

Table 10.3 Intensity of rains producing debris flows in Jinlong Gully

Year of major debris flow	Depth of rainfall in stated time period (millimetres)		
	10 minutes	1 hour	24 hours
1974		60	124
1983	15.2	48	118.7
1984	20.0	37.1	107.8
1986	14.8	55.6	133.2

(*Source*: After He Qixiu 1991.)

The debris flow problems in northern Yunnan are well illustrated by the Xiaojiang basin (Du Ronghuan *et al*. 1987). The middle reaches of the river drain barren mountains where landslides and rockfalls are frequent. Many debris flow gullies occur on both sides of the river. Large depositional fans coalesce into a continuous zone of deposited debris covering the entire river bed. Debris flows are triggered by high and intense rainfalls (Table 10.3) and may carry huge boulders up to 250 m^3 in volume. The sudden occurrence and rapid movement of debris flows causes severe damage and risk to life and limb. Rapid aggradation of river channels means that many bridges have to be raised repeatedly and the water supply projects are threatened by rapid siltation. Huge check dams and diversion dikes have to be built to try to direct the courses of debris flow and to protect farmland.

The ultimate reduction of the debris flow problem lies in comprehensive management of the catchment areas: re-establishment of forest cover, sustainable forest management, declaration of areas of protective forest on mountains, solution to the land use conflict between forestry and grazing, attention to the fuelwood problem and management of firewood plantations in a sustainable manner (Tang Bangxing and Liu Suquing 1984).

Much of the Chang Jiang catchment has unstable slopes, especially in the gorge sections of rivers. Near Wanxian, downstream of Chongqing, for example, four landslides in a 16 km reach of river have a combined debris volume of over 50 million m^3 (Li and Wan 1989). In the whole Three Gorge area 177 landslides exist with a total rock material volume of about 1420 million m^3, including giant landslides of over 10 million m^3 each with a combined volume of about 1310 million m^3. These slides are mainly in Triassic and Jurassic sedimentary rocks containing weak mudstone beds which fail along bedding plane surfaces. On the river banks composed of subhorizontal strata, compression induces tensile fracturing and horizontal push type sliding occurs with slip surfaces cutting through bedding planes (State Commission of Science and Technology 1988).

The need to maximize the downstream use of the water resources of the

Chang Jiang and to exploit its hydroelectric potential has led to an intensive campaign by the river conservancy commission to improve soil conservation and to regulate runoff to streams. As slopes of 30 degrees or more are cultivated for vegetables in parts of the Sichuan basin, new terracing techniques have to be introduced which combine the creation of narrow strip terraces, often less than 2 m wide, with steep slope segments planted to commercially valuable trees, such as the mulberry. This combination renders all the land productive, but provides some permanent vegetation cover and structures to reduce the rate of runoff and to trap sediment on the slopes and enable it to be replaced, manually, on the cultivated terraces, rather than be washed downslope into the streams. To achieve widespread adoption of such erosion control methods, individual communities have to be persuaded of the value of the labour inputs to construct terraces and maintain the water control and sediment detention structures. In Tongliang county, Sichuan, this has been achieved by obtaining a 30 per cent increase in maize yields in the first year of terrace cultivation.

Soil erosion control on the slopes is all the more important because the storage of eroded material in reservoirs is relatively small. Sediment retention in over 10 000 reservoirs with a combined storage capacity of 18.9×109 m^3 in the Changjiang basin upstream has only slightly reduced the potential sedimentation in the Three Gorge Dam by 3.2 to 4.0 per cent of the annual sediment discharge at the dam site (Shi Guoyo and Cheng Xianwei 1992).

The Zhu Jiang (Pearl River)

The Zhu Jiang drains the hills of southern China which receive high rainfall from the south-west monsoon in the summer months. The mean annual depth of runoff is 820 mm, compared with 531 mm in the Chang Jiang and only 86.5 mm in the Huang He (Chen Zhizai 1985). Exceptional rains, particularly when associated with typhoons, can produce major flooding. In 1915 a flood on the Bejiang and Xijiang tributaries inundated 4.5 million ha of farmland and affected 3 million people. Large parts of Guangzhou city were flooded (Pan Qingshen et al. 1983). Since 1949 much has been done to build dikes and protect the delta against the flood risks which arise as tropical typhoons sweep into this part of southern China. Even so, the flow of the Zhujiang is much less variable than those of rivers further north, annual flow variability being less than 30 per cent. Parts of this area have sediment yields of up to 15 000 t km^{-2} a^{-1} (Lin 1992).

Much of the terrain is deeply weathered with red oxisols that erode relatively easily when vegetation is removed. While the average silt content for the Zhujiang basin as a whole is 300 mg l^{-1}, the Hongshui River draining the weathered red soils of the upper parts of the Xijiang has a mean silt content of 1000 mg l^{-1} (Ren Mei' E et al. 1985). Even the establishment of orchards, which provide a permanent tree cover, has been seen as damaging to the soil, as rills and gullies develop between the trees. Severe gullying of some of the deep soils is widespread in parts of the catchment area.

The catchment requires careful land management. Both a series of earth dams in major gullies (Xi Cheng-Fan 1990) and a careful scheme of soil conservation planting (Zhu Hejian 1990) have been advocated to reduce erosion. The suggested zoning is a forest on the summits of hills, below which is a belt of tea gardens, beneath which is another forest belt which gives way downslope to orchards. At the slope foot is an area of grass or forage crops, and on the valley floors and flood plains paddy rice cultivation. Adoption of such techniques in Wupi county, together with the blocking of gullies to trap silt and the mixing of coarse sandy material with finer silt has seen much eroded land restored to orchards and an overall reduction of the annual erosion rate from $6262 \text{ t km}^{-2} \text{a}^{-1}$ in 1952 to the present level of $217 \text{ t km}^{-2} \text{a}^{-1}$ (Lin 1992). Flood flows are now 37 per cent less than they used to be, indicating better retention of the water in the soil to support crop growth. Successes of this type are many, but cover only part of the originally severely eroded areas. Many gullies continue to enlarge and much remains to be done. The great economic expansion in Guangdong province is likely to increase pressures on land in the southern high rainfall area. Competition to supply the urban markets could precipitate more vegetable cultivation on steep slopes which might set off even more severe erosion than that now occurring around Chongqing in Sichuan. The environmental impact of the Guangdong boom on soil and water resources deserves more serious attention than it has so far received.

Conclusions

The water resource and soil conservation issues in China are so vast that both local, small-scale measures, essentially to retain the soil on the slopes and reduce runoff rates will have to proceed hand in hand with large-scale engineering works on the major rivers to regulate discharges, trap sediment and mitigate flooding. The growth of the rural population and the threat of tens of millions of rural unemployed or underemployed indicate difficulties in rural areas for some time to come. Land use controls must go hand in hand with soil conservation work. The labour availability makes it possible to undertake more terracing on steeper slopes than is possible in countries where labour costs are higher, but the real key is not only to improve conditions in existing areas, but to increase food production from present cultivated land so that people are not pressured into clearing plots on ever steeper slopes. In the north, the problems of grazing moving in to drier and drier areas as cultivation spreads on to former grazing land needs further attention. Yet it remains difficult to see how people can be excluded from many of the most fragile and unstable areas. Every encouragement must be given to the development of the appropriate technologies of land management.

Many authorities insist that reforestation can be the only long-term cure for the problem of rapid rates of runoff and severe soil erosion. Noting the trapping of silt behind man-made dams, Ding Zhao (1992) points out that dams cannot take the place of forests for conservation and argues that the nation must shift attention from the huge dam building programme to reforestation. Such policies are far less headline-making than major dam and reservoir projects and run into servere management problems, for the dependence of rural people on fuelwood makes forests a ready target for small-scale entrepreneurs interested in illicit wood marketing. Forests also consume land that may be used for cultivation or grazing, and only community-based forestry, in which local land holders have a stake, is likely to succeed. The massive windbreak forest planting in the middle reaches of the Changjiang is a thoroughly laudable exercise, but the effectiveness of the programme will be greatest where communities and individuals have a personal stake in the tree planting programme.

Several assumptions are made in the 'forests are a good thing' campaign. The first is that the forest provide as much protection against erosion as their proponents expect. In other countries, both temperate and tropical, plantation forests often leave sediment sources in the form of eroding drains and tracks established during the planting process. In some cases, particularly temperate uplands, sediment yields from forested areas are higher than from adjacent grazing lands. The second assumption is that forests contribute to good water management. Forests consume water, by transpiring it back to the atmosphere, and thus reduce the water available for runoff to rivers and ground water, and thus for industrial and domestic use. A third assumption is that plantation forests are self-perpetuating. Without good management and protection, they easily become degraded. Illicit grazing of domestic animals and fuelwood collection are the biggest risks. In the drier regions, establishment of a carefully managed ground cover may be the most effective protection against erosion.

Despite the emphasis on industrialization and urban growth by many contemporary commentators on China, the water resource and environmental hazards issues will remain major national concerns. While the massive engineering works of major dams and flood embankments on the great rivers have their place, the real solutions lie in catchment area management by the rural peoples themselves. The emphasis on rural development in the past was not entirely misplaced, for prevention of erosion at source and control of runoff in the headwaters are the best ways of reducing channel aggradation and the heights of flood peaks. In terms of social policy, the conservation of soil and water requires attention to appropriate rural environmental education and investment in training of rural extension officers and community level leadership to enable the people to see the relevance to their economic and social well-being of forest protection and soil conservation works. This may mean a large-scale transfer of financial resources from the developing coastal regions to the less wealthy interior headwater areas.

References

Aki A and Berthelot R (1974) 'Hydrology of humid tropical Asia', in Unesco (eds). *Natural Resources of Humid Tropical Asia*, Unesco, Paris, pp. 145–58.

Anon. (1987) 'Groundwater exploration and development in China', *UN/ ECAFE Water Resources Series* 62, 112–13.

Chen Zhizai (1985) 'China's water resources and its utilization', *Geojournal* 10, 167–71.

Cheng Xuemin (1989) 'Design criteria for flood discharge at China's hydro schemes', *International Water Power and Dam Construction* 41 (4), 14–17.

Derbyshire E (1990) 'Loess and the Loess Plateau of north China', in Cannon, T. and Jenkins, A. (eds). *The Geography of Contemporary China: The Impact of Deng Xiaoping's Decade*, Routledge, London, pp. 100–1.

Ding Zhao (1992) 'Forest cover', *World Water and Environmental Engineer* October, 33–7.

Douglas I (1989) 'Land degradation, soil conservation and the sediment load of the Yellow River, China: review and assessment', *Land Degradation and Rehabilitation* 1, 141–51.

Du Roughuan, Kang Zhicheng and Zhu Pingyi (eds) (1987) *Debris Flow of Xiaojiang Basin in Photographs*, Sichuan Publishing House of Science and Technology, Chendu.

Gao Jiacai (1989) 'Water resources in China', *UN ECAFE Water Resources Series* 64, 64–8.

Gu Hengyue and Douglas I (1989) 'Spatial and temporal dynamics of land degradation and fluvial erosion in the middle and upper Yangtze Basin, China', *Land Degradation and Rehabilitation* 1, 217–35.

He Qixiu (1991) 'Debris flows of the Jinlong Gully', *Mountain Research* 9, 59–62.

Huang Bingwei (1988) 'River conservancy and agricultural development of the North China Plains and loess highlands: strategies and research', *Great Plains Quarterly* 6, 218–24.

Institute of Hydrogeology and Engineering Geology, Chinese Academy of Geological Science (1976) *Karst in China*, Shanghai People's Publishing House, Shanghai.

Jiang Deqi, Qi Leidi and Tan Jiesheng (1981) 'Soil erosion and conservation in the Uding River Valley, China', in Morgan, R.P.C. (ed.) *Soil Conservation: Problems and prospects*, Wiley, Chichester, pp. 461–79.

Li J and Cheng K (1987) 'The erosion process in the middle and upper reaches of the Yangzi River'. *International Association of Hydrological Science Publication*, 165, 483–7.

Li Ping (1992) 'Trial resettlement of residents', *Beijing Review* 35 (14), 24–8.

Li Tranchi and Wan Shu Min (1989) 'Landslide 320 hazards regions in the middle river valley of the Chang Jiang. *Mountain Research* 6, 8–10.

Lin Bingnan (1992) 'Watershed and sediment management in China', in Larsen P and Eisenhauer N (eds), *Sediment Management Proceedings 5th International Symposium on River Sedimentation Karlsruhe 1992*, Institute of Hydraulic Structures and Agriculture Engineering, Karlsruhe

University, pp. 5–18.

Liu Jaixing and Cai Quaosheng (1988) 'A research in the groundwater reservoir in west suburb of Beijing, People's Republic of China', *Ministry of Geology and Mineral Resources Geological Memoirs Series 6 (5)* 1–113.

Liu Tungsheng 1988 *Loess in China*, 2nd edn, Springer, Heidelburg.

Macmillan, B. (1989) The Three Gorges Dam: Practical geography on the grand scale. *Geography Review*, 3 (2), 36–40.

Pan Qingshen, Zeng Jingxian, Yu Wenchen, Li Chunan, Wang Zhikun and Zhou Kaiping (1983) 'Experiences and flood prevention and control in China', *United Nations Department of Technical co-operation in Development Natural Resources/Water series 11*, 35–105.

Ren Mei'E, Yang Renzhang and Bao Haosheng (1985) *An Outline of China's Physical Geography*. Foreign Languages Press, Beijing.

Shi Guoyo and Cheng Xianwei (1992) 'The study on affecting of the reservoirs on the upper reaches of the Yangtze deposited for the sediment of the Three Gorges project', in Larson P and Eisenhauer N (eds), *Sediment Management Proceedings 5th International Symposium on River Sedimentation Karlsruhe 1992*, Institute of Hydraulic Structures and Agricultural Engineering, Karlsruhe University, pp. 801–7.

State Commission of Science and Technology, PRC and Ministry of Geology and Mineral Resources, PRC (1988) *Landslides and Rockfall of Yangtze Gorges*, Geological Publishing House, Beijing.

Tang Bangxing and Liu Suqing (1984) 'Dry valley environment and debris flow', in Yang Hanx, Zhu Zenda and Yang Youlin (eds), *International Symposium in Integrated Control of Land Desertification Proceedings*, National Committee of the People's Republic of China for MAB, Lanzshou, pp. 51–4.

Tong Guang-gun (1989) 'Irrigation development, financing and charges: China', *UN/ECAFE Water Resources Series* 63, 59–67.

Wei Zhongy and Zhao Chunian (1983) 'Natural conditions in the proposed water transfer region', in Biswas A K, Zuo Dankang, Nickum D E and Liu Changming (eds). *Long Distance Water Transfer: a Chinese case study and international experiences*, Tycooly, Dublin, pp. 97–125.

Wu Chuan-Jun (1990) 'Land utilization in China: its problems and prospects', *Geojournal* 20 347–52.

Xi Cheng-Fan (1990) 'Better land use and reclamation of 7 red soil hilly regions of southern China', *Geojournal* 20, 365–8.

Yao Jianguo (1992) 'Is Three Gorges project affordable?', *Beijing Review* 35 (22), 26–8.

Yen Kai, Xue Hongchao and Liu Jiaju (1986) 'Coastal and estuarine sedimentation problems in china', *Proceedings Third International Symposium on river Sedimentation*, University of Mississippi, Oxford, Miss., pp. 257–72.

Yuan Jiang (1991) 'Taming floods', *World Water and Environmental Engineer*, November, 45.

Yuan Meiqi, Li Bohai and Zhang Xiquin (1992) 'Study on the channel and harbour regulation in backwater fluctuation area of the Three Gorge project', in Larsen P and Eisenhauer N (eds), *Sediment Management*

Proceedings 5th International Symposium on River Sedimentation Karlsruhe 1992, Institute of hydraulic structures and Agricultural Engineering, Karlsruhe University, pp. 139–45.

Zeng Quinghua and Zhou Wenhao (1989) 'Soil erosion in the Yellow River basin and its impact on reservoir sedimentation and the lower Yellow River', *International Association of Hydrological Sciences Publication* **184**, 123–30.

Zhang Xinbao, Li Shaolong, Wang Chenghua, Tan Wanpei, Zhao Qingchang, Zhang Yiyun, Yan Mei Qiong, Liu Yalun, Jiang Jingjang, Ziao Jule and Zhou Jie (1989) 'Use of caesium 137 measurements to investigate erosion of sediment sources within a small drainage basin in the loess plateau of China', *Hydrological Processes* **3**, 317–23.

Zhu Hejian (1990) 'The present state and development orientation of land utilization in mountainous red earth region of China to take Fujian Province', *Geojournal* **20** 375–9.

Zuo Dakang and Zhang Peiyuan (1990) 'The Huang-Huai-Hai Plain', in Turner B L II, Clark W C, Kates R W, Richard J F, Mathews J T and Meyer W B (eds), *The Earth as Transferred by Human Action*, Cambridge University Press, Cambridge, pp. 473–7.

CHAPTER 11

The continuity of Hong Kong: key factors in retrospect and prospect*

Brian Hook

Whether Hong Kong continues, as one would hope, in its present form under the sovereignty of the People's Republic of China depends on many factors including notably the future political and legal system and the future level of economic performance. In the final analysis, however, it can continue only if sufficient numbers of its key residents are there to run the increasingly sophisticated system on which its sustained success has come to rely. In essence, this means that no matter how good the formal preparations by both the principals for the transition and the actual retrocession, the key element for success is the favourable perception of its residents not only of what has been done and will be done (or not done) but also of the prevailing spirit in which things are done.

It has been argued ever since the acknowledging of a serious brain-drain (Address by the Governor 1988) in 1987–88 that Hong Kong's viability is dependent on about 500 000 key personnel, including government officials, businessmen, professionals and technicians. Any shortfall in the supply of those categories to the system would adversely affect its efficiency and, if suffered over a long term, would result in changes that could undermine a remarkable human achievement. The aim of this chapter is to discuss, firstly in retrospect, how people's perceptions of China and Hong Kong contributed to the growth and development that led to the contemporary situation in Hong Kong and secondly, in prospect, how Hong Kong residents' perceptions as they affect their

*The data on which this chapter is based were collected during separate periods of field research in Hong Kong from 1988 to 1992. I would like to express my thanks to the staff of the relevant government departments, Immigration, Education, Information Services and Census, and also to those of the Canadian Commission, and the Australian and US Consulates General for their assistance. Thanks are also due to the Director and staff of the Centre of Asian Studies and to the Master and staff of Robert Black College, at the University of Hong Kong, who greatly contributed to making both my research work and my visits so agreeable. I am responsible for the interpretation of the data (and also, therefore, for any misinterpretation) and for the conclusions reached.

decisions whether or not to remain in Hong Kong, appear to have been formed in the light of events. These discussions will be followed by a concluding section on the prospects for the continuity of Hong Kong.

It was the people's perception of comparative advantage in terms of security and well-being that swelled the population of Hong Kong from half a million in 1945 to some 2.5 million in 1960 as they fled the vicissitudes of revolutionary and post-revolutionary China. This mass refugee migration, which strained the resources of the Hong Kong government and, unimaginable though it may appear in the light of its contemporary affluence, made the colony's plight a focus for international charity, occurred despite the post-war weakness of the UK, the imminent dissolution of the empire and precisely because of the refugees' experience and perception of life in China under Stalinist Communism.

A particularly graphic historical illustration of people's 'negative' perception of the prospects of a place in which to remain and to work exists in the rather sad history of Shanghai since the 1950s. For all its faults, and there were many in terms of urban deprivation, exploitation and unacceptable foreign domination, Shanghai was an international city and an unmatched powerhouse of commerce and industry in pre-war China. As such, it was a major source and pool of business talent which China could not afford to lose, much of which subsequently flowed to Hong Kong, to the benefit of the British colony. Despite claims that China was well rid of its 'comprador-bourgeoisie', the effect of their loss was, in the last analysis, to the detriment of the long-term prospects of the PRC in general and to Shanghai in particular.

While the massive influx of Chinese refugees in the 1950s presented the Hong Kong authorities with what at the time seemed an almost insuperable problem in meeting their basic needs of subsistence, it was shortly to provide the inexpensive labour resources and the rich talents for the recovery and comprehensive growth of Hong Kong in subsequent decades. One may also ascribe the success of Hong Kong in the second half of the twentieth century to reasonably good British-led government, in particular to the conduct of government within a rule of law unique in East Asia for much of the time that, by and large, protected the rights of the individual and created a reliable framework within which business could prosper.

In the perception of those who left China in the first decade of the PRC, during the famine that followed the Great Leap Forward, and the turmoil of the Cultural Revolution in the second decade, Hong Kong offered levels of security and well-being which, while still falling short of those in the developed world, nevertheless justified the immense personal risks involved in illegal immigration, both in the various stages leading to the act and subsequently in the alien environment. It was soon to be apparent that Hong Kong's gain was China's, particularly Shanghai's, loss. Over the ensuing decades the combination of reasonably good government, a policy of positive non-interventionism in the economy, consensus politics and a framework of law and order that protected the rights of the individual and encouraged business, together with a talented low cost labour force, provided most of the essential bases for the trends of development that brought Hong Kong to the impressive levels attained on the eve of the negotiations with China over its future.

The formal negotiations over some two years leading to the Sino-British Joint Declaration on the Future of Hong Kong (JD) in 1984 were preceded by UK attempts for several years to raise the question of the future of Hong Kong with China. There was concern over the prospects for investments in the New Territories (NT) beyond the 1997 expiry date of the lease governing that part of Hong Kong. Had the NT remained the rural hinterland it was until the development of new towns began the process of urbanization and accelerated its infrastructural and administrative integration with the already developed parts of the colony, there would have been less basis for concern. As it was, such concern was wholly justifiable.

Any form of self-determination having been ruled out for Hong Kong, there were three courses open to the UK: the first would have been to do nothing in the expectation that the PRC would permit 1997 to pass without comment on the ground that the lease had been signed under duress and was null and void from its inception; the second would have been to test the sensitivity of the PRC to the lease's imminent expiry by validating extensions of property leases and plans for development in the NT beyond 1997, thus enabling lawyers working for any company concerned, in which the PRC had an interest, to raise questions that would signal the PRC's unease; the third was to raise the question of Hong Kong's future formally with the PRC with a view to achieving a satisfactory solution. Although the first two courses had evident attractions – the second involving testing the PRC's sensitivities in an inconspicuous manner more in keeping with oriental diplomacy – neither of them could satisfy the legally binding criteria sought by the professions engaged in financial planning and development. Nor could the second be squared with the British position that the lease was lawful and binding, as were the treaties on which the occupation of Hong Kong was based. Accordingly, the decision was made formally to seek a solution to guarantee the future of Hong Kong beyond 1997.

While it is evident that unless the British government were to embark on a course that was both risky and uncharacteristic, ignoring the advice of its foreign affairs specialists, it had to seek to open formal negotiations, it is worth noting that all but the most inured pessimist around the beginning of the 1980s, remained, on balance, optimistic about the outcome. After all, the PRC had put behind it the Cultural Revolution, large-scale class struggle, Maoism and self-isolation; it had rehabilitated Deng Xiaoping who was a reformer (that he was a Marxist–Leninist reformer had become obscured at the time by the market characteristics of the reforms), espoused modernization and an open-door policy that was to encourage investment in China (particularly in special economic zones (SEZs) one of which, Shenzhen, was contiguous with Hong Kong), and there was a greater freedom of expression in the cultural sphere. This general perception of the prospects for the future generated an unprecedented degree of euphoria. This was initially supported by the evident success of Hong Kong under the Maclehose governorship and by the good international links developed between the British governmant under Mrs Thatcher's leadership and the Chinese government under Hua Guofeng, who visited the UK, and Deng Xiaoping's protégés Zhao Ziyang and Hu Yaobang. The actual fragility of the Sino-British relationship was not generally perceived until negotiations over the future of Hong Kong had become stalled in Peking and the differences exposed in thinly veiled statements and analogies, such as those that centred on the right (denied by the PRC) of Hong Kong people being represented at the negotiations, and we are told, in the chemistry of the Deng–Thatcher meeting.

Whether or not the Falklands War substantially affected the PRC approach to the Hong Kong issue is difficult to measure. It undoubtedly caused the PRC verbally to take sides, lest neglecting to do so be interpreted as a softening of attitude to imperialism in general and to the offshore island province of Taiwan in particular. In so doing, the PRC supported what most people viewed as the Galtieri military–Fascist dictatorship, presumably on the ground that the Falklands were, in fact, the illegally occupied and colonized Malvinas, whose future, ultimately, was an internal affair of Argentina. The most one can say is that the Falklands war occurred inopportunely for the negotiations over the future of Hong Kong. By raising the spectre of a colonial war, albeit fully justified as far as Britain was concerned, within the fissiparous ranks of the leadership of the Communist Party of China (CPC) it increased the inevitable tension between ideology and pragmatism when least tolerable. Furthermore, this tension was bound to be reflected in the stance taken by Deng Xiaoping over the Hong Kong question just as the determination evinced by Mrs Thatcher over the Falklands was likely to be present in some measure, though not in the same form, in her approach to the future of Hong Kong.

For the people of Hong Kong it was clear from the media reports and from the publicity given to China's unwillingness to compromise over the issue of sovereignty that their perception of the future would have to undergo review. On balance, even more important than what appeared in the media was what became common knowledge either through deliberate leaks in China or through clandestine sources with links in Taiwan and Hong Kong. It became evident that the formal British approach to the issue had been based on the assumption of legal occupation through a combination of the treaties and the lease which, it was hoped, could be continued either by simply extending the lease or by surrendering sovereignty for continued administration. Ironically, this was similar to a formula that had been explored to resolve the issue between Argentina and Britain over the Falklands and which, once Argentina had gone to war, was consigned, as Lenin might have said, to the dustbin of history. While there may be an impermanence to Lenin's having consigned certain things to the dustbin of history and to the abandoning of the Falklands formula, it was evident from Deng's well-publicized statement to the effect he would not be a twentieth century Li Hongzhang, that China would certainly resume both sovereignty and administration over Hong Kong in 1997. According to reports attributed to those present at the meeting, Deng had made it clear to Mrs Thatcher that, in his view, sovereignty and administration were inseparable.

It is clear from the available evidence of the negotiations that while people's perceptions of the future of Hong Kong were in flux there was as yet no major shift – 1997 was still far off and in terms of the development of Hong Kong there was still time for three economic booms. What did have an immediate effect, however, was the line adopted by the PRC that failure by the UK to come to a mutual agreement would leave it free to impose its own solution. Similarly, the collapse in the value of the Hong Kong dollar in 1983, although precipitated by perceptions in Hong Kong and overseas of PRC intransigence, was nevertheless perceived in Peking as a result of manipulation of the exchange rate by the UK (as an instrument of its diplomacy) and brought into sharp focus the complexities that lay ahead in the Sino-British relationship and in the future relationship between Hong Kong and China.

The delayed response to a changed perception of the future is shown in the relatively slow rise in the annual figures for emigration from Hong Kong in the 1980–85 period to the three favourite destinations of Hong Kong residents, Canada, Australia and the United States of America. Table 11.1, far from signalling alarm over the future such as that which spurred the exodus of talent from Shanghai in the 1950s, is consistent with a pattern that could be associated with travel to and from the continually developing Chinese diaspora. The pattern of movement was determined more by the aim of promoting business rather than an ultimate intention to resettle in another country. The figures for 1980–85 do not represent any expression of a lack of confidence in the future of the Hong Kong–China relationship since they are consistent with flows of people from Hong Kong for the creation of wealth overseas for remittance and for retirement in Hong Kong or China. In addition, the outflow was thought to be balanced by the inflow of those returning for retirement, education or family reunion.

Table 11.1 Hong Kong Immigrants to Canada,[1] Australia[2] and the USA[3], 1980–85

	1980	1981	1982	1983	1984	1985
Canada	6309	6461	6543	6710	7690	7380
Australia	2058	2139	2446	3030	4490	4610
USA						
(quota)		345	244	406	388	419
(non-quota)		1843	2170	2314	2345	2225

(*Source*: Statistics made available by the respective consular authorities in Hong Kong.)

Notes:
1. Total landings not immigrant visas issued; the latter exceeded total landings.
2. Settler arrivals.
3. Immigrant visas by fiscal year beginning fiscal year 1981 (Oct. 1980–Sept. 1981). During this period, until 1987, the quota was 600 a year; non-quota visas were those issued to Hong Kong residents who were close relatives of US citizens.

Although it has no *direct* relevance for the argument advanced in this chapter, namely that the future of Hong Kong will be determined by the people's response to their perception of China and to the prospects for the Hong Kong–China relationship, it must be added that the picture would be incomplete without information on immigration into Hong Kong. The lure of Hong Kong and of capitalism over Stalinist Communism was always evident from the long-standing immigration from the PRC and, since the fall of Saigon in 1975, from Vietnam. Immigration to Hong Kong from the by then reforming PRC had been brought under control by mutual agreement and averaged about 27 000 annually between 1980 and 1985. The figures for illegal immigration are difficult to ascertain but, for example, over 12 000 illegal Chinese immigrants were detained and repatriated in 1985. On the assumption that for every two arrested a third immigrant evaded capture, the total immigration from China to Hong Kong is less than 35 000 annually.

Immigration from Vietnam proved to be a much less manageable problem for the Hong Kong authorities: between 1975 and 1988, 133 000 refugee boat people arrived in Hong Kong, 69 000 in 1979 alone. While largely a UK–Hong Kong question with humanitarian and foreign policy overtones (in so far as the USA steadfastly opposed Vietnamese repatriation), the sanctuary given by the Hong Kong government to those 'alien' refugees led the PRC to demand a solution to the problem before 1997. Moreover, despite a large proportion of the local population having been refugees at some time in their lives, there was little sympathy for the so-called 'boat people'; they were deemed a source of social problems and an unnecessary burden on the exchequer. The latter they certainly were, costing HK$ 1316 million between 1979 and 1989.

The problem of illegal immigration from Vietnam dominated the immigration–emigration issues in the first half of the 1980s. For the remainder of the decade, however, that intractable problem was compounded by the dramatic rise in emigration from Hong Kong to Canada, Australia and the USA. Table 11.2 demonstrates the scale of this unprecedented increase.

As the Hong Kong government does not place any restriction on exit, its statistical system did not immediately highlight the steep upward trend of emigration. When the authorities became aware of it, the tendency was to downplay it by alluding to the historic flows of people in and out of a trading entrepôt like Hong Kong. This initial reaction was more a matter of genuine conviction and wishful thinking than dissimulation or misjudgement. However, it was unfortunate, since the populace knew roughly the extent of the exodus, the socio-economic origin of the type of person involved and the reasons for the decision to go. Hong Kong is a small densely populated place. The extended family system still flourishes despite the conflicting demands of capitalist individualism. In fact, there had developed a unique reconciliation between the claims of traditional and modern social values. Thus, there are few secrets that remain so for long. For example, the practice of holding farewell dinners and parties drew attention to the phenomenal growth of emigration; companies were constantly seeking to fill vacancies; load factors on the flights from Hong Kong to Vancouver (which became known as 'Hongcouver') and Sydney

Table 11.2   Hong Kong immigrants to Canada,[1] Australia[2] and the USA[3], 1986–90

	1986	1987	1988	1989	1990
Canada	6893	16170	23281	19981	28825[4]
Australia	4940	6420	9530	10380	17589[2]
USA					
(quota)	409	462	4200[3]	4099	3901
(non-quota)	1907	1628	1863	1831	2224

(*Source*: Statistics made available by the respective consular authorities in Hong Kong.)

Notes:

1. Figures are for total landings (of immigrants from Hong Kong with visas) not immigrant visas actually issued that year. For the 1987–90 period the annual figures in that category were 22 097, 21 843, 22 130 and 22 566, respectively, implying a considerable number of intending immigrants in the pipeline.

2. The migration categories were: Economic, 12 438 (Independents 7497, Business 3253 and Employer nomination scheme 1688); Family migration, 3679; Humanitarian, 1472 (Vietnamese refugees).

3. There was a numerical limitation of 600 p.a. before 1987. From 1987 this was increased to 5000 p.a. US immigration law was changed in 1990 to raise the total to 10 000 p.a. with visa validity extended to the year 2001 at the wish of the applicant. This total is expected to be raised in steps to 20 000 p.a. over the next few years.

4. The leap is explained by the results of applicants having their papers processed at Canadian missions outside Hong Kong where the delay, through pressure of numbers, was very long. Of this total, some 6000 applications for immigrant visas had been processed abroad (e.g. Singapore, Seattle) by lawyers, consultants and agents working for applicants who had merely a mailing address. This trend began in 1989.

were constantly above average; and the local Cantonese punned, as is their wont, on the plight of husbands whose absentee wives were establishing residence abroad and who commuted ennervatingly back and forth on conjugal duty, referring to them as *taikongren* (astronauts, but here *tai* means *taitai* wife and *kong* void or space), i.e. men without wives.

For a while, the government's reaction was low key. By downplaying the trend it actually succeeded to some extent in not drawing attention to the issue which in any case was politically sensitive. Emigration implied a lack of confidence in the long-term likelihood of political institutions dominated by an unreconstructed Communist Party of China (CPC) to maintain the successful development of Hong Kong as a special administrative region (SAR) of the PRC on the basis of *gangren zhigang* (Hong Kong people ruling Hong Kong) and *yiguo liangzhi* (one country two systems). The downplaying of the trend in emigration was, however, largely achieved only outside Hong Kong. On the spot, most residents were aware of it and knew the cause to be a changing perception, at the time, of the outcome of the modernization process in China coupled to the fall in the level of confidence felt about the future of Hong Kong as a SAR. When one says many residents knew the cause, it is impossible to quantify precisely how many; what is factually certain and quantifiably so, is the *effect*. It is clear that the perception of those who decided to go, and others who are still doing so, was and is affected chiefly by adverse political developments on the mainland. Moreover, the sensitivity to such developments, particularly if they actually involve Hong Kong–China relations, may be compounded by a delayed response, or by the inaction of the local authorities or of the two principals. Conversely, good news from China over an appropriate period, in particular good news on the economic front that eclipses or occludes political concerns, may produce the opposite reaction, such is the sensitivity and volatility of local public perception in the run-up to the retrocession.

Such sensitivities and volatility in the general perception of the situation that follows are the results of Hong Kong's enjoying not only a good formal news media network but also an unparalleled informal news network extending throughout most parts of China and fed by information from Taiwan that originates in anti-Communist networks. There is also a significant left-wing press controlled from the mainland which, to the extent that it serves the political centre uncritically (which as the Tiananmen crisis showed is not invariably), informs a rather sophisticated local readership by *negative example*. Accordingly, among the chief influences on the perception of a key socio-economic section of the Hong Kong population were the internal political struggles in China culminating, for example, in the sacking of Hu Yaobang, together with the manifest economic problems, including the seemingly unabated growth of corruption and nepotism. By virtue of experience and being Chinese, Hong Kong people could sense the difficulties, though obviously not their grisly consequences that were ultimately to lead to Tiananmen Square.

This perception of the future was bound to be affected by the debate in Hong Kong over the extent and pace of democratization. It is probably true that, as Lord Maclehose indicated later in a BBC interview (30/6/89) regarding his own period as governor, there was no great pressure in Hong Kong for democratization. We may assume that had the question been put to the population before the signing of the Joint Declaration in the form of a referendum the answer may well have been negative. Once the debate got under way, however, and once the head of the local branch of the Xinhua News Agency (XHNA: actually the representative of the Central Committee of the Communist Party of China) intervened, claiming that by allowing what the PRC deemed to be unacceptably fast democratization 'one side was deviating from the terms of the Joint Declaration', (Davies and Roberts, 1990, p. 524), perceptions changed. It would be far from the truth to say that there was anything like a *single* perception of the future that was changing: the debate on democratization had served to divide and factionalize Hong Kong's elites from whom the community leaders are selected by the government and to draw attention to the issues of the day. Thus there were different perceptions from different groups: with some exceptions the business community was not altogether happy with the prospect of democratization arguing that the existing executive-led system had been, and would remain, the best guarantee of Hong Kong's prosperity and stability.

The most explicit endorsement of this conservative position came from China and was expressed by supporters and official agencies in Hong Kong (Davies and Roberts, 1990, p. 524). Not only did China claim the moral high ground by referring to the principle of upholding the letter and spirit of the Joint Declaration, it too shared the pragmatic view of the business community. Both feared a legislature generated democratically, and dominated by members elected by and for the groups who would benefit from wealth redistributative policies, on the grounds that moves towards higher taxation would inevitably adversely affect investment. The Hong Kong administration remained overtly neutral in this debate, but it was clear that democratization on the scale envisaged by certain of its advocates implied a vastly changed role for the administration and amounted to a venture into *terra incognita* at a juncture when it might be better to remain on *terra firma*. Significantly, the group that was most vulnerable to the implications of the debate as to China's preferences, and the extent to which the UK would promote reform in face of Chinese resistance, was the young to middle-aged professionals. It appears that the perceptions of this group changed in the mid-1980s: firstly, as the implications for Hong Kong of the debate on the parameters of modernization in China itself became clearer; and secondly, as the implications of the potentially destabilizing debate within Hong Kong, and China's undoubted indirect role in it, were factored into their assessment of Hong Kong's future as a SAR within the polity of China. Their concern was compounded by the introduction of yet another nationality status for Hong Kong people, that of British National Overseas (BNO) and a related passport for use after 1997.

As the flow of normal emigration was swelled by emigrants from this socio-economic group most vital to Hong Kong's survival as a business and capital-intensive high-value-added manufacturing centre, the government became more concerned. The Governor, Sir David Wilson, who had taken office in April 1987 following the sudden death in Peking of Sir Edward Youde at the end of 1986, devoted much space to a wide-ranging review of the government perception of the twin emigration and immigration problems in his address at the opening of the 1988/89 session of the Legislative Council (Address by the Governor, 1988). Regarding emigration, he noted that recent increases had to be viewed against an historical and cultural background characterized by population mobility generated for various reasons. Significantly, it was noted that added to those traditional reasons for movement was a degree of uncertainty about the future and the search for some sort of insurance policy. He confirmed that a task force had been set up earlier in 1988 to gather information about emigration and that its estimate was that some 30 000 people had left in 1987 while some 3000 former emigrants had returned, using old Hong Kong documents. The task force had surmised that an unknown number of emigrants had returned on newly acquired travel documents, and that with some 45 000 people emigrating in 1988 the net outflow, on a similar basis, would exceed 40 000.

The Governor urged his audience to view the figures in a proper perspective: the net outflow in the 1970s had been 38 000 a year, and while the numbers for the late 1980s exceeded those for the first half of the decade when an estimated average of 20 000 a year emigrated, it was wrong to conclude that the net outflow for 1988 would be '45 000 professionals', as the true figure in that catagory was less than a quarter of the figure cited. The reference to the loss of professionals is very significant as it is the clearest recognition of the damage that a brain-drain could do to Hong Kong in the run-up to 1997. By September 1990 matters had grown much worse. The Tiananmen crisis coincided with visits to Hong Kong of the Australian and Canadian ministers of immigration, and there was wide speculation that the government might be seeking to persuade them either to curb entry or to adopt delayed-action (i.e. immigration visas of extended validity) schemes. There was public recognition that, in the absence of emergency measures to retard the outflow, Hong Kong could lose some 400 000 of its best educated and talented young people in the decade leading up to the transfer of sovereignty. Such a loss, no matter what efforts had been made to mitigate its effect, in a population of 6 million, would be intolerable. Not only would there be the threat that Hong Kong might cease to function as it had in the past, but its potential contribution to China's modernization would be irretrievably forgone.

In the same context, in his speech the Governor drew attention to the increased opportunities for emigration and to the points system which certain countries operated, the aim of which was to give strong preference to the better trained applicants. He added that while there would be no question of interfering with the freedom of people to travel and to settle, the intention would be to gather information about the qualifications and experience of the emigrants, the better to design education and training programmes to fill the gaps. At the same time, noting that knowledge at graduation could not be equated with knowledge gained from experience, the Governor drew attention to the need to encourage people to stay and those who had left to return. He envisaged steps to improve housing and the quality of life generally, and the need for international schools.

The seriousness of emigration, or the brain-drain as it became known popularly, was by now universally recognized. The administration, which had been slower than the public to accept what was happening, was now fully aware of the situation and the worst fears were confirmed by the trend evident both in the official long-run statistics (Table 11.3) and in applications for certificates of no criminal conviction (Table 11.4), the latter being required of intending emigrants by the consular representation in Hong Kong of the country of their choice.

Table 11.3   Hong Kong Government estimates of net emigration

1980	22 400	1986	19 000
1981	18 300	1987	30 000
1982	20 300	1988	45 800
1983	19 800	1989	42 000
1984	22 400	1990	62 000
1985	22 300	1991	60 000

(*Source*: Statistics provided by Government Information Services, Hong Kong Government.)

212

The statistics in Table 11.4 form the background to the action that the government was to take in 1989 and 1990 to counter the brain-drain. In this context it is relevant to note that whereas the rise in emigration in 1986 and 1987 can, to some extent, be ascribed to the main destination countries making entry easier by relaxing quotas, which at one time was the contention of the Hong Kong administration, on balance it cannot be denied that the chief factor involved was the changing perception of the candidate group of the future of the Hong Kong government under Chinese sovereignty. Indeed, it may be argued that rather than the destination countries so to speak sowing the seeds of emigration, the seeds were first sown by the perception of a deterioration in the prospects for tolerably smooth and uneventful modernization in China and the destination countries merely responded to the collective wish to emigrate, out of self-interest, when it became apparent that high quality, qualified professionals were available.

Table 11.4 Number of applications in Hong Kong for a certificate of no criminal conviction with estimates of emigration totals for resettlement in brackets, and actual landings in Australia, Canada and the USA

	1985	1986	1987	1988	1989	1990
Applications	23 080	38 200	53 471	40 448	57 339	69 275
Emigration estimates	(22 300)	(19 000)	(30 000)	(45 800)	(42 000)	(62 000)
Landings (3 countries)	14 634	14 149	10 180	38 874	36 291	23 714[1]

(*Source*: Statistics made available by the respective consular authorities in Hong Kong and by the Immigration Department, Hong Kong Government.)

Note
1. Excluding Canada.

There is no doubt that Australia, Canada and the USA have benefited and stand to benefit immensely from the influx of Hong Kong professionals in terms of their contributing skills acquired after years of training, their calibre and life style, not to mention their transferred wealth. For example, the Canadian Commission in Hong Kong confirmed that the declared assets alone (i.e. excluding undeclared assets) of the some 20 000 Hong Kong immigrants to Canada in 1989 were HK 30 000 million. These considerations were not lost on British politicians who were critical of the UK immigration restrictions, since they foresaw that in the worst-case scenario, 'Armageddon' as it became known, the UK could be forced to accept those who had remained in Hong Kong, who would, on balance, be from lower socio-economic cohorts. While the argument that other countries made it easier to immigrate and thus actually caused greater emigration may have been convincing in 1987–88, it was manifestly no longer the case in 1989–90 when the political struggle in China brought the violent suppression of the democracy movement. At a most difficult juncture for Hong Kong, immediately following the shootings around Tiananmen Square on 4 June 1989, it was obvious to those in government that the brutal outcome of events could not fail fundamentally to change people's perceptions of China.

At that time, official statements in Hong Kong were perforce diplomatically restrained, but the message was clear. Confidence in the future Hong Kong SAR depended on confidence in the future of a modernized, stable China. The Tiananmen Square crisis was the tragic culmination of a stage in China's modernization in which Hong Kong, by virtue of its contiguity with Guangdong and in particular with the thriving SEZ of Shenzhen, was symbiotically linked. The Hong Kong economy had recently been systematically restructured to take advantage of the lower labour costs and ample space in Shenzhen and the Pearl River Delta and, in consequence, some 2 million people were then employed by companies and units linked to Hong Kong (and even through Hong Kong with Taiwan) interests in 'outward processing'. In contrast, manufacturing industry in Hong Kong itself had declined in terms of employment to fewer than 1 million people. Simultaneously, the service sector of the Hong Kong economy had been expanding as it adjusted to meet the growing demands of re-exporting and transhipment.

As we have seen, while Hong Kong was thus becoming economically more integrated with China, the perception of a section of the population of Hong Kong about the future had already undergone a significant change. This had resulted in a steep upward trend in emigration amounting to a serious brain-drain that, unchecked, could threaten the viability of Hong Kong in its existing form. In retrospect, the reasons for the apparently contradictory decisions by Hong Kong emigrants is much clearer than it was when, before the Tiananmen crisis, they appeared set to benefit from Hong Kong's greater economic integration with a modernizing, open-door China. Besides the anxieties generated by the political struggle in China over the appropriate road to economic modernization, a struggle that presented serious ideological problems for the CPC both nationally and, in the light of trends in Eastern Europe and the USSR, internationally, confidence in Hong Kong was understandably most affected by the relations between Hong Kong itself and China. Even before the tragedy of Tiananmen Square, confidence had been sensitive to issues such as the drafting of the Basic Law, Human Rights and the question of native Hong Kong citizens' rights to live in the United Kingdom.

The drafting of the Hong Kong Basic Law was a task assigned to the PRC in the 1984 Joint Declaration (JD). The Basic Law (BL) is perceived by most people as a constitution for the Hong Kong SAR, though that is probably elevating it to a status not actually acknowledged by the PRC where basic laws are those laws subordinate to the state constitution and approved by a plenary session of the National People's Congress (NPC). The BL is, nevertheless, a constitutional document for the Hong Kong SAR and as such it was expected to incorporate what were viewed as the essential guarantees made in the JD. Accordingly, as the debate over the text of the BL was widely reported, attention focused in particular on the future political system.

In this regard, the inability of the aspiring democratizers in Hong Kong such as Martin Lee and Szeto Wah sufficiently to get their ideas about the Hong Kong political system through the Basic Law Consultative Committee

(BLCC) and adopted by the Basic Law Drafting Committee (BLDC) was seen by some Hong Kong residents as a shift away from the spirit, if not the letter, of the JD. Although many did not support the democratizers in all their demands, the level of debate and evidence of disagreement over the BL drafts could not fail to intensify anxieties among people who, in the light of the struggle in China that had already brought the demise of Hu Yaobang and appeared to threaten other modernizers, were already worried about their future and that of their families. By the time of the Tiananmen crisis, two drafts had been produced. It was clear, however, that the second draft, in which the BLDC sought to incorporate acceptable criticisms of the first, did not meet the expectations of many in Hong Kong, and, we must assume, the concerns expressed confidentially through diplomatic channels by the British government. A senior Hong Kong official speaking shortly after the Tiananmen crisis 'pointed towards some of the areas in the second draft needing further examination . . .' (Cheng and Wong 1990, p.X. Text released by Government Information Services, Hong Kong).

These latter concerns, made public in August 1989, included the issue of the PLA's future role in the Hong Kong SAR and other matters affecting public order, the existence of possible sources of conflict between provisions in the State Constitution and the BL, the role of the BL Standing Committee of the NPC in regard to determining the application of articles concerning the respective powers of the central authorities and those of the Hong Kong SAR, the future political system and democratization, the relationship between the Executive and Legislative Councils and the preparation of the Hong Kong SAR budget. The aim was, on the one hand, to encourage an articulate middle class audience to address issues of concern before time ran out and, on the other, obliquely to signal to the PRC side that in the circumstances more time and effort was needed to arrive at a satisfactory draft that would restore confidence in the future. Well intentioned though these aims were it was, as events showed, unlikely they would be achieved: the suppression of the democracy movement had cast a dark shadow over the BL drafting process and had evoked more protest and despair than reasoned comment. Moreover, in China the authorities had already drawn their own conclusions about the role of Hong Kong in a movement they perceived to have as its aim the toppling of the legitimate government of another sovereign power. The conclusions of the PRC authorities about the role of Hong Kong in the democracy movement had already been published. Addressing the Eighth Session of the 7th NPC Standing Committee on 30 June 1989 Chen Xitong, Mayor of Peking and concurrently a State Councillor, referred *inter alia* to Hong Kong newspapers and journals, including *The Economic Journal, Emancipation Monthly, Mirror Monthly, Ming Pao Daily News* and the *Express*, publishing articles variously advocating explicit changes in the leadership and in the system of government, and seeking a reversal of the verdict on liberalization and a rehabilitation of Hu Yaobang (*Renmin Ribao Wenxuan*, Beijing, 10/7/89). He referred to 'reactionary political forces in Hong Kong, Taiwan, the USA and other Western countries having been involved in the turmoil through various channels and by various means'. Hong Kong supporters, it was stated, had provided tents for those in the Square, enabling the occupation to be maintained. These had been used to set up 'villages of freedom' and to launch a 'democratic university' that was intended to become the 'Huangpu military school of the new era'. Referring to financial contributions, Chen Xitong spoke of some people in the US, Britain and Hong Kong offering US$1 million and millions of Hong Kong dollars, money that, he claimed, went in part towards sabotaging law enforcement.

For those Hong Kong residents who were concerned about the possible implications of the retrocession, the events of 1989 confirmed their worst fears. China had experienced a destabilizing power struggle in which elements whose policies, at the time, appeared to augur well for the future, had been defeated while Hong Kong itself had been identified as a source of subversion. Furthermore, for the time being, as the international community reacted to the movement and the means of its suppression, there was a threat to the economic prosperity that in the past had enabled Hong Kong to overcome periods of extreme pessimism. In the circumstances it is not surprising that the combined effect of, on the one hand, doubts accumulated over the period after the signing of the JD (doubts that were until 1989 probably not wholly beyond dispelling given a more flexible approach to issues affecting the future), and on the other the suppression of the democracy movement, led more Hong Kong people to initiate procedures leading to emigration. As Table 11.4 shows, applications for certificates of no criminal conviction having stood at 23 080 in 1985 reached 57 339 in 1989 and rose to 69 275 in 1990.

Even before the tragic events of 1989, the Hong Kong authorities, concerned about emigration trends at the time of the early debates on democratization when local XHNA spokespersons were stressing the need for 'convergence', had set up a working party to identify the implications of the exodus for the economy. Once the implications were clear, the government had orchestrated a significant response aimed at ensuring the supply of well-educated professionally qualified persons for the economy. It had become evident that unless such a supply was assured, no matter what the future political structure, Hong Kong could not continue in its present form let alone develop beyond it as a SAR within the PRC.

Noting that some 23 per cent of all those emigrating were in the 'professional, administrative and managerial' category of the workforce (though that category was only 5.7 per cent of the population), the government raised the targets set in 1988 for first degree places in tertiary level institutions. The effect of this was to raise the existing number of first year degree places from 7100 in 1990 to 15 000 by 1994–95, enabling 18 per cent of the age group to take a degree course and, 25 per cent to proceed to some form of post-secondary education. The programme, which must be regarded as among the most significant socio-economic initiatives of the difficult five years spanning the governorship of Sir David (now Lord) Wilson, would give a total of 67 000 tertiary places (in a system of universities, polytechnics and colleges) in 1995 and some 88 000 first degree places between 1989 and 1996, at a cost, in additional recurrent expenditure of HK$2341 million.

Confronted by a further and precipitate drop in confidence in the summer of 1989, the Hong Kong government made three additional major policy initiatives aimed at maintaining stability and containing emigration within parameters that the Hong Kong political and economic system could tolerate, pending, it was hoped, a return to political reform and economic progress in China. These initiatives were the adoption of the Port and Airport Development Strategy (PADS), the drafting of a Bill of Rights and the introduction of a British Nationality Selection Scheme (Address by the Governor 1989). The PADS initiative, by world standards a huge infrastructural project costing, at 1989 prices, some HK$130 billion, was conceived to meet the needs of the Hong Kong SAR's role as the principal port and airport serving a population of 70 million in southern China. Its core projects, to be completed by 1997, would provide the boost to investment, international involvement and employment that should carry Hong Kong prosperously and vigorously into the twenty-first century. The Bill of Rights was designed to ensure that certain rights provided by international conventions were guaranteed in law in Hong Kong. The British Nationality Selection Scheme was designed, not as its designation might be construed to confer the right, forthwith, to 50 000 selected heads of families (plus dependants) to move to Britain, but to provide a carefully selected key group with an insurance policy that would induce them to *remain* in Hong Kong in the belief that their collective contribution to the concepts of 'one country two systems' and 'Hong Kong people running Hong Kong' could be successfully applied in the Hong Kong SAR beyond 1997.

Since their introduction, the record shows that none of these measures has been well received by the PRC. The latter two have, however, been implemented and both appear to be having some effect: the Bill of Rights is being applied by the courts and some 200 laws are affected by its provisions, many by shifting an onus of proof back to the prosecution when, hitherto, there was an assumption of culpability unless otherwise proved by the defendant. The British Nationality scheme, while itself providing an insurance policy for a large number of people, has encouraged the emergence of a number of delayed or protracted visa validity schemes for other countries that will retard the loss of human resources.

While all three initiatives designed to restore confidence in Hong Kong encountered varying degrees of suspicion, criticism and hostility from the PRC authorities the greatest challenge has been mounted on PADS. In retrospect, with the benefit of hindsight, it now appears that it would have been more prudent to have sought to convince the PRC authorities of the aims of and need for PADS at a much earlier stage rather than to launch it literally in the wake of the Tiananmen crisis. For a while after the announcement of PADS Hong Kong, much to the displeasure of the PRC, was evidently being used as an escape conduit for refugees fleeing from arrest and punishment for involvement in the democracy movement. Moreover, although the large-scale sympathy demonstrations that in Hong Kong had marked the June events had ceased, sporadic lawful demonstrations and protests were a constant possibility. An indication of the distrust that existed occurred when the international swimmer Yang Yang was not returned to the PRC having sought asylum but permitted to leave for the USA. Such instances, and allegations of the complicity of members of some PRC organs in Hong Kong (among them members of the XHNA and associated media which culminated in the 'unauthorized departure' of the XHNA head, Xu Jiatun, for the USA), convinced the Beijing authorities that their adverse perception of Hong Kong was correct.

It was evident at the outset that the Hong Kong government would require private investment in PADS. For private investors to participate, it was equally evident that PRC support for the strategy would be needed since the concept was predicated on yields to the Airport Authority to repay debt from fees starting in 1997. From the PRC standpoint, setting aside political factors, there was the need to be confident about the implications for sovereign debt after 1997. Once the politics of 1989 and 1990 were factored into the equation, the outcome was the 18 months delay that appeared to be brought to an end by the visit of the British Prime Minister John Major to Peking and the signing of a memorandum of understanding on PADS, in which certain guarantees were entered into by Britain about the level of accumulated reserves in Hong Kong in 1997. Even so, the climate of mutual suspicion that characterized the post-1989 period has proved very difficult to dispel, and political relations between Britain and China over Hong Kong have been slow to improve. (The airport controversy had not been resolved by late 1992). Moreover, on occasion even when agreement by the two principals has been reached in the JLG, there has been less certainty it would be accepted by the post-1991 in part directly elected and consequently highly politicized Hong Kong legislature, (reported to have been characterized by Lord Maclehose as 'the wild card in the pack') as was shown by the vote of the legislature against the agreement between Britain and China on the post-1997 arrangement for the Court of Final Appeal early in 1992.

Such a protracted period of difference and discord rather than consensus and harmony at the political level will inevitably have made an impression on those contemplating emigration. Had it not been for a unique combination of factors, Hong Kong might by now be facing a much worse brain-drain than actually exists and one which could have determined that the territory would not continue in its present form. These factors are: firstly, the economic recession in the developed world; secondly, the resumption of economic reform policies in China and the confirmation of the open-door policy; and thirdly, the effectiveness of the various measures to provide key Hong Kong residents with the insurance policy they needed to persuade them to stay.

The economic recession of the late 1980s and early 1990s affected all the developed economies, among them those of the countries most favoured by intending Hong Kong emigrants, namely, in order of preference, Canada, Australia and the USA. While the life styles of Hong Kong emigrants in their countries of adoption were customarily imagined, or frequently depicted through self-propagandizing, as superior to those in Hong Kong, particularly in terms of the quality of housing, education, welfare and the environment, in reality, this was seldom the case. Even in Cantonese-acculturated centres such as Vancouver, with which through

Cathay Pacific Airways there was a direct link and which had attracted much Hong Kong investment in real estate, the lot of the Hong Kong emigrant has often been far from satisfactory. The sources of dissatisfaction in all the countries of adoption were in varying degrees both cultural and material. No matter how much the emigrant tried it was impossible faithfully to replicate the unique combination of culturalism and materialism, that remained, for the time being, in a dynamic cosmopolitan Hong Kong.

These considerations of human ecology apart, more importantly for a working, as distinct from a retiring emigrant, the translation from Hong Kong to Canada, or to any of the other destinations, involved job relocation too. Normally, in the position of supplicant, the change in employment seldom involved promotion; more often it involved settling for a less rewarding, less prestigious and less promising post in a more highly taxed alien environment. Once the recession began to take effect, the mid-1980s comparative advantage perceived to be gained from emigration began seriously to be eroded.

The Hong Kong authorities, aware of the changing conditions, were by the early 1990s approaching the problem of the brain-drain more systematically and in a more coordinated way. As was noted above, education and training facilities were increased. To these were added the greater availability in Hong Kong of international schooling, a feature that encouraged professional parents to remain with their children in the territory. In addition, regular attempts were made, with considerable success, to encourage Hong Kong residents abroad to return to take up posts in Hong Kong. These measures, together with the British Nationality Selection Scheme (BNSS), taken against a background of a serious economic recession in the countries of adoption, were indeed attractive. They were not, however, by themselves, likely to stem the flow of emigration from Hong Kong. What was much more likely to do so was the added factor of a significant improvement in political–economic conditions in China.

For well over a year after the event, political–economic conditions in the PRC were dominated by the consequences, both external and internal, of the suppression of the democracy movement. These remained a major concern to Hong Kong residents. Moreover, the critical reaction in Hong Kong to the coercive measures, coupled with the sympathy expressed for the erstwhile leadership had, in turn, generated considerable criticism, suspicion and hostility in the new leadership group. This was reflected in the final draft of the BL. In it, as if in retaliation to a perception of the BNSS as a plot to retain a 'fifth column' of British loyalists in the Hong Kong SAR administration, more senior government posts in Hong Kong were apparently effectively brought under future *nomenklatura* control, being stipulated solely for Chinese nationals. Similarly, no more than 20 per cent of the future Legco membership could be composed of persons with a right of abode other than that enjoyed in the Hong Kong SAR.

By the early 1990s, however, it was possible to take careful stock of a changing situation in political–economic conditions in the PRC. These showed a rapidly evolving scene. At the centre, the reform policies and open-door championed by Deng Xiaoping were evidently gaining more general support in a stabilized political environment. Conversely, the faction in the central leadership advocating a more conservative approach was losing ground. This trend was confirmed in a triumphal visit by Deng Xiaoping to Guangdong and more significantly for Hong Kong, to Shenzhen, in the spring of 1992. The visit consolidated politically what had been evident economically, namely that reform and development accomplished by southern China should continue. Hong Kong residents could now look at the structural changes in the PRC economy that had led to the growth in the south generally, and to the exponential growth and promise of institutional reform in Shenzhen in particular, as a trend that had now reached an almost irreversible stage.

Together with the negative effects on would-be emigrants of the recession in the developed world, the favourable evolution of political–economic conditions in southern China led to a changing perception of the future. For the moment, and for the foreseeable future, Hong Kong was shielded from the recession in the developed world by increasing intraregional demand, in particular the growing demand of consumers in the PRC. When the third factor, the BNSS, to which reference had already been made, was taken into account, the case for emigrating from Hong Kong in the early 1990s was further weakened. Although the BNSS did not, in fact, attract the huge number of applications anticipated at the outset, confirming the relative unattractiveness of life in Britain to the average Hong Kong emigrant, who preferred the prospects of Canada, Australia and the USA, it was not in effect seriously undersubscribed. In the three-month period from 1 December 1990 to 28 February 1991, some 65 600 applications were received for the first tranche of 43 000 of the 50 000 places available.

Reviewing the evidence of emigration from Hong Kong over the past decade can one say with confidence that the evolving relationship between Hong Kong and China is such that a sufficient proportion of the half million or so key residents will remain in the future Hong Kong SAR to maintain its system alongside the other system under PRC sovereignty? The 1991 figures for applications for certificates of non-criminality and those for emigration, at 73 783 and 60 000 respectively, do not indicate the likelihood of a fall in emigration. More likely than a fall, however, would be a levelling off of emigration at around 60 000 a year. The implication of this trend is that the combined effect of all the factors affecting the decision to emigrate has been to retard the loss of talent. It would follow that any change affecting the main factors, such as on the positive side a continued improvement in the political and economic development of the PRC or on the negative side the opposite, would be reflected in the trend.

In addressing the fundamental question as to whether Hong Kong will continue, as one would hope, in its present form under the sovereignty of the PRC, supported by the decision of sufficient numbers of its key residents to remain, the absolute importance of their perception of the relationship with China in the run-up to the retrocession is inescapable. Such is their sensitivity to this relationship, any perceived change in it, as was shown in 1985 and 1986 on the negative side and, as far as the economic prospects are concerned, as was evident in 1991 on the positive side, is certain to be reflected in the emigration statistics. Furthermore, on the negative side, is now controversy over the so-called 'Patten Proposals' for the 1994-95 elections in Hong Kong (Address by the Governor 1992) since these proposals are perceived by the PRC to unacceptably promote democratization beyond the limits defined in the JD and the BL. On the positive side, it is possible to argue that a sustained period of political and economic reform maintaining the upward trend in net disposable income in China, coupled with a willingness by the PRC to reach a compromise on the 'Patten proposals' thus facilitating a modest extension of democratization, would not only persuade more would-be emigrants from the key group to remain but also induce more who have left actually to return. This would be an optimum scenario for both Hong Kong and China.

At present, the level of emigration is just manageable and, arguably, could be tolerated in a future Hong Kong SAR under a 'one country two systems', 'Hong Kong people running Hong Kong' arrangement. A significant difference between the situations in the 1980s and in the 1990s is that in addition to the favourable economic trends, a growing proportion of the group of key personnel, although remaining sensitive to political risk, is in fact, because of the BNSS and similar arrangements made by other governments and multinationals in Hong Kong, under less pressure to move than in the past. This suggests that such schemes are serving Hong Kong well. The corollary is that a vital section of the Hong Kong population is now potentially much more mobile than ever before. This single fact, while it guarantees the short-term future operation of a sophisticated international city, and may therefore both see Hong Kong successfully through the transition and offer it a good long-term future, cannot be overlooked by those concerned as the politics of the future unfold.

References

Address by the Governor (1988) at the opening of the 1988/9 Session of the Legislative Council, 12/10/88. Government Printer, Hong Kong, pp.52–6.

Address by the Governor (1989) at the opening of the 1989/90 Session of the Legislative Council, 11/10/89. Government Printer, Hong Kong.

Address by the Governor (1992) at the opening of the 1992/93 Session of the Legislative Council, 7/10/92. Government Printer, Hong Kong.

Cheng Joseph Y S and **Wong Paul C K** (1990) *The Other Hong Kong Report* Chinese University Press, Hong Kong.

Davies Stephen and **Roberts Elfed** (1990) *Political Dictionary for Hong Kong*, Macmillan, Hong Kong.

CHAPTER 12

China and Taiwan

Jack F. Williams

Perched high on a bluff overlooking the entrance to Xiamen (Amoy) harbour in Fujian province is a giant statue of Zheng Chenggong (Koxinga), gazing out to sea toward the island of Taiwan, which lies some 90 miles away across the Strait of Taiwan. Zheng was the pirate/ adventurer and Ming loyalist who drove the Dutch from Taiwan in the 1640s in order to establish a base from which to regroup his forces and prepare for a retaking of the mainland from the Manchus, who had just conquered China and established the Qing Dynasty (1644–1911). Zheng, ironically, is revered on both the mainland and in Taiwan, but for different reasons. In many ways, he symbolizes the ambivalence of the relationship between the People's Republic of China (PRC) and the Republic of China (ROC) in Taiwan. The PRC built that enormous statue of Zheng expressly to symbolize the historical linkages between Taiwan and the mainland, and the 'natural' role Taiwan has waiting for it as a province of Greater China. The ROC government, in turn, sees itself as something of a modern-day successor to Zheng and his forces, far more successful than Zheng in terms of building up Taiwan into a powerful military force but, even more important, a giant economic power in East Asia that has the capacity to deal with the PRC on terms of the ROC's own choosing. Who will win in this David/Goliath struggle, which is really just the latest stage of the Chinese Civil War that went into suspended animation in 1949 when the ROC government was forced to flee in exile to Taiwan, remains to be seen.

The best prediction is probably for continued stalemate, rather than checkmate by either side, for the foreseeable future. Yet, while Taiwan remains adamant about not accepting continued Communist domination of the mainland and still sticks officially to its so-called 'Three No's' (no contact, no compromise, no negotiations), forces are at work that are inexorably leading to increased linkages between the PRC and Taiwan (FCR 1991, p. 22). Those linkages or ties are primarily economic at the present time, represented by growing trade, investment and tourism. None the less, those ties are growing precisely because of the historical and cultural linkages between Taiwan and the mainland, in terms of ethnicity, settlement patterns, trade, and other factors, and are leading to increased contacts between Taiwan and mainland authorities in respect of international bodies, such as APEC, GATT, the Olympics, etc. This chapter is an examination of Taiwan's position *vis-à-vis* the PRC in the 1990s, and an attempt to project where the relationship between the 'two Chinas' is likely to head in the next decade or two. Will the 'two Chinas' eventually unite or continue locked in a sort of love – hate relationship?*

Prelude: 1949–1987

For almost 40 years after fleeing to Taiwan, the ROC operated under a basic policy known as 'Recovery of the Mainland'. All actions and policy decisions were directly or indirectly aimed at strengthening the military, political and economic forces of Taiwan so that eventually, somehow, the ROC government could be re-established on the mainland and the Communists expelled. Even though the number of people, in or out of Taiwan, who actually believed this would happen diminished rapidly over the years, the ROC government was compelled periodically to state this policy in public, because the government's legitimacy on Taiwan was based on the notion that there is but one China and Taiwan is part of that. This was basically the only substantive policy that both the PRC and ROC governments agreed on in those days. The dispute was over who had the legitimate right to rule Greater China. Since neither side recognized the other's legitimacy, the two had nothing whatever to do with each other. There was no trade, no communications, no linkages whatever. Both sides maintained formidable military forces on either side of the Taiwan Strait, and the ROC continued occupation of Matsu and Quemoy islands just off the coast of Fujian. The United States played a key role in this period in helping the ROC defend itself, by signing a Mutual Defense Treaty with Taiwan in 1954 and by stationing the 7th Fleet on patrol in the Strait of Taiwan to prevent a Communist invasion of the island. As it was, Communist forces attempted a military takeover of Quemoy (Chinmen) in 1958 that resulted in a fierce military engagement with the Nationalist forces, which defeated the Communists. The attempt was not repeated by the PRC.

This situation began to change with the end of the Maoist era in China, starting in 1976 when Mao died. China's reform era began in the late 1970s, and renewed overtures were made by the PRC to the ROC to reconsider its hardline position. The signing of the 1984 accord between Britain and China over the future transfer of Hong Kong to the PRC in 1997 provided an additional opportunity for the PRC to restate its policy toward Taiwan. Basically, the PRC was telling the ROC that Taiwan would be given the same guarantees that Hong Kong had, that Taiwan would also become a special administrative region (SAR) in which nothing would

*Myers (1992) presents an interesting collection of pieces about the development paths of the 'two Chinas' since 1949.

change except for the relinquishment of the claim by the ROC that it is the sole legitimate government of China. In short, the PRC offered Taiwan the 'one government, two systems' formula. Since this position requires the ROC to abandon its most basic principles, it is hardly surprising that Taiwan has said no to the Beijing government.

David and Goliath

The two 'Chinas' are very different entities today, of course, from what they were in 1949–50. Geographically, the two very much fit the image of David and Goliath. The PRC with its 1.2 billion people and 9.6 million square kilometres dwarfs Taiwan's mere 21 million people and approximately 36 000 square kilometres. Taiwan would be the second smallest in land area of China's 29 provinces, if reunited (Hainan, made a province in 1988, is slightly smaller than Taiwan) and seventh from the bottom in population. Economically, however, David does not look so little compared to Goliath, and one might even ask who really is Goliath. Today, Taiwan is the world's 12th largest exporter. In 1991, Taiwan had a total export trade of US$76 billion, compared with the PRC's US$72 billion (FCJ 24/3/92). Per capita income in Taiwan soared to over US$8000 in 1991, 20 times the average figure of under US$400 for the mainland. Even China's richest area, the Shenzhen Special Economic Zone with its per capita income of about US$2000, is still far behind Taiwan (Tyson 1992a, 1992b). While the economic gap between Taiwan and parts of China may be narrowing, the gap with the mainland as a whole continues to widen. Politically, Taiwan also is distancing itself from the mainland. The Tiananmen events of 1989 made clear, contrary to what some outsiders naively believed to be the case in the mid-1980s, that the Communist Party has no intention of sharing political power with any other party or organization on the mainland. The PRC government is resolutely determined to maintain a unitary and harsh political system, while trying to pursue only as much economic liberalization as necessary to move China ahead.

Taiwan, by contrast, had reached the point in the mid-1980s when the Kuomintang (Nationalist) Party, which had ruled Taiwan with a similar authoritarianism up until the 1980s, realized that true political reform was essential in order to maintain the ability of Taiwan to advance economically and maintain its strength *vis-à-vis* the mainland. From 1949 until the early 1980s, most people on Taiwan in effect traded political rights for economic growth. Very rapid increases in per capita income and the quality of life (at least measured in purchasing power) satisfied most people during this period. By the 1980s, however, basic human needs had been more than satisfied and an increasingly well-to-do middle-class-dominated society had emerged; people demanded increased human rights and political liberalization. The critical turning point proved to be July 1987, when martial law was finally lifted. This occurred, in part, because President Chiang Ching-kuo, who had ruled Taiwan since the death of his father, Chiang Kai-shek, in 1975, had seen the writing on the wall and started the liberalization process in the early 1980s. Political and social forces were released that hastened dramatic reforms within Taiwan. For the first time ever, a native Taiwanese, Lee Teng-hui, became leader of the government in January 1988, after the death of Chiang Ching-kuo. An opposition political party, the Democratic Progressive Party (DPP), was formed. A rash of new civic organizations sprouted, devoted to sundry causes, such as environmental protection, women's rights, and others. The press was freed of most of its previous shackles and blossomed into a lively and contentious force that criticized developments on the island with a candour previously unknown there, thus hastening still further the pace of change. Inevitably, pressure mounted for reviewing and changing government policies towards the mainland.

The new era: 1987 onward

In some respects, the ROC government was compelled by public pressure to relax its rules about contact with the mainland. But in part, the new policies also reflected the fact that times had indeed changed and that the ROC might have a better chance of changing the mainland through peaceful linkages and contact than with the confrontational policies of the past. Moreover, the natural evolution of Taiwan's economic system was forcing a rethinking of past strategies. What exactly, then, are the new policies, and what is their impact likely to be?

Trade

Economics really has been the driving force leading to increased ties between Taiwan and the mainland. The explanation is quite simple: Taiwan and the PRC have developed a natural economic complementarity that transcends political differences (Yeung and Hu 1992). That complementarity rests on the simple fact that Taiwan has a surplus of manufactured goods and capital, both of which the mainland needs. Hence, the PRC has rapidly grown in the past five years as a major trading partner and investment outlet for Taiwan. The relationship is very lopsided, primarily a one-way flow from Taiwan to the mainland. Yet, it is not so simple to say precisely who needs whom the most.

The trade relationship is shown in Table 12.1. There are several significant characteristics to Taiwan-PRC trade:

1. The trade consists primarily of *indirect* trade, that is, trade handled by middlemen (mostly Hong Kong businesses), as direct trade is still expressly forbidden by the ROC government. The ROC government's position has softened over the years from trying to track down and prosecute those attempting to trade with the mainland (pre-1980 era), to accepting the fact that trade is going to occur and to tolerate it as long as it is not direct trade (which implies political recognition of the mainland government).
2. Total trade with the mainland grew from a trifling US$47 million in

Table 12.1 Two-way trade between Taiwan and mainland China (through Hong Kong)

Year	Exports	Imports	Total	% Growth	Taiwan's
	(US$ million)		(US$ million)	over previous year	Trade surplus (US$ million)
1978	–	47	47	–	−47
1979	21	56	77	64	−35
1980	235	76	311	300	+160
1981	384	75	459	48	+309
1982	195	84	279	−39	+111
1983	158	90	248	−11	+68
1984	426	138	564	127	+288
1985	987	116	1103	99	+871
1986	811	144	955	−13	+667
1987	1227	289	1516	59	+938
1988	2242	479	2721	80	+1763
1989	2896	587	3483	28	+2309
1990	3278	765	4043	16	+2513
1991	4670	1130	5800	43	+3540

(*Source*: Board of Foreign Trade, Ministry of Economic Affairs, Taipei and Hong Kong Census and Statistics Department.)

1978 to US$5.8 billion in 1991. Taiwan has had a large and growing surplus in its trade with the mainland, reaching over US$3.5 billion in 1991. Imports have grown sharply, but not as rapidly as exports to the PRC.

3. The island's 1991 total world trade volume was US$140 billion (larger, incidentally, than the PRC's total trade), with a surplus of US$13.2 billion. The PRC trade accounted for over 4 per cent of the total (*FCJ* 31/2/92, 11/2/92). While the mainland still accounts for a relatively small percentage share of Taiwan's trade, the proportion is growing faster than trade with any other country in the world. Moreover, the mainland is supplying by far the largest share of Taiwan's trade surplus.

4. Taiwan's trade relationship with Hong Kong has thus grown enormously in recent years (Fig. 12.1). Exports to Hong Kong have increased far faster than imports, resulting in a growing trade surplus that soared beyond US$10 billion in 1991, of which a large proportion is due to re-exports to the mainland (*FCJ* 30/7/92, 24/3/92). Since April, 1991, Taiwan has operated a Taipei Trade Centre in a huge complex in Hong Kong, to assist Taiwan investors establishing trade bases.

5. In addition, there is an undetermined amount of direct trade that Taiwanese businessmen carry on illegally, in spite of government restrictions, and which thus does not show up in the Hong Kong trade figures. Some of this involves smuggling directly across the Taiwan

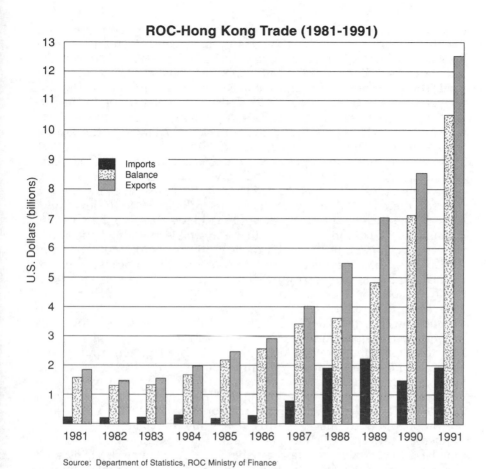

Source: Department of Statistics, ROC Ministry of Finance

Fig. 12.1 ROC–Hong Kong trade 1981–91. (*Source:* Department of Statistics, ROC Ministry of Finance)

Strait, primarily by fishermen trying to make bigger profits than sea-food will provide. The press in Taiwan occasionally has reports about government agents catching such people in the act, but it is increasingly difficult to police this kind of activity in today's looser social/political climate in Taiwan. In short, the desire to make bigger money is an irresistible lure to promote two-way trade, regardless of what the government may think of it. None the less, the government is considering using 20 000 new army conscripts (Taiwan still has compulsory military service for all males, in spite of the easing of tensions) for increasing the patrolling of Taiwan's coastline against smugglers. These forces would be supported by an additional 150 coast guard vessels (Lin 1992).

The ROC government is concerned about several potential problems with trade. One is the fear that if Taiwan–PRC trade gets too large, especially exports, Taiwan will then be so heavily dependent on mainland markets that the PRC government could increase political leverage to coerce Taiwan into accepting the PRC's terms for reunification. To help counteract the problem, Taiwan's Board of Foreign Trade (BOFT) recently unveiled a new system for monitoring the ebb and flow of mainland trade (*FCJ* 21/1/92). The system determines the growth rate and market share of Taiwan's 30 leading imports and exports transhipped via Hong Kong, and grades the level of danger on the basis of 'cold, cool, normal, warm, or overheated' 'Overheated' exports for 1991 included polymer and copolymer products, knitted textiles, machine tools, leather, paper and plastic goods. Overheated imports for the same period were tobacco, yarns, medicines and dyestuffs. Since the trade is indirect, there is little the government can realistically do to slow down trade of 'overheated' products except to issue warnings to the business community. A second concern is that Taiwan's exports will encounter increasing competition with PRC goods in the key markets of Japan and the US. To counteract this problem, Taiwan must keep one step ahead of the mainland in moving up the economic ladder. So far, Taiwan has been relatively successful in working towards higher quality, higher value-added products for its export markets, while the mainland still tends to produce lower quality goods which typified Taiwan's exports in the 1960s or 1970s. But the pressure is relentless on Taiwan.

A third problem, already occurring, is Taiwan getting drawn into China's trade disputes with the United States. The PRC, desperate to boost exports and willing to cut corners and circumvent rules when it can get away with it, has been shipping textiles to other countries, e.g. in Latin America or Asia, where new labels are affixed and then the goods are shipped on to the US, thus disguising the country of origin. Numerous Taiwan textile makers have relocated production lines to the mainland to capitalize on cheaper labour and raw materials. They then ship the finished textiles to their home plants in Taiwan for relabelling as 'Made in Taiwan' and shipment on to the US. This skews US import quotas and adds to negative feelings in the US towards both Taiwan and the PRC. Taiwan's BOFT, under pressure from the US, recently adopted stricter requirements for place-of-origin labels on textiles coming through Hong Kong (*FCJ* 1/4/92). How effective these measures will be in the long run remains to be seen.

A fourth potential problem looms on the horizon. Dependency is a two-way street. Localities in the PRC that have received large amounts of Taiwan investment or depend on Taiwan for a large share of their trade, such as Xiamen, may find themselves in the uncomfortable position of facing difficult times in the event of an economic downturn in Taiwan. What might happen if Taiwanese investors, for whatever reason, pull out of mainland operations, either reducing production or shutting down completely? Jobs would be lost and economic hardship felt. How might such developments affect attitudes toward Taiwan by the PRC, both government and public? This is an issue in virtually every part of the world where foreign investment is avidly courted by governments desperate to industrialize and develop local economies. The situation is complicated further in China because of the unique nature of Taiwan's relationship with the mainland.

Already by mid-1992 it was estimated by some that Taiwan manufacturers were responsible for more than 40 per cent of the mainland's export value, suggesting that the mainland may find itself irreversibly dependent on Taiwan for export manufacturing (Chen 1992). It is increasingly clear that Taiwan's investment in mainland manufacturing, mainly in the labour-intensive light industry sector, has played a key role in the rapid growth of the PRC's total export volume. The mainland's sales of goods abroad surged in 1992, reaching a record in August (Pun 1992c). At this rate, the PRC was predicted to surpass Taiwan in total trade volume in 1992 for the first time ever.

Politics aside, direct trade with the mainland could bypass Hong Kong and save as much as 10–20 per cent in transport costs for bulk commodities such as coal or cement, and up to 50 per cent of transport costs for containers to destinations other than Guangdong or Fujian (Baum 1991a). The lack of direct trade is also said to make Taiwan more dependent on Hong Kong, reducing Taiwan's competitive edge in international trade. Manufacturers who now export large amounts of semi-finished goods and equipment to China for further processing would particularly benefit from direct trade. Proposals have also been made to open free-trade zones on Taiwan's west coast expressly for mainland trade. Taichung would be especially ideal because of (i) its proximity to Xiamen directly across the Strait and (ii) Taichung port's still underdeveloped potential. Nonetheless, the general consensus is that legalization of direct trade is not likely to occur soon.

Investment

The other side of the trade coin is investment. In this case it is truly one way, consisting entirely of a flow of Taiwan capital to the mainland. The reason for it is again quite simple: labour costs in Taiwan are now so high as to make many manufacturing operations on the island no longer internationally competitive. Taiwan needs cheaper labour; the mainland has plenty of it. Taiwan is thus simply a newcomer to the international division of labour, in what is increasingly a global economy.

Taiwan investors actually began covertly transferring money into the mainland as early as 1983, when such activity was strictly illegal and a serious crime. Even after mid-1985, when indirect trade with the mainland was legalized, the volume of investment was negligible. The key turning point was in 1987, when foreign exchange restrictions were relaxed to allow outward remittances of US$5 million per person per year (Chin 1991, p. 41). Movements of capital out of Taiwan increased dramatically after that. The PRC stimulated the investment by passing a statute in July 1988 known as 'Encouragement of Taiwan Compatriots' Investment'. Taiwan businessmen responded to the tune of some US$500 million by the end of 1988. Tiananmen in June 1989 caused a temporary slowdown (Liu 1991), but the pace of investment quickened again and has continued to grow. As of March 1992, 2552 Taiwan companies had formally registered mainland investments with the ROC government's Ministry of Economic Affairs, which monitors the situation. The total volume of investment was reported to be US$821 million (Peng 1992d). This figure is believed to be a serious under-reporting, however. *Beijing Review* reported that as of December 1990, there were 2080 Taiwan-funded enterprises on the mainland, with a total investment of about US$2 billion (Jing 1992, p. 21). Part of the discrepancy may be due to the fact that the ROC is reporting actual investment, while the PRC may be including investment contracted for but not yet actually spent. Officials on Taiwan admit that probably not all investment has been reported to the ROC government, for various reasons. Estimates of actual investment run as high as US$4 billion by over 3000 companies (Peng 1992h; Goldstein 1992).

Since all investment, like trade, must be indirect, it is difficult for the government to maintain accurate monitoring of these activities. The government has a list of over 3000 items approved for indirect investment (about 47 per cent of the total custom classification categories). Most of these are labor-intensive products that have lost or are losing their comparative advantage in Taiwan, including synthetic leather, textiles, bicycles, toys, plastics and some electronics. Through this list, the government is legalizing the activities of small and medium-sized enterprises that have already invested on the mainland and trying to bring them under government regulation. Undoubtedly, taxation is also a motive of the government. The 'stick' in this carrot-and-stick approach to regulation is the imposition of heavy fines and administrative punishments, such as exit bans on foreign travel, for businesspeople violating the rules (Chin 1991). Since the probability of getting caught is low, there is believed to be a large volume of both trade and investment that operates in a 'black economy' of technically illegal operations. Short of investing a much greater effort and cost in policing the situation (for which the government does not appear to have the stomach), the government must rely largely on the goodwill of businesspeople, who must balance patriotism and national welfare against their profit and loss ledgers.

In spite of distaste for the PRC's political activities, especially from 1989 on, Taiwan businesspeople have found the mainland very attractive for several reasons: cheap and abundant labour, low cost land and buildings, and the language and cultural compatibility. On the other hand, the mainland has some definite drawbacks: lack of administrative efficiency, incomplete laws and legal systems, out-of-date banking operations and concocted expenses designed to fleece foreign investors (Chen, 1992, p. 43).

Taiwan actually still plays a relatively small role in mainland investment as a whole. As of June 1991, Hong Kong was by far the leader, with over US$26 billion in investment, most of this in Guangdong province. The United States was second, with US$4.6 billion in investments. Japan was third at about US$3.4 billion; Britain fourth at US$1.7 billion, if one accepts Taiwan reported figures (Yang 1992; Yang and Li 1992, p. 21). If one accepts the PRC figure for Taiwan investment, then Taiwan would be fourth, behind the US and Japan.

The nature of Taiwan's investment has changed over the five years or so of activity. Initially, investments were small, under US$500 000, and for short term. The investors rented a factory and operated on a fly-by-night strategy, since there seemed to be little security at that time. By the early 1990s, individual investments had grown to multimillion dollar figures, and tenure of contracts had increased to as long as 50 years. The types of investment also evolved, from such things as footwear, garments, toys and umbrellas initially, to today's petrochemicals, real estate, construction materials, electric appliances, computers and precision machines. The indication clearly is one of increased confidence in the mainland as an investment site. A survey of 320 Taiwan firms which have invested in the mainland found that 85 per cent were yielding profits of 7–13 per cent. This was partly due to production costs 25 per cent lower than in Taiwan. Of the goods produced by these Taiwan entrepreneurs, 19 per cent were sold on the mainland, 12 per cent were sent to Taiwan for sale, and the remaining 69 per cent were marketed overseas (*FCJ* 24/1/92). Another survey of 239 investors found that two-thirds reported returns of more than 10 per cent, and one-twelfth had earnings above 25 per cent. By contrast, profits from operations within Taiwan by the 1000 largest manufacturers averaged merely 8 per cent in 1991 (Liu 1992a). A report by the Ministry of Economic Affairs (MOEA) in Taiwan found that the average Taiwan-invested mainland operation had a capital outlay of US$1.2 million, employed 210 workers and had annual sales of US$3 million (Liu 1992a).

The location of Taiwan investments is an extremely important factor in understanding the situation (Fig. 12.2). About half of Taiwanese investment capital has gone into the Xiamen Special Economic Zone, in Fujian province, although this accounted for only about one-fifth of Taiwan-funded projects on the mainland (Cheng 1990a, 1990b; Reardon 1991; Jing 1992, p. 21). That means, of course, that Xiamen has tended to attract larger individual investments than the rest of China. Xiamen is a natural outlet for Taiwanese capital, because of its location closest to Taiwan, and the common language (the Min dialect) shared by Chinese on both sides of the Strait. Although the Xiamen SEZ was founded in 1980, when this author visited Xiamen in 1986 he found the SEZ largely a ghost town, with many modern buildings and roads going in, but very little economic activity. Today, Xiamen is the second most developed of the SEZs, after Shenzhen, and is booming. Total foreign investment in Xiamen by the end of 1990 came to US$2.12 billion, with just over 500 foreign enterprises at work (Jing 1992, p. 17). Taiwan capital thus accounted for nearly half of all contracted foreign investment in the SEZ. Most of the remaining foreign capital has been from Hong Kong. Most analysts seem to agree that Xiamen is likely to remain the primary target in the PRC for Taiwan capital for the foreseeable future. Most of the remaining Taiwan investment has been directed at Guangdong province, particularly the Shenzhen SEZ and the Pearl River Delta economic area, which is the fastest growing region in China today. Hainan, which became a separate province and the fifth SEZ in 1988, has also tried to attract Taiwan capital as part of its effort to elevate itself from one of the most backward parts of China to one of the most advanced (Williams 1992).

Hainan has not yet been very successful in this effort, especially to lure Taiwan capital, because it is competing with the other already well established SEZs that have geographical location and other investment advantages (especially infrastructure). Taiwan investors have shown some interest in food processing and agriculture in Hainan, but the volume of investment is not yet significant and is not likely to become so in the near future.

The footwear industry is a good illustration of the movement from Taiwan to the mainland, and why it is occurring. In the 1970s and 1980s, footwear manufacturing in Taiwan became one of the most lucrative operations and footwear became a prime export product of the island, peaking in 1987 with exports of 800 million pairs of shoes valued at US$3.7 billion (Liu 1992a pp. 54–6). However, driven by high labour costs, labour shortages, appreciation of the NT (New Taiwan) dollar, and monstrous land prices, footwear manufacturers were among the first to flee to the mainland as barriers fell after 1987. By 1992, more than 200 Taiwan-

Fig. 12.2 Taiwan and South East China.

invested shoe factories were in operation on the mainland, employing 100 000 workers, and exporting over US$2 billion worth annually to leading American footwear importers such as Nike, Reebok and Payless. Production on Taiwan declined proportionately, such that membership in the Taiwan Footwear Exporters Association dwindled from 1600 to 600, and footwear exports from Taiwan came to just somewhat over US$2 billion in 1991. The shift across the Strait was virtually certain to lead to mainland production exceeding Taiwan production in 1992 and for the gap to widen steadily after that. Dependency, however, has really become a two-way street in this particular industry. Taiwan-invested mainland factories rely on Taiwan for leather and shoe accessories, as well as new materials and models, production samples, experienced managers and technicians, and marketing know-how (Liu 1992a, 56). Toys are predicted to follow the path of footwear in the very near future (Goldstein 1992, p. 24).

A Chinese Common Market?

As part of the economic linkages and growing rapprochement between Taiwan and the PRC, there is growing talk of forging new types of cooperation. One of the bolder ideas is to create a sort of Chinese Common Market. This was publicly discussed in an International Symposium on the Coordination of Chinese Economic Systems, held in Hong Kong in January 1992 (Peng, 1992b).* Perhaps not surprisingly, the PRC delegates to the conference were more optimistic than the Taiwan delegates about the prospects for such an organization, which would be designed to combine Taiwan's financial resources and marketing skills, the PRC's huge market and labour supply, and Hong Kong's financial and information systems (Duckworth 1992, p. 3; FCJ 24/1/92; Pun 1992).

In general, Taiwan's position is that an economic union will not be possible until all political roadblocks are removed (see below). None the less, a *de facto* economic triangle of sorts is developing already between Taiwan, Hong Kong and South China as a result of indirect trade and investment (Sheng 1991). There is no question that Hong Kong is increasingly important to Taiwan. In 1991, US$4.7 billion of goods made in Taiwan flowed through Hong Kong to the PRC, while US$1.2 billion made the reverse trip. Taiwan is also becoming one of the principal sources of foreign investment in Hong Kong, even while others are having second thoughts with 1997 looming on the horizon. The ROC's trade representative in Hong Kong estimates there were more than 2500 Taiwan-invested companies in Hong Kong by mid-1992, including some of the biggest names in Taiwan manufacturing, such as Formosa Plastics, Far Eastern Textile, San Yang Industry, Cheng Shin Rubber, Evergreen

*The conference was organized by Hong Kong Baptist College's Centre for East–West Studies, headed by William Liu, in cooperation with Taiwan's Democracy Foundation (a group that supports reunification of Taiwan and China), headed by John Kuan, former KMT Deputy Secretary-General. The conference brought together some 100 scholars, entrepreneurs and other experts to discuss the idea of a 'Greater China Economic Sphere'.

Marine Corporation, and others (Liu 1992b, p.57). The strong presence of Taiwan investors is seen as a reflection of the colony's ability to remain a major trade and financial centre after 1997. The argument goes that Hong Kong will continue to serve as the principal intermediary between Taiwan and the mainland for a long time to come.

Person-to-person: the human factor in Taiwan/ China relations

Economics and politics aside, the human factor is very important in the growing relationship between Taiwan and the mainland. There are two forces shaping this trend. The first is the fact that the majority of people on Taiwan, the 'Taiwanese', can trace their ancestral roots back to the mainland, primarily Fujian province, even though most of the Taiwanese had never seen the mainland until after the mid-1980s. Although most of the Taiwanese do not have direct relatives living on the mainland, they have an intense curiosity about China, a place that the ROC government, through the educational system and public media on Taiwan, has tried for four decades to indoctrinate them to regard as their true homeland (FCR 1991). The second force is the fact that about 2 million or more so-called 'mainlanders', who came over after 1949 to escape the Communist takeover, also have family ties to various places in China (Chung 1991; Peng 1992c). Many of these mainlanders left parents, spouses and other living relatives behind when they fled or were forced to go to Taiwan. Many of these mainlanders were in the military. Even after four decades, most of these people still think of the mainland as their real 'home', although offspring born in Taiwan after 1949 typically have much weaker identification with the mainland and sometimes ambivalence about whether they regard themselves as mainlanders or Taiwanese. This younger generation commonly speaks Taiwanese as well as Mandarin and the native dialect of their parents. Even the government in recent years has been downplaying the significance of place of birth of oneself or one's parents, and saying that anyone born and living in Taiwan is a true 'Taiwanese', albeit emphasizing at the same time that everyone on Taiwan is 'Chinese' and a citizen of China. The 'us' versus 'them' division of Taiwan society that grew out of the '2–28 Incident'* of 1947, while still evident, has diminished significantly.

Thus, there has been a huge movement of people between Taiwan and the mainland, again primarily a one-way flow, since the government eased restrictions on travel and person-to-person contacts with the mainland, starting in November 1987. Total flow of visitors from Taiwan

---

*The '2–28 Incident' in 1947 was a rebellion by native Taiwanese against the mainlanders who took over Taiwan from the Japanese in 1945. The rebellion was ruthlessly crushed, at great loss of Taiwanese lives, and embittered the Taiwanese against mainlanders. The enmity still has not totally disappeared among those of that generation, although younger Taiwanese have fewer hard feelings about it. One of the best comprehensive studies about this complex and controversial event in modern Taiwan history is the recent publication by Lai et al. (1991).

to the mainland reached more than 3.5 million by mid-1992 (*FCJ* 7/1/92; Goldstein 1992, p.23). This averages out at about 750 000 per annum over the roughly four-year period, a significant volume in relation to Taiwan's 21 million population. The official data does not accurately distinguish between the different types of visitors. The composition of these visitors has varied, consisting of ordinary tourists just curious to see the mainland, people visiting ancestral villages and relatives, males seeking brides, businessmen pursuing investments and economic opportunity, and others. Ordinary tourists have been the majority group, however.

Cross-strait marriages have totalled at least 20 000 since 1987, according to one report (Baum 1991b). These do not include marriages that occurred before then. Spousal reunions have become one of the more intense issues in Taiwan/mainland relations, as a result. On 3 January, 1992, the ROC began accepting applications for mainland spouses to immigrate to Taiwan. The flow is being tightly controlled, with many restrictions and regulations (*FCJ* 31/1/92, 7/1/92, 17/1/92).

Movement of mainlanders to Taiwan, other than spouses, has been extremely limited so far. Partly, this is a reflection of the greatly differing income levels between the PRC and Taiwan. Mainlanders are lucky in most cases to be able to travel within their own country; foreign travel is a luxury few can afford. But government restrictions on foreign travel are the main impediment. For example, Taiwan forbade any Communist Party members to visit Taiwan, only just recently lifting the restriction. Faced with a growing demand for travel, the PRC government issued new regulations in January 1992, effective 1 May, for Chinese desiring to visit Taiwan (*BR* 20–26/1/92, p. 9). While these new rules clarify some of the legal and technical issues involved, they are not likely to contribute to a significant immediate increase in mainland visitors to Taiwan.

This might change, however, if the ROC opens the doors to mainlanders seeking employment in Taiwan. Taiwan has been debating this issue for some time. Again, natural economic complementarity is pushing Taiwan in this direction. Taiwan has a labour shortage, particularly for low paid jobs at the bottom of the economic ladder, which Taiwanese increasingly do not want. The mainland, in turn, has huge numbers of surplus labourers who are willing to do just about anything for a job (*FCJ* 6/8/91). In late January 1992, Taiwan agreed to accept mainland workers under tight controls, which include a time limit of one year in Taiwan and numerous other restrictions (*FCJ* 31/1/92). None the less, if significant numbers of mainlanders eventually are allowed in, they could have a real impact on Taiwan, and not just on the economy.

Taiwan faces a dilemma on this issue. On the one hand, there is a growing labour shortage that is driving up wages and forcing manufacturers to other locations. The shortage is also being felt in the government's ambitious US$300 billion Six Year National Development Plan (*FCJ* 24/1/92). Yet, if large numbers of outside workers are allowed into Taiwan, there are all sorts of economic and social problems that can occur. This is especially true of mainlanders. In August, the quota was increased to 32 000 foreign workers (compared to just 15 000 allowed in 1991), although this still fell far short of the 180 000 labourers recommended by the Chinese National Federation of Industries to maintain Taiwan's industrial development (Pun 1992b).

Bridging the gap: SEF and ARATS

Both Taiwan and the PRC have set up quasi-governmental bodies designed to help resolve problems in the growing linkages between the 'two Chinas'. Taiwan took the initiative. As linkages began to expand after 1987, Taiwan set up the Mainland Affairs Task Force in August 1988 to oversee these matters. In October 1990, the Executive Yuan's Mainland Affairs Council, headed by the Vice-Premier, took over the responsibilities of the two-year-old Task Force. At the same time, the National Unification Council was established, with President Lee as its head, to provide the highest level of policy consultation for the Mainland Affairs Council (*ROC Yearbook* 1990–91, pp. 199–209). These are formal governmental organizations, however, and as such are unable to deal officially and directly with mainland authorities, without violating the sacred 'Three No's'.

Hence, in November 1990, the quasi-private Foundation for Exchanges Across the Taiwan Straits (or simply known as the Straits Exchange Foundation, SEF), was established to act as an intermediary between the ROC government and mainland authorities (Lo 1991). C.F. Koo, a member of the KMT Central Standing Committee, is chair of the Foundation. The SEF acts as coordinator and arbitrator for business, cultural and other contacts with the mainland. More than half its funds come from the private sector; the rest are from the ROC government. The foundation board has 43 members drawn from a broad cross-section of Taiwan's society, with half consisting of businessmen. With this organization Taiwan can deal with the mainland while still pretending that it is not having official contact with the PRC government.

To reciprocate, the PRC in December 1991 organized its own organization, the Association for Relations Across the Taiwan Straits (ARATS), likewise ostensibly a non-governmental organization with Rong Yiren, vice-chairman of the Standing Committee of the National People's Congress and president of the China International Trust and Investment Corporation, as honorary chair, and Wang Daohan, former mayor of Shanghai, as chairman (*BR* 30/12/91–5/1/92; Yang and Li 1992). ARATS is designed to complement the official government body, the Taiwan Affairs Office of the Central Committee of the Chinese Communist Party, in a manner similar to the Taiwan arrangement. Membership of ARATS' 65-member council consists likewise of a mixture of government, business and academic figures. Noted Taiwanese living on the mainland, including Shang Kehui, Lin Liyun and Cai Zimin, are advisers to the association.

A SEF delegation met in March 1992 in Beijing for the first time with ARATS counterparts to discuss pending issues, particularly the verification of documents related to growing person-to-person ties between Taiwan and the mainland, such as mainland spouses of Taiwan residents (*FCJ* 6/3/92; Peng 1992d). The meeting was reportedly a great disappointment, however, because of deep-rooted suspicions and efforts by the PRC side to drag in the 'one China' issue. SEF cancelled a second planned visit. Clearly, much bridge building between the two sides remains to be done before the hostility built up over many decades can be dissipated (Song 1992).

Political differences: the PRC, the KMT, and the Taiwan independence movement

In spite of all the progress made in just five years in relations between Taiwan and the mainland, fundamental political differences persist and present formidable obstacles to anything approaching true reunification. Not only are the interests of the PRC and the ROC governments involved, but there is also the wild card of the Taiwan independence movement.

At the governmental level, the two sides are still stuck on a fundamental disagreement. The PRC insists on Taiwan accepting the mainland's 'one country, two systems' formula, which implies that there is but one China that includes Taiwan, ruled by the Beijing government, but that another 'system' operates autonomously on the island of Taiwan. In short, this is the formula for a Taiwan Special Administrative Region, based on the Hong Kong and Macau models set to come into existence in 1997 and 1999, respectively. Taiwan would be allowed to keep everything in its current economic/political/social system except the notion that the ROC is a legitimate government of China. To set up this model for Taiwan, the PRC insists on party-to-party negotiations with Taiwan's ruling KMT. The ROC, in turn, insists on the formula of 'one country, two governments', which agrees with the PRC position that there is but one China and Taiwan is part of it, but diverges with the idea that there are two legitimate governments controlling China, and hence the PRC should stop interfering with Taiwan's efforts to participate in international affairs, rejoin the United Nations and other organizations such as GATT, just as there are two Koreas and used to be two Germanies. Both sides refuse to give an inch on their fundamental positions, even while economic and other ties are rapidly growing. However, until the mainland renounces the threat to use force to achieve reunification, Taiwan has made it clear that direct links through the *san tong* 'three communications' – direct mail, direct shipping and air services, and direct commercial links – will not be permitted (Baum 1992, p.21). This means that relations between the two sides remain mired in the first stage of the National Unification Guidelines adopted by the ROC in 1991, which includes an end to hostilities, building mutual trust through private exchanges, and solving disputes by peaceful means. The second stage, involving direct talks and linkages, is impossible at this time and may well not occur until the next century. The third stage, outright political reunification, is probably at least a generation away, if not longer.

Where do the Taiwanese people fit into all of this? Overt opposition to

KMT rule was a dangerous activity until the late 1980s. Those Taiwanese unwilling to accept the system on Taiwan either went to jail or fled Taiwan. Thousands emigrated, often initially as college students, most to the US, the rest to Europe and Japan. Large numbers of Taiwanese emigrés formed various political opposition groups loosely aligned around the goal of independence for Taiwan. Although highly splintered, these groups argued that Taiwan should be independent of either Communist or KMT rule, and should be recognized in the world community as an independent Republic of Taiwan. To even state this publicly in Taiwan until very recently was a criminal offence subject to severe punishment.

The situation changed dramatically on 28 September 1986, when a group of political oppositionists from the loosely organized but technically legal *tang wai* ('outside the KMT party') organization formed the Democratic Progressive Party (DPP) (Huang 1992b). Although this was an illegal action, the government was effectively unable to stop or control the DPP after that, simply because the political liberalization process was already too far along and the Taiwanese majority population would no longer stand for harsh repression. Moreover, Chiang Ching-kuo and his successor, Lee Teng-hui, had determined that democratization was essential for the survival of Taiwan in its dealings with the mainland government. Since that date in 1986, the Emergency Decree and Martial Law have ended, thus legitimizing opposition political parties, and Taiwan has been experiencing the growth pains of democratization. The social and political stability of the old days are gone, resulting in turmoil and change that disturb many people, especially the older generation.

One of the striking features of the political changes is the failure of the DPP to gain as large a representation in the island's government as might be expected. In fact, in the Second National Assembly election held in late 1991, the DPP actually lost some ground. Of the 325 seats in the national assembly, the DPP captured only 66, and had only 24 per cent of the total votes. The KMT got the other three-quarters (Li 1992). Political scientists both in Taiwan and abroad have made careers out of analysing the political system in Taiwan, and the DPP has been scrutinized with special intensity. It has been found that the DPP has not lost ground because of voters being scared off by the Taiwan independence platform of the party (as the KMT would have people believe). Rather, voters have been dismayed by the crude behaviour, lack of political sophistication, and common corruption of many DPP legislators and candidates (Wu, 1992). The failings of many DPP members are not too surprising, given the decades of denial of political participation and the short history of the party. In the long run, there is a strong likelihood for the continued 'Taiwanization' of the political process, with Taiwanese becoming increasingly dominant within the KMT itself, while the DPP acquires a higher degree of sophistication and professionalism, and in turn greater voter support. In short, Taiwan unquestionably is headed toward a real multi-party political system.

As for the independence issue, the argument has been made that the only true way to determine the feelings of the majority population is to have a popular plebiscite on the independence issue. The KMT has adamantly refused such a move, and probably will continue to do so, on the grounds that independence is the one issue that the PRC is most resolutely opposed to, and could well trigger military action by the mainland to prevent independence from being implemented. Taiwan has been *de facto* independent since 1949, but most nations of the world have not accepted it as such, and this is what most counts in the eyes of both the PRC and the ROC governments. Moreover, it is unlikely that the key nations, especially the United States, would recognize an independent Taiwan even if it were proclaimed, simply because the bottom line is that relations with the PRC are more important to the national interest than relations with Taiwan. The US, of course, hopes it will never have to make such a decision.

Conclusion

Governments really have limited ability to control events and relations with other countries in the face of inexorable forces of change. Such is the case with the PRC and ROC governments. The Beijing government, in spite of its determination to maintain one party control over China, is facing an unstoppable economic liberalization that is propelling the country into the modern era of a dynamic East Asia (*Economist* 1991; Yeung and Hu 1992). Whether the political straitjacket can withstand the changes sweeping China remains to be seen. Likewise, the ROC government is struggling to remain in control of forces drawing Taiwan into increasingly close ties with the mainland. As one report put it, Taiwan's 'Three No's' have really become the 'Three Maybe's' (Brick and Aurini 1992, p. 16). While Taiwan may not have had any direct contact, negotiation, or compromise with the mainland in any official sense, there has been plenty of indirect, or unofficial, contact, negotiation and compromise. Some 15 000 Taiwan residents per month travel to the mainland; billions of dollars in Taiwan capital have flowed and continue to flow into mainland investments; indirect trade and illegal trade in billions of dollars moves across the Taiwan Strait; ROC and PRC officials are talking to each other in all kinds of forums in various parts of the world. Taiwan now is locked into what may well be an irreversible commitment to the mainland.

Nonetheless, serious obstacles still stand in the way. The principal problem would appear to be the intransigence of both sides on basic political principles. A ROC official recently made the following statement, which sums up the situation well (Lo 1991, p. 18):

'There is one thing we have to convince Peking about, and that is to give up their 'big brother" manner,' . . . 'If they want unification for China, they must first respect us and give us equal status. Then we can talk. But if they treat us as a subordinate part of their polity, there is no use trying to talk. Our per capita income is US$8000 and we lead a very good life. Why should we become poorer in the process of unifying with them? On the contrary, it's they who need our help, including our capital, technology, and business management. Why should we be lowered to the level of a local government when we are actually the central government? The fact is, they must give up this 'one country, two systems" model.'

Since it is most unlikely that the PRC will accept the ROC's demands, the *status quo* appears likely to continue for the foreseeable future. The ROC and PRC, like two uncertain suitors, will continue to court each other but without taking the final step to tie the knot, i.e. political reunification. That final step is likely to be a long time coming.

References

Abbreviations:
    AWSJ = Asian Wall Street Journal (Hong Kong)
    BR = Beijing Review (Beijing)
    CBR = China Business Review
    CSM = Christian Science Monitor
    FCJ = Free China Journal (Los Angeles)
    FCR = Free China Review (Taipei)
    FEER = Far Eastern Economic Review (Hong Kong)
Baum J (1991a) 'Strait expectations: Taiwan businessmen prepare for direct trade with China', *FEER* 6 June.
Baum J (1991b) 'Belated reunions', *FEER* 30 January.
Baum J (1992) 'Flags follow trade', *FEER* 17 September.
BR (1992) 'Association founded for Taiwan contacts', 30 Dec.–5 January.
BR (1992) 'Regulations for citizens visiting Taiwan issued', 20-26 January.
Brick A B and **Aurini G** (1992) 'Taiwan's three noes becoming maybes', *AWSJ* 6 April.
Chen D (1992) 'Politics taking backseat to economy', *FCJ* 30 June.
Cheng E (1990a) 'China's changing tide: coastal cities rush to offer land after Peking policy shift', *FEER* 28 June.
Cheng E (1990b) 'Down but not out: SEZs aim to regain their pioneering role in China's development', *FEER* 8 February.
Chin C (1991) 'Trade across the Straits', *FCR* January.
Chung K S (1991) 'Separations and reunions', *FCR* January.
Duckworth M (1992) 'Political differences cloud prospects for Greater Chinese Economic Zone', *AWSJ* 27 January.
FCJ (1991) 'Taiwan-Hong Kong trade boom seen as alarming', 30 July.
FCJ (1991) 'Officials, scholars illuminate key problems in hiring of mainlanders', 6 August.
FCJ (1992) 'MAC wants door opened for Taiwan ARATS office', 7 January.
FCJ (1992) 'Spouse permits attract hundreds in wind, rain', 7 January.
FCJ (1992) 'Greater China triangle foreseen', 17 January.
FCJ (1992) 'Level of mainland trade nears overheated mark', 21 January.
FCJ (1992) 'Mainland investments profiting; guidelines recommended in report', 24 January.
FCJ (1992) 'Law covers mainland's work force', 31 January.
FCJ (1992) 'Trade with mainland exceeds forecast', 11 February.

FCJ (1992) 'ARATS OKs document-verification talks', 6 March.
FCJ (1992) 'Direct link legal basis approved', 6 March.
FCJ (1992) 'Local funds boost mainland export rank', 24 March.
FCJ (1992) 'First Peking meet a flop between SEF and ARATS', 27 March.
FCJ (1992) 'Trade growth with mainland stumbles', 1 April.
FCJ (1992) 'Businessmen eye mainland boycott', 24 April.
FCJ (1992) 'Mainland workers security risk', 5 June.
FCJ (1992) 'Steps eye mainland trade growth', 31 December.
FCR (1991) 'Adjustments in policies', January.
FCR (1991) 'Imagination linked with decisiveness', January.
FCR (1991) 'Visiting the home front', January.
FCR (1992) 'Mainland trade high but tolerable', 28 February.
Goldstein C (1992) 'The bottom line, Taiwan capital, factories pour into China', FEER 17 September.
Huang H (1992a) 'If Peking wants peaceful coexistence, ROC willing', FCJ 17 January.
Huang H (1992b) 'Happy birthday, DPP, and thanks for pushing reform', FCJ 2 October.
Jing F (1992) 'Xiamen: ten years of tremendous change', BR 27 January–2 February.
Lai T H, Myers R H and Wei W (1991) A Tragic Beginning: the Taiwan Uprising of February 28, 1947, Stanford University Press.
Li J (1992) 'Taiwan independence, independent Taiwan, and reunification', BR 10–16 August.
Lin D (1992) 'Conscripts may police coast', FCJ 14 April.
Liu P (1991) 'Investment slows down', FCR January.
Liu P (1992a) 'No turning back', FCR July.
Liu P (1992b) 'The Hong Kong connection', FCR July.
Lo A (1991) 'Strait talk', FCR January.
Myers R M (ed.) (1991) Two Societies in Opposition: the Republic of China and the People's Republic of China after Forty Years, Hoover Institution Press, Stanford.
Peng T C (1992a) 'Mainland-Taiwan Feb. 4 spouse reunion doubtful', FCJ 17 January.
Peng T C (1992b) 'Chinese common market idea probed in HK', FCJ 24 January.
Peng T C (1992c) 'Taiwan welcoming stranded home', FCJ 31 January.
Peng T C (1992d) 'SEF delegates finally meet mainland ARATS counterpart', FCJ 24 March.
Peng T C (1992e) 'Mainland relations bill gets 1st OK', FCJ 27 March.
Peng T C (1992f) 'Peking discriminates against Taiwan people', FCJ 17 April.
Peng T C (1992g) 'Peking backing down verbally on visa rule against Taiwan people', FCJ 17 April.
Peng T C (1992h) 'SEF prospecting for mainland business ventures', FCJ 16 June.
Pun A (1992) 'Politics cloud economic sphere issue at Hong Kong symposium', FCJ 28 January.
Pun A (1992b) '32 000 foreign workers coming', FCJ 7 August.

Pun A (1992c) 'Taiwan investment helps put mainland exports over top', *FCJ* 18 September.

Reardon L C (1991) 'The SEZs come of age', *CBR* November–December.

Republic of China Yearbook 1990–91, Kwang Hwa Publishing Company, Taipei, Taiwan.

Sheng F (1991) 'Economic cooperation between Mainland, Taiwan and Hong Kong, *BR* 25 November–1 December.

Song S F (1992) 'SEF official foresees higher tide of Taiwan–mainland exchanges', *FCJ* 10 January.

Tyson J L (1992a) 'China coast's Taiwan experience', *CSM* 10 January.

Tyson J L (1992b) 'Taiwan touts its model for mainland reformers', *CSM* 18 February.

The Economist (1991) 'Where tigers breed: a survey of Asia's emerging economies', 16 November.

Williams J F (1992) The development of Hainan Island, China: past strategies and future options', *Proceedings, International Conference on Dynamic Transformation, Seoul, 1991.*

Wu N (1992) 'Voter answer to independence moot', *FCJ* 22 September.

Yang X (1992) 'Foreign-funded enterprises in China', *BR* 3–16 February.

Yang Y and **Li D** (1992) 'Promoting exchanges across the Taiwan Straits', *BR* 3–16 February.

Yeung Y M and **Hu X W** (eds) (1992) *China's Coastal Cities: Catalysts for Modernization*, University of Hawaii Press, Honolulu.

CHAPTER 13

The prospect for China
Denis Dwyer

In some respects it is not difficult to be bullish about China; indeed, less than four years after the Tiananmen massacre, bullishness seems to be abounding on all sides. According to official statistics, China's GNP increased by 7 per cent in 1991. In October 1992, the Xinhua News Agency reported that GNP growth in 1992 was likely to reach 12 per cent, double the official target set in March the same year (*Hong Kong Standard*, 15/10/92). This spurt in growth has followed the severe downturn of 1989–90, when the economic retrenchment of autumn of 1988, necessitated by the development of runaway inflation in excess of 30 per cent a year, had been followed by the international ostracism of China resulting from the massacre. Foreign investment in 1992, it has now been announced, will exceed all previous levels. It soared to a record US $6.6 billion in the first nine months of the year, up 131 per cent from the equivalent period in 1991, according to the official *China Daily* (quoted in the *South China Morning Post*, Hong Kong, 19/10/92). China approved about 27 000 foreign investment projects between January and September as compared to 12 978 projects in the whole of 1991. About 70 per cent of the new projects were Sino-foreign joint ventures with, significantly, Taiwan becoming the second biggest investing 'country' after Hong Kong. 'One trend we see', said Lin Kun of the Trade Ministry's foreign investment division, 'is the wholesale transfer of entire industries from Taiwan to the mainland'. Further, the renewed confidence of international financiers in China comes at a time when, again according to Chinese reports, the grain harvest is set to exceed even that of 1990, which at 435 million tonnes was itself a record (*South China Morning Post*, Hong Kong, 30/9/92).

The scholarship of benevolence

The local results of these impressive national achievements are unprecedented prosperity, we are told. For example, in the village of Daqiuzhuang, near Tianjin, everybody is now rich (Crothall 1992). It was

243

not long ago that the parents of Li Fuenzhuang, who holds a senior position in the village hierarchy, lived in a rundown mud brick house with only the most rudimentary plumbing. Today, they occupy a three-storey, six bedroom villa, with half a dozen colour television sets and a gleaming black Cadillac in the garage. Their villa is furnished with stylish leather sofas on which the family recline while watching satellite TV. This is not unusual, for the villages' 4500 permanent residents have on average well over 100 000 yuan in the bank, and some have savings in excess of 1 million yuan. The village has about 20 top-range Mercedes, as well as Cadillacs and Buicks, and an extensive fleet of Japanese limousines. Its gross domestic product in 1991 was 1.8 billion yuan. In mid-1992 that figure had already reached 3 billion yuan and by the end of 1992 it is planned to touch 5 billion yuan. Daqiuzhuang aims to become the richest village in the world by the end of the century, and more than 1000 people a day visit it from all over China to learn the secrets of its success. With a dozen hotels, the village has no problem in accommodating them all. It has become a latter-day Dazhai, the rural commune in Shanxi which in the 1960s was elevated by Mao to the status of a national model. Whether it will ultimately suffer Dazhai's fate of being denounced as a fraud remains to be seen.

There are a multitude of other Dazhais. They fill the pages of China's own publications, and a good deal of this material is subsequently reproduced, quite uncritically, in the West, even in Hong Kong, where it might be thought there would be rather more local knowledge of the actual situation in China. Chen Zhongmin, we are told in the *South China Morning Post* (Kwan 1991), is delighted that his once-impoverished farm outside Hangzhou, the capital of Zhejiang province, is now connected to the rest of the world by IDD telephone service. In the early 1960s his collective farm in Hongshan was in an area known locally as 'Siberia on the edge of a paradise' in comparison with its prosperous neighbour, Hangzhou. 'This used to be a saltpan where nothing would grow . . . we had barely enough to eat', Chen says. Now Hongshan is one of the richest rural areas in China, with an average personal income of more than 20 000 yuan a year as compared with 73 yuan only 20 years ago. This is because township industries have flourished since the economic reforms were introduced in 1979. Nine out of ten farmers have left their farms to join such enterprises and the fixed assets of Hongshan have grown in value from 3 million yuan in 1978 to almost 100 million in 1992. 'No, I won't move to Hangzhou even if I am allowed to', says Dong Peihua, formerly a farmer and now a factory director. Overseas investors in Hongshan are equally pleased. The Japanese partners of the new garment factory like not just the cheapness and discipline of the local labour force but equally the comparative freedom from regulation they enjoy as their price for bringing in scarce capital and international industrial know-how to this impoverished area. As they say, 'Here we can set our own company rules'.

In Britain, similar articles are produced in the press, though not perhaps with such regularity as in Hong Kong. One recent example was that by William Rees-Mogg (1992) which appeared in *The Independent*, generally regarded as a heavyweight newspaper. 'Last Wednesday I was in China', Rees-Mogg tells his readership (actually, it emerges from the article, Rees-Mogg was making a brief visit to the Shenzen Special Economic Zone, just over the border from Hong Kong). Having bought in Hong Kong a painted wooden parasol for HK$20, or about £1.50, he became very worried. The cost was so low because of the cheapness of China's labour. Yet there is so much labour in China that China has a massive international advantage that will continue at least until the middle of the next century. 'The scale of the potential development is staggering', for 'if all of China reached the economic level of Taiwan [presumably in per capita terms], its GDP would exceed that of the United States, or the European Community'. 'China will reach that level well before the middle of the next century . . .'

The *naïveté* of this kind of optimistic assessment – with all its echoes of the Maoist thinking on population that underpinned the Great Leap Forward of the late 1950s ('For China a big population is a good thing', to quote the Great Helmsman) – would be laughable were it not for the fact that a combination of economic optimism and exaggerated respect for China's perceived world status has become embodied in a good deal of influential official thinking outside of China (Dwyer 1992). The complaisant attitude of former President Bush towards China, even during the immediate aftermath of the Tiananmen massacre, has been very evident and has given rise to much controversy within the United States. The British government has been scrupulous to avoid offending China over Hong Kong, to the point of being accused of 'supine acquiescence' to China by the International Commission of Jurists (*The Independent*, 29/4/92). Hong Kong government officials even quote Rees-Mogg *in extenso*. The Commissioner for the Hong Kong Government told a businessmen's conference in London in July 1922:

> By now I hope that some of my enthusiasm for the great opportunities [in Hong Kong and China] which present themselves to businessmen all over the world, including the United Kingdom, has affected you but just in case I have failed let me, in conclusion, quote from a recent article by Lord Rees-Mogg: 'The clock of China is still in the early morning, perhaps three o'clock. Hong Kong itself, with Taiwan, Malaysia and Singapore, is perhaps at six o'clock, half way to the zenith. Japan is at 11.30, still a little before noon, but with a long afternoon of relative decline not so far away. In Tokyo, they tell you that China is bound to pass them at sometime in the next century. They are right.'
>
> (Hong Kong Government Office, London, 1992)

The academic equivalent of these rosy journalistic representations of China's future consists of a body of work that Mosher (1990, p.200) has characterized as 'the scholarship of benevolence'; work that essentially is underpinned by the overall assessment of the communist regime enunciated by John King Fairbank, who for so long was the generally accepted dean of United States sinologists, that '. . . the revolution has been a magnificent achievement, a victory not only for Mao Tse-tung, but for several hundreds of millions of the Chinese people' (Fairbank, 1974, p.xvii). At its extremes, such scholarship stretches to the largely uncritical and wholesale acceptance in learned papers and books of China's own claims of substantial progress. Such work, as Mosher has convincingly demonstrated, runs in a continuous, and sometimes the preponderant, stream in the scholarly assessment of China's prospects, virtually from the founding of the Communist state in 1949 to the present day.

In his path-breaking book *China Misperceived: American Illusions and Chinese Reality*, Mosher (1990, pp.86–101) draws attention to the Chinese claim of a phenomenal increase in GNP of 68 per cent over the period of the First Five Year Plan from 1952 to 1957, and demonstrates how this claim, as well as most of the even more exaggerated ones made during the Great Leap Forward, were immediately accepted as valid by many academics in the West. Elements of the same situation exist today, and were particularly characteristic of the period of reform and partial liberalization from early 1979 until the Tiananmen massacre. Perhaps the best example of the genre is Vogel's widely-noticed book *One Step Ahead in China: Guangdong Under Reform*, published in 1989, which resulted from seven months spent in Guangdong province as a guest of the Provincial Economic Commission, investigating Guangdong's overall economic development during the post-1978 period of economic liberalization. Vogel (1989, p.5) states that he was not aware of any other foreign scholar being given a comparable opportunity to study a Chinese province. He makes it clear that he insisted upon complete freedom of expression for his findings and that his finished manuscript was not subject to any kind of official review by the Chinese authorities. Yet, as an analysis of recent development in Guangdong the end-product is profoundly disappointing, the book largely consisting of little more than edited transcriptions of interviews with a multitude of officials throughout the province, each complete with claims of substantial progress in virtually every direction. Only the chapter on 'Reforming foreign trade', which was not written by Vogel but contributed by John Kamm, stands up as a balanced, properly analytical account of one of the development topics of current major importance.

At one point in the book, when discussing the inner delta counties, Vogel (pp.173–4) describes his visit to Beijiao township, where industrial production is recorded as having risen in value from 14 million to 305 million yuan between 1979 and 1986 and agricultural production from 30 to 55 million yuan. The best known factory, he writes, is the Yuhua Electric Fan Factory which in 1987 employed 1200 people and produced about 1.2 million fans a year, about 4 per cent of all the electric fans produced in China. The factory manager, Ou Jianchang, he records, was honoured by the state in 1987 as being one of the ten great national entrepreneurs from a peasant background. The factory had originally been a commune factory making soya sauce and plastic tops for thermos bottles, and Ou became head of it in 1967. Towards the end of the 1970s, he decided to move into the manufacture of plastic fans. 'They originally learned the basic technology from a state factory in Guangzhou but later gained new technology from Hong Kong. Ou himself went to Hong Kong frequently to get advice about technology and markets from people he met through personal channels' (Vogel 1989, p.174).

However, when visited by the present writer in August 1988, it was clear that this factory was, at least by then, a joint venture with a Hong Kong company which had closed down its manufacturing operation in the Chai Wan district of Hong Kong and transferred the machinery, much of it quite old, to Beijiao. The plant consisted of a mixture of old and new machinery, and not all of its floor area was fully utilized. All the design and marketing operations were taking place in Hong Kong, and Hong Kong managers came periodically to supervise the manufacturing processes. The plant did not appear to be working at full capacity, and its electroplating section was discharging effluent directly into a nearby stream. What had attracted the Hong Kong investment and technical know-how was possibly not so much the personal efforts of Ou Jianchang as cheap local labour and industrial land, plus an official tolerance of levels of industrial pollution that would not have been permitted even in Hong Kong.

Reality and China's aspirations

In any serious discussion of China's past and future progress there clearly needs to be a great deal of reservation and caution over both the statistical base and the other developmental information supplied by Chinese sources at all levels. At the national level, the State Statistical Bureau was abolished soon after the start of the Cultural Revolution in 1966. Well before then, however, in the late 1950s and early 1960s, statistics had become only figments of the imagination of cadres and officials, even at the highest levels, seeking to please the political masterminds of the Great Leap Forward. During the middle 1950s, the government had conducted several nationwide surveys of development, but with regard to the critical sector of rural development, for example, Vermeer (1982) has shown that there was obvious political bias, with the results of the surveys, in the end, showing what they were officially intended to show. Then, 'when in 1957 statistical methods started to improve, the anti-rightist campaign of the Chinese Communist Party made objective sampling and representation of data virtually impossible. The 1957 model survey of 228 agricultural producers co-operatives throughout China . . . is, therefore, of little use' (Vermeer, 1982, pp.6-7). Typically, surveys would be heavily biased towards high-income, activist co-operatives; and although during the 1980s a climate of greater openness developed and, at least ostensibly, comprehensive national statistics began to be produced once more by the resurrected State Statistical Bureau, doubts still remain.

Burns (1981, pp.638-40) has emphasized the methods and scale of the problem of false reporting in Guangdong Province in the early 1970s and he draws attention to the fact which still obtains today that whilst the national system of statistical collection and centralized national planning rests heavily on reporting from local production units, it is frequently in the best interests of these units to conceal true production figures in reports to higher levels. This must be particularly true of the many loss-

247

making factories in the state industrial sector. Such concealment takes two forms in the countryside, according to Burns. One is the hiding of production in order to reduce payments in cash or kind to the state. As one former production team leader pointed out. 'In our place, hidden production became a custom. Those units which could not do it were considered crazy' (Burns, 1981, p.638). The obverse of the falsification coin is over-reporting, a practice which is rife today even at quite high levels: for example, the GNP of Chongqing, the municipality claims, has increased by a factor of 5 since 1978 and the average annual wage in the urban area of 4.4 million people from 585 yuan to 2355 yuan (*South China Morning Post* Hong Kong, 30/8/92). Over-reporting has, of course, been particularly associated with enterprises or units attempting to become designated as models, with consequential state investment and subsidies. By the early 1980s the publication of basic national statistics had become well established once more. However, to take a further example, according to Hartford (1992, p.113), the officially reported grain harvest for 1989, which at 407 million tonnes equalled the previous best for the decade (1984), remains disputable'. . . given the clamp-down on press reporting, and the pressure on the Li Peng government to display some economic successes'. 'I have queried a number of agricultural experts concerning the credibility of the claim', Hartford writes (1992, p.113), 'some find it plausible, others (especially some who had paid local rural visits in 1989) do not.'

Even taking the most recently published national economic statistics at face value, as Kueh (1991, p.10.6) has pointed out, the apparently more optimistic position of China by mid-1992 has resulted from the necessity from early 1990 onwards to rescue the economy from the possibility of near-collapse. By the beginning of 1990, not only was the economic situation marked by a negative growth in industrial output, unemployment was increasing rapidly and a rising peasant exodus towards the towns was becoming apparent as the result of the closure of tens of thousands of the new rural factories through the impact of the severe credit squeeze designed to halt the rise in inflation.

The basic reasons for the subsequent recovery have been three-fold. First, a rapid increase in industrial output, though very largely one of light industrial production, and industrial production outside the state sector. This has been very largely the result of the second factor, however: the greater availability of finance once more, not only from foreign investment but, more importantly, provincial and local finance through the relaxation of bank lending and credit control. (According to Kueh, 1991, p.10.5, bank loans increased by 22 per cent in 1990). Thirdly, the agricultural sector has given significant impetus to GNP growth through the rise in foodgrain output and the gross value of agricultural output generally, though as shown below, this achievement can in the main also be related to increased financial inputs, largely by the state. The present spurt in development, both industrial and agricultural, has thus predominantly been investment-led rather than productivity-led. The prospect remains of another serious overheating of the economy, which would in turn necessitate a return to the retrenchment of the 1988–89 period. This would perpetuate the record of China's economic development under the Communist Party of two steps forward followed by one, two, or on occasion even three steps back: booms followed by slumps which have as often been caused by political as by economic factors.

Population: the central issue

In addition to the problem of the severe cyclical fluctuations that occur regularly in the Chinese economy, there are more profound, underlying factors affecting China's future prospects which are both deeply structural and of immense scale: factors which at present seem insurmountable obstacles to China's emergence into the ranks even of the poorer middle-income countries within the foreseeable future. The central group of these is surely population and population-related problems.

The 1990 census returned a population of 1.134 billion, which means that China has virtually doubled its population since the first modern census in 1953, the interim increase of 546 million being equivalent to the 1990 size of the population of the United States, Northern Europe and Western Europe combined. Every year 16 million people are currently added to China's population. The birth rate figure produced by the 1990 census was 2.1 per cent, which is the equivalent of 2.6 to 2.8 children per couple, or the same level attained during the early 1980s. The import of this aspect of the 1990 census is, according to Kwong (1991, p.18.4), that 'the family planning campaign has hit a solid barrier'.

One result of the famine of the early 1960s was that immediately after it the birth rate exploded. It reached 4.3 per cent in 1963 and did not fall below 3 per cent until 1972. For the decade of the 1970s as a whole, the total fertility rate was 4.01 children per couple. The one child family policy introduced in 1979 had substantial effect in the urban areas but much less in the countryside, despite such draconian measures as forced abortions (see Mosher 1983, pp.224-61) because tolerated exceptions became widespread. However, the total fertility rate did decline nationally, to an average of 2.47 during the period 1980 to 1987 (Kwong 1991, p.18.4). This kind of level, given the evidence of the 1990 census, now appears to be somewhat beyond the capability of birth control policy and practice as at present constituted. What this means is that the announced census figure was 15 million over the target for the Five Year Plan of 1986 to 1990; and that China's official population target of 1.2 billion, adopted in the early 1980s for the year 2000, has had first to be modified and more recently to be abandoned. The 1.2 billion level will, in fact, be reached by the end of 1994 or early in 1995 and by the middle of the year 2000 China will have more than 1.3 billion inhabitants (Kwong 1991, p.18.7). To reduce the population of China, as opposed to causing it to grow more slowly, the total fertility rate would need to fall to below 2.03.

As Kwong demonstrates, there has been much dispute both within and outside China as to the causes of the present apparent impasse in population limitation. Clearly, intensive propaganda coupled with extreme compulsion in such matters as abortion has not fully worked, perhaps because the intensive efforts required could be sustained only for relatively short periods and in circumstances of very tight control over individual lives, circumstances which have been undermined by the changed climate of local control – the loosening of the authority of local party organizations and individual cadres – brought about by the liberalization of the economy in the 1980s. Kwong claims (p.18.13) that '. . . the whole state apparatus, previously well integrated for the task of fertility control had by the late 1980s deteriorated to a point close to collapse'. He points out that the extremely low total fertility rates of 1984 and 1985 were artificially attained through extraordinary family planning campaigns which were unsustainable; and he outlines other consequences of the changed spirit of the times that work against further progress in population reduction, for example the rise of migration, particularly rural–urban migration, which has both seriously undermined the household registration system, which previously had been a major element in birth control programmes, and frequently produced additional wealth from which financial penalties for having extra children could be paid (as also in the latter respect has the institution of the household responsibility system in agriculture as a major part of the economic reforms).

The fact that there is also a complex of socio-demographic factors involved in the present overall problem of population – such as the relationship of the present age structure of the country to its fertility and current tendencies towards both earlier marriage and earlier childbearing – adds to its intractibility. As Kwong warns (p.18.2), if China has indeed 'lost control of population', a prospect which has produced much discussion within the country of late, then its future prospects will be considerably dimmed. At the most basic level, the matter of future food supply will become more central in both political and economic terms even than it is at present. To maintain foodgrain production at the per capita 1989 level, which at 370 kg was hardly extravagant, China would need to be producing 481 million tonnes of foodgrains annually by the year 2000 (Ma 1991, p.257). The official target for the Eighth Five Year Plan is, in fact, 500 million tonnes of foodgrains by the year 2000.

During the 1980s, the foodgrain output fluctuated considerably, from a low of 325 million tonnes in 1980 to a high of 407 million tonnes in 1984 and 1989, with an average for the decade of 383 million tonnes. In 1990, however, a record output of 435 million tonnes was achieved, according to the official statistics. The critical question in terms of future prospects is whether this improved yield is sustainable, and indeed capable of further significant improvement. In a recent examination of this question, You and Wang (1991, pp.12.2–12.9) are quite pessimistic. In macro-terms, they attribute the good harvest of 1990 to a policy shift from the development strategy of the 1980s, and in particular to the sense of social crisis that followed the Tiananmen massacre forcing the leadership of the party to re-emphasize the key role of agriculture in national socio-economic development and to re-embrace the veteran Stalinist economist Chen Yun's idea of 'no stability without grain'. As a result, agriculture has been given an enhanced allocation of financial inputs compared with the situation of the 1980s when its percentage of total investment had been allowed to shrink from even the meagre 6.1 per cent of 1981 to levels of just over 3 per cent during the years 1984 to 1988. Specifically, the level of various state investments has been raised, and more funds have been made available for loans for rural development. Official prices for grain and some other crops such as cotton have been raised in 1989 and again in 1990 to motivate the peasantry to increased production; and the costs of essential inputs for agriculture from the industrial sector, such as pesticides and chemical fertilizers, have been controlled in such a way as to preserve for the peasants much of the financial benefit from increased production. Further, there has been some re-emphasis of collective labour in order, for example, to repair irrigation works and to rectify some of the more general neglect to the communal facilities necessary for agriculture that has occurred since the introduction of the household responsibility system.

Whether these policies are sustainable is very doubtful, however, according to You and Wang (1991, pp.12.6–12.7). They demonstrate that since 1984 increases in agricultural productivity have been virtually negligible. 'Labour productivity has declined constantly, and its general level has remained stagnant. On the other hand, the productivity of capital has been declining too. As a result more investment is needed to achieve the same amount of growth . . .' It is even unlikely that the state could afford the investment level of 1990 for a sustained period; while to meet a grain production target of 500 million tonnes by the year 2000 . . .' requires an additional outlay of 170 billion yuan in total or an annual investment of 15.4 billion yuan on top of the current level. This would be a huge burden on the state's treasury. Therefore, we submit that the impressive growth of grain production in 1990 is rather exceptional and does not mark a new period of sustained agricultural development in China.'

The industrial and urban consequences of surplus labour

These are disturbing findings for they indicate not only the severe financial limitations to China's possible future grain output but also the constraints in terms of the availability of capital for the agricultural sector to any possible future switch on a large scale of labour out of agriculture and into secondary and tertiary activates. Should such financial constraints to sectoral change become critical within the medium-term future, it will be in large part because of another significant aspect of the country's overall population problem: the need to provide finance for ever-increasing increments of employment in the towns and cities for the non-peasant sector of the population, a sector that has been deliberately and disproportionately favoured by the state since the institution of communist rule in 1949. As has been widely recognized (see, for example, Kirkby 1985), the Chinese revolution in economic terms has been primarily an industrial revolution. The allocation of state development capital has been heavily biased towards industrial development, and especially towards heavy industry (see details in Brodsgaard 1991, pp.180–1) partly following both earlier Stalinist traditions and the modernization paradigms accepted internationally in the 1950s, and partly for reasons of national prestige, international influence and defence. In a command economy that was self-contained to a high degree until the 1980s, for defence reasons locational decisions frequently favoured relatively remote interior locations (see Naughton 1988; Dwyer 1986a). These virtually guaranteed a considerable measure of industrial inefficiency for geographical reasons alone, quite apart from other factors.

Yet in terms of the generality of industry, a complex of additional factors has been even more significant in terms of producing today a state sector quite unable to compete internationally and equally, it seems, now virtually impossible to reform (Dwyer 1993). In particular, the idea of welfare, in terms of the maximum provision of industrial employment as a response to the situation of over-abundance of labour, has by and large prevailed over the idea of efficiency, and as a consequence the 'iron ricebowl' (or jobs for life regardless of performance) policy has become an entrenched industrial feature.

In a situation in which the point was reached in 1978 at which a 'substitution' option was given to all retiring state employees enabling them to designate one of their children as a 'successor' in their old unit (Davis, 1990, p.95), the possible future consequences for China's industrial prospects of the perpetuation of the 'iron ricebowl' mentality must be extremely serious. However, this is only one of a large number of fundamental reforms necessary in the industrial sector if China is to have a viable international industrial future. Other important reforms include the rationalization of systems of supply of raw materials and the chaotic distribution network, the modernization of management practices and the separation of management from political control, the upgrading of generally antiquated industrial equipment and the fundamental reform of the accounting and pricing systems.

The bizarre results of the present system of Chinese industrial organization have been commented upon *ad nauseam* in the West since the period of greater openness began in the late 1970s. There are estimates that in 1991 China was holding industrial products worth more than US$42 billion, or 12 per cent of GDP, that are of such bad quality that nobody in the country will buy them (*Economist*, 30/11/91); and it is commonly held that at least one-third of the state industrial enterprises are loss-making. Yet to reform them could lead to loss of employment for more than half of the total state industrial workforce of 103 million, according to Zhu Rongji, the official responsible for reviving state industries (*Sunday Times*, London, 2/8/92).

In the present population circumstances – with an estimated 20 to 30 per cent of the massive rural labour force already surplus to requirements – this is clearly an impossibility, despite the official commitments to such reform at an unspecified future date that are frequently published. Further, there is always the possibility of labour unrest to be considered, particularly since the participation of the urban workers in the events immediately before and after the Tiananmen massacre, in Beijing, Shanghai and other cities. For these reasons there will, it seems, be no large-scale outbreak of industrial bankruptcies in China within the foreseeable future, and half of the profits and taxes derived from state industry will continue to be devoted to bailing out loss-making units.

Spatially until the last decade, because of the emergence of this industrial situation since 1949, because of the lack of growth in – indeed the Maoist antagonism towards – the logical alternative to industrial employment in the urban areas, which was in services, and because of the massive surpluses of labour in the countryside, nationally the population became increasingly fossilized in functional terms. The peasantry was excluded from participation in higher order economic activities in the towns and cities by a system of pass regulations and the close supervision of personal movement by rural cadres and urban street committees. Now this whole system is in process of disintegration under pressures of surplus labour which, it seems, can no longer be resisted in the somewhat changed climate since 1978. Between 1980 and 1987, according to Davis (1990, p.86), 35 million left their villages to work in factories, take up construction work or travel daily to urban markets as itinerant sellers; and by the end of the 1980s in some large cities rural migrants made up 20 per cent of the workforce, many without any formal permission to shift residence from the rural to the urban areas and existing as a 'floating' population of indeterminate status. By the end of April 1986, for example, 644 000 people from outside Beijing had registered there as temporary residents, including interestingly enough for a communist society 15 000 housemaids; and by October 1989 the Beijing Municipal Government was formulating regulations aimed at getting workers from other provinces out of the capital in order to provide more opportunities for employment for young people from Beijing (Linge and Forbes 1990, pp.195–6). In addition to the future economic consequences of such large-scale migration for China's urban economies – for undoubtedly the surge in non-state industrial and service activities produced by the economic reforms since 1979 will be able to take up only a fraction of the available surplus rural labour – the social consequences are also disturbing. As (Hartford 1992, p.101) describes;

> 'With the loosening of urban migration restrictions in the mid-1980s, millions of peasants voted with their feet. Thousands of young women from rural Anhui province flocked to Beijing to find work as maids; tens of thousands of young men from Gansu moved to Guangzhou (Canton) and the Pearl River Delta area for temporary and contract labour in construction and other unskilled jobs. Beggars appeared on the streets of the capital city (notably, near the major hotels catering to foreigners) and prostitutes appeared in hotel lobbies.'

Government and authority

Begging, prostitution, theft, smuggling and other similar antisocial activities have risen dramatically as a consequence of the official endorsement of material incentives (Dwyer 1986b), individualism and individual, or at best family, enrichment that has characterized the last decade. The situation is worst in the Pearl River Delta area where the greatest measure of economic progress in the country – largely through investment from Hong Kong – has been accompanied by a rising tide of official corruption and lawlessness. The most notorious single incident of recent years has probably been the Hainan vehicle smuggling ramp of 1984 (see Vogel 1989, pp.291–4), in which permissions to import new vehicles, mostly vans, were corruptly organized by local and regional government officials and the vehicles sold outside Hainan at huge profits to units which had no such permissions. In all, the import of more than 80 000 vehicles was approved before higher authorities stepped in and discovered that Chen Yuyi, the deputy director of the island in charge of foreign economic work, had personally approved the import of 73 000 vehicles. It is estimated that this smuggling racket alone used up over US $1 billion of China's foreign currency. During the last five years, much of this lawlessness has even spilled over into Hong Kong, with armed robbers, some from the mainland, using a variety of sophisticated weapons, including hand grenades obtained from People's Liberation Army and Chinese security sources. In the first nine months of 1992, 5000 cars were stolen in Hong Kong. It is estimated by the Hong Kong police that about 2000 of them, almost exclusively large luxury models, were smuggled by sea into the Pearl River Delta area. Only six of the smuggled cars have been returned by the Chinese authorities, despite the fact that as right-hand drive models they would be instantly recognizable in China (*South China Morning Post*, Hong Kong, 7/10/92).

The 'Guangdong miracle' of the 1980s – the rapid growth of light industry outside of the state sector on the dual basis of international capital and cheap labour (see Sit, 1989) – clearly has some ugly sides, and in this it mirrors the contemporary national situation. Maoist-oriented writers such as Hinton (1991, pp.7–8) have not been slow to emphasize the negative aspects of development since the late 1970s, claiming, for example:

'Mao Zedong was far more astute. More than twenty years ago during the Cultural Revolution, he exposed Deng Xiaoping, Yang Shangkun and most of their 'hardline" colleagues as capitalist roaders. He accurately predicted that if such persons ever came to power they would transform the Communist Party into a revisionist party and finally into a fascist party and then the whole of China would change colour . . . Make no mistake. The leaders in Beijing are not motivated by communist ideals; they are not revolutionary planners or socialist builders. They are newly constituted bureaucratic capitalists, busy carving the economy into gigantic family fiefs, ready, in true comprador style, to sell China out to the highest bidder.'

While substantial corruption at the highest levels is undeniable, the ultimate results of the mixing of international capitalism with Chinese nationalism and what remains of communist economic theory and policy in China are as yet unclear, and thus judgement on Hinton's assessment must be suspended. What is much more certain is that the Communist Party in China has failed in the eyes of the nation to create a new legitimacy based upon economic success to replace Maoism. Saich (1992, p.50) claims that by 1989 it had become clear that 'the party's incompetence and moral laxness had eroded any vestigial notions that the party was a moral force in Chinese society'. Further, it can be argued that the very success of some aspects of the new rural and urban policies of the Dengist period has in fact served only to undermine what Hartford (1992, p.75) has termed 'the implicit social contract that bound together the Chinese body politic', a contract that 'represented certain concrete guarantees to certain social groups and created a political elite whose authority vested ultimately on their capacity to sustain those guarantees'. With the discrediting of the Maoist system, Hartford asserts, a new social contract is essential. However '. . . with an ageing, unimaginative, and illegitimized group of leaders at the helm . . . China is unlikely to enjoy such a new social contract in the foreseeable future' (Hartford, 1992, p.75).

During the last decade, the development of a massive personality cult centering on Deng Xiaoping, the relentless barrage of propaganda concerning economic achievement and national progress, and the savage imposition of repression and the re-emphasis of Party of authority in 1989, have in fact been paralleled by the steady weakening of Party authority and control throughout the country. There is now no consistent ideological framework for change: pragmatism rules. Policies are liable to abrupt and fundamental change as circumstances dictate, and such circumstances are no long predominantly internal, for in the process of recent change China has become integrated into the world capitalist economy and without unacceptable levels of hardship to privileged individual and group interests it would be impossible to reverse this. China's future is thus difficult to foretell, especially in view of the advanced age not only of Deng himself but of several others of the present leadership.

The challenge China now faces is not the challenge of achieving communist or even socialist development. It has become the challenge of achieving development in a much more typical Third World context. It is the challenge of now confronting a range of factors inhibiting development that has resulted from the contradictions of communist rule during the first 30 years since 1949 plus a new range of factors very well known already in the Third World which result from interdependence with the industrially advanced capitalist nations. Apart from enclaves of success in the material sense – geographical enclaves like that of the Pearl River Delta area, and personal and family enclaves, for example as a result of some of the workings of the family responsibility system and the development of the township industrial enterprises in the countryside – enclaves which it has to be said have in aggregate proved of considerable national importance in the development record of the last decade, China as at present led is still a considerable distance away from formulating and prosecuting a realistic, coherent and sustainable programme of national development. This is, of course, but another reflection of how much more 'Third World' rather than 'communist' its development characteristics have now become. So far this century, China has experienced three revolutions: nationalist, Maoist and Dengist. A fourth revolution, the nature of which is at present unknown, may well be the response to the working through the body politic of the present combination of socio-economic circumstances.

References

Brodsgaard Kjeld Erik (1991) 'China's political economy in the nineties', *China Report* **27** 177–95.

Burns John P (1981) 'Rural Guangdong's Second Economy', *China Quarterly* **88**, 629–44.

Crothall Geoffrey (1992) 'Inside the Beverly Hills of China', *South China Sunday Morning Post*, Hong Kong, 30/8/92.

Davis Deborah (1990) 'Urban job mobility', in Davis Deborah and Vogel Ezra F. (eds). *Chinese Society in the Eve of Tiananmen*, Harvard University Press, Harvard, Mass., pp.86–108.

Dwyer D J (1986a) 'Chengdu, Sichuan, the modernization of a Chinese city', *Geography* **71**, 215–27.

Dwyer D J (1986b) 'Urban housing and planning in China', *Transactions of the Institute of British Geographers* **11**, 479–89.

Dwyer D J (1992) 'Doubts surround China's economic future', *Independent*, 8/2/92.

Dwyer D J (1993) 'China: the consequences of liberalization', in Drakakis-Smith David and Dixon Chris (eds) *Economic and Social Development in Pacific Asia*, Routledge, London.

Fairbank John K (1974) *China Perceived*, Random House, New York.

Hartford Kathleen (1992) 'No way out? Rural reforms and food policy in China', in Dassu Marta and Saich Tony (eds). *The Reform Decade in China: from hope to dismay*, Kegan Paul, London, pp.74–114.

Hinton William (1991) *The Privatization of China*, Earthscan Publications, London.

Hong Kong Government Office, London (1992) Press Circular: Commissioner's speech to Department of Trade and Industry, Port and Airport Strategy Conference, Heathrow, London, 7/7/92.

Kirkby R J R (1985) *Urbanization in China: Town and county in a developing economy*, Croom Helm, London.

Kueh Y Y (1991) 'The state of the economy and economic reform', in Kuan Hsin-chi and Maurice Brosseau (eds.), *China Review*, Hong Kong: Chinese University Press, pp.10.1–10.25.

Kwan Daniel (1991) 'Farmers find prosperity away from the state', *South China Morning Post*, Hong Kong, 7/9/91.

Kwong Chun-Kuen Paul (1991) 'The 1990 census and the fertility policy debate', in Hsin-chi Kuan and Brosseau Maurice (eds), *China Review*,

Chinese University Press, Hong Kong, pp.18.1–18.27.

Linge G J R and **Forbes D K** (1990) 'Definition of urban in the PRC', in Linge G J R and Forbes D K (eds). *China's Spatial Economy*, Oxford University Press, Hong Kong, pp.193–8.

Ma Jiali (1991) 'Prospects of China's economic development', *China Report* **27**, 259–66.

Mosher Stephen W (1983) *Broken Earth: the rural Chinese*, The Free Press, New York.

Mosher Stephen W (1990) *China Misperceived: American Illusions and Chinese Reality*, Harper Collins, New York.

Naughton Barry (1988) 'The Third Front: defence industrialization in the Chinese interior', *China Quarterly* **115**, 351–86.

Rees-Mogg William (1992) 'The clock counts down to China's economic dawn', *Independent*, 3/2/92.

Saich Tony (1992) 'The reform decade in China: the limits to revolution from above', in Saich Tony and Dassu Marta (eds). *The Reform Decade in China: from Hope to Dismay*, Kegan Paul, London.

Sit Victor F S (1989) 'Hong Kong's new industrial partnership with the Pearl River Delta', *Asian Geographer* **8**, 103–15.

Vermeer E B (1982) 'Income differentials in rural China', *China Quarterly* **89**, 1–33.

Vogel Ezra F (1989) *One Step Ahead in China: Guangdong Under Reform*, Harvard University Press, Cambridge, Mass.

You Ji and **Wang Yuesheng** (1991) 'China's agricultural development and reform in 1990', in Kuan Hsin-chi and Maurice Brosseau (eds). *China Review*, Chinese University Press, Hong Kong, pp.12.1–12.20.

Index